TAKING SIDES

Clashing Views on

Educational Issues

SIXTEENTH EDITION

Selected, Edited, and with Introductions by

James Wm. Noll
University of Maryland

W9-BZM-095

Connect
Learn
Succeed™

TAKING SIDES: CLASHING VIEWS ON EDUCATIONAL ISSUES,
SIXTEENTH EDITION

Published by McGraw-Hill, a business unit of The McGraw-Hill Companies, Inc., 1221 Avenue of the Americas, New York, NY 10020. Copyright © 2011 by The McGraw-Hill Companies, Inc. All rights reserved. Previous edition(s) 2010, 2009, and 2008. No part of this publication may be reproduced or distributed in any form or by any means, or stored in a database or retrieval system, without the prior written consent of The McGraw-Hill Companies, Inc., including, but not limited to, in any network or other electronic storage or transmission, or broadcast for distance learning.

Some ancillaries, including electronic and print components, may not be available to customers outside the United States.

Taking Sides® is a registered trademark of The McGraw-Hill Companies, Inc.
Taking Sides is published by the **Contemporary Learning Series** group within the McGraw-Hill Higher Education division.

1 2 3 4 5 6 7 8 9 0 DOC/DOC 0

MHID: 0-07-804997-0
ISBN: 978-0-07-804997-2
ISSN: 1091-8817

Managing Editor: *Larry Loeppke*
Senior Managing Editor: *Faye Schilling*
Developmental Editor: *Jade Benedict*
Editorial Coordinator: *Mary Foust*
Editorial Assistant: *Cindy Hedley*
Production Service Assistant: *Rita Hingtgen*
Permissions Coordinator: *Shirley Lanners*
Senior Marketing Manager: *Julie Keck*
Marketing Communications Specialist: *Mary Klein*
Marketing Coordinator: *Alice Link*
Senior Project Manager: *Jane Mohr*
Design Specialist: *Brenda Rolwes*
Cover Design: *Rick Noel*

Compositor: MPS Limited, A Macmillan Company
Cover Image: © Getty Images-RF

Library of Congress Cataloging-in-Publication Data

Main entry under title:
Taking Sides: Clashing Views on Educational Issues/Selected, Edited, and with Introductions by James Wm. Noll—16th edition

Includes bibliographical references.
1. Education-United States. I. Noll, James Wm. *comp.*

370-973

Editors/Academic Advisory Board

Members of the Academic Advisory Board are instrumental in the final selection of articles for each edition of TAKING SIDES. Their review of articles for content, level, and appropriateness provides critical direction to the editors and staff. We think that you will find their careful consideration well reflected in this volume.

TAKING SIDES: Clashing Views on EDUCATIONAL ISSUES
Sixteenth Edition

EDITOR

James Wm. Noll
University of Maryland

ACADEMIC ADVISORY BOARD MEMBERS

Editors/Academic Advisory Board continued

Preface

Controversy is the basis of change and often of improvement. Its lack signifies the presence of complacency, the authoritarian limitation of viewpoint expression, or the absence of realistic alternatives to the existing circumstances. An articulate presentation of a point of view on a controversial matter breathes new life into abiding human and social concerns. Controversy prompts reexamination and perhaps renewal.

Education is controversial. Arguments over the most appropriate aims, the most propitious means, and the most effective control have raged over the centuries. Particularly in the United States, where the systematic effort to provide education has been more democratically dispersed and more varied than elsewhere, educational issues have been contentiously debated. Philosophers, psychologists, sociologists, professional educators, lobbyists, government officials, school boards, local pressure groups, taxpayers, parents, and students have all voiced their views.

This book presents opposing or sharply varying viewpoints on educational issues of current concern. Unit 1 offers consideration of five basic theoretical issues that have been discussed by scholars and practitioners in past decades and are still debated today: the purpose of education, curriculum content and its imposition upon the young, the motivational atmosphere of schools, the philosophical underpinning of the process of education, and the effect of global competition. Unit 2 features five issues that are fundamental to understanding the present circumstances that shape American education: democratic classrooms for citizenship preparation, legitimization of school vouchers, federal initiatives in school improvement, programs for children of poverty, and the redefinition of "public" education. Unit 3 examines more specific issues currently being discussed: undocumented immigrants, universal preschool, privatization, inclusive classrooms, high school reform and the dropout problem, the "intelligent design" theory in science education, single-sex instruction, zero-tolerance policies, computer usage, alternative teacher training, and merit pay for teachers.

I have made every effort to select views from a wide range of thinkers—philosophers, psychologists, sociologists, professional educators, political leaders, historians, researchers, and gadflies.

Each issue is accompanied by an *introduction,* which sets the stage for the debate, and each issue concludes with a *postscript* that considers other views on the issue and suggests additional readings. I have also provided relevant Internet site addresses (URLs) on the *Internet References* page that accompanies each part opener. By combining the material in this volume with the informational background provided by a good introductory textbook, students should be prepared to address the problems confronting schools today.

My hope is that students will find challenges in the material presented here—provocations that will inspire them to better understand the roots of educational controversy, to attain a greater awareness of possible alternatives in dealing with the various issues, and to stretch their personal powers of creative thinking in the search for more promising resolutions of the problems.

Changes to this edition   This sixteenth edition offers seven new issues (two of which were featured in the expanded version of the previous edition) and one reconstituted issue, *Is the Inclusive Classroom Model Workable?* (Issue 14). These are the new issues: *Are Truly Democratic Classrooms Possible?* (Issue 6), *Is No Child Left Behind Irretrievably Flawed?* (Issue 8), *Does a "Deficit Model" Serve Poor Children Well?* (Issue 9), *Are Undocumented Immigrants Entitled to Public Education?* (Issue 11), *Has the Time Arrived for Universal Preschool?* (Issue 12), *Are Single-Sex Schools and Classes Effective?* (Issue I7), and *Can Zero Tolerance Violate Students Rights?* (Issue 18). There are 16 new articles in this edition.

A word to the instructor   *An Instructor's Resource Guide with Test Questions* (multiple choice and essay) is available through the publisher for the instructor using *Taking Sides* in the classroom. A general guidebook, called *Using Taking Sides in the Classroom,* which discusses methods and techniques for integrating the pro/con approach into any classroom setting, is also available. An online version of *Using Taking Sides in the Classroom* and a correspondence service for Taking Sides adopters can be found at http://www.mhcls.com/usingts/.
   Taking Sides: Clashing Views on Educational Issues is only one title in the Taking Sides series. If you are interested in seeing the table of contents for any of the other titles, please visit the Taking Sides Web site at http://www.mhcls .com/takingsides/.

Acknowledgments   I am thankful for the kind and efficient assistance given to me by Jade Benedict, Larry Loeppke, and the other members of the production staff at McGraw-Hill Contemporary Learning Series.

James Wm. Noll
University of Maryland

Contents In Brief

UNIT 1 Basic Theoretical Issues   1

Issue 1. Should Schooling Be Based on Social Experiences?   2
Issue 2. Should the Curriculum Be Standardized for All?   16
Issue 3. Should Behaviorism Shape Educational Practices?   31
Issue 4. Is Constructivism the Best Philosophy of Education?   48
Issue 5. Should Global Competition Steer School Reform?   64

UNIT 2 Current Fundamental Issues   83

Issue 6. Are Truly Democratic Classrooms Possible?   84
Issue 7. Has the Supreme Court Reconfigured American Education?   103
Issue 8. Is No Child Left Behind Irretrievably Flawed?   120
Issue 9. Does a "Deficit Model" Serve Poor Children Well?   133
Issue 10. Should "Public Schooling" Be Redefined?   149

UNIT 3 Current Specific Issues   175

Issue 11. Are Undocumented Immigrants Entitled to Public Education?   176
Issue 12. Has the Time Arrived for Universal Preschool?   195
Issue 13. Is Privatization the Hope of the Future?   216
Issue 14. Is the Inclusive Classroom Model Workable?   230
Issue 15. Can Current High School Reform Curtail Dropouts?   245
Issue 16. Is "Intelligent Design" a Threat to the Curriculum?   262
Issue 17. Are Single-Sex Schools and Classes Effective?   283
Issue 18. Can Zero Tolerance Violate Students Rights?   302
Issue 19. Do Computers Negatively Affect Student Growth?   316
Issue 20. Should Alternative Teacher Training Be Encouraged?   333
Issue 21. Can Merit Pay Accelerate School Improvement?   356

Contents

Preface   v

Correlation Guide   xv

Introduction   xvii

UNIT 1   BASIC THEORETICAL ISSUES   1

Issue 1.   Should Schooling Be Based on Social Experiences?   2

YES: John Dewey, from *Experience and Education* (Macmillan, 1938)   *4*

NO: Robert M. Hutchins, from *The Conflict in Education in a Democratic Society* (Harper & Row, 1953)   *11*

Philosopher John Dewey suggests a reconsideration of traditional approaches to schooling, giving fuller attention to the social development of the learner and the quality of his or her total experience. Robert M. Hutchins, noted educator and one-time chancellor of the University of Chicago, argues for a liberal arts education geared to the development of intellectual powers.

Issue 2.   Should the Curriculum Be Standardized for All?   16

YES: Mortimer J. Adler, from "The Paideia Proposal: Rediscovering the Essence of Education," *American School Board Journal* (July 1982)   *18*

NO: John Holt, from *Escape from Childhood* (E. P. Dutton, 1974)   *25*

Philosopher Mortimer J. Adler contends that democracy is best served by a public school system that establishes uniform curricular objectives for all students. Educator John Holt argues that an imposed curriculum damages the individual and usurps a basic human right to select one's own path of development.

Issue 3.   Should Behaviorism Shape Educational Practices?   31

YES: B. F. Skinner, from *Beyond Freedom and Dignity* (Alfred A. Knopf, 1971)   *33*

NO: Carl R. Rogers, from *Freedom to Learn for the Eighties* (Merrill, 1983)   *39*

B. F. Skinner, an influential proponent of behaviorism and professor of psychology, critiques the concept of "inner freedom" and links learning and motivation to the influence of external forces. Professor of psychology and psychiatry Carl R. Rogers offers the "humanistic" alternative to behaviorism, insisting on the reality of subjective forces in human motivation.

Issue 4.   Is Constructivism the Best Philosophy of Education?   48

YES: **David Elkind,** from "The Problem with Constructivism," *The Educational Forum* (Summer 2004)   *50*

NO: **Jamin Carson,** from "Objectivism and Education: A Response to David Elkind's 'The Problem with Constructivism'," *The Educational Forum* (Spring 2005)   *57*

Child development professor David Elkind contends that the philosophical positions found in constructivism, though often difficult to apply, are necessary elements in a meaningful reform of educational practices. Jamin Carson, an assistant professor of education and former high school teacher, offers a close critique of constructivism and argues that the philosophy of objectivism is a more realistic and usable basis for the process of education.

Issue 5.   Should Global Competition Steer School Reform?   64

YES: **Marc Tucker,** from "Charting a New Course for Schools," *Educational Leadership* (April 2007)   *66*

NO: **Herb Childress,** from "A Subtractive Education," *Phi Delta Kappan* (October 2006)   *73*

Marc Tucker, president of the National Center on Education and the Economy, summarizes the work of the New Commission on the Skills of the American Workforce on which he served as vice chairman. Herb Childress, director of liberal studies at the Boston Architectural College, argues for a completely different approach to improvement of our efforts to educate.

UNIT 2   CURRENT FUNDAMENTAL ISSUES   83

Issue 6.   Are Truly Democratic Classrooms Possible?   84

YES: **Kristan A. Morrison,** from "Democratic Classrooms: Promises and Challenges of Student Voice and Choice, Part One," *Educational Horizons* (Fall 2008)   *86*

NO: **Gary K. Clabaugh,** from "Second Thoughts About Democratic Classrooms," *Educational Horizons* (Fall 2008)   *96*

Associate professor of education Kristan A. Morrison explores historical and theoretical bases for implementing democratic practices in schools that would make student experience more appealing and productive. Professor of education Gary K. Clabaugh examines such factors as top-down management, compulsory attendance, business world influences, and federal mandates to declare Morrison's ideas to be "out of touch" with reality.

Issue 7.   Has the Supreme Court Reconfigured American Education?   103

YES: **Charles L. Glenn,** from "Fanatical Secularism," *Education Next* (Winter 2003)   *105*

NO: **Paul E. Peterson,** from "Victory for Vouchers?" *Commentary* (September 2002)   *112*

Professor of education Charles L. Glenn argues that the Supreme Court's decision in *Zelman v. Simmons-Harris* is an immediate antidote to the public school's secularist philosophy. Professor of government Paul E. Peterson, while welcoming the decision, contends that the barricades against widespread use of vouchers in religious schools will postpone any lasting effects.

Issue 8.   Is No Child Left Behind Irretrievably Flawed?   120

YES: **Sharon L. Nichols and David C. Berliner,** from "Testing the Joy Out of Learning," *Educational Leadership* (March 2008)   *122*

NO: **Dianne Piché,** from "Basically a Good Model," *Education Next* (Fall 2007)   *128*

Education professors Sharon Nichols and David Berliner cite evidence of the negative effects of test-dominated schooling under the influence of No Child Left Behind (NCLB). Dianne Piché, executive director of the Citizen's Commission on Civil Rights, supports the testing and accountability measures of the federal law as the best way to advance the interests of the poor and minorities.

Issue 9.   Does a "Deficit Model" Serve Poor Children Well?   133

YES: **Ruby Payne,** from "Nine Powerful Practices," *Educational Leadership* (April 2008)   *135*

NO: **Mistilina Sato and Timothy J. Lensmire,** from "Poverty and Payne: Supporting Teachers to Work with Children of Poverty," *Phi Delta Kappan* (January 2009)   *141*

Ruby Payne, president of aha!Process, Inc., a company that offers guidance to educators in poverty-area districts, puts forth specific ideas for overcoming deficits in students' lives. Assistant professor of education Mistilina Sato and associate professor of education Timothy J. Lensmire find that Payne's approach offers only simplistic solutions based on a grossly overgeneralized, deficit-laden portrayal of poor children.

Issue 10.   Should "Public Schooling" Be Redefined?   149

YES: **Frederick M. Hess,** from "What Is a 'Public School?' Principles for a New Century," *Phi Delta Kappan* (February 2004)   *151*

NO: **Linda Nathan et al.,** from "A Response to Frederick Hess," *Phi Delta Kappan* (February 2004)   *160*

Frederick M. Hess, a resident scholar at the American Enterprise Institute, advocates a broadening of the definition of "public schooling" in light of recent developments such as vouchers, charter schools, and home schooling. Linda Nathan, Joe Nathan, Ray Bacchetti, and Evans Clinchy express a variety of concerns about the conceptual expansion that Hess proposes.

UNIT 3   CURRENT SPECIFIC ISSUES   175

Issue 11.   Are Undocumented Immigrants Entitled to Public Education?   176

YES: **William J. Brennan, Jr.**, from Majority Opinion in
Plyler v. Doe (June 15, 1982)   *178*

NO: **Warren Burger**, from Dissenting Opinion in *Plyler v. Doe*
(June 15, 1982)   *188*

Justice William Brennan argues that the action of the Texas state legislature to authorize local school districts to deny enrollment in public schools to children not "legally admitted" to the country violates the Fourteenth Amendment. Chief Justice Warren Burger, in dissent, counters that the Court has no business assuming a policymaking role simply because the legislative branches of government fail to act appropriately.

Issue 12.   Has the Time Arrived for Universal Preschool?   195

YES: **David L. Kirp**, from *Big Ideas for Children: Investing in Our Nation's Future* (First Focus, 2008)   *197*

NO: **Douglas J. Besharov and Douglas M. Call**, from "The New Kindergarten," *The Wilson Quarterly* (Autumn 2008)   *206*

David L. Kirp, a professor of public policy and author of *The Sandbox Investment,* calls for expansion of federal support for universal preschool and other child care services. Professor Douglas J. Besharov and research associate Douglas M. Call of the University of Maryland School of Public Policy examine the development of child care programs and conclude that the case for universal preschool is not as strong as it seems.

Issue 13.   Is Privatization the Hope of the Future?   216

YES: **Chris Whittle**, from "Dramatic Growth Is Possible," *Education Next* (Spring 2006)   *218*

NO: **Henry Levin**, from "Déjà Vu All Over Again," *Education Next* (Spring 2006)   *224*

Chris Whittle, founder and CEO of Edison Schools, contends that public school systems still operate in an eighteenth-century mindset and offers an "independent learning" model as a replacement. Professor of economics and education Henry Levin criticizes the assumptions on which Whittle bases his prediction of successful operation of schools by for-profit management organizations such as Edison.

Issue 14.   Is the Inclusive Classroom Model Workable?   230

YES: **Mara Sapon-Shevin**, from "Learning in an Inclusive Community," *Educational Leadership* (September 2008)   232

NO: **Wade A. Carpenter**, from "The Other Side of Inclusion," *Educational Horizons* (Spring 2008)   *239*

Professor of inclusive education Mara Sapon-Shevin presents a redefinition of the inclusive classroom and offers specific strategies for bringing it about in practice. Associate professor of education Wade A. Carpenter expresses concerns about the inclusive ideology's uncritical infatuation with socialization.

Issue 15. Can Current High School Reform Curtail Dropouts? 245

YES: Thomas Toch, Craig D. Jerald, and Erin Dillon, from "Surprise—High School Reform Is Working," *Phi Delta Kappan* (February 2007) *247*

NO: Robert Epstein, from "Why High School Must Go: An Interview with Leon Botstein," *Phi Delta Kappan* (May 2007) *254*

Thomas Toch, Craig D. Jerald, and Erin Dillon, think-tank researchers at Education Sector, review recent efforts at high school reform by the Gates Foundation, the National Governors Association, and other groups, identifying many signs of progress. Scholar, author, and editor Robert Epstein, interviewing college president Leon Botstein, explores the abolition of high school as it now exists.

Issue 16. Is "Intelligent Design" a Threat to the Curriculum? 262

YES: Mark Terry, from "One Nation, Under the Designer," *Phi Delta Kappan* (December 2004) *264*

NO: Dan Peterson, from "The Little Engine That Could . . . Undo Darwinism," *The American Spectator* (June 2005) *274*

Biology teacher and science department administrator Mark Terry warns of the so-called Wedge Strategy being employed by the Discovery Institute to incorporate the "intelligent design" approach into the public school science curriculum. Attorney Dan Peterson presents fact-based arguments that separate "intelligent design" from previous campaigns for inclusion of "creation science" in the biology curriculum and cause evolution theorists to possibly adjust their standard positions.

Issue 17. Are Single-Sex Schools and Classes Effective? 283

YES: Peter Meyer, from "Learning Separately: The Case for Single-Sex Schools," *Education Next* (Winter 2008) *285*

NO: Vincent A. Anfara, Jr. and Steven B. Mertens, from "Do Single-Sex Classes and Schools Make a Difference?" *Middle School Journal* (November 2008) *291*

Journalist Peter Meyer examines the history of single-sex schools and recent concerns about "shortchanging" girls and the "crisis" in boys' education and lauds the current resurgence of single-sex schooling. Associate professor of education Vincent A. Anfara, Jr. and assistant professor of education Steven B. Mertens review research on student culture, academic climate, and attitudinal effects, concluding that the benefits of single-sex schooling remain unclear.

Issue 18. Can Zero Tolerance Violate Students Rights? 302

YES: Hon. David Souter, from Majority Opinion in *Safford Unified School District #1 v. Redding* (June 25, 2009) *304*

NO: Hon. Clarence Thomas, from Dissenting Opinion in *Safford Unified School District #1 v. Redding* (June 25, 2009) *310*

Supreme Court justice David Souter, delivering the opinion of the Court, hold that school officials, in carrying out a zero-tolerance policy on drug possession, violated a student's Fourth Amendment right against unreasonable search and seizure when they included a strip search of the girl. Justice Clarence Thomas, in dissent, states that the majority opinion imposes too vague a standard on school officials and that it grants judges sweeping authority to second-guess measures those officials take to maintain discipline and ensure safety.

Issue 19. Do Computers Negatively Affect Student Growth? 316

YES: **Lowell Monke,** from "The Human Touch," *Education Next* (Fall 2004) *318*

NO: **Frederick M. Hess,** from "Technical Difficulties," *Education Next* (Fall 2004) *325*

Lowell Monke, an assistant professor of education, expresses deep concerns that the uncritical faith in computer technology in schools has led to sacrifices in intellectual growth and creativity. Frederick M. Hess, while sharing some of Monke's observations, believes that the tools of technology, used appropriately, can support innovation and reinvention in education.

Issue 20. Should Alternative Teacher Training Be Encouraged? 333

YES: **Robert Holland,** from "How to Build a Better Teacher," *Policy Review* (April & May 2001) *335*

NO: **Linda Darling-Hammond,** from "How Teacher Education Matters," *Journal of Teacher Education* (May/June 2000) *345*

Public policy researcher Robert Holland argues that current certification programs are inadequate, especially given the growing shortage of teachers. Educational professor Linda Darling-Hammond offers evidence of failure among alternative programs and responds to criticism of standard professional preparation.

Issue 21. Can Merit Pay Accelerate School Improvement? 356

YES: **Steven Malanga,** from "Why Merit Pay Will Improve Teaching," *City Journal* (Summer 2001) *358*

NO: **Al Ramirez,** from "How Merit Pay Undermines Education," *Educational Leadership* (February 2001) *364*

Steven Malanga, a senior fellow of the Manhattan Institute, draws on examples from the corporate world and from public school systems in Cincinnati, Iowa, and Denver to make his case for performance-based merit pay for teachers. Associate professor of education Al Ramirez contends that merit pay programs misconstrue human motivation and devalue the work of teachers.

Contributors 371

Correlation Guide

The *Taking Sides* series presents current issues in a debate-style format designed to stimulate student interest and develop critical thinking skills. Each issue is thoughtfully framed with an issue summary, an issue introduction, and a postscript. The pro and con essays—selected for their liveliness and substance—represent the arguments of leading scholars and commentators in their fields.

Taking Sides: Clashing Views on Educational Issues, 16/e is an easy-to-use reader that presents issues on important topics such as *democratic classrooms, universal preschool, and merit pay for teachers.* For more information on *Taking Sides* and other *McGraw-Hill Contemporary Learning Series* titles, visit www.mhcls.com.

This convenient guide matches the issues in **Taking Sides: Educational Issues, 16/e** with the corresponding chapters in two of our best-selling McGraw-Hill Education textbooks by Nelson et al. and Spring.

Taking Sides: Educational Issues, 16/e	Critical Issues in Education: Dialogues and Dialectics, 7/e by Nelson et al.	American Education, 14/e by Spring
Issue 1: Should Schooling Be Based on Social Experiences?	**Chapter 11:** Values/Character Education: Traditional or Liberational	**Chapter 1:** The History and Goals of Public Schooling
Issue 2: Should the Curriculum Be Standardized for All?	**Chapter 5:** Standards-Based Reform: Real Change or Political Smoke Screen	**Chapter 2:** Education and Equality of Opportunity
Issue 3: Should Behaviorism Shape Educational Practices?	**Chapter 11:** Values/Character Education: Traditional or Liberational	**Chapter 1:** The History and Goals of Public Schooling
Issue 4: Is Constructivism the Best Philosophy of Education?	**Chapter 11:** Values/Character Education: Traditional or Liberational	**Chapter 1:** The History and Goals of Public Schooling
Issue 5: Should Global Competition Steer School Reform?	**Chapter 8:** Corporations, Commerce, and Schools: Complementing or Competing Interests	**Chapter 1:** The History and Goals of Public Schooling **Chapter 7:** Power and Control at State and National Levels: Political Party Platforms, High-Stakes Testing, and School Violence
Issue 6: Are Truly Democratic Classrooms Possible?	**Chapter 12:** Multicultural Education: Democratic or Divisive **Chapter 17:** Academic Freedom: Teacher Rights or Responsibilities	**Chapter 4:** Student Diversity

(Continued)

Taking Sides: Educational Issues, 16/e	Critical Issues in Education: Dialogues and Dialectics, 7/e by Nelson et al.	American Education, 14/e by Spring
Issue 7: Has the Supreme Court Reconfigured American Education?	**Chapter 6:** Religion and Public Schools: Unification or Separation	**Chapter 10:** The Courts and the Schools
Issue 8: Is No Child Left Behind Irretrievably Flawed?	**Chapter 5:** Standards-Based Reform: Real Change or Political Smoke Screen **Chapter 7:** Privatization of Schools: Boon or Bane	**Chapter 7:** Power and Control at State and National Levels: Political Party Platforms, High-Stakes Testing, and School Violence
Issue 9: Does a "Deficit Model" Serve Poor Children Well?	**Chapter 12:** Multicultural Education: Democratic or Divisive	**Chapter 3:** Equality of Educational Opportunity: Race, Gender, and Special Needs
Issue 10: Should "Public Schooling" Be Redefined?	**Chapter 7:** Privatization of Schools: Boon or Bane	**Chapter 9:** Textbooks, Curriculum, E-Learning, Cyber Bullying, and Global Models of Curriculum and Instruction
Issue 11: Are Undocumented Immigrants Entitled to Public Education?	**Chapter 9:** New Immigrants and the Schools: Unfair Burden or Business as Usual	**Chapter 4:** Student Diversity
Issue 12: Has the Time Arrived for Universal Preschool?	**Chapter 7:** Privatization of Schools: Boon or Bane	**Chapter 2:** Education and Equality of Opportunity
Issue 13: Is Privatization the Hope of the Future?	**Chapter 7:** Privatization of Schools: Boon or Bane	**Chapter 6:** Local Control, Choice, Charter Schools, and Home Schooling
Issue 14: Is the Inclusive Classroom Model Workable?	**Chapter 18:** Inclusion and Mainstreaming: Common or Special Education	**Chapter 3:** Equality of Educational Opportunity: Race, Gender, and Special Needs
Issue 15: Can Current High School Reform Curtail Dropouts?	**Chapter 12:** Multicultural Education: Democratic or Divisive	**Chapter 2:** Education and Equality of Opportunity
Issue 16: Is "Intelligent Design" a Threat to the Curriculum?	**Chapter 6:** Religion and Public Schools: Unification or Separation	**Chapter 10:** The Courts and the Schools
Issue 17: Are Single-Sex Schools and Classes Effective?	**Chapter 4:** Gender Equity: Eliminating Discrimination or Accommodating Difference **Chapter 7:** Privatization of Schools: Boon or Bane	**Chapter 5:** Multicultural and Multilingual Education
Issue 18: Can Zero Tolerance Violate Student Rights?	**Chapter 15:** Discipline and Justice: Zero Tolerance or Discretion	**Chapter 10:** The Courts and the Schools
Issue 19: Do Computers Negatively Affect Student Growth?	**Chapter 4:** Gender Equity: Eliminating Discrimination or Accommodating Difference	**Chapter 9:** Textbooks, Curriculum, E-Learning, Cyber Bullying, and Global Models of Curriculum and Instruction
Issue 20: Should Alternative Teacher Training Be Encouraged?	**Chapter 13:** Technology and Learning: Enabling or Subverting	**Chapter 8:** The Profession of Teaching
Issue 21: Can Merit Pay Accelerate School Improvement?	**Chapter 1:** Introduction: Critical Issues and Critical Thinking	**Chapter 8:** The Profession of Teaching

Introduction

Ways of Thinking About Educational Issues

James Wm. Noll

Concern about the quality of education has been expressed by philosophers, politicians, and parents for centuries. There has been a perpetual and unresolved debate regarding the definition of education, the relationship between school and society, the distribution of decision-making power in educational matters, and the means for improving all aspects of the educational enterprise.

In recent decades the growing influence of thinking drawn from the humanities and the behavioral and social sciences has brought about the development of interpretive, normative, and critical perspectives, which have sharpened the focus on educational concerns. These perspectives have allowed scholars and researchers to closely examine the contextual variables, value orientations, and philosophical and political assumptions that shape both the status quo and reform efforts.

The study of education involves the application of many perspectives to the analysis of "what is and how it got that way" and "what can be and how we can get there." Central to such study are the prevailing philosophical assumptions, theories, and visions that find their way into real-life educational situations. The application situation, with its attendant political pressures, sociocultural differences, community expectations, parental influence, and professional problems, provides a testing ground for contending theories and ideals.

This "testing ground" image applies only insofar as the status quo is malleable enough to allow the examination and trial of alternative views. Historically, institutionalized education has been characteristically rigid. As a testing ground of ideas, it has often lacked an orientation encouraging innovation and futuristic thinking. Its political grounding has usually been conservative.

As social psychologist Allen Wheelis points out in *The Quest for Identity* (1958), social institutions by definition tend toward solidification and protectionism. His depiction of the dialectical development of civilizations centers on the tension between the security and authoritarianism of "institutional processes" and the dynamism and change-orientation of "instrumental processes."

The field of education seems to graphically illustrate this observation. Educational practices are primarily tradition bound. The twentieth-century reform movement, spurred by the ideas of John Dewey, A. S. Neill, and a host of critics who campaigned for change in the 1960s, challenged the structural rigidity of schooling. In more recent decades, reformers have either attempted to restore uniformity in the curriculum and in assessment of results or campaigned for the support of alternatives to the public school monopoly. The latter group comes from both the right and the left of the political spectrum.

We are left with the abiding questions: What is an "educated" person? What should be the primary purpose of organized education? Who should control the decisions influencing the educational process? Should the schools follow society or lead it toward change? Should schooling be compulsory?

Long-standing forces have molded a wide variety of responses to these fundamental questions. The religious impetus, nationalistic fervor, philosophical ideas, the march of science and technology, varied interpretations of "societal needs," and the desire to use the schools as a means for social reform have been historically influential. In recent times other factors have emerged to contribute to the complexity of the search for answers—social class differences, demographic shifts, increasing bureaucratization, the growth of the textbook industry, the changing financial base for schooling, teacher unionization, and strengthening of parental and community pressure groups.

The struggle to find the most appropriate answers to these questions now involves, as in the past, an interplay of societal aims, educational purposes, and individual intentions. Moral development, the quest for wisdom, citizenship training, socioeconomic improvement, mental discipline, the rational control of life, job preparation, liberation of the individual, freedom of inquiry—these and many others continue to be topics of discourse on education.

A detailed historical perspective on these questions and topics may be gained by reading the interpretations of noted scholars in the field. R. Freeman Butts has written a brief but effective summary portrayal in "Search for Freedom—The Story of American Education," *NEA Journal* (March 1960). A partial listing of other sources includes R. Freeman Butts and Lawrence Cremin, *A History of Education in American Culture;* S. E. Frost, Jr., *Historical and Philosophical Foundations of Western Education;* Harry Good and Edwin Teller, *A History of Education;* Adolphe Meyer, *An Educational History of the American People;* Robert L. Church and Michael W. Sedlak, *Education in the United States: An Interpretive History;* Merle Curti, *The Social Ideas of American Educators;* Henry J. Perkinson, *The Imperfect Panacea: American Faith in Education, 1865–1965;* Clarence Karier, *Man, Society, and Education;* V. T. Thayer, *Formative Ideas in American Education;* H. Warren Button and Eugene F. Provenzo, Jr., *History of Education and Culture in America;* David Tyack and Elisabeth Hansot, *Managers of Virtue: Public School Leadership in America, 1820–1980;* Joel Spring, *The American School, 1642–1990;* S. Alexander Rippa, *Education in a Free Society: An American History;* John D. Pulliam, *History of Education in America;* Edward Stevens and George H. Wood, *Justice, Ideology, and Education;* and Walter Feinberg and Jonas F. Soltis, *School and Society.*

These and other historical accounts of the development of schooling demonstrate the continuing need to address educational questions in terms of cultural and social dynamics. A careful analysis of contemporary education demands attention not only to the historical interpretation of developmental influences but also to the philosophical forces that define formal education and the social and cultural factors that form the basis of informal education.

Examining Viewpoints

In his book *A New Public Education* (1976), Seymour Itzkoff examines the interplay between informal and formal education, concluding that economic and technological expansion have pulled people away from the informal culture by placing a premium on success in formal education. This has brought about a reactive search for less artificial educational contexts within the informal cultural community, which recognizes the impact of individual personality in shaping educational experiences.

This search for a reconstructed philosophical base for education has produced a barrage of critical commentary. Those who seek radical change in education characterize the present schools as mindless, manipulative, factory-like, bureaucratic institutions that offer little sense of community, pay scant attention to personal meaning, fail to achieve curricular integration, and maintain a psychological atmosphere of competitiveness, tension, fear, and alienation. Others deplore the ideological movement away from the formal organization of education, fearing an abandonment of standards, a dilution of the curriculum, an erosion of intellectual and behavioral discipline, and a decline in adult and institutional authority.

Students of education (whether prospective teachers, practicing professionals, or interested laypeople) must examine closely the assumptions and values underlying alternative positions in order to clarify their own viewpoints. This tri-level task may best be organized around the basic themes of purpose, power, and reform. These themes offer access to the theoretical grounding of actions in the field of education, to the political grounding of such actions, and to the future orientation of action decisions.

A general model for the examination of positions on educational issues includes the following dimensions: identification of the viewpoint, recognition of the stated or implied assumptions underlying the viewpoint, analysis of the validity of the supporting argument, and evaluation of the conclusions and action-suggestions of the originator of the position. The stated or implied assumptions may be derived from a philosophical or religious orientation, from scientific theory, from social or personal values, or from accumulated experience. Acceptance by the reader of an author's assumptions opens the way for a receptive attitude regarding the specific viewpoint expressed and its implications for action. The argument offered in justification of the viewpoint may be based on logic, common experience, controlled experiments, information and data, legal precedents, emotional appeals, and a host of other persuasive devices.

Holding the basic model in mind, readers of the positions presented in this volume (or anywhere else, for that matter) can examine the constituent elements of arguments—basic assumptions, viewpoint statements, supporting evidence, conclusions, and suggestions for action. The careful reader will accept or reject the individual elements of the total position. One might see reasonableness in a viewpoint and its justification but be unable to accept the assumptions on which it is based. Or one might accept the flow of argument from assumptions to viewpoint to evidence but find illogic or impracticality in the stated conclusions and suggestions for action. In any event, the reader's personal view is tested and honed through the process of analyzing the views of others.

Philosophical Considerations

Historically, organized education has been initiated and instituted to serve many purposes—spiritual salvation, political socialization, moral uplift, societal stability, social mobility, mental discipline, vocational efficiency, and social reform, among others. The various purposes have usually reflected the dominant philosophical conception of human nature and the prevailing assumptions about the relationship between the individual and society. At any given time, competing conceptions may vie for dominance—social conceptions, economic conceptions, conceptions that emphasize spirituality, or conceptions that stress the uniqueness and dignity of the individual, for example.

These considerations of human nature and individual—society relationships are grounded in philosophical assumptions, and these assumptions find their way to such practical domains as schooling. In Western civilization there has been an identifiable (but far from consistent and clear-cut) historical trend in the basic assumptions about reality, knowledge, values, and the human condition. This trend, made manifest in the philosophical positions of idealism, realism, pragmatism, and existentialism, has involved a shift in emphasis from the spiritual world to nature to human behavior to the social individual to the free individual, and from eternal ideas to fixed natural laws to social interaction to the inner person.

The idealist tradition, which dominated much of philosophical and educational thought until the eighteenth and nineteenth centuries, separates the changing, imperfect, material world and the permanent, perfect, spiritual or mental world. As Plato saw it, for example, human beings and all other physical entities are particular manifestations of an ideal reality that in material existence humans can never fully know. The purpose of education is to bring us closer to the absolute ideals, pure forms, and universal standards that exist spiritually, by awakening and strengthening our rational powers. For Plato, a curriculum based on mathematics, logic, and music would serve this purpose, especially in the training of leaders whose rationality must exert control over emotionality and baser instincts.

Against this tradition, which shaped the liberal arts curriculum in schools for centuries, the realism of Aristotle, with its finding of the "forms" of things *within* the material world, brought an emphasis on scientific investigation and on environmental factors in the development of human potential. This fundamental view has influenced two philosophical movements in education: naturalism, based on following or gently assisting nature (as in the approaches of John Amos Comenius, Jean-Jacques Rousseau, and Johann Heinrich Pestalozzi), and scientific realism, based on uncovering the natural laws of human behavior and shaping the educational environment to maximize their effectiveness (as in the approaches of John Locke, Johann Friedrich Herbart, and Edward Thorndike).

In the twentieth century, two philosophical forces (pragmatism and existentialism) have challenged these traditions. Each has moved primary attention away from fixed spiritual or natural influences and toward the individual as shaper of knowledge and values. The pragmatic position, articulated in America by Charles Sanders Peirce, William James, and John Dewey, turns from metaphysical abstractions toward concrete results of action. In a world of change and relativity, human beings must forge their own truths and values as they interact with their environments and each other. The European-based philosophy of existentialism, emerging from such thinkers as Gabriel Marcel, Martin Buber, Martin Heidegger, and Jean-Paul Sartre, has more recently influenced education here. Existentialism places the burdens of freedom, choice, and responsibility squarely on the individual, viewing the current encroachment of external forces and the tendency of people to "escape from freedom" as a serious diminishment of our human possibilities.

These many theoretical slants contend for recognition and acceptance as we continue the search for broad purposes in education and as we attempt to create curricula, methodologies, and learning environments that fulfill our stated purposes. This is carried out, of course, in the real world of the public schools in which social, political, and economic forces often predominate.

Power and Control

Plato, in the fourth century B.C., found existing education manipulative and confining and, in the *Republic,* described a meritocratic approach designed to nurture intellectual powers so as to form and sustain a rational society. Reform-oriented as Plato's suggestions were, he nevertheless insisted on certain restrictions and controls so that his particular version of the ideal could be met.

The ways and means of education have been fertile grounds for power struggles throughout history. Many educational efforts have been initiated by religious bodies, often creating a conflict situation when secular authorities have moved into the field. Schools have usually been seen as repositories of culture and social values and, as such, have been overseen by the more conservative forces in society. To others, bent on social reform, the schools have been treated as a spawning ground for change. Given these basic political forces, conflict is inevitable.

When one speaks of the control of education, the range of influence is indeed wide. Political influences, governmental actions, court decisions, professional militancy, parental power, and student assertion all contribute to the phenomenon of control. And the domain of control is equally broad—school finances, curriculum, instructional means and objectives, teacher certification, accountability, student discipline, censorship of school materials, determination of access and opportunity, and determination of inclusion and exclusion.

The general topic of power and control leads to a multitude of questions: Who should make policy decisions? Must the schools be puppets of the government? Can the schools function in the vanguard of social change? Can cultural indoctrination be avoided? Can the schools lead the way to full social integration? Can the effects of social class be eradicated? Can and should the schools teach values? Dealing with such questions is complicated by the increasing power of the federal government in educational matters. Congressional legislation has broadened substantially from the early land grants and aid to agricultural and vocational programs to more recent laws covering aid to federally impacted areas, school construction aid, student loans and fellowships, support for several academic areas of the curriculum, work-study programs, compensatory education, employment opportunities for youth, adult education, aid to libraries, teacher preparation, educational research, career education, education of the handicapped, and equal opportunity for females. This proliferation of areas of influence has caused the federal administrative bureaucracy to blossom from its meager beginnings in 1867 into a cabinet-level Department of Education in 1979.

State legislatures and state departments of education have also grown in power, handling greater percentages of school appropriations and controlling basic curricular decisions, attendance laws, accreditation, research, and so on. Local school boards, once the sole authorities in policy making, now share the role with higher governmental echelons as the financial support sources shift away from the local scene. Simultaneously, strengthened teacher organizations and increasingly vocal pressure groups at the local, state, and national levels have forced a widening of the base for policy decisions.

Some Concluding Remarks

The schools often seem to be either facing backward or completely absorbed in the tribulations of the present, lacking a vision of possible futures that might guide current decisions. The present is inescapable, obviously, and certainly the historical and philosophical underpinnings of the present situation must be understood, but true improvement often requires a break with conventionality—a surge toward a desired future.

The radical reform critique of government-sponsored compulsory schooling has depicted organized education as a form of cultural or political imprisonment that traps young people in an artificial and mainly irrelevant environment and rewards conformity and docility while inhibiting curiosity and creativity. Constructive reform ideas that have come from this critique include the creation of open classrooms, the de-emphasis of external motivators, the diversification of educational experience, and the building of a true sense of community within the instructional environment.

Starting with Francis Wayland Parker's schools in Quincy, Massachusetts, and John Dewey's laboratory school at the University of Chicago around the turn of the twentieth century, the campaign to make schools into more productive and humane places has been relentless. The duplication of A. S. Neill's Summerhill model in the free school movement in the 1960s, the open classroom/open space experiments, the several curricular variations, and the emergence of schools without walls, charter schools, privatization of management, and home schooling across the country testify to the desire to reform the present system or to build alternatives to it.

The progressive education movement, the development of "life adjust-ment" goals and curricula, and the "whole person" theories of educational psychology moved the schools toward an expanded concept of schooling that embraced new subject matters and new approaches to discipline during the first half of this century. Since the 1950s, however, pressure for a return to a narrower concept of schooling as intellectual training has sparked new waves of debate. Out of this situation have come attempts by educators and academi-cians to design new curricular approaches in the basic subject matter areas, efforts by private foundations to stimulate organizational innovations and to improve the training of teachers, and federal government support of educa-tional technology. Yet criticism of the schools abounds. The schools, according to many who use their services, remain too factorylike, too age-segregated, and too custodial. Alternative paths are still sought—paths that would allow action-learning, work-study, and a diversity of ways to achieve success.

H. G. Wells has told us that human history becomes more and more a race between education and catastrophe. What is needed in order to win this race is the generation of new ideas regarding cultural change, human relation-ships, ethical norms, the uses of technology, and the quality of life. These new ideas, of course, may be old ideas newly applied. One could do worse, in think-ing through the problem of improving the quality of education, than to turn to the third-century philosopher Plotinus, who called for an education directed to "the outer, the inner, and the whole." For Plotinus, "the outer" represented the public person, or the socioeconomic dimension of the total human being; "the inner" reflected the subjective dimension, the uniquely experiencing individual, or the "I"; and "the whole" signified the universe of meaning and relatedness, or the realm of human, natural, and spiritual connectedness. It would seem that education must address all of these dimensions if it is to truly help people in the lifelong struggle to shape a meaningful existence. If educa-tional experiences can be improved in these directions, the end result might be people who are not just filling space, filling time, or filling a social role, but who are capable of saying something worthwhile with their lives.

Internet References . . .

The Center for Dewey Studies

Southern Illinois University site offers a wealth of source materials on the ideas of philosopher-educator John Dewey and the progressive education movement.

http://www.siu.edu/~deweyctr

The National Paideia Center

Promotes and supports efforts of educators who are implementing the long-term systemic school reform known as the Paideia Program based on the ideas of philosopher Mortimer J. Adler.

http://www.paideia.org

Learn in Freedom!

Provides ideas, resources, and encouragement for unschoolers, homeschoolers, and all learners within or without school.

http://www.learninfreedom.org

Behaviorism

Stanford Encyclopedia of Philosophy offers articles on B. F. Skinner and other behaviorists plus links to other sites.

http://plato.stanford.edu/entries/behaviorism

The Association for Humanistic Psychology

Features material on the theories of Carl Rogers, Abraham Maslow, Rollo May, and others, as well as links to Web resources.

http://ahpweb.org

Constructivism vs. Instructivism

Offers research on two dominant pedagogical approaches and the philosophical assumptions lying behind them.

http://www.ed.sc.edu/caw/webbarton.htm

Skills Commission

Contains information on the New Commission on the Skills of the American Workforce report and the research findings on which it was based.

http://www.skillscommission.org

Basic Theoretical Issues

*W*hat is the basic purpose of education? How should the curriculum be organized and how much control should students have over their own development? What is the best way to teach and motivate students to learn? What philosophy of education should guide the process of education? These questions have been discussed throughout the history of American education and continue to be debated today. In this section, some major figures from the 20th century—John Dewey, Robert M. Hutchins, Mortimer J. Adler, John Holt, B. F. Skinner, and Carl R. Rogers—and four current scholars in the field of education—David Elkind, Jamin Carson, Marc Tucker, and Herb Childress address these basic questions.

- Should Schooling Be Based on Social Experiences?

- Should the Curriculum Be Standardized for All?

- Should Behaviorism Shape Educational Practices?

- Is Constructivism the Best Philosophy of Education?

- Should Global Competition Steer School Reform?

ISSUE 1

Should Schooling Be Based on Social Experiences?

YES: John Dewey, from *Experience and Education* (Macmillan, 1938)

NO: Robert M. Hutchins, from *The Conflict in Education in a Democratic Society* (Harper & Row, 1953)

ISSUE SUMMARY

YES: Philosopher John Dewey suggests a reconsideration of traditional approaches to schooling, giving fuller attention to the social development of the learner and the quality of his or her total experience.

NO: Robert M. Hutchins, noted educator and one-time chancellor of the University of Chicago, argues for a liberal arts education geared to the development of intellectual powers.

T hroughout history, organized education has served many purposes—the transmission of tradition, knowledge, and skills; the acculturation and socialization of the young; the building and preserving of political-economic systems; the provision of opportunity for social mobility; the enhancement of the quality of life; and the cultivation of individual potential, among others. At any given time, schools pursue a number of such goals, but the elucidation of a primary or overriding goal, which gives focus to all others, has been a source of continuous contention.

Schooling in America has been extended in the last 100 years to vast numbers of young people, and during this time the argument over aims has gained momentum. At the turn of the century, John Dewey was raising serious questions about the efficacy of the prevailing approach to schooling. He believed that schooling was often arid, pedantic, and detached from the real lives of children and youths. In establishing his laboratory school at the University of Chicago, Dewey hoped to demonstrate that experiences provided by schools could be meaningful extensions of the normal social activities of learners, having as their primary aim the full experiential growth of the individual.

In order to accomplish this, Dewey sought to bring the learner into an active and intimate relationship with the subject matter. The problem-solving, or inquiry, approach that he and his colleagues at Columbia University in New York City devised became the cornerstone of the "new education"—the progressive education movement.

In 1938 Dewey himself (as expressed in the selection that follows) sounded a note of caution to progressive educators who may have abandoned too completely the traditional disciplines in their attempt to link schooling with the needs and interests of the learners. Having spawned an educational revolution, Dewey, in his later years, emerges as more of a compromiser.

In that same year, William C. Bagley, in "An Essentialists' Platform for the Advancement of American Education," harshly criticized what he felt were anti-intellectual excesses promulgated by progressivism. In the 1950s and 1960s this theme was elaborated on by other academics, among them Robert M. Hutchins, Hyman Rickover, Arthur Bestor, and Max Rafferty, who demanded a return to intellectual discipline, higher standards, and moral guidance.

Hutchins' critique of Dewey's pragmatic philosophy was perhaps the best reasoned. He felt that the emphasis on immediate needs and desires of students and the focus on change and relativism detracted from the development of the intellectual skills needed for the realization of human potential.

A renewal of scholarly interest in the philosophical and educational ideas of both Dewey and Hutchins has resulted in a number of books, among which are *Hutchins' University: A Memoir of the University of Chicago* by William H. O'Neill (1991); *Robert M. Hutchins: Portrait of an Educator* by Mary Ann Dzuback (1991); *John Dewey and American Democracy* by Robert B. Westbrook (1991); *The End of Epistemology: Dewey and His Allies on the Spectator Theory of Knowledge* by Christopher B. Kulp (1992); and *The Promise of Pragmatism* by John Patrick Diggins (1994). Their continuing influence is charted by Rene Vincente Arcilla in "Metaphysics in Education After Hutchins and Dewey," *Teachers College Record* (Winter 1991).

More recent articles on the legacies of Dewey's progressivism and the traditionalism of Hutchins include "Why Traditional Education Is More Progressive," by E. D. Hirsch, Jr., *The American Enterprise* (March 1997); "The Plight of Children Is Our Plight," by William H. Schubert, *Educational Horizons* (Winter 1998); Diana Schaub's "Can Liberal Education Survive Liberal Democracy?" *The Public Interest* (Spring 2002); Roger Scruton's "Schools and Schooling," *The American Spectator* (June 2006) and Stanley Pogrow's "The Bermuda Triangle of American Education: Pure Traditionalism, Pure Progressivism, and Good Intentions," *Phi Delta Kappan* (October 2006).

In the following selections, Dewey charts what he considers a necessary shift from the abstractness and isolation of traditional schooling to the concreteness and vitality of the newer concept. Hutchins dissects the assumptions underlying Dewey's position and puts forth his own theory based on the premise that human nature is constant and functions the same in every society.

YES

John Dewey

Experience and Education

Mankind likes to think in terms of extreme opposites. It is given to formulating its beliefs in terms of *Either-Ors*, between which it recognizes no intermediate possibilities. When forced to recognize that the extremes cannot be acted upon, it is still inclined to hold that they are all right in theory but that when it comes to practical matters circumstances compel us to compromise. Educational philosophy is no exception. The history of educational theory is marked by opposition between the idea that education is development from within and that it is formation from without; that it is based upon natural endowments and that education is a process of overcoming natural inclination and substituting in its place habits acquired under external pressure.

At present, the opposition, so far as practical affairs of the school are concerned, tends to take the form of contrast between traditional and progressive education. If the underlying ideas of the former are formulated broadly, without the qualifications required for accurate statement, they are found to be about as follows: The subject-matter of education consists of bodies of information and of skills that have been worked out in the past; therefore, the chief business of the school is to transmit them to the new generation. In the past, there have also been developed standards and rules of conduct; moral training consists of forming habits of action in conformity with these rules and standards. Finally, the general pattern of school organization (by which I mean the relations of pupils to one another and to the teachers) constitutes the school as a kind of institution sharply marked off from other social institutions. Call up in imagination the ordinary schoolroom, its time schedules, schemes of classification, of examination and promotion, of rules of order, and I think you will grasp what is meant by "pattern of organization." If then you contrast this scene with what goes on in the family, for example, you will appreciate what is meant by the school being a kind of institution sharply marked off from any other form of social organization.

The three characteristics just mentioned fix the aims and methods of instruction and discipline. The main purpose or objective is to prepare the young for future responsibilities and for success in life, by means of acquisition of the organized bodies of information and prepared forms of skill which comprehend the material of instruction. Since the subject-matter as well as standards of proper conduct are handed down from the past, the attitude of pupils must, upon the whole, be one of docility, receptivity, and obedience. Books, especially textbooks, are the chief representatives of the lore and wisdom of the past, while teachers are the organs through which pupils are brought into effective connection with the material. Teachers are the agents through which knowledge and skills are communicated and rules of conduct enforced.

I have not made this brief summary for the purpose of criticizing the underlying philosophy. The rise of what is called new education and progressive schools is of itself a product of discontent with traditional education. In effect it is a criticism of the latter. When the implied criticism is made explicit it reads somewhat as follows: The traditional scheme is, in essence, one of imposition from above and from outside. It imposes adult standards, subject-matter, and methods upon those who are only growing slowly toward maturity. The gap is so great that the required subject-matter, the methods of learning and of behaving are foreign to the existing capacities of the young. They are beyond the reach of the experience the young learners already possess. Consequently, they must be imposed; even though good teachers will use devices of art to cover up the imposition so as to relieve it of obviously brutal features.

But the gulf between the mature or adult products and the experience and abilities of the young is so wide that the very situation forbids much active participation by pupils in the development of what is taught. Theirs is to do—and learn, as it was the part of the six hundred to do and die. Learning here means acquisition of what already is incorporated in books and in the heads of the elders. Moreover, that which is taught is thought of as essentially static. It is taught as a finished product, with little regard either to the ways in which it was originally built up or to changes that will surely occur in the future. It is to a large extent the cultural product of societies that assumed the future would be much like the past, and yet it is used as educational food in a society where change is the rule, not the exception.

If one attempts to formulate the philosophy of education implicit in the practices of the new education, we may, I think, discover certain common principles amid the variety of progressive schools now existing. To imposition from above is opposed expression and cultivation of individuality; to external discipline is opposed free activity; to learning from texts and teachers, learning through experience; to acquisition of isolated skills and techniques by drill, is opposed acquisition of them as means of attaining ends which make direct vital appeal; to preparation for a more or less remote future is opposed making the most of the opportunities of present life; to static aims and materials is opposed acquaintance with a changing world.

Now, all principles by themselves are abstract. They become concrete only in the consequences which result from their application. Just because the principles set forth are so fundamental and far-reaching, everything depends upon the interpretation given them as they are put into practice in the school and the home. It is at this point that the reference made earlier to *Either-Or* philosophies becomes peculiarly pertinent. The general philosophy of the new education may be sound, and yet the difference in abstract principles will not decide the way in which the moral and intellectual preference involved shall be worked out in practice. There is always the danger in a new movement that in rejecting the aims and methods of that which it would supplant, it may develop its principles negatively rather than positively and constructively. Then it takes its clew in practice from that which is rejected instead of from the constructive development its own philosophy.

I take it that the fundamental unity of the newer philosophy is found in the idea that there is an intimate and necessary relation between the processes of actual experience and education. If this be true, then a positive and constructive development of its own basic idea depends upon having a correct idea of experience. Take, for example, the question of organized subject-matter. . . . The problem for progressive education is: What is the place and meaning of subject-matter and of organization *within* experience? How does subject-matter function? Is there anything inherent in experience which tends towards progressive organization of its contents? What results follow when the materials of experience are not progressively organized? A philosophy which proceeds on the basis of rejection, of sheer opposition, will neglect these questions. It will tend to suppose that because the old education was based on ready-made organization, therefore it suffices to reject the principle of organization *in toto*, instead of striving to discover what it means and how it is to be attained on the basis of experience. We might go through all the points of difference between the new and the old education and reach similar conclusions. When external control is rejected, the problem becomes that of finding the factors of control that are inherent within experience. When external authority is rejected, it does not follow that all authority should be rejected, but rather that there is need to search for a more effective source of authority. Because the older education imposed the knowledge, methods, and the rules of conduct of the mature person upon the young, it does not follow, except upon the basis of the extreme *Either-Or* philosophy, that the knowledge and skill of the mature person has no directive value for the experience of the immature. On the contrary, basing education upon personal experience may mean more multiplied and more intimate contacts between the mature and the immature than ever existed in the traditional school, and consequently more, rather than less, guidance by others. The problem, then, is: how these contacts can be established without violating the principle of learning through personal experience. The solution of this problem requires a well thought-out philosophy of the social factors that operate in the constitution of individual experience.

What is indicated in the foregoing remarks is that the general principles of the new education do not of themselves solve any of the problems of the actual or practical conduct and management of progressive schools. Rather, they set new problems which have to be worked out on the basis of a new philosophy of experience. The problems are not even recognized, to say nothing of being solved, when it is assumed that it suffices to reject the ideas and practices of the old education and then go to the opposite extreme. Yet I am sure that you will appreciate what is meant when I say that many of the newer schools tend to make little or nothing of organized subject-matter of study; to proceed as if any form of direction and guidance by adults were an invasion of individual freedom, and as if the idea that education should be concerned with the present and future meant that acquaintance with the past has little or no role to play in education. Without pressing these defects to the point of exaggeration, they at least illustrate what is meant by a theory and practice of education which proceeds negatively or by reaction against what has been current in education rather than by a positive and constructive development of purposes, methods, and subject-matter on the foundation of a theory of experience and its educational potentialities.

It is not too much to say that an educational philosophy which professes to be based on the idea of freedom may become as dogmatic as ever was the traditional education which is reacted against. For any theory and set of practices is dogmatic which is not based upon critical examination of its own underlying principles. Let us say that the new education emphasizes the freedom of the learner. Very well. A problem is now set. What does freedom mean and what are the conditions under which it is capable of realization? Let us say that the kind of external imposition which was so common in the traditional school limited rather than promoted the intellectual and moral development of the young. Again, very well. Recognition of this serious defect sets a problem. Just what is the role of the teacher and of books in promoting the educational development of the immature? Admit that traditional education employed as the subject-matter for study facts and ideas so bound up with the past as to give little help in dealing with the issues of the present and future. Very well. Now we have the problem of discovering the connection which actually exists *within* experience between the achievements of the past and the issues of the present. We have the problem of ascertaining how acquaintance with the past may be translated into a potent instrumentality for dealing effectively with the future. We may reject knowledge of the past as the *end* of education and thereby only emphasize its importance as a *means*. When we do that we have a problem that is new in the story of education: How shall the young become acquainted with the past in such a way that the acquaintance is a potent agent in appreciation of the living present? . . .

In short, the point I am making is that rejection of the philosophy and practice of traditional education sets a new type of difficult educational problem for those who believe in the new type of education. We shall operate blindly and in confusion until we recognize this fact; until we thoroughly appreciate that departure from the old solves no problems. What is said in the following pages is, accordingly, intended to indicate some of the main problems with which the newer education is confronted and to suggest the main lines along which their solution is to be sought. I assume that amid all uncertainties there is one permanent frame of reference: namely, the organic connection between education and personal experience; or, that the new philosophy of education is committed to some kind of empirical and experimental philosophy. But experience and experiment are not self-explanatory ideas. Rather, their meaning is part of the problem to be explored. To know the meaning of empiricism we need to understand what experience is.

The belief that all genuine education comes about through experience does not mean that all experiences are genuinely or equally educative. Experience and education cannot be directly equated to each other. For some experiences are miseducative. Any experience is miseducative that has the effect of arresting or distorting the growth of further experience. An experience may be such as to engender callousness; it may produce lack of sensitivity and of responsiveness. Then the possibilities of having richer experience in the future are restricted. Again, a given experience may increase a person's automatic skill in a particular direction and yet tend to land him in a groove or rut; the effect again is to narrow the field of further experience. An experience may be immediately enjoyable and yet promote the formation of a slack and careless attitude; this attitude then operates to modify the quality of subsequent experiences so as to prevent a person from getting out of them what they have to give. Again, experiences may be so disconnected from one another that, while each is agreeable or even exciting in itself, they are not linked cumulatively to one another. Energy is then dissipated and a person becomes scatter-brained. Each experience may be lively, vivid, and "interesting," and yet their disconnectedness may artificially generate dispersive, disintegrated, centrifugal habits. The consequence of formation of such habits is inability to control future experiences. They are then taken, either by way of enjoyment or of discontent and revolt, just as they come. Under such circumstances, it is idle to talk of self-control.

Traditional education offers a plethora of examples of experiences of the kinds just mentioned. It is a great mistake to suppose, even tacitly, that the traditional schoolroom was not a place in which pupils had experiences. Yet this is tacitly assumed when progressive education as a plan of learning by experience is placed in sharp opposition to the old. The proper line of attack is that the experiences which were had, by pupils and teachers alike, were largely of a wrong kind. How many students, for example, were rendered callous to ideas, and how many lost the impetus to learn because of the way in which learning was experienced by them? How many acquired special skills by means of automatic drill so that their power of judgment and capacity to act intelligently in new situations was limited? How many came to associate the learning process with ennui and boredom? How many found what they did learn so foreign to the situations of life outside the school as to give them no power of control over the latter? How many came to associate books with dull drudgery, so that they were "conditioned" to all but flashy reading matter?

If I ask these questions, it is not for the sake of wholesale condemnation of the old education. It is for quite another purpose. It is to emphasize the fact, first, that young people in traditional schools do have experiences; and, secondly, that the trouble is not the absence of experiences, but their defective and wrong character—wrong and defective from the standpoint of connection with further experience. The positive side of this point is even more important in connection with progressive education. It is not enough to insist upon the necessity of experience, nor even of activity in experience. Everything depends upon the *quality* of the experience which is had. The quality of an experience has two aspects. There is an immediate aspect of agreeableness or disagreeableness, and there is its influence upon later experiences. The first is obvious and easy to judge. The *effect* of an experience is not borne on its face. It sets a problem to the educator. It is his business to arrange for the kind of experiences which, while they do not repel the student, but rather engage his activities are, nevertheless, more than immediately enjoyable since they promote having desirable future experiences. Just as no man lives or dies to himself, so no experience lives or dies to itself. Wholly independent of desire or intent, every experience lives on in further experiences. Hence the central problem of an education based upon experience is to select the kind of present experiences that live fruitfully and creatively in subsequent experiences.

. . . Here I wish simply to emphasize the importance of this principle [of the continuity of experience] for the philosophy of educative experience. A philosophy of education, like my theory, has to be stated in words, in symbols. But so far as it is more than verbal it is a plan for conducting education. Like any plan, it must be framed with reference to what is to be done and how it is to be done. The more definitely and sincerely it is held that education is a development within, by, and for experience, the more important it is that there shall be clear conceptions of what experience is. Unless experience is so conceived that the result is a plan for deciding upon subject-matter, upon methods of instruction and discipline, and upon material equipment and social organization of the school, it is wholly in the air. It is reduced to a form of words which may be emotionally stirring but for which any other set of words might equally well be substituted unless they indicate operations to be initiated and executed. Just because traditional education was a matter of routine in which the plans and programs were handed down from the past, it does not follow that progressive education is a matter of planless improvisation.

The traditional school could get along without any consistently developed philosophy of education. About all it required in that line was a set of abstract words like culture, discipline, our great cultural heritage, etc., actual guidance being derived not from them but from custom and established routines. Just because progressive schools cannot rely upon established traditions and institutional habits, they must either proceed more or less haphazardly or be directed by ideas which, when they are made articulate and coherent, form a philosophy of education. Revolt against the kind of organization characteristic of the traditional school constitutes a demand for a kind of organization based upon ideas. I think that only slight acquaintance with the history of education is needed to prove that educational reformers and innovators alone have felt the need for a philosophy of education. Those who adhered to the established system needed merely a few fine-sounding words to justify existing practices. The real work was done by habits which were so fixed as to be institutional. The lesson for progressive education is that it requires in an urgent degree, a degree more pressing than was incumbent upon former innovators, a philosophy of education based upon a philosophy of experience.

I remarked incidentally that the philosophy in question is, to paraphrase the saying of Lincoln about democracy, one of education of, by, and for experience. No one of these words, *of, by,* or *for,* names anything which is self-evident. Each of them is a challenge to discover and put into operation a principle of order and organization which follows from understanding what education experience signifies.

It is, accordingly, a much more difficult task to work out the kinds of materials, of methods, and of social relationships that are appropriate to the new education than is the case with traditional education. I think many of the difficulties experienced in the conduct of progressive schools and many of the criticisms leveled against them arise from this source. The difficulties are aggravated and the criticisms are increased when it is supposed that the new education is somehow easier than the old. This belief is, I imagine, more or less current. Perhaps it illustrates again the *Either-Or* philosophy, springing from the idea that about all which is required is not to do what is done in traditional schools.

I admit gladly that the new education is *simpler* in principle than the old. It is in harmony with principles of growth, while there is very much which is artificial in the old selection and arrangement of subjects and methods, and artificiality always leads to unnecessary complexity. But the easy and the simple are not identical. To discover what is really simple and to act upon the discovery is an exceedingly difficult task. After the artificial and complex is once institutionally established and ingrained in custom and routine, it is easier to walk in the paths that have been beaten than it is, after taking a new point of view, to work out what is practically involved in the new point of view. The old Ptolemaic astronomical system was more complicated with its cycles and epicycles than the Copernican system. But until organization of actual astronomical phenomena on the ground of the latter principle had been effected the easiest course was to follow the line of least resistance provided by the old intellectual habit. So we come back to the idea that a coherent *theory* of experience, affording positive direction to selection and organization of appropriate educational methods and materials, is required by the attempt to give new direction to the work of the schools. The process is a slow and arduous one. It is a matter of growth, and there are many obstacles which tend to obstruct growth and to deflect it into wrong lines.

. . . [W]e must escape from the tendency to think of organization in terms of the *kind* of organization, whether of content (or subject-matter), or of methods and social relations, that mark traditional education. I think that a good deal of the current opposition to the idea of organization is due to the fact that it is so hard to get away from the picture of the studies of the old school. The moment "organization" is mentioned imagination goes almost automatically to the kind of organization that is familiar, and in revolting against that we are led to shrink from the very idea of any organization. On the other hand, educational reactionaries, who are now gathering force, use the absence of adequate intellectual and moral organization in the newer type of school as proof not only of the need of organization, but to identify any and every kind of organization with that instituted before the rise of experimental science. Failure to develop a conception of organization upon the empirical and experimental basis gives reactionaries a too easy victory. But the fact that the empirical sciences now offer the best type of intellectual organization which can be found in any field shows that there is no reason why we, who call ourselves empiricists, should be "pushovers" in the matter of order and organization.

Robert M. Hutchins

The Basis of Education

The obvious failures of the doctrines of adaptation, immediate needs, social reform, and of the doctrine that we need no doctrine at all may suggest to us that we require a better definition of education. Let us concede that every society must have some system that attempts to adapt the young to their social and political environment. If the society is bad, in the sense, for example, in which the Nazi state was bad, the system will aim at the same bad ends. To the extent that it makes men bad in order that they may be tractable subjects of a bad state, the system may help to achieve the social ideals of the society. It may be what the society wants; it may even be what the society needs, if it is to perpetuate its form and accomplish its aims. In pragmatic terms, in terms of success in the society, it may be a "good" system.

But it seems to me clearer to say that, though it may be a system of training, or instruction, or adaptation, or meeting immediate needs, it is not a system of education. It seems clearer to say that the purpose of education is to improve men. Any system that tries to make them bad is not education, but something else. If, for example, democracy is the best form of society, a system that adapts the young to it will be an educational system. If despotism is a bad form of society, a system that adapts the young to it will not be an educational system, and the better it succeeds in adapting them the less educational it will be.

Every man has a function as a man. The function of a citizen or a subject may vary from society to society, and the system of training, or adaptation, or instruction, or meeting immediate needs may vary with it. But the function of a man as man is the same in every age and in every society, since it results from his nature as a man. The aim of an educational system is the same in every age and in every society where such a system can exist: it is to improve man as man.

If we are going to talk about improving men and societies, we have to believe that there is some difference between good and bad. This difference must not be, as the positivists think it is, merely conventional. We cannot tell this difference by any examination of the effectiveness of a given program as the pragmatists propose; the time required to estimate these effects is usually too long and the complexity of society is always too great for us to say that the consequences of a given program are altogether clear. We cannot discover the difference between good and bad by going to the laboratory, for men and societies are not laboratory animals. If we believe that there is no truth, there is no knowledge, and there are no values except those which are validated by laboratory experiment, we cannot talk about the improvement of men and societies, for we can have no standard of judging anything that takes place among men or in societies.

Society is to be improved, not by forcing a program of social reform down its throat, through the schools, or otherwise, but by the improvement of the individuals who compose it. As Plato said, "Governments reflect human nature. States are not made out of stone or wood, but out of the characters of their citizens: these turn the scale and draw everything after them." The individual is the heart of society. . . .

Man is by nature free, and he is by nature social. To use his freedom rightly he needs discipline. To live in society he needs the moral virtues. Good moral and intellectual habits are required for the fullest development of the nature of man.

To develop fully as a social, political animal man needs participation in his own government. A benevolent despotism will not do. You cannot expect the slave to show the virtues of the free man unless you first set him free. Only democracy, in which all men rule and are ruled in turn for the good life of the whole community, can be an absolutely good form of government. . . .

Education deals with the development of the intellectual powers of men. Their moral and spiritual powers are the sphere of the family and the church. All three agencies must work in harmony; for, though a man has three aspects, he is still one man. But the schools cannot take over the role of the family and the church without promoting the atrophy of those institutions and failing in the task that is proper to the schools.

We cannot talk about the intellectual powers of men, though we can talk about training them, or amusing them, or adapting them, and meeting their immediate needs, unless our philosophy in general tells us that there is knowledge and that there is a difference between true and false. We must believe, too, that there are other means of obtaining knowledge than scientific experimentation. If knowledge can be sought only in the laboratory, many fields in which we thought we had knowledge will offer us nothing but opinion or superstition, and we shall be forced to conclude that we cannot know anything about the most important aspects of man and society. If we are to set about developing the intellectual powers of man through having them acquire knowledge of the most important subjects, we have to begin with the proposition that experimentation and empirical data will be of only limited use to us, contrary to the convictions of many American social scientists, and that philosophy, history, literature, and art give us knowledge, and significant knowledge, on the most significant issues.

If the object of education is the improvement of men, then any system of education that is without values is a contradiction in terms. A system that seeks bad values is bad. A system that denies the existence of values denies the possibility of education. Relativism, scientism, skepticism, and anti-intellectualism, the four horsemen of the philosophical apocalypse, have produced that chaos in education which will end in the disintegration of the West.

The prime object of education is to know what is good for man. It is to know the goods in their order. There is a hierarchy of values. The task of education is to help us understand it, establish it, and live by it. This Aristotle had in mind when he said: "It is not the possessions but the desires of men that must be equalized, and this is impossible unless they have a sufficient education according to the nature of things."

Such an education is far removed from the triviality of that produced by the doctrines of adaptation, of immediate needs, of social reform, or of the doctrine of no doctrine at all. Such an education will not adapt the young to a bad environment, but it will encourage them to make it good. It will not overlook immediate needs, but it will place these needs in their proper relationship to more distant, less tangible, and more important goods. It will be the only effective means of reforming society.

This is the education appropriate to free men. It is liberal education. If all men are to be free, all men must have this education. It makes no difference how they are to earn their living or what their special interests or aptitudes may be. They can learn to make a living, and they can develop their special interests and aptitudes, after they have laid the foundation of free and responsible manhood through liberal education. It will not do to say that they are incapable of such education. This claim is made by those who are too indolent or unconvinced to make the effort to give such education to the masses.

Nor will it do to say that there is not enough time to give everybody a liberal education before he becomes a specialist. In America, at least, the waste and frivolity of the educational system are so great that it would be possible through getting rid of them to give every citizen a liberal education and make him a qualified specialist, too, in less time than is now consumed in turning out uneducated specialists.

A liberal education aims to develop the powers of understanding and judgment. It is impossible that too many people can be educated in this sense, because there cannot be too many people with understanding and judgment. We hear a great deal today about the dangers that will come upon us through the frustration of educated people who have got educated in the expectation that education will get them a better job, and who then fail to get it. But surely this depends on the representations that are made to the young about what education is. If we allow them to believe that education will get them better jobs and encourage them to get educated with this end in view, they are entitled to a sense of frustration if, when they have got the education, they do not get the jobs. But, if we say that they should be educated in order to be men, and that everybody, whether he is ditch-digger or a bank president, should have this education because he is a man, then the ditch-digger may still feel frustrated, but not because of his education.

Nor is it possible for a person to have too much liberal education, because it is impossible to have too much understanding and judgment. But it is possible to undertake too much in the name of liberal education in youth. The object of liberal education in youth is not to teach the young all they will ever need to know. It is to give them the habits, ideas, and techniques that they need to continue to educate themselves. Thus the object of formal institutional liberal education in youth is to prepare the young to educate themselves throughout their lives.

I would remind you of the impossibility of learning to understand and judge many of the most important things in youth. The judgment and under-standing of practical affairs can amount to little in the absence of experience with practical affairs. Subjects that cannot be understood without experience should not be taught to those who are without experience. Or, if these subjects are taught to those who are without experience, it should be clear that these subjects can be taught only by way of introduction and that their value to the student depends on his continuing to study them as he acquires experience. The tragedy in America is that economics, ethics, politics, history, and litera-ture are studied in youth, and seldom studied again. Therefore the graduates of American universities seldom understand them.

This pedagogical principle, that subjects requiring experience can be learned only by the experienced, leads to the conclusion that the most impor-tant branch of education is the education of adults. We sometimes seem to think of education as something like the mumps, measles, whooping cough, or chicken pox. If a person has had education in childhood, he need not, in fact he cannot, have it again. But the pedagogical principle that the most important things can be learned only in mature life is supported by a sound philosophy in general. Men are rational animals. They achieve their terrestrial felicity by the use of reason. And this means that they have to use it for their entire lives. To say that they should learn only in childhood would mean that they were human only in childhood.

And it would mean that they were unfit to be citizens of a republic. A re-public, a true *res publica*, can maintain justice, peace, freedom, and order only by the exercise of intelligence. When we speak of the consent of the governed, we mean, since men are not angels who seek the truth intuitively and do not have to learn it, that every act of assent on the part of the governed is a prod-uct of learning. A republic is really a common educational life in process. So Montesquieu said that, whereas the principle of a monarchy was honor, and the principle of a tyranny was fear, the principle of a republic was education.

Hence the ideal republic is the republic of learning. It is the utopia by which all actual political republics are measured. The goal toward which we started with the Athenians twenty-five centuries ago is an unlimited republic of learning and a worldwide political republic mutually supporting each other.

All men are capable of learning. Learning does not stop as long as a man lives, unless his learning power atrophies because he does not use it. Political freedom cannot endure unless it is accompanied by provision for the unlim-ited acquisition of knowledge. Truth is not long retained in human affairs without continual learning and relearning. Peace is unlikely unless there are continuous, unlimited opportunities for learning and unless men continu-ously avail themselves of them. The world of law and justice for which we yearn, the worldwide political republic, cannot be realized without the world-wide republic of learning. The civilization we seek will be achieved when all men are citizens of the world republic of law and justice and of the republic of learning all their lives long.

POSTSCRIPT

Should Schooling Be Based on Social Experiences?

Intellectual training versus social-emotional-mental growth—the argument between Dewey and Hutchins reflects a historical debate that flows from the ideas of Plato and Aristotle and that continues today. Psychologists, sociologists, curriculum and instruction specialists, and popular critics have joined philosophers in commenting on this central concern.

Followers of Dewey contend that training the mental powers cannot be isolated from other factors of development and, indeed, can be enhanced by attention to the concrete social situations in which learning occurs. Critics of Dewey worry that the expansion of effort into the social and emotional realm only detracts from the intellectual mission that is schooling's unique province.

Was the progressive education movement ruinous, or did it lay the foundation for the education of the future? A reasonably even-handed appraisal can be found in Lawrence Cremin's *The Transformation of the School* (1961). The free school movement of the 1960s, at least partly derived from progressivism, is analyzed in Allen Graubard's *Free the Children* (1973) and Jonathan Kozol's *Free Schools* (1972). Diane Ravitch's *Troubled Crusade* (1983) and Mary Eberstadt's "The Schools They Deserve," *Policy Review* (October/November 1999) offer effective critiques of progressivism.

Among the best general explorations of philosophical alternatives are Gerald L. Gutek's *Philosophical and Ideological Perspectives on Education* (1988); Edward J. Power's *Philosophy of Education: Studies in Philosophies, Schooling, and Educational Policies* (1990); and *Philosophical Foundations of Education* by Howard Ozmon and Samuel Craver (1990).

Also worth perusing are Philip W. Jackson's "Dewey's *Experience and Education* Revisited," *The Educational Forum* (Summer 1996); Jerome Bruner's 1996 book *The Culture of Education* (particularly chapter 3, "The Complexity of Educational Aims"); Christine McCarthy's "Dewey's Ethics: Philosophy or Science?" *Education Theory* (Summer 1999); Debra J. Anderson and Robert L. Major, "Dewey, Democracy, and Citizenship," *The Clearing House* (November/December 2001); Julie Webber, "Why Can't We Be Deweyan Citizens?" *Educational Theory* (Spring 2001); David B. Ackerman, "Taproots for a New Century: Tapping the Best of Traditional and Progressive Education," *Phi Delta Kappan* (January 2003); and William Hayes, "The Future of Progressive Education," *Educational Horizons* (Spring 2008).

Questions that must be addressed include: Can the "either/or" polarities of this basic argument be overcome? Is the articulation of overarching general aims essential to the charting of a worthwhile educational experience? And how can the classroom teacher relate to general philosophical aims?

ISSUE 2

Should the Curriculum Be Standardized for All?

YES: Mortimer J. Adler, from "The Paideia Proposal: Rediscovering the Essence of Education," *American School Board Journal* (July 1982)

NO: John Holt, from *Escape from Childhood* (E. P. Dutton, 1974)

ISSUE SUMMARY

YES: Philosopher Mortimer J. Adler contends that democracy is best served by a public school system that establishes uniform curricular objectives for all students.

NO: Educator John Holt argues that an imposed curriculum damages the individual and usurps a basic human right to select one's own path of development.

$\mathbf{C}$ontroversy over the content of education has been particularly keen since the 1950s. The pendulum has swung from learner-centered progressive education to an emphasis on structured intellectual discipline to calls for radical reform in the direction of "openness" to the recent rally to go "back to basics."

The conservative viewpoint, articulated by such writers as Robert M. Hutchins, Clifton Fadiman, Jacques Barzun, Arthur Bestor, and Mortimer J. Adler, arises from concerns about the drift toward informalism and the decline in academic achievement in recent decades. Taking philosophical cues from Plato's contention that certain subject matters have universal qualities that prompt mental and characterological development, the "basics" advocates argue against incidental learning, student choice, and diminution of structure and standards. Barzun summarizes the viewpoint succinctly: "Nonsense is at the heart of those proposals that would replace definable subject matters with vague activities copied from 'life' or with courses organized around 'problems' or 'attitudes.'"

The reform viewpoint, represented by John Holt, Paul Goodman, Ivan Illich, Charles Silberman, Edgar Friedenberg, and others, portrays the typical traditional school as a mindless, indifferent, social institution dedicated to producing fear, docility, and conformity. In such an atmosphere, the viewpoint holds, learners either become alienated from the established curriculum or learn to play the school "game" and thus achieve a hollow success. Taking cues from the ideas of John Dewey and A. S. Neill, the "radical reformers" have given rise to a flurry of alternatives to regular schooling during recent decades. Among these are free schools, which follow the Summerhill model; urban storefront schools, which attempt to develop a true sense of "community"; "schools without walls," which follow the Philadelphia Parkway Program model; "commonwealth" schools, in which students, parents, and teachers share responsibility; and various "humanistic education" projects within regular school systems, which emphasize students' self-concept development and choice-making ability.

The utilitarian tradition that has descended from Benjamin Franklin, Horace Mann, and Herbert Spencer, Dewey's theory of active experiencing, and Neill's insistence on free and natural development support the reform position. The ideology rejects the factory model of schooling with its rigidly set curriculum, its neglect of individual differences, its social engineering function, and its pervasive formalism. "Basics" advocates, on the other hand, express deep concern over the erosion of authority and the watering down of demands upon students that result from the reform ideology.

Arguments for a more standardized curriculum have been embodied most recently in Theodore R. Sizer's Coalition of Essential Schools and the Core Knowledge Schools of E. D. Hirsch, Jr., whose 1996 book *The Schools We Need and Why We Don't Have Them* summarizes the basic points of this view. An interview with Hirsch by Mark F. Goldberg titled "Doing What Works" appeared in the September 1997 issue of *Phi Delta Kappan*. A thorough critique of Hirsch's position is presented by Kristen L. Buras in "Questioning Core Assumptions," *Harvard Educational Review* (Spring 1999). In 1998 Terry Roberts and the staff of the National Paideia Center at the University of North Carolina released *The Power of Paideia Schools: Defining Lives Through Learning*.

A broad spectrum of ideas on the curriculum may be found in John I. Goodlad's *A Place Called School* (1984), Maxine Green's *The Dialectic of Freedom* (1987), Theodore R. Sizer's *Horace* trilogy, and Ernest L. Boyer's *The Basic School* (1995). Some provocative ideas on this and related issues may be found in "The Goals of Education" by Richard Rothstein and Rebecca Jacobsen in *Phi Delta Kappan* (December 2006).

In the following selections, Mortimer J. Adler outlines his "Paideia Proposal," which calls for a uniform and unified curriculum and methodological approach—a common schooling for the development of a truly democratic society. In opposition, John Holt goes beyond his earlier concerns about the oppressiveness of the school curriculum to propose complete freedom for the learner to determine all aspects of his or her educational development.

YES

Mortimer J. Adler

The Paideia Proposal: Rediscovering the Essence of Education

In the first 80 years of this century, we have met the obligation imposed on us by the principle of equal educational opportunity, but only in a quantitative sense. Now as we approach the end of the century, we must achieve equality in qualitative terms.

This means a completely on-track system of schooling. It means, at the basic level, giving all the young the same kind of schooling, whether or not they are college bound.

We are aware that children, although equal in their common humanity and fundamental human rights, are unequal as individuals, differing in their capacity to learn. In addition, the homes and environments from which they come to school are unequal—either predisposing the child for schooling or doing the opposite.

Consequently, the Paideia Proposal, faithful to the principle of equal educational opportunity, includes the suggestion that inequalities due to environmental factors must be overcome by some form of preschool preparation at least one year for all and two or even three for some. We know that to make such preschool tutelage compulsory at the public expense would be tantamount to increasing the duration of compulsory schooling from 12 years to 13, 14, or 15 years. Nevertheless, we think that this preschool adjunct to the 12 years of compulsory basic schooling is so important that some way must be found to make it available for all and to see that all use it to advantage.

The Essentials of Basic Schooling

The objectives of basic schooling should be the same for the whole school population. In our current two-track or multitrack system, the learning objectives are not the same for all. And even when the objectives aimed at those on the upper track are correct, the course of study now provided does not adequately realize these correct objectives. On all tracks in our current system, we fail to cultivate proficiency in the common tasks of learning, and we especially fail to develop sufficiently the indispensable skills of learning.

The uniform objectives of basic schooling should be threefold. They should correspond to three aspects of the common future to which all the children are destined: (1) Our society provides all children ample opportunity for personal development. Given such opportunity, each individual is under a moral obligation to make the most of himself and his life. Basic schooling must facilitate this accomplishment. (2) All the children will become, when of age, full-fledged citizens with suffrage and other political responsibilities. Basic schooling must do everything it can to make them good citizens, able to perform the duties of citizenship with all the trained intelligence that each is able to achieve. (3) When they are grown, all (or certainly most) of the children will engage in some form of work to earn a living. Basic schooling must prepare them for earning a living, but not by training them for this or that specific job while they are still in school.

To achieve these three objectives, the character of basic schooling must be general and liberal. It should have a single, required, 12-year course of study for all, with no electives except one—an elective choice with regard to a second language, to be selected from such modern languages as French, German, Italian, Spanish, Russian, and Chinese. The elimination of all electives, with this one exception, excludes what *should* be excluded—all forms of specialization, including particularized job training.

In its final form, the Paideia Proposal will detail this required course of study, but I will summarize the curriculum here in its bare outline. It consists of three main columns of teaching and learning, running through the 12 years and progressing, of course, from the simple to the more complex, from the less difficult to the more difficult, as the students grow older. Understand: The three columns (see Table 1) represent three distinct modes of teaching and learning. They do not represent a series of courses. A specific course or class may employ more than one mode of teaching and learning, but all three modes are essential to the overall course of study.

Table 1

The Paideia Curriculum

	Column One	Column Two	Column Three
Goals	Acquisition of Organized Knowledge	Development of Intellectual Skills and Skills of Learning	Improved Understading of Ideas and Values
	by means of	*by means of*	*by means of*
Means	Didactic Instruction, Lecturing, and Textbooks	Coaching, Exercises, Supervised Practice	Maieutic or Socratic Questioning and Active Participation
	in these three subject areas	*in these operations*	*in these activities*
Subject Areas, Operations, and Activities	Language, Literature, and Fine Arts; Mathematics and Natural Science; History, Geography, and Social Studies	Reading, Writing, Speaking, Listening, Calculating, Problem Solving, Observing, Measuring, Estimating, Exercising Critical Judgment	Discussion of Books (Not Textbooks) and Other Works of Art; Involvement in Music, Drama, and Visual Arts

The three columns do not correspond to separate courses, nor is one kind of teaching and learning necessarily confined to any one class.

The first column is devoted to acquiring knowledge in three subject areas: (A) language, literature, and the fine arts; (B) mathematics and natural science; (C) history, geography, and social studies.

The second column is devoted to developing the intellectual skills of learning. These include all the language skills necessary for thought and communication—the skills of reading, writing, speaking, listening. They also include mathematical and scientific skills; the skills of observing, measuring, estimating, and calculating; and skills in the use of the computer and of other scientific instruments. Together, these skills make it possible to think clearly and critically. They once were called the liberal arts—the intellectual skills indispensable to being competent as a learner.

The third column is devoted to enlarging the understanding of ideas and values. The materials of the third column are books (*not* textbooks), and other products of human artistry. These materials include books of every variety—historical, scientific, and philosophical as well as poems, stories, and essays—and also individual pieces of music, visual art, dramatic productions, dance productions, film or television productions. Music and works of visual art can be used in seminars in which ideas are discussed; but as with poetry and fiction, they also are to be experienced aesthetically, to be enjoyed and admired for their excellence. In this connection, exercises in the composition of poetry, music, and visual works and in the production of dramatic works should be used to develop the appreciation of excellence.

The three columns represent three different kinds of learning on the part of the student and three different kinds of instruction on the part of teachers.

In the first column, the students are engaged in acquiring information and organized knowledge about nature, man, and human society. The method of instruction here, using textbooks and manuals, is didactic. The teacher lectures, invites responses from the students, monitors the acquisition of knowledge, and tests that acquisition in various ways.

In the second column, the students are engaged in developing habits of performance, which is all that is involved in the development of an art or skill. Art, skill, or technique is nothing more than a cultivated, habitual ability to do a certain kind of thing well, whether that is swimming and dancing, or reading and writing. Here, students are acquiring linguistic, mathematical, scientific, and historical *know-how* in contrast to what they acquire in the first column, which is *know-that* with respect to language, literature, and the fine arts, mathematics and science, history, geography, and social studies. Here, the method of instruction cannot be didactic or monitorial; it cannot be dependent on textbooks. It must be coaching, the same kind used in the gym to develop bodily skills; only here it is used by a different kind of coach in the classroom to develop intellectual skills.

In the third column, students are engaged in a process of enlightenment, the process whereby they develop their understanding of the basic and controlling ideas in all fields of subject matter and come to appreciate better all the human values embodied in works of art. Here, students move progressively from understanding less to understanding more—understanding better what they already know and appreciating more what they already have experienced. Here, the method of instruction cannot be either didactic or coaching. It must be the Socratic, or maieutic, method of questioning and discussing. It should not occur in any ordinary classroom with the students sitting in rows and the teacher in front of the class, but in a seminar room, with the students sitting around a table and the teacher sitting with them as an equal, even though a little older and wiser.

Of these three main elements in the required curriculum, the third column is completely innovative. Nothing like this is done in our schools, and because it is completely absent from the ordinary curriculum of basic schooling, the students never have the experience of having their minds addressed in a challenging way or of being asked to think about the important ideas, to express their thoughts, to defend their opinions in a reasonable fashion.

The only thing that is innovative about the second column is the insistence that the method of instruction here must be coaching carried on either with one student at a time or with very small groups of students. Nothing else can be effective in the development of a skill, be it bodily or intellectual. The absence of such individualized coaching in our schools explains why most of the students cannot read well, write well, speak well, listen well, or perform well any of the other basic intellectual operations.

The three columns are closely interconnected and integrated, but the middle column—the one concerned with linguistic, mathematical, and scientific skills—is central. It both supports and is supported by the other two columns. All the intellectual skills with which it is concerned must be exercised in the study of the three basic subject-matters and in acquiring knowledge about them, and these intellectual skills must be exercised in the seminars devoted to the discussion of books and other things.

In addition to the three main columns in the curriculum, ascending through the 12 years of basic schooling, there are three adjuncts: One is 12 years of physical training, accompanied by instruction in bodily care and hygiene. The second, running through something less than 12 years, is the development of basic manual skills, such as cooking, sewing, carpentry, and the operation of all kinds of machines. The third, reserved for the last year or two, is an introduction to the whole world of work—the range of occupations in which human beings earn their livings. This is not particularized job training. It is the very opposite. It aims at a broad understanding of what is involved in working for a living and of the various ways in which that can be done. If, at the end of 12 years, students wish training for specific jobs, they should get that in two-year community or junior colleges, or on the job itself, or in technical institutes of one sort or another.

Everything that has not been specifically mentioned as occupying the time of the school day should be reserved for after-hours and have the status of extracurricular activities.

Please, note: The required course of study just described is as important for what it *displaces* as for what it introduces. It displaces a multitude of elective courses, especially those offered in our secondary schools, most of which make little or no contribution to general, liberal education. It eliminates all narrowly specialized job training, which now abounds in our schools. It throws out of the curriculum and into the category of optional extracurricular activities a variety of things that have little or no educational value.

If it did not call for all these displacements, there would not be enough time in the school day or year to accomplish everything that is essential to the general, liberal learning that must be the content of basic schooling.

The Quintessential Element

So far, I have set forth the bare essentials of the Paideia Proposal with regard to basic schooling. I have not yet mentioned the quintessential element—the *sine qua non*—without which nothing else can possibly come to fruition, no matter how sound it might be in principle. The heart of the matter is the quality of learning and the quality of teaching that occupies the school day, not to mention the quality of the homework after school.

First, the learning must be active. It must use the whole mind, not just the memory. It must be learning by discovery, in which the student, never the teacher, is the primary agent. Learning by discovery, which is the only genuine learning, may be either unaided or aided. It is unaided only for geniuses. For most students, discovery must be aided.

Here is where teachers come in—as aids in the process of learning by discovery not as knowers who attempt to put the knowledge they have into the minds of their students. The quality of the teaching, in short, depends crucially upon how the teacher conceives his role in the process of learning, and that must be as an aid to the student's process of discovery.

I am prepared for the questions that must be agitating you by now: How and where will we get the teachers who can perform as teachers should? How will we be able to staff the program with teachers so trained that they will be competent to provide the quality of instruction required for the quality of learning desired?

The first part of our answer to these questions is negative: We *cannot* get the teachers we need for the Paideia program from schools of education as *they are now constituted*. As teachers are now trained for teaching, they simply will not do. The ideal—an impracticable ideal—would be to ask for teachers who are, themselves, truly educated human beings. But truly educated human beings are too rare. Even if we could draft all who are now alive, there still would be far too few to staff our schools.

Well, then, what can we look for? Look for teachers who are actively engaged in the process of *becoming* educated human beings, who are themselves deeply motivated to develop their own minds. Assuming this is not too much to ask for the present, how should teachers be schooled and trained in the future? First, they should have the same kind of basic schooling that is recommended in the Paideia Proposal. Second, they should have additional schooling, at the college and even the university level, in which the same kind of general, liberal learning is carried on at advanced levels—more deeply, broadly, and intensively than it can be done in the first 12 years of schooling. Third, they must be given something analogous to the clinical experience in the training of physicians. They must engage in practice-teaching under supervision, which is another way of saying that they must be *coached* in the arts of teaching, not just given didactic instruction in educational psychology and in pedagogy. Finally, and most important of all, they must learn how to teach well by being exposed to the performances of those who are masters of the arts involved in teaching.

It is by watching a good teacher at work that they will be able to perceive what is involved in the process of assisting others to learn by discovery. Perceiving it, they must then try to emulate what they observe, and through this process, they slowly will become good teachers themselves.

The Paideia Proposal recognizes the need for three different kinds of institutions at the collegiate level: The two-year community or junior college should offer a wide choice of electives that give students some training in one or another specialized field, mainly those fields of study that have something to do with earning a living. The four-year college also should offer a wide variety of electives, to be chosen by students who aim at the various professional or technical occupations that require advanced study. Those elective majors chosen by students should be accompanied, for all students, by one required minor, in which the kind of general and liberal learning that was begun at the level of basic schooling is continued at a higher level in the four years of college. And we should have still a third type of collegiate institution—a four-year college in which general, liberal learning at a higher level constitutes a required course of study that is to be taken by all students. *It is this third type of college, by the way, that should be attended by all who plan to become teachers in our basic schools.*

At the university level, there should be a continuation of general, liberal learning at a still higher level to accompany intensive specialization in this or that field of science or scholarship, this or that learned profession. Our insistence on the continuation of general, liberal learning at all the higher levels of schooling stems from our concern with the worst cultural disease that is rampant in our society—*the barbarism of specialization.*

There is no question that our technologically advanced industrial society needs specialists of all sorts. There is no question that the advancement of knowledge in all fields of science and scholarship, and in all the learned professions, needs intense specialization. But for the sake of preserving and enhancing our cultural traditions, as well as for the health of science and scholarship, we need specialists who also are generalists—generally cultivated human beings, not just good plumbers. We need truly educated human beings who can perform their special tasks better precisely because they have general cultivation as well as intensely specialized training.

Changes indeed are needed in higher education, but those improvements cannot reasonably be expected unless improvement in basic schooling makes that possible.

The Future of Our Free Institutions

I already have declared as emphatically as I know how that the quality of human life in our society depends on the quality of the schooling we give our young people, both basic and advanced. But a marked elevation in the quality of human life is not the only reason improving the quality of schooling is so necessary—not the only reason we must move heaven and earth to stop the deterioration of our schools and turn them in the opposite direction. The other reason is to safeguard the future of our free institutions.

They cannot prosper, they may not even survive, unless we do something to rescue our schools from their current deplorable deterioration. Democracy, in the full sense of that term, came into existence only in this century and only in a few countries on earth, among which the United States is an outstanding example. But democracy came into existence in this century, only in its initial conditions, all of which hold out promises for the future that remain to be fulfilled. Unless we do something about improving the quality of basic schooling for all and the quality of advanced schooling for some, there is little chance that those promises ever will be fulfilled. And if they are not, our free institutions are doomed to decay and wither away.

We face many insistently urgent problems. Our prosperity and even our survival depend on the solution of those problems—the threat of nuclear war, the exhaustion of essential resources and of supplies of energy, the pollution or spoilage of the environment, the spiraling of inflation accompanied by the spread of unemployment.

To solve these problems, we need resourceful and innovative leadership. For that to arise and be effective, an educated populace is needed. Trained intelligence—not only on the part of leaders, but also on the part of followers— holds the key to the solution of the problems our society faces. Achieving peace, prosperity and plenty could put us on the threshold of an early paradise. But a much better educational system than now exists also is needed, for that alone can carry us across the threshold. Without it, a poorly schooled population will not be able to put to good use the opportunities afforded by the achievement of the general welfare. Those who are not schooled to enjoy society can only despoil its institutions and corrupt themselves.

Escape from Childhood

Young people should have the right to control and direct their own learning, that is, to decide what they want to learn, and when, where, how, how much, how fast, and with what help they want to learn it. To be still more specific, I want them to have the right to decide if, when, how much, and by whom they want to be *taught* and the right to decide whether they want to learn in a school and if so which one and for how much of the time.

No human right, except the right to life itself, is more fundamental than this. A person's freedom of learning is part of his freedom of thought, even more basic than his freedom of speech. If we take from someone his right to decide what he will be curious about, we destroy his freedom of thought. We say, in effect, you must think not about what interests and concerns you, but about what interests and concerns *us*.

We might call this the right of curiosity, the right to ask whatever questions are most important to us. As adults, we assume that we have the right to decide what does or does not interest us, what we will look into and what we will leave alone. We take this right for granted, cannot imagine that it might be taken away from us. Indeed, as far as I know, it has never been written into any body of law. Even the writers of our Constitution did not mention it. They thought it was enough to guarantee citizens the freedom of speech and the freedom to spread their ideas as widely as they wished and could. It did not occur to them that even the most tyrannical government would try to control people's minds, what they thought and knew. That idea was to come later, under the benevolent guise of compulsory universal education.

This right to each of us to control our own learning is now in danger. When we put into our laws the highly authoritarian notion that someone should and could decide what all young people were to learn and, beyond that, could do whatever might seem necessary (which now includes dosing them with drugs) to compel them to learn it, we took a long step down a very steep and dangerous path. The requirement that a child go to school, for about six hours a day, 180 days a year, for about ten years, whether or not he learns anything there, whether or not he already knows it or could learn it faster or better somewhere else, is such gross violation of civil liberties that few adults would stand for it. But the child who resists is treated as a criminal. With this requirement we created an industry, an army of people whose whole work was to tell young people what they had to learn and to try to make them learn it.

Some of these people, wanting to exercise even more power over others, to be even more "helpful," or simply because the industry is not growing fast enough to hold all the people who want to get into it, are now beginning to say, "If it is good for children for us to decide what they shall learn and to make them learn it, why wouldn't it be good for everyone? If compulsory education is a good thing, how can there be too much of it? Why should we allow anyone, of any age, to decide that he has had enough of it? Why should we allow older people, any more than young, not to know what we know when their ignorance may have bad consequences for all of us? Why should we not *make* them know what they *ought* to know?"

They are beginning to talk, as one man did on a nationwide TV show, about "womb-to-tomb" schooling. If hours of homework every night are good for the young, why wouldn't they be good for us all—they would keep us away from the TV set and other frivolous pursuits. Some group of experts, somewhere, would be glad to decide what we all ought to know and then every so often check up on us to make sure we knew it—with, of course, appropriate penalties if we did not.

I am very serious in saying that I think this is coming unless we prepare against it and take steps to prevent it. The right I ask for the young is a right that I want to preserve for the rest of us, the right *to decide what goes into our minds*. This is much more than the right to decide whether or when or how much to go to school or what school you want to go to. That right is important, but it is only part of a much larger and more fundamental right, which I might call the right to Learn, as opposed to being Educated, *i.e.*, made to learn what someone else thinks would be good for you. It is not just compulsory schooling but compulsory Education that I oppose and want to do away with.

That children might have the control of their own learning, including the right to decide if, when, how much, and where they wanted to go to school, frightens and angers many people. They ask me, "Are you saying that if the parents wanted the child to go to school, and the child didn't want to go, that he wouldn't have to go? Are you saying that if the parents wanted the child to go to one school, and the child wanted to go to another, that the child would have the right to decide?" Yes, that is what I say. Some people ask, "If school wasn't compulsory, wouldn't many parents take their children out of school to exploit their labors in one way or another?" Such questions are often both snobbish and hypocritical. The questioner assumes and implies (though rarely says) that these bad parents are people poorer and less schooled than he. Also, though he appears to be defending the right of children to go to school, what he really is defending is the right of the state to compel them to go whether they want to or not. What he wants, in short, is that children should be in school, not that they should have any choice about going.

But saying that children should have the right to choose to go or not to go to school does not mean that the ideas and wishes of the parents would have no weight. Unless he is estranged from his parents and rebelling against them, a child cares very much about what they think and want. Most of the time, he doesn't want to anger or worry or disappoint them. Right now, in families where the parents feel that they have some choice about their children's schooling, there is much bargaining about schools. Such parents, when their children are little, often ask them whether they want to go to nursery school or kindergarten. Or they may take them to school for a while to try it out. Or, if they have a choice of schools, they may take them to several to see which they think they will like the best. Later, they care whether the child likes his school. If he does not, they try to do something about it, get him out of it, find a school he will like.

I know some parents who for years had a running bargain with their children. "If on a given day you just can't stand the thought of school, you don't feel well, you are afraid of something that may happen, you have something of your own that you very much want to do—well, you can stay home." Needless to say, the schools, with their supporting experts, fight it with all their might—Don't Give in to Your Child, Make Him Go to School, He's Got to Learn. Some parents, when their own plans make it possible for them to take an interesting trip, take their children with them. They don't ask the schools' permission, they just go. If the child doesn't want to make the trip and would rather stay in school, they work out a way for him to do that. Some parents, when their child is frightened, unhappy, and suffering in school, as many children are, just take him out. Hal Bennett, in his excellent book *No More Public School*, talks about ways to do this.

A friend of mine told me that when her boy was in third grade, he had a bad teacher, bullying, contemptuous, sarcastic, cruel. Many of the class switched to another section, but this eight-year-old, being tough, defiant, and stubborn, hung on. One day—his parents did not learn this until about two years later—having had enough of the teacher's meanness, he just got up from his desk and without saying a word, walked out of the room and went home. But for all his toughness and resiliency of spirit, the experience was hard on him. He grew more timid and quarrelsome, less outgoing and confident. He lost his ordinary good humor. Even his handwriting began to go to pieces—it was much worse in the spring of the school year than in the previous fall. One spring day he sat at breakfast, eating his cereal. After a while he stopped eating and sat silently thinking about the day ahead. His eyes filled up with tears, and two big ones slowly rolled down his cheeks. His mother, who ordinarily stays out of the school life of her children, saw this and knew what it was about. "Listen," she said to him, "we don't have to go on with this. If you've had enough of that teacher, if she's making school so bad for you that you don't want to go any more, I'll be perfectly happy just to pull you right out. We can manage it. Just say the word." He was horrified and indignant. "No!" he said, "I couldn't do that." "Okay," she said, "whatever you want is fine. Just let me know." And so they left it. He had decided that he was going to tough it out, and he did. But I am sure knowing that he had the support of his mother and the chance to give it up if it got too much for him gave him the strength he needed to go on.

To say that children should have the right to control and direct their own learning, to go to school or not as they choose, does not mean that the law would forbid the parents to express an opinion or wish or strong desire on the matter. It only means that if their natural authority is not strong enough the parents can't call in the cops to make the child do what they are not able to persuade him to do. And the law may say that there is no limit to the amount of pressure or coercion the parents can apply to the child to deny him a choice that he has a legal right to make.

When I urge that children should control their learning, there is one argument that people bring up so often that I feel I must anticipate and meet it here. It says that schools are a place where children can for a while be protected against the bad influences of the world outside, particularly from its greed, dishonesty, and commercialism. It says that in school children may have a glimpse of a higher way of life, of people acting from other and better motives than greed and fear. People say, "We know that society is bad enough as it is and that if children go out into the larger world as soon as they wanted, they would be tempted and corrupted just that much sooner."

They seem to believe that schools are better, more honorable places than the world outside—what a friend of mine at Harvard once called "museums of virtue." Or that people in school, both children and adults, act from higher and better motives than people outside. In this they are mistaken. There are, of course, some good schools. But on the whole, far from being the opposite of, or an antidote to, the world outside, with all its envy, fear, greed, and obsessive competitiveness, the schools are very much like it. If anything, they are worse, a terrible, abstract, simplified caricature of it. In the world outside the school, some work, at least, is done honestly and well, for its own sake, not just to get ahead of others; people are not everywhere and always being set in competition against each other; people are not (or not yet) in every minute of their lives subject to the arbitrary, irrevocable orders and judgement of others. But in most schools, a student is every minute doing what others tell him, subject to their judgement, in situations in which he can only win at the expense of other students.

This is a harsh judgement. Let me say again, as I have before, that schools are worse than most of the people in them and that many of these people do many harmful things they would rather not do, and a great many other harmful things that they do not even see as harmful. The whole of school is much worse than the sum of its parts. There are very few people in the U.S. today (or perhaps anywhere, any time) in *any* occupation, who could be trusted with the kind of power that schools give most teachers over their students. Schools seem to me among the most anti-democratic, most authoritarian, most destructive, and most dangerous institutions of modern society. No other institution does more harm or more lasting harm to more people or destroys so much of their curiosity, independence, trust, dignity, and sense of identity and worth. Even quite kindly schools are inhibited and corrupted by the knowledge of children and teachers alike that they are *performing* for the judgement and approval of others—the children for the teachers; the teachers for the parents, supervisors, school board, or the state. No one is ever free from feeling that he is being judged all the time, or soon may be. Even after the best class experiences teachers must ask themselves, "Were we right to do that? Can we prove we were right? Will it get us in trouble?"

What corrupts the school, and makes it so much worse than most of the people in it, or than they would like it to be, is its power—just as their powerlessness corrupts the students. The school is corrupted by the endless anxious demand of the parents to know how their child is doing—meaning is he ahead of the other kids—and their demand that he be kept ahead. Schools do not protect children from the badness of the world outside. They are at least as bad as the world outside, and the harm they do to the children in their power creates much of the badness of the world outside. The sickness of the modern world is in many ways a school-induced sickness. It is in school that most people learn to expect and accept that some expert can always place them in some sort of rank or hierarchy. It is in school that we meet, become used to, and learn to believe in the totally controlled society. We do not learn much science, but we learn to worship "scientists" and to believe that anything we might conceivably need or want can only come, and someday will come, from them. The school is the closest we have yet been able to come to Huxley's *Brave New World*, with its alphas and betas, deltas and epsilons—and now it even has its soma. Everyone, including children, should have the right to say "No!" to it.

POSTSCRIPT

Should the Curriculum Be Standardized for All?

The free/open school movement values small, personalized educational settings in which students engage in activities that have personal meaning. One of the movement's ideological assumptions, emanating from the philosophy of Jean-Jacques Rousseau, is that given a reasonably unrestrictive atmosphere, the learner will pursue avenues of creative and intellectual self-development. This confidence in self-motivation is the cornerstone of Holt's advocacy of freedom for the learner, a position he elaborates upon in his books *Instead of Education* (1988) and *Teach Your Own* (1982). The argument has gained some potency with recent developments in home-based computer-assisted instruction.

Adler's proposal for a unified curricular and methodological approach, released in 1982 by the Institute for Philosophical Research, was fashioned by a group of distinguished scholars and practitioners and has its roots in such earlier works as Arthur Bestor's *Educational Wastelands* (1953), Mortimer Smith's *The Diminished Mind* (1954), and Paul Copperman's *The Literacy Hoax* (1978). The proposal has been widely discussed since its release, and it has been implemented in a number of school systems. See, for example, "Launching Paideia in Chattanooga," by Cynthia M. Gettys and Anne Wheelock, *Educational Leadership* (September 1994) and Terry Roberts and Audrey Trainor, "Performing for Yourself and Others: The Paideia Coached Project," *Phi Delta Kappan* (March 2004).

Holt's plea for freedom from an imposed curriculum has a champion in John Taylor Gatto, New York City and New York State Teacher of the Year. Gatto has produced two provocative books, *Dumbing Us Down: The Hidden Curriculum of Compulsory Schooling* (1992) and *Confederacy of Dunces: The Tyranny of Compulsory Schooling* (1992). Two other works that build upon Holt's basic views are Lewis J. Perelman's *School's Out: The New Technology and the End of Education* (1992) and George Leonard's "Notes: The End of School," *The Atlantic Monthly* (May 1992).

Among recent provocative books and articles dealing with the topic are Susan Ohanian, *Caught in the Middle: Nonstandard Kids and a Killing Curriculum* (2001); John Berlau, "What Happened to the Great Ideas?" *Insight on the News* (August 27, 2001); and Elliott W. Eisner, "The Kind of Schools We Need," *Phi Delta Kappan* (April 2002), which is a balanced and thoughtful presentation of needed alterations. Excellent articles by E. D. Hirsch, Jr., and Alfie Kohn may be found in *Principal Leadership* (March 2003). Also see Terry Roberts and Laura Billings, "Thinking Is Literacy, Literacy Thinking," *Educational Leadership* (February 2008).

ISSUE 3

Should Behaviorism Shape Educational Practices?

YES: B. F. Skinner, from *Beyond Freedom and Dignity* (Alfred A. Knopf, 1971)

NO: Carl R. Rogers, from *Freedom to Learn for the Eighties* (Merrill, 1983)

ISSUE SUMMARY

YES: B. F. Skinner, an influential proponent of behaviorism and professor of psychology, critiques the concept of "inner freedom" and links learning and motivation to the influence of external forces.

NO: Professor of psychology and psychiatry Carl R. Rogers offers the "humanistic" alternative to behaviorism, insisting on the reality of subjective forces in human motivation.

Intimately enmeshed with considerations of aims and purposes and determination of curricular elements are the psychological base that affects the total setting in which learning takes place and the basic means of motivating learners. Historically, the atmosphere of schooling has often been characterized by harsh discipline, regimentation, and restriction. The prison metaphor often used by critics in describing school conditions rings true all too often.

Although calls to make schools pleasant have been sounded frequently, they have seldomly been heeded. Roman rhetorician Marcus Fabius Quintilian (ca. A.D. 35–100) advocated a constructive and enjoyable learning atmosphere. John Amos Comenius in the seventeenth century suggested a gardening metaphor in which learners were given kindly nurturance. Johann Heinrich Pestalozzi established a model school in the nineteenth century that replaced authoritarianism with love and respect.

Yet school as an institution retains the stigma of authoritarian control—attendance is compelled, social and psychological punishment is meted out, and the decision-making freedom of students is limited and often curtailed. These practices lead to rather obvious conclusions: the prevailing belief is either that young people are naturally evil and wild and therefore must be tamed in a restricting environment or that schooling as such is so unpalatable that people must be forced and cajoled to reap its benefits—or both.

31

Certainly, philosopher John Dewey (1895–1952) was concerned about this circumstance, citing at one time the superintendent of his native Burlington, Vermont, school district as admitting that the schools were a source of "grief and mortification" and were "unworthy of patronage." Dewey rejected both the need for "taming" and the defeatist attitude that the school environment must remain unappealing. He hoped to create a motivational atmosphere that would engage learners in real problem-solving activities, thereby sustaining curiosity, creativity, and attachment. The rewards were to flow from the sense of accomplishment and freedom, which was to be achieved through the disciplined actions necessary to solve the problem at hand.

More recent treatment of the allied issues of freedom, control, and motivation has come from the two major camps in the field of educational psychology: the behaviorists (rooted in the early-twentieth-century theories of Ivan Pavlov, Edward L. Thorndike, and John B. Watson) and the humanists (emanating from the Gestalt and field theory psychologies developed in Europe and America earlier in the twentieth century).

B. F. Skinner has been the dominant force in translating behaviorism into recommendations for school practices. He and his disciples, often referred to as "neobehaviorists," have contributed to widely used innovations such as behavioral objectives in instruction and testing, competency-based education, mastery learning, assertive discipline, and outcome-based education. The humanistic viewpoint has been championed by Carl R. Rogers, Abraham Maslow, Fritz Perls, Rollo May, and Erich Fromm, most of whom ground their psychological theories in the philosophical assumptions of existentialism and phenomenology.

Skinner believes that "inner" states are merely convenient myths, that motives and behaviors are shaped by environmental factors. These shaping forces, however, need not be negative, nor must they operate in an uncontrolled manner. Our present understanding of human behavior allows us the freedom to shape the environmental forces, which in turn shape us. With this power, Skinner contends, we can replace aversive controls in schooling with positive reinforcements that heighten the students' motivation level and make learning more efficient.

Recent manifestations of the continuing interest in Skinner's behaviorism and the humanistic psychology of Rogers include Virginia Richardson's "From Behaviorism to Constructivism in Teacher Education," *Teacher Education and Special Education* (Summer 1996) and Tobin Hart's "From Category to Contact: Epistemology and the Enlivening and Deadening of Spirit in Education," *Journal of Humanistic Education and Development* (September 1997).

Skinner deals with the problem of freedom and control in the selection that follows. In the second selection, Carl R. Rogers critiques Skinner's behaviorist approach and sets forth his argument supporting the reality of freedom as an inner human state that is the wellspring of responsibility, will, and commitment.

YES

B. F. Skinner

Beyond Freedom and Dignity

Almost all living things act to free themselves from harmful contacts. A kind of freedom is achieved by the relatively simple forms of behavior called reflexes. A person sneezes and frees his respiratory passages from irritating substances. He vomits and frees his stomach from indigestible or poisonous food. He pulls back his hand and frees it from a sharp or hot object. More elaborate forms of behavior have similar effects. When confined, people struggle ("in rage") and break free. When in danger they flee from or attack its source. Behavior of this kind presumably evolved because of its survival value; it is as much a part of what we call the human genetic endowment as breathing, sweating, or digesting food. And through conditioning similar behavior may be acquired with respect to novel objects which could have played no role in evolution. These are no doubt minor instances of the struggle to be free, but they are significant. We do not attribute them to any love of freedom; they are simply forms of behavior which have proved useful in reducing various threats to the individual and hence to the species in the course of evolution.

A much more important role is played by behavior which weakens harmful stimuli in another way. It is not acquired in the form of conditioned reflexes, but as the product of a different process called operant conditioning. When a bit of behavior is followed by a certain kind of consequence, it is more likely to occur again, and a consequence having this effect is called a reinforcer. Food, for example, is a reinforcer to a hungry organism; anything the organism does that is followed by the receipt of food is more likely to be done again whenever the organism is hungry. Some stimuli are called negative reinforcers; any response which reduces the intensity of such a stimulus—or ends it—is more likely to be emitted when the stimulus recurs. Thus, if a person escapes from a hot sun when he moves under cover, he is more likely to move under cover when the sun is again hot. The reduction in temperature reinforces the behavior it is "contingent upon"—that is, the behavior it follows. Operant conditioning also occurs when a person simply avoids a hot sun—when, roughly speaking, he escapes from the *threat* of a hot sun.

Negative reinforcers are called aversive in the sense that they are the things organisms "turn away from." The term suggests a spatial separation—moving or running away from something—but the essential relation is temporal. In a standard apparatus used to study the process in the laboratory, an arbitrary response simply weakens an aversive stimulus or brings it to an end.

A great deal of physical technology is the result of this kind of struggle for freedom. Over the centuries, in erratic ways, men have constructed a world in which they are relatively free of many kinds of threatening or harmful stimuli—extremes of temperature, sources of infection, hard labor, danger, and even those minor aversive stimuli called discomfort.

Escape and avoidance play a much more important role in the struggle for freedom when the aversive conditions are generated by other people. Other people can be aversive without, so to speak, trying; they can be rude, dangerous, contagious, or annoying, and one escapes from them or avoids them accordingly. They may also be "intentionally" aversive—that is, they may treat other people aversively because of what follows. Thus, a slave driver induces a slave to work by whipping him when he stops; by resuming work the slave escapes from the whipping (and incidentally reinforces the slave driver's behavior in using the whip). A parent nags a child until the child performs a task; by performing the task the child escapes nagging (and reinforces the parent's behavior). The blackmailer threatens exposure unless the victim pays; by paying, the victim escapes from the threat (and reinforces the practice). A teacher threatens corporal punishment or failure until his students pay attention; by paying attention the students escape from the threat of punishment (and reinforce the teacher for threatening it). In one form or another intentional aversive control is the pattern of most social coordination—in ethics, religion, government, economics, education, psychotherapy, and family life.

A person escapes from or avoids aversive treatment by behaving in ways which reinforce those who treated him aversively until he did so, but he may escape in other ways. For example, he may simply move out of range. A person may escape from slavery, emigrate or defect from a government, desert from an army, become an apostate from a religion, play truant, leave home, or drop out of a culture as a hobo, hermit, or hippie. Such behavior is as much a product of the aversive conditions as the behavior the conditions were designed to evoke. The latter can be guaranteed only by sharpening the contingencies or by using stronger aversive stimuli.

Another anomalous mode of escape is to attack those who arrange aversive conditions and weaken or destroy their power. We may attack those who crowd us or annoy us, as we attack the weeds in our garden, but again the struggle for freedom is mainly directed toward intentional controllers—toward those who treat others aversively in order to induce them to behave in particular ways. Thus, a child may stand up to his parents, a citizen may overthrow a government, a communicant may reform a religion, a student may attack a teacher or vandalize a school, and a dropout may work to destroy a culture.

It is possible that man's genetic endowment supports this kind of struggle for freedom: when treated aversively people tend to act aggressively or to be reinforced by signs of having worked aggressive damage. Both tendencies should have had evolutionary advantages, and they can easily be demonstrated. If two organisms which have been coexisting peacefully receive painful shocks, they immediately exhibit characteristic patterns of aggression toward each other. The aggressive behavior is not necessarily directed toward the actual source of stimulation; it may be "displaced" toward any convenient person or object.

Vandalism and riots are often forms of undirected or misdirected aggression. An organism which has received a painful shock will also, if possible, act to gain access to another organism toward which it can act aggressively. The extent to which human aggression exemplifies innate tendencies is not clear, and many of the ways in which people attack and thus weaken or destroy the power of intentional controllers are quite obviously learned.

What we may call the "literature of freedom" has been designed to induce people to escape from or attack those who act to control them aversively. The content of the literature is the philosophy of freedom, but philosophies are among those inner causes which need to be scrutinized. We say that a person behaves in a given way because he possesses a philosophy, but we infer the philosophy from the behavior and therefore cannot use it in any satisfactory way as an explanation, at least until it is in turn explained. The literature of freedom, on the other hand, has a simple objective status. It consists of books, pamphlets, manifestoes, speeches, and other verbal products, designed to induce people to act to free themselves from various kinds of intentional control. It does not impart a philosophy of freedom; it induces people to act.

The literature often emphasizes the aversive conditions under which people live, perhaps by contrasting them with conditions in a freer world. It thus makes the conditions more aversive, "increasing the misery" of those it is trying to rescue. It also identifies those from whom one is to escape or those whose power is to be weakened through attack. Characteristic villains of the literature are tyrants, priests, generals, capitalists, martinet teachers, and domineering parents.

The literature also prescribes modes of action. It has not been much concerned with escape, possibly because advice has not been needed; instead, it has emphasized how controlling power may be weakened or destroyed. Tyrants are to be overthrown, ostracized, or assassinated. The legitimacy of a government is to be questioned. The ability of a religious agency to mediate supernatural sanctions is to be challenged. Strikes and boycotts are to be organized to weaken the economic power which supports aversive practices. The argument is strengthened by exhorting people to act, describing likely results, reviewing successful instances on the model of the advertising testimonial, and so on.

The would-be controllers do not, of course, remain inactive. Governments make escape impossible by banning travel or severely punishing or incarcerating defectors. They keep weapons and other sources of power out of the hands of revolutionaries. They destroy the written literature of freedom and imprison or kill those who carry it orally. If the struggle for freedom is to succeed, it must then be intensified.

The importance of the literature of freedom can scarcely be questioned. Without help or guidance people submit to aversive conditions in the most surprising way. This is true even when the aversive conditions are part of the natural environment. Darwin observed, for example, that the Fuegians seemed to make no effort to protect themselves from the cold; they wore only scant clothing and made little use of it against the weather. And one of the most striking things about the struggle for freedom from intentional control is how often it has been lacking. Many people have submitted to the most obvious religious, governmental, and economic controls for centuries, striking for free-dom only sporadically, if at all. The literature of freedom has made an essential contribution to the elimination of many aversive practices in government, religion, education, family life, and the production of goods.

The contributions of the literature of freedom, however, are not usually described in these terms. Some traditional theories could conceivably be said to define freedom as the absence of aversive control, but the emphasis has been on how the condition *feels*. Other traditional theories could conceivably be said to define freedom as a person's condition when he is behaving under nonaversive control, but the emphasis has been upon a state of mind associ-ated with doing what one wants. According to John Stuart Mill, "Liberty con-sists in doing what one desires." The literature of freedom has been important in changing practice (it has changed practices whenever it has had any effect whatsoever), but it has nevertheless defined its task as the changing of states of mind and feelings. Freedom is a "possession." A person escapes from or destroys the power of a controller in order to feel free, and once he feels free and can do what he desires, no further action is recommended and none is prescribed by the literature of freedom, except perhaps eternal vigilance lest control be resumed.

The feeling of freedom becomes an unreliable guide to action as soon as would-be controllers turn to nonaversive measures, as they are likely to do to avoid the problems raised when the controllee escapes or attacks. Nonaversive measures are not as conspicuous as aversive and are likely to be acquired more slowly, but they have obvious advantages which promote their use. Productive labor, for example, was once the result of punishment: the slave worked to avoid the consequences of not working. Wages exemplify a different principle; a person is paid when he behaves in a given way so that he will continue to behave in that way. Although it has long been recognized that rewards have useful effects, wage systems have evolved slowly. In the nineteenth century it was believed that an industrial society required a hungry labor force; wages would be effective only if the hungry worker could exchange them for food. By making labor less aversive—for instance, by shortening hours and improving conditions—it has been possible to get men to work for lesser rewards. Until recently teaching was almost entirely aversive: the student studies to escape the consequences of not studying, but nonaversive techniques are gradually being discovered and used. The skillful parent learns to reward a child for good behavior rather than punish him for bad. Religious agencies move from the threat of hellfire to an emphasis on God's love, and governments turn from aversive sanctions to various kinds of inducements. . . . What the layman calls a reward is a "positive reinforcer," the effects of which have been exhaustively studied in the experimental analysis of operant behavior. The effects are not as easily recognized as those of aversive contingencies because they tend to be deferred, and applications have therefore been delayed, but techniques as powerful as the older aversive techniques are now available. . . .

The literature of freedom has never come to grips with techniques of con-trol which do not generate escape or counterattack because it has dealt with the problem in terms of states of mind and feelings. In his book *Sovereignty*,

Bertrand de Jouvenel quotes two important figures in that literature. According to Leibnitz, "Liberty consists in the power to do what one wants to do," and according to Voltaire, "When I can do what I want to do, there is my liberty for me." But both writers add a concluding phrase: Leibnitz, ". . . or in the power to want what can be got," and Voltaire, more candidly, ". . . but I can't help wanting what I do want." Jouvenel relegates these comments to a footnote, saying that the power to want is a matter of "interior liberty" (the freedom of the inner man!) which falls outside the "gambit of freedom."

A person wants something if he acts to get it when the occasion arises. A person who says "I want something to eat" will presumably eat when something becomes available. If he says "I want to get warm," he will presumably move into a warm place when he can. These acts have been reinforced in the past by whatever was wanted. What a person *feels* when he feels himself wanting something depends upon the circumstances. Food is reinforcing only in a state of deprivation, and a person who wants something to eat may feel parts of that state—for example, hunger pangs. A person who wants to get warm presumably feels cold. Conditions associated with a high probability of responding may also be felt, together with aspects of the present occasion which are similar to those of past occasions upon which behavior has been reinforced. Wanting is not, however, a feeling, nor is a feeling the reason a person acts to get what he wants. Certain contingencies have raised the probability of behavior and at the same time have created conditions which may be felt. Freedom is a matter of contingencies of reinforcement, not of the feelings the contingencies generate. The distinction is particularly important when the contingencies do not generate escape or counterattack. . . .

The literature of freedom has encouraged escape from or attack upon all controllers. It has done so by making any indication of control aversive. Those who manipulate human behavior are said to be evil men, necessarily bent on exploitation. Control is clearly the opposite of freedom, and if freedom is good, control must be bad. What is overlooked is control which does not have aversive consequences at any time. Many social practices essential to the welfare of the species involve the control of one person by another, and no one can suppress them who has any concern for human achievements. . . . [I]n order to maintain the position that all control is wrong, it has been necessary to disguise or conceal the nature of useful practices, to prefer weak practices just because they can be disguised or concealed, and—a most extraordinary result indeed!—to perpetuate punitive measures.

The problem is to be free men, not from control, but from certain kinds of control, and it can be solved only if our analysis takes all consequences into account. How people feel about control, before or after the literature of freedom has worked on their feelings, does not lead to useful distinctions.

Were it not for the unwarranted generalization that all control is wrong, we should deal with the social environment as simply as we deal with the nonsocial. Although technology has freed men from certain aversive features of the environment, it has not freed them from the environment. We accept the fact that we depend upon the world around us, and we simply change the nature of the dependency. In the same way, to make the social environment as free as possible of aversive stimuli, we do not need to destroy that environment or escape from it; we need to redesign it.

❦

Man's struggle for freedom is not due to a will to be free, but to certain behavioral processes characteristic of the human organism, the chief effect of which is the avoidance of or escape from so-called "aversive" features of the environment. Physical and biological technologies have been mainly concerned with natural aversive stimuli; the struggle for freedom is concerned with stimuli intentionally arranged by other people. The literature of freedom has identified the other people and has proposed ways of escaping from them or weakening or destroying their power. It has been successful in reducing the aversive stimuli used in intentional control, but it has made the mistake of defining freedom in terms of states of mind or feelings, and it has therefore not been able to deal effectively with techniques of control which do not breed escape or revolt but nevertheless have aversive consequences. It has been forced to brand all control as wrong and to misrepresent many of the advantages to be gained from a social environment. It is unprepared for the next step, which is not to free men from control but to analyze and change the kinds of control to which they are exposed.

Carl R. Rogers

 NO

Freedom to Learn

One of the deepest issues in modern life, in modern man, is the question as to whether the concept of personal freedom has any meaning whatsoever in our present-day scientific world. The growing ability of the behavioral scientist to predict and to control behavior has brought the issue sharply to the fore. If we accept the logical positivism and strictly behavioristic emphases which are predominant in the American psychological scene, there is not even room for discussion. . . .

But if we step outside the narrowness of the behavioral sciences, this question is not only *an* issue, it is one of the primary issues which define modern man. Friedman in his book (1963, p. 251) makes his topic "the problematic of modern man—the alienation, the divided nature, the unresolved tension between personal freedom and psychological compulsion which follows on 'the death of God'." The issues of personal freedom and personal commitment have become very sharp indeed in a world in which man feels unsupported by a supernatural religion, and experiences keenly the division between his awareness and those elements of his dynamic functioning of which he is unaware. If he is to wrest any meaning from a universe which for all he knows may be indifferent, he must arrive at some stance which he can hold in regard to these timeless uncertainties.

So, writing as both a behavioral scientist and as one profoundly concerned with the human, the personal, the phenomenological and the intangible, I should like to contribute what I can to this continuing dialogue regarding the meaning of and the possibility of freedom.

Man Is Unfree

. . . In the minds of most behavioral scientists, man is not free, nor can he as a free man commit himself to some purpose, since he is controlled by factors outside of himself. Therefore, neither freedom nor commitment is even a possible concept to modern behavioral science as it is usually understood.

To show that I am not exaggerating, let me quote a statement from Dr. B. F. Skinner of Harvard, who is one of the most consistent advocates of a strictly behavioristic psychology. He says,

> The hypothesis that man is not free is essential to the application of scientific method to the study of human behavior. The free inner man

who is held responsible for his behavior is only a prescientific substitute for the kinds of causes which are discovered in the course of scientific analysis. All these alternative causes lie *outside* the individual (1953, p. 477).

This view is shared by many psychologists and others who feel, as does Dr. Skinner, that all the effective causes of behavior lie outside of the individual and that it is only through the external stimulus that behavior takes place. The scientific description of behavior avoids anything that partakes in any way of freedom. For example, Dr. Skinner (1964, pp. 90–91) describes an experiment in which a pigeon was conditioned to turn in a clockwise direction. The behavior of the pigeon was "shaped up" by rewarding any movement that approximated a clockwise turn until, increasingly, the bird was turning round and round in a steady movement. This is what is known as operant conditioning. Students who had watched the demonstration were asked to write an account of what they had seen. Their responses included the following ideas: that the pigeon was conditioned to *expect* reinforcement for the right kind of behavior; that the pigeon *hoped* that something would bring the food back again; that the pigeon *observed* that a certain behavior seemed to produce a particular result; that the pigeon *felt* that food would be given it because of its action; that the bird came to *associate* his action with the clock of the food dispenser. Skinner ridicules these statements because they all go beyond the observed behavior in using such words as *expect, hope, observe, felt,* and *associate.* The whole explanation from his point of view is that the bird was reinforced when it emitted a given kind of behavior; the pigeon walked around until the food container again appeared; a certain behavior produced a given result; food was given to the pigeon when it acted in a given way; the click of the food dispenser was related in time to the bird's action. These statements describe the pigeon's behavior from a scientific point of view.

Skinner goes on to point out that the students were undoubtedly reporting what they would have expected, felt and hoped under similar circumstances. But he then makes the case that there is no more reality to such ideas in the human being than there is in the pigeon, that it is only because such words have been reinforced by the verbal community in which the individual has developed, that such terms are used. He discusses the fact that the verbal community which conditioned them to use such terms saw no more of their behavior than they had seen of the pigeon's. In other words the internal events, if they indeed exist, have no scientific significance.

As to the methods used for changing the behavior of the pigeon, many people besides Dr. Skinner feel that through such positive reinforcement human behavior as well as animal behavior can be "shaped up" and controlled. In his book *Walden Two,* Skinner says,

> Now that we know how positive reinforcement works and how negative doesn't, we can be more deliberate and hence more successful in our cultural design. We can achieve a sort of control under which the controlled, though they are following a code much more scrupulously than was ever the case under the old system, nevertheless *feel free.* They are

doing what they want to do, not what they are forced to do. That's the source of the tremendous power of positive reinforcement—there is no restraint and no revolt. By a careful cultural design we control not the final behavior but the *inclination* to behave—the motives, the desires, the wishes. The curious thing is that in that case *the question of freedom never arises* (1948, p. 218).

. . . I think it is clear from all of this that man is a machine—a complex machine, to be sure, but one which is increasingly subject to scientific control. Whether behavior will be managed through operant conditioning as in *Walden Two* or whether we will be "shaped up" by the unplanned forms of conditioning implied in social pressure, or whether we will be controlled by electrodes in the brain, it seems quite clear that science is making out of man an object and that the purpose of such science is not only understanding and prediction but control. Thus it would seem to be quite clear that there could be no concept so foreign to the facts as that man is free. Man is a machine, man is unfree, man cannot commit himself in any meaningful sense; he is simply controlled by planned or unplanned forces outside of himself.

Man Is Free

I am impressed by the scientific advances illustrated in the examples I have given. I regard them as a great tribute to the ingenuity, insight, and persistence of the individuals making the investigations. They have added enormously to our knowledge. Yet for me they leave something very important unsaid. Let me try to illustrate this, first from my experience in therapy.

I think of a young man classed as schizophrenic with whom I had been working for a long time in a state hospital. He was a very inarticulate man, and during one hour he made a few remarks about individuals who had recently left the hospital; then he remained silent for almost forty minutes. When he got up to go, he mumbled almost under his breath, "If some of *them* can do it, maybe I can too." That was all—not a dramatic statement, not uttered with force and vigor, yet a statement of choice by this young man to work toward his own improvement and eventual release from the hospital. It is not too surprising that about eight months after that statement he was out of the hospital. I believe this experience of responsible choice is one of the deepest aspects of psychotherapy and one of the elements which most solidly under-lies personality change.

I think of another young person, this time a young woman graduate student, who was deeply disturbed and on the borderline of a psychotic break. Yet after a number of interviews in which she talked very critically about all of the people who had failed to give her what she needed, she finally concluded: "Well, with that sort of a foundation, it's really up to *me*. I mean it seems to be really apparent to me that I can't depend on someone else to *give* me an education." And then she added very softly: "I'll really have to get it myself." She goes on to explore this experience of important and responsible choice. She finds it a frightening experience, and yet one which gives her a feeling of strength. A force seems to surge up within her which is big and strong, and yet she also feels very much alone and sort of cut off from support. She adds: "I am going to begin to do more things that I know I should do." And she did.

I could add many other examples. One young fellow talking about the way in which his whole life had been distorted and spoiled by his parents finally comes to the conclusion that, "Maybe now that I *see* that, it's up to *me*." . . .

For those of you [who] have seen the film *David and Lisa*—and I hope that you have had that rich experience—I can illustrate exactly what I have been discussing. David, the adolescent schizophrenic, goes into a panic if he is touched by anyone. He feels that "touching kills," and he is deathly afraid of it, and afraid of the closeness in human relationships which touching implies. Yet toward the close of the film he makes a bold and positive choice of the kind I have been describing. He has been trying to be of help to Lisa, the girl who is out of touch with reality. He tries to help at first in an intellectually contemptuous way, then increasingly in a warmer and more personal way. Finally, in a highly dramatic movement, he says to her, "Lisa, take my hand." He *chooses*, with obvious conflict and fear, to leave behind the safety of his untouchableness, and to venture into the world of real human relationships where he is literally and figuratively in *touch* with another. You are an unusual person if the film does not grow a bit misty at this point.

Perhaps a behaviorist could try to account for the reaching out of his hand by saying that it was the result of intermittent reinforcement of partial movements. I find such an explanation both inaccurate and inadequate. It is the *meaning* of the *decision* which is essential to understanding the act.

What I am trying to suggest in all of this is that I would be at a loss to explain the positive change which can occur in psychotherapy if I had to omit the importance of the sense of free and responsible choice on the part of my clients. I believe that this experience of freedom to choose is one of the deepest elements underlying change.

The Meaning of Freedom

Considering the scientific advances which I have mentioned, how can we even speak of freedom? In what sense is a client free? In what sense are any of us free? What possible definition of freedom can there be in the modern world? Let me attempt such a definition.

In the first place, the freedom that I am talking about is essentially an inner thing, something which exists in the living person quite aside from any of the outward choices of alternatives which we so often think of as constituting freedom. I am speaking of the kind of freedom which Viktor Frankl vividly describes in his experience of the concentration camp, when everything—possessions, status, identity—was taken from the prisoners. But even months and years in such an environment showed only "that everything can be taken from a man but one thing: the last of the human freedoms—to choose one's own attitude in any given set of circumstances, to choose one's own way" (1959, p. 65). It is this inner, subjective, existential freedom which I have observed. It is the realization that "I can live myself, here and now, by my own choice." It is the quality of courage which enables a person to step into the uncertainty of the unknown as he chooses himself. It is the discovery of meaning from within oneself, meaning which comes from listening, sensitively and openly to the complexities of what one is experiencing. It is the burden of being responsible for the self one chooses to be. It is the recognition of a person that he is an emerging process, not a static end product. The individual who is thus deeply and courageously thinking his own thoughts, becoming his own uniqueness, responsibly choosing himself, may be fortunate in having hundreds of objective outer alternatives from which to choose, or he may be unfortunate in having none. But his freedom exists regardless. So we are first of all speaking of something which exists within the individual, something phenomenological rather than external, but nonetheless to be prized.

The second point in defining this experience of freedom is that it exists not as a contradiction of the picture of the psychological universe as a sequence of cause and effect, but as a complement to such a universe. Freedom rightly understood is a fulfillment by the person of the ordered sequence of his life. The free man moves out voluntarily, freely, responsibly, to play his significant part in a world whose determined events move through him and through his spontaneous choice and will.

I see this freedom of which I am speaking, then, as existing in a different *dimension* than the determined sequence of cause and effect. I regard it as a freedom which exists in the subjective person, a freedom which he courageously uses to live his potentialities. The fact that this type of freedom seems completely irreconcilable with the behaviorist's picture of man is something which I will discuss a bit later. . . .

The Emergence of Commitment

I have spoken thus far primarily about freedom. What about commitment? Certainly the disease of our age is lack of purpose, lack of meaning, lack of commitment on the part of individuals. Is there anything which I can say in regard to this?

It is clear to me that in therapy, as indicated in the examples that I have given, commitment to purpose and to meaning in life is one of the significant elements of change. It is only when the person decides, "I am someone; I am someone worth being: I am committed to being myself," that change becomes possible.

At a very interesting symposium at Rice University recently, Dr. Sigmund Koch sketched the revolution which is taking place in science, literature and the arts, in which a sense of commitment is again becoming evident after a long period in which that emphasis has been absent.

Part of what he meant by that may be illustrated by talking about Dr. Michael Polanyi, the philosopher of science, formerly a physicist, who has been presenting his notions about what science basically is. In his book, *Personal Knowledge*, Polanyi makes it clear that even scientific knowledge is personal knowledge, committed knowledge. We cannot rest comfortably on the belief that scientific knowledge is impersonal and "out there," that it has nothing to do with the individual who has discovered it. Instead, every aspect of science is pervaded by disciplined personal commitment, and Polanyi makes the case very persuasively that the whole attempt to divorce science from the person is a completely unrealistic one. I think I am stating his belief correctly when I say that in his judgment logical positivism and all the current structure of science cannot save us from the fact that all knowing is uncertain, involves risk, and is grasped and comprehended only through the deep, personal commitment of a disciplined search.

Perhaps a brief quotation will give something of the flavor of his thinking. Speaking of great scientists, he says:

> So we see that both Kepler and Einstein approached nature with intellectual passions and with beliefs inherent in these passions, which led them to their triumphs and misguided them to their errors. These passions and beliefs were theirs, personally, even universally. I believe that they were competent to follow these impulses, even though they risked being misled by them. And again, what I accept of their work today, I accept personally, guided by passions and beliefs similar to theirs, holding in my turn that my impulses are valid, universally, even though I must admit the possibility that they may be mistaken (1959, p. 145).

Thus we see that a modern philosopher of science believes that deep personal commitment is the only possible basis on which science can firmly stand. This is a far cry indeed from the logical positivism of twenty or thirty years ago, which placed knowledge far out in impersonal space.

Let me say a bit more about what I mean by commitment in the psychological sense. I think it is easy to give this word a much too shallow meaning, indicating that the individual has, simply by conscious choice, committed himself to one course of action or another. I think the meaning goes far deeper than that. Commitment is a total organismic direction involving not only the conscious mind but the whole direction of the organism as well.

In my judgment, commitment is something that one *discovers* within oneself. It is a trust of one's total reaction rather than of one's mind only. It has much to do with creativity. Einstein's explanation of how he moved toward his formulation of relativity without any clear knowledge of his goal is an excellent example of what I mean by the sense of commitment based on a total organismic reaction. He says:

> During all those years there was a feeling of direction, of going straight toward something concrete. It is, of course, very hard to express that feeling in words but it was decidedly the case and clearly to be distinguished from later considerations about the rational form of the solution (quoted in Wertheimer, 1945, pp. 183–184).

Thus commitment is more than a decision. It is the functioning of an individual who is searching for the directions which are emerging within himself. Kierkegaard has said, "The truth exists only in the process of becoming, in the process of appropriation" (1941, p. 72). It is this individual creation of a tentative personal truth through action which is the essence of commitment.

Man is most successful in such a commitment when he is functioning as an integrated, whole, unified individual. The more that he is functioning in this total manner the more confidence he has in the directions which he unconsciously chooses. He feels a trust in his experiencing, of which, even if he is fortunate, he has only partial glimpses in his awareness.

Thought of in the sense in which I am describing it, it is clear that commitment is an achievement. It is the kind of purposeful and meaningful direction which is only gradually achieved by the individual who has come increasingly to live closely in relationship with his own experiencing—a relationship in which his unconscious tendencies are as much respected as are his conscious choices. This is the kind of commitment toward which I believe individuals can move. It is an important aspect of living in a fully functioning way.

The Irreconcilable Contradiction

I trust it will be very clear that I have given two sharply divergent and irreconcilably contradictory points of view. On the one hand, modern psychological science and many other forces in modern life as well, hold the view that man is unfree, that he is controlled, that words such as purpose, choice, commitment have no significant meaning, that man is nothing but an object which we can more fully understand and more fully control. Enormous strides have been and are being made in implementing this perspective. It would seem heretical indeed to question this view.

Yet, as Polanyi has pointed out in another of his writings (1957), the dogmas of science can be in error. He says:

> In the days when an idea could be silenced by showing that it was contrary to religion, theology was the greatest single source of fallacies. Today, when any human thought can be discredited by branding it as unscientific, the power previously exercised by theology has passed over to science; hence science has become in its turn the greatest single source of error.

So I am emboldened to say that over against this view of man as unfree, as an object, is the evidence from therapy, from subjective living, and from objective research as well, that personal freedom and responsibility have a crucial significance, that one cannot live a complete life without such personal freedom and responsibility, and that self-understanding and responsible choice make a sharp and measurable difference in the behavior of the individual. In this context, commitment does have meaning. Commitment is the emerging and changing total direction of the individual, based on a close and acceptant relationship between the person and all of the trends in his life, conscious and unconscious. Unless, as individuals and as a society, we can make constructive use of this capacity for freedom and commitment, mankind, it seems to me, is set on a collision course with fate. . . .

A part of modern living is to face the paradox that, viewed from one perspective, man is a complex machine. We are every day moving toward a more precise understanding and a more precise control of this objective mechanism which we call man. On the other hand, in another significant dimension of his existence, man is subjectively free; his personal choice and responsibility account for the shape of his life; he is in fact the architect of himself. A truly crucial part of his existence is the discovery of his own meaningful commitment to life with all of his being.

POSTSCRIPT

Should Behaviorism Shape Educational Practices?

The freedom-determinism or freedom-control argument has raged in philosophical, political, and psychological circles down through the ages. Is freedom of choice and action a central, perhaps *the* central, characteristic of being human? Or is freedom only an illusion, a refusal to acknowledge the external shaping of all human actions?

Moving the debate into the field of education, John Dewey depicted a developmental freedom that is acquired through improving one's ability to cope with problems. A. S. Neill (*Summerhill: A Radical Approach to Child Rearing*, 1984), who advanced the ideas of early-twentieth-century progressive educators and the establishment of free schools, sees a more natural inborn freedom in human beings, which must be protected and allowed to flourish. Skinner refuses to recognize this "inner autonomous man" but sees freedom resulting from the scientific reshaping of the environment that influences us.

Just as Skinner has struggled to remove the stigma from the word *control*, arguing that it is the true gateway to freedom, John Holt, in *Freedom and Beyond* (1972), contends that freedom and free activities are not "unstructured"—indeed, that the structure of an open classroom is vastly more complicated than the structure of a traditional classroom.

If both of these views have validity, then we are in a position, as Dewey counselled, to go beyond either-or polemics on these matters and build a more constructive educational atmosphere. Jerome S. Bruner has consistently suggested ways in which free inquiry and subject matter structure can be effectively blended. Arthur W. Combs, in a report titled *Humanistic Education: Objectives and Assessment* (1978), helped to bridge the ideological gap between humanists and behaviorists by demonstrating that subjective outcomes can be assessed by direct or modified behavioral techniques.

Skinner's death in 1990 prompted a number of evaluations, among them "Skinner's Stimulus: The Legacy of Behaviorism's Grand Designer," by Jeff Meade, *Teacher* (November/December 1990); "The Life and Contributions of Burrhus Frederic Skinner," by Robert P. Hawkins, *Education and Treatment of Children* (August 1990); and Carson M. Bennett, "A Skinnerian View of Human Freedom," *The Humanist* (July/August 1990). Recently, neuroscience has come forward. See, for instance, "Brain-Compatible Learning: Fad or Foundation?" *The School Administrator* (December 2006) by Patricia Wolfe; "Which Brain Research Can Educators Trust?" *Phi Delta Kappan* (May 2007) by Judy Willis, M.D., and "A Fresh Look at Brain-Based Education," *Phi Delta Kappan* (February 2008), by Eric P. Jensen.

ISSUE 4

Is Constructivism the Best Philosophy of Education?

YES: David Elkind, from "The Problem with Constructivism," *The Educational Forum* (Summer 2004)

NO: Jamin Carson, from "Objectivism and Education: A Response to David Elkind's 'The Problem with Constructivism'," *The Educational Forum* (Spring 2005)

ISSUE SUMMARY

YES: Child development professor David Elkind contends that the philosophical positions found in constructivism, though often difficult to apply, are necessary elements in a meaningful reform of educational practices.

NO: Jamin Carson, an assistant professor of education and former high school teacher, offers a close critique of constructivism and argues that the philosophy of objectivism is a more realistic and usable basis for the process of education.

For years the term *constructivism* appeared only in journals read primarily by philosophers, epistemologists, and psychologists. Nowadays, *constructivism* regularly appears in the teacher's manuals of textbook series, state education department curriculum frameworks, education reform literature, and education journals. Constructivism now has a face and a name in education. So say educators Martin G. Brooks and Jacqueline Grennon Brooks in "The Courage to Be Constructivist," *Educational Leadership* (November 1999). According to them, the heart of the constructivist approach to education is that learners control their learning. This being the case, the philosophical orientation provided by John Dewey, John Holt, and Carl R. Rogers here in Part 1 would seem to feed into the development of David Elkind's ideas on this educational theory. The contrary positions taken by Hutchins, Adler, and Skinner would seem to contribute to the objectivist philosophy espoused by Jamin Carson.

Constructivism, which is additionally influenced by the theories of Jean Piaget, Lev Vygotsky, and Jerome Bruner, is an approach to learning in which students construct new understandings through active engagement with their past and present experiences. Constructivists contend that traditional instructional models emphasize knowledge transmission without producing deeper levels of understanding and internalization.

Objectivists and other critics of constructivism say that this approach to learning is imprecise, overly permissive, and lacking in rigor. This argument is quite well illustrated in a *Phi Delta Kappan* exchange between Lawrence A. Baines and Gregory Stanley on one hand and Lynn Chrenka on the other (Baines and Stanley, "We Want to See the Teacher: Constructivism and the Rage Against Expertise," in the December 2000 issue and Chrenka, "Misconstructing Constructivism," in the May 2001 issue). Baines and Stanley condemn the constructivists' adamant stand against direct instruction by lecturing and the sin of memorization. Chrenka replies that expertise is central in a constructivist classroom in which the teacher must develop "scaffolding strategies" needed for the learners to begin to construct their own meanings.

David N. Perkins of the Harvard Graduate School of Education, in "The Many Faces of Constructivism," *Educational Leadership* (November 1999), describes a tension between ideological constructivism and pragmatic constructionism, the former being seen as a rather rigid cure-all for traditional school ills and the latter as a flexible, circumstance-driven means of school improvement. While the constructivists' goal of producing active, collaborative, creative learners is certainly an antidote to the often prevalent emphasis on knowledge absorption by passive learners, the techniques for moving toward that goal are often difficult to implement and most always require more time than traditional methods.

These "theory-into-practice" difficulties have been elaborated upon by Mark Windschitl in "The Challenges of Sustaining a Constructivist Classroom Culture," *Phi Delta Kappan* (June 1999), and by Peter W. Airasian and Mary E. Walsh in "Constructivist Cautions," *Phi Delta Kappan* (February 1997). Windschitl sees constructivism as a culture, not a mere collection of practices, so its effectiveness as a guiding philosophy is realized only through major changes in curriculum, scheduling, and assessment. Airasian and Walsh insist that the "catch phrases" that flow from theorists to teachers are inadequate for dealing with implementation complexities.

These and similar concerns are addressed in the first of the following articles, in which constructivism advocate David Elkind examines three major barriers—societal, curricular, and pedagogical—that must be removed if the philosophy is to flourish in school settings. In the second article, Jamin Carson, an objectivist, attacks not only the practical aspects of constructivism's implementation but the very basic principles on which it is based.

YES

David Elkind

The Problem with Constructivism

Constructivism, in all of its various incarnations, is now a major educational philosophy and pedagogy. What the various interpretations of constructivism have in common is the proposition that the child is an active participant in constructing reality and not just a passive recorder of it. Constructivism thus echoes the philosophy implicit in Rousseau's *Emile* (1962) in which he argued that children have their own ways of knowing and that these have to be valued and respected. It also reflects the Kantian (Kant 2002) resolution of the nature/nurture controversy. Kant argued that the mind provides the categories of knowing, while experience provides the content. Piaget (1950) created the contemporary version of constructivism by demonstrating that the categories of knowing, no less than the contents of knowledge, are constructed in the course of development. Vygotsky (1978) added the importance of social context to the constructivist epistemology—a theory of knowledge and knowledge acquisition.

Constructivism in education has been approached at many different levels and from a variety of perspectives (e.g., Larochelle, Bednarz, and Garrison 1998). In this essay, I will limit the discussion to those writers who have attempted to translate constructivism into a practical pedagogy (e.g., Brooks and Brooks 1993; Fosnot 1996; Gagnon and Collay 2001; Lambert et al. 1997). Though many different models have been created and put to test, none have been satisfactorily implemented. The failure of the constructivist reform movement is yet another in the long list of ill-fated educational reform movements (Gibboney 1994).

The inability to implement constructivist reforms is particularly instructive with regard to the failures of educational reforms in general. Constructivist reforms start from an epistemology. This sets constructivism apart from those educational reforms inspired by political events (such as the curriculum reform movement spurred by the Russian launching of the Sputnik) or by social events (such as the school reforms initiated by the Civil Rights Movement) or by a political agenda (e.g., *A Nation at Risk* [National Commission on Excellence in Education 1983]; the No Child Left Behind initiative). That is to say, the constructivist movement is generated by genuine pedagogical concerns and motivations.

The lack of success in implementing this widely accepted educational epistemology into the schools can be attributed to what might be called *failures of readiness*. Consider three types of readiness: teacher readiness, curricular

From *The Educational Forum*, vol. 68, Summer 2004, pp. 306–312. Copyright © 2004 by Kappa Delta Pi. Reprinted by permission.

readiness, and societal readiness. Teacher readiness requires teachers who are child development specialists with curricular and instructional expertise. Curriculum readiness requires courses of study that have been researched as to what, when, and how the subject matter should be taught. Societal readiness requires a nation that is willing—indeed eager—to accept educational change. For a reform movement to succeed, all three forms of readiness must be in alignment.

Teacher Readiness

Those who have tried to implement a constructivist pedagogy often argue that their efforts are blocked by unsupportive teachers. They claim that some teachers are wedded to an objectivist view that knowledge has an independent existence and needs only to be transmitted. Others have difficulty understanding how to integrate the learner's intuitive conceptions into the learning process. Still others are good at getting children actively involved in projects but are not able to translate them effectively into learning objectives. These problems are aggravated by an increasingly test-driven curriculum with little opportunity for creativity and innovation.

The problem, however, is not primarily with teachers but with teacher training. In the United States, many universities and colleges have done away with the undergraduate major in education. In Massachusetts, for example, a student with a bachelor's degree in any field can get a provisional certification after a year of supervised internship. After five years and the attainment of a master's degree, the candidate is eligible for permanent certification.

The demise of the undergraduate major in education can be attributed to a number of different factors that were enunciated in *Tomorrow's Schools of Education* (Holmes Group 1995) written by the deans of 80 of some of the nation's most prestigious schools of education. The report (1995, 45–46) targeted the education faculty who "ignore public schools to concentrate on theoretical research or to work with graduate students who do not intend careers as classroom teachers." In effect, the education faculty has failed to provide the kind of research that would be useful to teachers. As the report (1995, 45–46) argued, "Traditional forms of academic scholarship have a place in professional schools, but such institutions are obliged as well to learn from practice and to concern themselves with questions of applying knowledge." These observations are supported by the facts. Few teachers read the educational research journals, and few educational researchers read the journals directed at teachers such as *Educational Leadership* and *Young Children*. This also is true for researchers in the field of child development. Much of the research on children's cognitive, social, and emotional development is directly relevant to teaching. Yet, the educational implications of these studies are rarely, if ever, discussed in the literature.

The end result is that much of teaching as a profession has to be learned in the field. While this is true for all professions to a certain extent, it is particularly true of education. Indeed, one could make the case that teaching is, as yet, more art than profession. Professional training implies a body of knowledge and skills that are unique and that can be acquired only through a prescribed course of study. It is not clear that such a body of knowledge and skills exists for education. In fact, each educational reform movement challenges the practices currently in play. Perhaps it is because there is no agreed upon body of knowledge and skills that reform in education is so frequent and so unsuccessful. To be sure, all professions have disagreements but they all share some fundamental common ground, whether it is anatomy in medicine or legal precedence in the field of law. There is, however, no such common base in education.

Teaching will become a true profession only when we have a genuine science of education. Such a science will have to be multidisciplinary and include workers from traditional educational psychology, developmental psychology, sociology, and various subject matter disciplines. Researchers would investigate individual and group differences in learning styles in relation to the acquisition of the various tool subjects (i.e., reading, writing, arithmetic, science, and social studies) at different age levels. Teacher training would provide not only a solid grounding in child development but also would require domain specific knowledge as it applies to young people at different age levels. Teachers also would be knowledgeable about research and would have access to journals that serve both teachers and investigators.

The failure to treat education as a profession has a long history but was made patent by Flexner's (1910) report *Medical Education in the United States and Canada*. That report was critical of medical education in the United States and suggested that training in medicine should be a graduate program with an undergraduate major. It also argued for the establishment of teaching hospitals as a means of practical training under supervision. Though the report was mandated by the Carnegie Foundation for the Advancement of Teaching, no comparable critique and suggestions were made for teachers and teacher training. The only innovation taken from this report was the founding of lab schools which would serve the same function as teaching hospitals at various universities. These schools, however, were more often used for research than for training. Today, only a few lab schools remain in operation.

Before any serious, effective reform in education can be introduced, we must first reinvent teacher training. At the very least, teachers should be trained as child development specialists. But teachers need much more. Particularly today, with the technological revolution in our schools, teacher training should be a graduate program. Even with that, teaching will not become a true profession unless and until we have a true science of education (Elkind 1999).

Curricular Readiness

A constructivist approach to education presupposes a thorough understanding of the curriculum to be taught. Piaget understood this very well. Much of his research was aimed at shedding light on what might be called the *logical substructure* of the discipline. That is to say, to match the subject matter to the child's level of developing mental abilities, you have to understand the logical demands it makes upon the child's reasoning powers. In his research with Inhelder (1964), Piaget demonstrated that for a child to engage in the addition and multiplication of classes, relations, and numbers, children first need to attain concrete operations. Similarly, Inhelder and Piaget (1958) showed that true experimental thinking and dealing with multiple variables require the formal mental operations not attained until adolescence. Task analysis of this sort is required in all curricular domains. Only when we successfully match children's ability levels with the demands of the task can we expect them to reconstruct the knowledge we would like them to acquire.

In addition to knowing the logical substructure of the task, we also need research regarding the timing of the introduction of various subject matters. For example, the planets often are taught at second grade. We know that children of seven or eight do not yet have a firm grasp of celestial space and time. Does teaching the planets at grade two give the child an advantage when studying astronomy at the college level? Similar questions might be asked about introducing the explorers as a social study topic in the early elementary grades. I am not arguing against the teaching of such material; I am contending that we need to know whether this is time well spent. We have little or no research on these issues.

Another type of curriculum information has to do with the sequence of topics within any particular course of study. In elementary math, is it more effective to teach coins before or after we teach units of distance and weight? Some sequences of concepts are more effective for learning than others. In most cases, we don't have data upon which to make that kind of decision. In most public school textbooks, the order of topical instruction is determined more by tradition, or by the competition, than by research. We find this practice even at the college level. Most introductory courses begin with a chapter on the history of the discipline. Yet many students might become more engaged in the subject if the first topic was one to which they could immediately relate. Again, we have little or no research on such matters. This is true for teaching in an integrated or linear curriculum format.

The argument that there is little connection between academic research and practical applications has many exceptions. Nonetheless, as long as these remain exceptions rather than the rule, we will not move toward a true science of education.

Societal Readiness

If the majority of teachers are not ready to adopt a constructivist pedagogy, neither are educational policy makers and the larger society. To be successfully implemented, any reform pedagogy must reflect a broad and energized social consensus. John Dewey was able to get broad backing for his Progressive Education Reform thanks to World War I and the negative reaction to all things European. Up until the First World War, our educational system followed the European classical model. It was based on the doctrine of formal discipline whereby training in Greek and Latin, as well as the classics, rigorously trained the mind. In contrast, Dewey (1899) offered a uniquely American functional pedagogy. He wanted to prepare students for the demands and occupations of everyday life. There was general consensus that this was the way to go.

The launching of the Russian Sputnik in 1957 was another event that energized the nation to demand curriculum reform. Russia, it seemed, had outstripped us scientifically, and this reflected badly on our math and science education. The National Science Foundation embarked on a program of science and math curriculum reform. To this end, the foundation recruited leading figures in the fields of science and math to construct new, up-to-date curricula in these fields. These scholars knew their discipline but, for the most part, they did not know children. The new curricula, which included variable-base arithmetic and teaching the principles of the discipline, were inappropriate for children. When these curricula failed, a new consensus emerged to advocate the need to go "back to basics." The resulting teacher-made curricula dominated education prior to the entrance of the academicians. While "back to basics" was touted as a "get tough" movement, it was actually a "get easier" movement because it reintroduced more age-appropriate material.

Many of the educational reforms of any category have not had much success since that time. Though *A Nation at Risk* (NCEE 1983) created a number of reforms, the report itself did not energize the nation, and there was not sufficient motivation to bring about real change. In large part, I believe that this was because there was no national consciousness of a felt need for change. The current educational movement, No Child Left Behind, was introduced for political rather than pedagogical reasons. This legislation was avowedly for the purpose of improving student achievement and changing the culture of American schools. These aims are to be achieved by requiring the states to test all children every year from grades three through eight. Schools that do not meet statewide or national standards may be closed or parents given an opportunity to send their children to other schools.

This is an ill-conceived program based on a business model that regards education as akin to a factory turning out products. Obviously, children are not containers to be filled up to a certain amount at each grade level. The program forces schools to focus on tests to the exclusion of what is really important in the educational process. Testing is expensive and depletes already scarce educational resources. Students are being coached to do well on the tests without regard to their true knowledge and understanding. The policy is corrupt in that it encourages schools to cheat. The negative results of this policy already are being felt. A number of states are choosing to opt out of the program. The No Child Left Behind legislation is a good example of bad policy promoted for political gain that is not in the best interests of children.

Other than a national crisis, there is another way for social consensus to bring about educational reform. In Kuhn's (1996) innovative book on scientific revolutions, he made the point that such revolutions do not come about by the gradual accretion of knowledge. Rather they come about as a result of conflicts between opposing points of view with one eventually winning out over the other. Evolution, for example, is still fighting a rearguard action against those who believe in the biblical account of the origin of man. In education, the long-running battle between nature and nurture (read development and learning) is not likely to be resolved soon by a higher order synthesis.

An alternative view was offered by Galison (1997), who argued that the history of science is one of tools rather than ideas. He used the history of particle physics as an example. The tools of particle physics are optical-like cloud chambers and electronic-like photographic emulsions that display particle interactions by way of images. One could make equal claims for the history of biology and astronomy. As both Kuhn and Galison acknowledged, scientific progress can come about by conflict or the introduction of new technologies.

Education seems likely to be changed by new tools rather than conflicting ideas. Computers are changing education's successive phases. In the first phase, computers simply replaced typewriters and calculators. In the second phase, computers began to change the ways in which we teach. The widespread use of e-mail, Blackboard, PowerPoint, and simulations are examples. And there is an active and growing field of computer education with its own journals and conferences (e.g., Advancement of Computer Education and Association for the Advancement of Computing in Education). The third phase already has begun, and we are now seeing changes in math and science curricula as a direct result of the availability of technology. Education is one of the last social institutions to be changed by technology, but its time has come.

Conclusion

In this paper, I have used the failure of the constructivist reform movement to illustrate what I believe is necessary for any true educational innovation to succeed. There must be teacher, curricular, and societal readiness for any educational innovation to be accepted and put into practice. In the past, reforms were generated by one or the other form of readiness, but without the support of the others. I believe that technology will change this. It is my sense that it will move us toward making teaching a true profession, the establishment of a multidisciplinary science of education, and a society ready and eager to embrace a technologically based education.

Education is, however, more than technology. It is, at its heart, people dealing with people. That is why any successful educational reform must build upon a human philosophy that makes clear its aims and objectives. Technology without a philosophy of education is mechanical, and a philosophy without an appropriate technology will be ineffective. Technology is forcing educational reform, but we need to harness it to the best philosophy of education we have available. I believe this to be constructivism. The current failure to implement constructivism is not because of its merits but because of a lack of readiness for it. We need to make every effort to ensure that the technological revolution in education creates the kinds of teachers, curricula, and social climate that will make constructivism a reality in our classrooms.

References

Brooks, J. G., and M. G. Brooks. 1993. *In search of understanding: The case for constructivist classrooms*. Alexandria, Va.: Association for Supervision and Curriculum Development.

Dewey, J. 1899. *The school and society*. Chicago: University of Chicago Press.

Elkind, D. 1999. Educational research and the science of education. *Educational Psychology* 11(3): 171–87.

Flexner, A. 1910. *Medical education in the United States and Canada*. New York: Carnegie Foundation for the Advancement of Teaching.

Fosnot, C. T. 1996. *Constructivism: Theory, perspectives, and practice*. New York: Teachers College Press.

Gagnon, G. W. J., and M. Collay. 2001. *Designing for learning: Six elements in constructivist classrooms*. Thousand Oaks, Calif.: Corwin Press.

Galison, P. L. 1997. *Image and logic: A material culture of microphysics*. Chicago: University of Chicago Press.

Gibboney, R. A. 1994. *The stone trumpet: A story of practical school reform*. Albany, N.Y.: State University of New York Press.

Holmes Group. 1995. *Tomorrow's schools of education*. Ann Arbor: University of Michigan.

Inhelder, B., and J. Piaget. 1958. *The growth of logical thinking from childhood to adolescence: An essay on the construction of formal operational structures*, trans. A. Parsons and S. Milgram. New York: Basic Books.

Inhelder, B., and J. Piaget. 1964. *The early growth of logic in the child, classification and seriation*, trans. E. A. Lunzer and D. Papert. New York: Harper and Row.

Kant, I. 2002. *Immanuel Kant: Theoretical philosophy after 1781*, trans. G. Hatfield and M. Friedman. New York: Cambridge University Press.

Kuhn, T. S. 1996. *The structure of scientific revolutions*, 3rd ed. Chicago: University of Chicago Press.

Lambert, L., M. Collay, M. Dietz, K. Kent, and A. E. Richert. 1997. *Who will save our schools? Teachers as constructivist leaders*. Thousand Oaks, Calif.: Corwin Press.

Larochelle, M., N. Bednarz, and J. Garrison. 1998. *Constructivism and education*. Cambridge, England: Cambridge University Press.

National Commission on Excellence in Education. 1983. *A nation at risk: The imperative for educational reform*. Washington, D.C.: U.S. Government Printing Office.

Piaget, J. 1950. *The psychology of intelligence*, trans. M. Piercy and D. E. Berlyne. London: Routledge and Paul.

Rousseau, J. J. 1962. *Emile*, trans. W. Boyd. New York: Teachers College Press.

Vygotsky, L. S. 1978. *Mind in society: The development of higher psychological processes*, ed. M. Cole. Cambridge, Mass.: Harvard University Press.

Jamin Carson

Objectivism and Education: A Response to David Elkind's 'The Problem with Constructivism'

In "The Problem with Constructivism," David Elkind (2004) made several claims about why constructivism has not been implemented in schools. He argued that constructivism will be implemented only when we have *teacher*, *curricular*, and *societal readiness*; that teaching needs to become a science before it can be a true profession; and that constructivism is the only philosophy that will reform education. In this essay, I present counterarguments for each of these claims.

Constructivism is the theory that students learn by individually or socially transforming information (Slavin 1997). This theory necessarily entails certain metaphysical and epistemological assumptions. To accept constructivism, one must believe that:

- reality is dependent upon the perceiver, and thus constructed;
- reason or logic is not the only means of understanding reality, but one of many; and
- knowledge or truth is subjective and relative to the individual or community.

One philosophy of education that challenges this theory is objectivism, which asserts that students must be engaged actively in the subject matter to learn. This theory does not advocate, however, that students "transform" or "construct" reality, reason, knowledge, or truth. Objectivism holds that one reality exists independent of anyone perceiving it, humankind is capable of knowing this reality only by the faculty of reason, and objective knowledge and truth is possible (Peikoff 1993). I argue against Elkind's claims primarily from an objectivist viewpoint.

Failures of Readiness

Elkind's main thesis was that constructivism has not been implemented in schools because of failures of teacher, curricular, and societal readiness. Teacher readiness requires that a teacher be educated in a science of education such as child development. Curricular readiness involves knowing exactly when and

From *The Educational Forum*, vol. 69, Spring 2005, pp. 232–238. Copyright © 2005 by Kappa Delta Pi. Reprinted by permission.

how students are developmentally ready to learn specific information. Societal readiness is when society is eager for educational reform or change.

Elkind did not explain the causal relationship between these states of readiness and the implementation of constructivism. He only implied that a causal relationship exists. There is no reason to believe that a relationship exists or that any state of readiness would lead to a specific philosophy of education. A teacher must accept the metaphysical and epistemological assumptions of a pedagogic practice before he or she can implement it.

Elkind's definitions of readiness also were problematic. When defining teacher readiness as having good teacher "training"—which comes only from scientific knowledge (e.g., child development)—he stated (2004, 308), "Teaching will become a true profession only when we have a genuine science of education." Though education is not a true science, teachers generally are taught one unique body of knowledge. Most college and university teacher preparation programs, alternative certification programs, and professional development seminars teach the same information, and a great deal of it is constructivist in nature or a variant of it.

Elkind's definition of curricular readiness also has problems. He (2004, 307–08) defined curricular readiness as knowledge of "what, when, and how the subject matter should be taught" and then claimed that "only when we successfully match children's ability levels with the demands of the task can we expect them to reconstruct the knowledge we would like them to acquire." The phrase "we would like them to acquire" contradicts constructivist metaphysics and epistemology. If constructivism assumes that students construct their own knowledge, then how can a constructivist teacher choose the knowledge they would like students to acquire? The phrase "we would like them to acquire" presupposes an objective philosophy which holds that given a specific context, some knowledge is objectively superior to other knowledge. For a constructivist, this is a contradiction, if one views reality, reason, knowledge, and truth as subjective and relative to the perceiver, then what is the basis for arguing for any knowledge at all, let alone one over another? Any curricular choice, according to constructivist philosophy, should be as valid as any other. When constructivists make absolute claims about what, when, and how something should be taught, they are either objectivists or making arbitrary claims.

Finally, there are problems with societal readiness. Elkind (2004, 310) suggested that "to be successfully implemented, any reform pedagogy must reflect a broad and energized social consensus," which the United States currently does not have. Yet, a broad and energized social consensus in the United States does exist. The consensus is that public education has not adequately educated its students, particularly those of lower socioeconomic status. This societal readiness has paved the way for programs like No Child Left Behind. Progressive reform pedagogies like constructivism are usually prescribed by administrators to improve education or raise test scores. Despite the social consensus that education needs reform pedagogy and constructivism has been one of those pedagogies, education still has not closed the gap between rich and poor—assuming that is education's aim in the first place.

Science of Education

Most teachers receive the same education, but not all teachers readily accept what they are taught, whether it be constructivism or some other philosophy of education. Unlike medical practitioners, for example, educators disagree about nearly all issues within their field. Medical practitioners simply observe whether or not the treatment cured the patient. They may disagree about why or how a treatment worked, but at least they have objective and verifiable evidence of whether or not the treatment worked. Education, on the other hand, possesses many more points of disagreement. How do people learn? What should people learn? How do we measure learning? The complexity of these questions results in virtually no consensus about what works among all educators. Though education draws from a unique body of knowledge to prepare its teachers, it is not scientific and probably never will be because there is so much disagreement about the definition of education.

Assuming that Elkind is correct in believing that education must become a science, his argument is still flawed. It is contradictory for a constructivist to advocate a science of education. The philosophical foundation of constructivism rejects an objectively knowable reality. The philosophical foundation of science claims that one reality is objectively knowable through the senses and reason. Science, therefore, undermines constructivism rather than serves as a prerequisite to it.

If Elkind used Kuhn's (1996) definition of science—reality is observed by a perceiver who sees it through the lens of socially constructed paradigms that are periodically overthrown by new paradigms that are incommensurate with past paradigms—then any science of education still has no claim of truth over any other method of inquiry within education. Claims like "teaching will become a true profession only when we have a genuine science of education" are equivalent to saying that teaching will be a profession only when it becomes an art. If we construct our own reality, what is the difference?

If Elkind believes that most of what educators consider science comes from constructivists like Rousseau, Kant, Piaget, and Vygotsky, his argument is flawed. It is circular logic for a constructivist to claim that a science of education is needed and then to select only constructivists as the founders of that science. Though some beliefs are obtained in experiments, most are not—especially philosophical views about *literally* constructing reality, which are not testable or falsifiable and thus should not be accepted as scientific.

Philosophy of Education

Elkind seems to have overlooked the role of the educator's metaphysical and epistemological assumptions in accepting constructivism or any philosophy of education. He admitted that educators who "are wedded to an objectivist view that knowledge has an independent existence" have resisted constructivism, but he quickly dismissed this cause in favor of teacher readiness. Ironically, teacher readiness is more likely the cause of resistance to constructivism. For an educator to implement a pedagogical practice, he or she must consciously or unconsciously accept its metaphysical and epistemological assumptions. Constructivists possess certain metaphysical and epistemological assumptions that lead to constructivist practices, while objectivists possess other metaphysical and epistemological assumptions that lead to objectivist practices. Elkind overlooked the possibility that not everyone holds the same assumptions about reality, reason, knowledge, and truth that lead to constructivist practices. Some have other worldviews and, therefore, reject constructivism as a theory of learning because it contradicts their philosophical assumptions.

Elkind said that constructivism is the "best philosophy of education we have available," and that it has been "widely accepted." This is true only at the university level, where the majority of professors possess the metaphysical and epistemological assumptions that lead to constructivism. It is not true at other levels of education, where one is likely to encounter different metaphysical and epistemological assumptions that lead to other pedagogical practices.

Constructivism is not the best philosophy of education. Objectivism is more reasonable from a theoretical and practical perspective than constructivism. Objectivism holds that there is one reality independent of anyone perceiving it. This means that regardless of whether or not someone perceives something, it still exists. For example, I can leave the room with a table in it and be convinced that the table still exists. Most people probably would agree with this statement. Constructivism, on the other hand, holds that reality is dependent upon the perceiver. This means that something exists only if someone perceives it. From a constructivist perspective, if I leave a room with a table in it, the table ceases to exist. Most people would disagree with such a statement or at least have difficulty accepting it.

Objectivism also holds that humankind takes in data through the senses and uses reason to obtain knowledge. Constructivism does not deny the efficacy of reason completely, but does consider it as only one of many ways of knowing. This belief is another theory that does not stand up in practice. The theory of multiple intelligences, for example, proposes at least ten "intelligences" or ways of knowing: verbal, logical, musical, physical, spatial, inter- and intra-personal, natural, existential, and spiritual. When analyzed or reduced to their epistemological foundation, these intelligences seem more like specialized bodies of acquired knowledge than actual processors of information. Reason exists in all of them, which suggests that each is the *primary* way of knowing.

Objectivism also holds that we have objective knowledge and truth. A person observes reality via his or her senses, forms concepts through the use of noncontradictory (i.e., Aristotelian) logic, and thus acquires knowledge and truth. Constructivism posits that only subjective knowledge and relative truth are possible. If knowledge is subjective or relative to an individual or a group, then *any* knowledge could be true. Sacrificing virgins to appease the gods or believing that the universe revolves around the earth would count as knowledge and truth. Notable constructivists (Lawson 1989; Noddings 1998; Rorty 2003) have raised these criticisms about constructivist metaphysics and epistemology and have admitted that they have no answer to them.

Constructivism in Practice

Practically, objectivism is more reasonable than constructivism. As a high school English teacher, I implemented constructivism in my classes by allowing the students to construct what an English class is—choosing its purpose, curriculum, and instruction. Most of the students did not understand how they could "construct" an English class. They expected me to define the English class for them—a very reasonable assumption considering how young they were and how limited their experience. After a fair amount of prompting, a few bold students thought English should be spelling and grammar. Some might argue that the students' answer proves only that they had been prevented from constructing previous curriculums, and thus had not learned to think for themselves or to question the curriculum. I concede that the students' previous conception of what constitutes schooling was part of their inability to construct the course. However, perhaps children naturally look to adults to share with them their learned and acquired knowledge. They expect teachers to pass on to them a body of knowledge, imperfect though it may be, that they can update according to their discoveries. Many practicing constructivists refuse to do this, believing instead that a child's knowledge is equal to that of an adult's and a student is no less an authority on a subject than a teacher. This assumption is untrue and dangerous. It assumes that children are better off entering a world with no knowledge and creating their own rather than entering a world full of knowledge, learning it, and then updating it if it does not stand the test of their scrutiny.

The students in my English class could not be pure constructivists in the context of day-to-day assignments either. For example, when we read *Romeo and Juliet* by William Shakespeare, the reality of the story presented obstacles. If the students would have said that the story was about an aging salesman who imagines he is a success when he is not, a constructivist teacher would have to accept their response—right or wrong—because reality is constructed. For an objectivist English teacher, however, every claim must be supported by textual evidence and logic—by reality. *Romeo and Juliet*, therefore, must be about what the text supports and what logic dictates, not about the subjective feelings of the reader, which may not be in accordance with reality. Constructivist English teachers who tell students that there are no right-or-wrong answers or that their interpretation is as correct as anyone else's only encourage students to be careless and uncritical readers, writers, and thinkers.

I shifted to giving students a choice supported by evidence and logic because of the flaws in the practical application of constructivism. Students could choose the purpose, curriculum, and assignments of the course, but ultimately their choices had to conform to reality, not to their subjective whims. In other words, their choices had to have a compelling connection to their literacy development.

Conclusion

Constructivists must ask themselves whether they want to cling to the literal interpretation of constructivism that sees reality as constructed or simply believe that students learn best when they are actively engaged in the learning process. The two definitions are not the same metaphysically or epistemo-logically. The former entails an untenable theory and practice and should be modified or rejected.

Noddings (1998, 117–18) addressed the distinction between moderate and radical constructivism in this way:

> [I]f radical constructivists are just saying that our perception and cognition are theory-laden, that all knowledge is mediated by our cognitive struc-tures and theories, then they have lots of company among contemporary theorists. However, if they are saying that there is no mind-independent reality, then they seem to be arguing a line long ago rejected.

Though Noddings seemed to advocate a moderate constructivist view that denies a mind-dependent reality, I maintain that constructivists cannot be moderates. All constructivists necessarily must believe that reality is dependent upon the perceiver. It is logically impossible to believe that a person's perception and cognitive structures are theory-laden, while simultaneously believing that reality is independent of the perceiver. If reality is perceived by a theory-laden perceiver, then the reality is theory-laden too. The moment that one becomes theory-laden, one is prevented from knowing an objective reality.

Objectivists believe humans are not theory-laden in the pejorative sense of that word. Objectivists do not consider prior knowledge or cognitive struc-tures as a subjective lens through which one views reality. Rather, one possesses prior knowledge that informs new knowledge and, consequently, makes the new knowledge meaningful. If the prior knowledge or cognitive structure is incorrect, eventually the new correct knowledge will conflict with it and a per-son will be forced to update his or her old knowledge. If constructivists believe in an independent reality, then they not only must believe in it, but also must possess an objective method of perceiving it and, therefore, have objective knowledge and truth. There is no middle ground.

References

Elkind, D. 2004. The problem with constructivism. *The Educational Forum* 68(4): 306–12.

Kuhn, T. S. 1996. *The structure of scientific revolutions*, 3rd ed. Chicago: The University of Chicago Press.

Lawson, H. 1989. Stories about stories. In *Dismantling truth: Reality in the post-modern world*, ed. H. Lawson and L. Appignanesi, xi–xxviii. London: Weidenfeld and Nicolson.

Noddings, N. 1998. *Philosophy of education*. Boulder, CO: Westview Press.

Piekoff, L. 1993. *Objectivism: The philosophy of Ayn Rand*. New York: Penguin Books.

Rorty, R. 2003. Dismantling truth: Solidarity versus objectivity. In *The theory of knowledge: Classical and contemporary readings*, 3rd ed., ed. L. P. Pojman, 324–30. Belmont, CA: Wadsworth/Thomson Learning.

Slavin, R. E. 1997. *Educational psychology: Theory and practice*, 5th ed. Boston: Allyn & Bacon.

POSTSCRIPT

Is Constructivism the Best Philosophy of Education?

So it can be seen that present-day constructivists like David Elkind draw a lot of inspiration from Dewey's portrayal of the active, probing learner immersed in social experience, Holt's learners who steer their own personal development unfettered by imposed curricula, and Rogers' self-exploring students whose subjective knowledge takes precedence. In contrast, objectivists like Carson most likely find comfort in Hutchins's timeless rationality, Adler's concept of a single best curriculum for all, and Skinner's use of scientific principles and quantitative methods to create effective learners.

Elkind responded to Carson's critique in the Summer 2005 issue of *Educational Forum*, primarily refuting the accusation that constructivists deny that a physical world exists outside our sensory experiences. He states that "it is not that an external reality does not exist, only that we have to reconstruct it to know it . . . it is because humans share a common sensory apparatus that we can agree upon an external reality existing outside our experience." Our senses can be mistaken but "objective" reasoning is fallible as well, he concludes.

In the past decade, the philosophy of constructivism has been widely treated by those who praise it and those who deplore it. A sampling of sources includes Jacqueline Grennon Brooks and Martin G. Brooks, *In Search of Understanding: The Case for Constructivist Classrooms* (1993); Susan Ohanian, *One Size Fits Few* (1999); Karen R. Harris and Steve S. Graham, "Memo to Constructivists: Skills Count, Too," *Educational Leadership* (February 1996); Tony Wagner, "Change as Collaborative Inquiry: A 'Constructivist' Methodology for Reinventing Schools," *Phi Delta Kappan* (March 1998); Heinrich Mintrop, "Educating Students to Teach in a Constructivist Way—Can It All Be Done?" *Teachers College Record* (April 2001); and Rhoda Cummings and Steve Harlow, "The Constructivist Roots of Moral Education," *The Educational Forum* (Summer 2000).

Additional commentary may be found in Michael Glassman, "Running in Circles: Chasing Dewey," *Educational Theory* (August 2004); Donald G. Hackmann, "Constructivism and Block Scheduling: Making the Connection," *Phi Delta Kappan* (May 2004); Ian Moll, "Towards a Constructivist Montessori Education," *Perspectives in Education* (June 2004); and David Chicoine, "Ignoring the Obvious: A Constructivist Critique of a Traditional Teacher Education Program," *Educational Studies* (December 2004).

The discussion launched by Elkind and Carson has been continued in the Spring 2006, Fall 2006, and Summer 2007 issues of *Educational Forum*. See especially the Henry Pegues article, "Of Paradigm Wars: Constructivism, Objectivism, and Postmodern Stratagems," in the Summer 2007 issue.

ISSUE 5

Should Global Competition Steer School Reform?

YES: Marc Tucker, from "Charting a New Course for Schools," *Educational Leadership* (April 2007)

NO: Herb Childress, from "A Subtractive Education," *Phi Delta Kappan* (October 2006)

ISSUE SUMMARY

YES: Marc Tucker, president of the National Center on Education and the Economy, summarizes the work of the New Commission on the Skills of the American Workforce on which he served as vice chairman.

NO: Herb Childress, director of liberal studies at the Boston Architectural College, argues for a completely different approach to improvement of our efforts to educate.

Positions presented in Unit 1 of this book have been based primarily on philosophical reasoning and theoretical discourse. Dewey, Hutchins, Adler, Holt, Skinner, Rogers, Elkind, and Carson drew on basic assumptions about human nature and motivation to shape their arguments. But discussions about educational aims, policy, and practice have not been limited to such discourse. In the last half-century, particularly, considerations of economic factors and, most recently, the emergence of global competition, have come to dominate these discussions and in turn influence policymakers in the field of education.

Beginning with the Soviet Union's technological challenge in the 1950s and the growth of Japan and Germany as economic powers in the 1960s to present-day advances by China, South Korea, and India, Americans have been prompted to measure the effectiveness of our school systems against those in other countries. In the 1970s, the Council for Basic Education cited foreign competition to spur the public's acceptance of its "back to basics" campaign, which called for the trimming of "frills and fads" from the curriculum. Poor comparative performance of American schools, as documented in a number of international studies, fueled many of the recommendations of the 1983

"A Nation at Risk" report. Former Secretary of Education William J. Bennett, in "A Nation Still at Risk," *Policy Review* (July/August 1998), cites the Third International Math and Science Study in which the United States ranked nineteenth in math and sixteenth in science out of 21 nations. Bennett believes that too many educators in this country have "responded to the persistence of mediocre performance by engaging in denial, self-delusion, and blame-shifting" and that our current system has a rigid bureaucratic structure that is resistant to any meaningful reform. Other critics contend that the "education establishment" is either unwilling or incapable of improving the schools in which young Americans are not learning enough for their own or their nation's good.

In the current decade, increasing numbers of business leaders and economists are sounding alarms about the fast pace of a globalization process spurred by the Internet. Employers say that they cannot find people who possess the necessary skills, knowledge, attitudes, and habits to do acceptable work. The crux of the problem was identified by William J. Reese in "Why Americans Love to Reform the Public Schools" in *Educational Horizons* (Summer 2007). Reese states that "schools have become multi-purpose institutions . . . expected to feed the hungry, discipline the wayward, identify and encourage the talented, treat everyone alike yet not forget that everyone is an individual, raise not only test scores but also feelings of self-worth, ensure winning sports teams without demeaning academics, improve not only standards but also graduation rates, provide for differing learning styles and capacities while administering common tests, and counter the crass materialism of the larger society while they provide the young with the skills and sensibilities to thrive in it as future workers."

Time magazine (December 18, 2006) featured an article by Claudia Wallis and Sonja Steptoe, "How to Bring Our Schools Out of the 20th Century," that calls for a public conversation about "whether an entire generation of kids will fail to make the grade in the global economy because they can't think their way through abstract problems, work in teams, distinguish good information from bad, or speak a language other than English." The focus of the article was on the New Commission's report "Tough Choices or Tough Times." Today's economy, the report holds, demands not only high-level competence in academic disciplines but also knowing more about the world, thinking outside the box, becoming smarter about new sources of information, and developing good people skills.

The following articles offer New Commission leader Marc Tucker's depiction of the kind of school system that will produce competitive students and some dissenting thought by Herb Childress who worries about an over-emphasis on preparing the young for appropriate places in the business world.

YES

Marc Tucker

Charting a New Course for Schools

Developing countries, such as China, India, and Korea, have learned how to produce highly educated workers who offer world-class skills at low wages. Those workers, who are now available to global employers over the Internet, directly compete with the U.S. workforce. Why, asks the New Commission on the Skills of the American Workforce, would global employers pay U.S. workers more than twice as much for the same skills?

The Commission's new report, *Tough Choices or Tough Times*, considers this issue. It continues a discussion that began in 1990, when the first Commission released a report titled *America's Choice: High Skills or Low Wages*, which called attention to the steady loss of low-skill jobs to countries that could offer cheaper labor. The 1990 report proposed raising education standards in the United States so U.S. workers could migrate to better-paying work requiring higher-level skills. *Tough Choices or Tough Times* ups the ante by suggesting what it will take to vault the U.S. education system to top performance and ensure that graduates have the skills and knowledge that they, and the nation, need.

A Clear and Present Danger

Given the dynamics of global competition, the need for highly skilled U.S. graduates is becoming more pressing. For one thing, people in other countries are becoming more educated. In 1960, the United States led the world in the percentage of working-age adults who had completed high school (Organisation for Economic Co-operation and Development [OECD], 2006a). This is no longer the case. Also, 30 years ago, U.S. students accounted for 30 percent of the world's population of college students. That percentage has now plunged to 14 percent and continues to fall (OECD, 2006b).

The United States' low rankings in international comparative studies of achievement are another cause for concern. Moreover, rapid advances in technology are resulting in the automation of jobs—not just low-skill jobs, as used to be the case, but any job that involves routine work. Many well-paying middle-class jobs fall in this category and are becoming increasingly vulnerable.

With this in mind, how can the United States ensure that its workers continue to command high wages and maintain their standard of living?

From *Educational Leadership,* April 2007, pp. 48–52. Copyright © 2007 by ASCD. Reprinted by permission. The Association for Supervision and Curriculum Development is a worldwide community of educators advocating sound policies and sharing best practices to achieve the success of each learner. To learn more, visit ASCD at www.ascd.org.

We can do so only by meeting two criteria: We must match the best academic performance in the world and, at the same time, offer the most creative and innovative workers.

Only companies at the leading edge of their industries will be able to pay premium wages. And what will they pay a premium for? For workers who have a high level of preparation in reading, writing, speaking, mathematics, science, literature, history, and the arts; who are comfortable with ideas and abstractions; who are creative and can imagine useful and innovative products; who can solve problems by integrating knowledge from multiple fields; and who function well in groups and adapt easily to change.

Unfortunately, we're stuck in an education system that is not geared to produce these kinds of graduates. But it's not for lack of trying to change it. We have implemented a plethora of programs, policies, and interventions in schools, yet our academic performance remains mediocre and our costs continue to rise. We have the second most expensive system in the world,[1] which is not surprising, given that the per-pupil cost of our elementary and secondary education system has increased 240 percent over the last 30 years, after accounting for inflation. The one option that we have not tried is to overhaul the entire U.S. education system.

Investing in a System that Works

The Commission has proposed radical departures from the United States' current education system, whose main features were put in place a century ago to meet the needs of a different era. *Tough Choices or Tough Times* holds up a vision of what a more effective system might look like. Seven steps can take us there.

Step One: Chart a New Course for Student Progression Through the System

Let's begin with a thought experiment. Suppose we created state examinations of the same type and quality as the College Board advanced placement examinations. Suppose they were set to the standard required to do college-level work in the state's community and technical colleges. Now suppose that students—or, for that matter, adults—could take these exams whenever they thought they were sufficiently prepared and as often as they liked. Also, suppose for a moment that the majority of our high school students could pass these examinations at age 16 and that 95 percent could meet the standard by the time they left high school.

In this thought experiment, students who passed the exam could, if they chose, continue their studies in the state's community and technical colleges. Those who received somewhat higher scores could choose to stay in high school and continue in the International Baccalaureate program, a program consisting of advanced placement courses, a similar program developed by ACT, or one of the international equivalents of these programs. When they completed their program of study, they could apply to the colleges of their choice.

If you think this scenario sounds farfetched, it's not. Denmark graduates the majority of its students ready for college at 16 years old. And England and India permit students or schools to choose from a limited group of state-approved syllabus-based exams.

Step Two: Reinvest Available Resources Where it Counts

If our thought experiment were to become a reality, we could save enormous sums of money. Because most students would be prepared at 16 years old for college-level work, savings would be realized in high schools (because students would have the opportunity to exit early) and in colleges (because remediation costs would decrease). In fact, our analysis found that close to $60 billion would be available for strategic reinvestment in schools.

We would invest this money in three crucial areas: (1) building a high-quality early education system; (2) recruiting, training, and deploying a high-quality teaching force; and (3) providing additional resources to disadvantaged students so they meet rigorous education standards. Reinvestment in these areas, combined with other features of the plan, could get most students ready for college by age 16 and 95 percent of students ready for college by the end of high school.

Step 3: Invest in Universal Preschool Education

The United States has long trailed behind many other countries in providing universal, high-quality early childhood education. This is where we would spend the first third of our investment fund—a little more than $19 billion. That sum would buy high-quality early childhood education for all 4-year-olds in the United States whose families chose to enroll them (close to 3.5 million children) and for all low-income 3-year-olds (more than 600,000 children; National Center for Children in Poverty, 2004; National Center for Education Statistics, 2005).

Scores of studies indicate that high-quality early education programs can ameliorate or reverse learning disparities (Burr & Guinewald, 2006; King, 2006). However, for early childhood education to lead to improved outcomes for children, services must be made available equitably across states and be supported by an infrastructure that ensures high quality. States would need to create an infrastructure that would establish and monitor standards for children's learning and program quality, provide enriched professional development and adequate compensation, establish governance systems to promote the efficient use of resources, establish links among schools and other institutions that promote children's healthy development, and provide parents and policymakers with evaluative data to inform decision making. (For an update on how states are grappling with these issues, see Sacks & Ruzzi, 2005.)

Step 4: Recruit Teachers from the Top Third of Those Entering College

How can we expect to produce highly skilled students if teachers are not highly skilled? Unlike the United States, Singapore recruits its teachers from the top third of its high school graduates. Moreover, graduates with a BA or BS in education earn more than most other university graduates, with the exception of students graduating with law, business, computer engineering, and medical degrees (Singapore Ministry of Manpower, 2005). Increasing compensation can make teaching more appealing to top-performing students, especially to young teachers, who typically are more interested in higher salaries than in retirement benefits or pensions that come at the end of a career.

In our thought experiment, we would invest approximately $19 billion in teachers' compensation. Teachers would work through a four-step career ladder, with starting pay at approximately $45,000, which is now the median pay for teachers. Teachers at the top of the ladder would earn approximately $95,000. Those who were willing to work year-round would make $110,000 annually. Polling we conducted showed that college students in the top third of the distribution might elect to be teachers if teacher compensation reflected these higher amounts.

Step 5: Adopt High-Performance Management Models to Improve Schools and Districts

We would dramatically change the role of school districts. Under the plan, school districts would no longer operate schools. Instead, schools would be run by third-party organizations—preferably teams of teachers organized as limited liability corporations—working under contract to school districts (see Kolderie, 2002, for a discussion of teacher ownership). Districts and local boards would have a demanding and focused role: to manage a portfolio of schools working under performance contracts that would reward school operators that meet the district's student performance goals. The district would try hard to help those whose performance lagged, but if operators failed to meet their goals despite this help, the district would seek proposals from qualified operators who thought they could do a better job. Both the Netherlands and Flemish Belgium, the two countries with the highest mathematics performance in Europe, permit third-party groups—namely, families—to own and run schools.

All these schools would be public schools. They could not limit admission; if there were more applicants than spaces, they would have to admit students by lottery. Everyone would be accountable for student performance against state standards and for teaching the state curriculum. Beyond that, however, schools would have great latitude in establishing their own particular character and would be encouraged to develop distinctive programs.

The state would directly fund these public schools. (The United States is one of the few industrialized nations in the world that funds its schools locally, and often with poor results.) Funds would be distributed to the schools according to a formula based on the characteristics of the school's student body. Each student would get the same base funding. However, there would be various increments for students from low-income families, for students from homes in which English is not spoken, for mildly disabled students, for severely disabled students, and so on.

Teachers would be recruited, trained, certified, and employed by the state on a standard schedule of salary and benefits, with adjustments for significant differences in cost of living in different parts of the state. But they would be paid only when a particular school hired them. Each school would get its funds in one lump sum, with the amounts needed to pay its teachers deducted from the total. The school would be free to decide on how it would spend the remaining money in its budget.

School operators could only get a contract through association with a helping organization approved by the state. Helping organizations could be universities, for-profit organizations, independent not-for-profits, museums, technology companies, teachers unions, or such organizations as the Asia Society, the College Board, Cisco Systems, or KIPP Schools.

The kinds of organizations that would sponsor contract schools are very like those that have sponsored the best charter schools. To get approval, the helping agency would need to show a strong track record in providing high-quality technical assistance and professional development as well as support on matters ranging from budget and leadership training to curriculum and pedagogy.

Excerpts from Tough Choices or Tough Times?

- The United States will have to be number one or two in technology leadership in every industry in which it expects to be a major competitor. (p. 8)
- Americans are not likely to succeed unless many more of us than at present understand a good deal about the other peoples of the world. (p. 27)
- Being good at math will entail not just being able to do math well but being very good at mathematical reasoning. (p. 29)
- History, music, drawing and painting, and economics will give our students an edge just as surely as math and science will. (p. 29)
- Our curricula and our pedagogy heavily emphasize analysis over synthesis, the distinguishing feature of the creative impulse. (p. 30)
- The United States . . . has managed to construct a system that could not be better designed to deprive the vast majority of our students of a reason to take tough courses or to study hard. (p. 37)
- To visit the typical American school is to practice a certain kind of archaeology. We do not throw anything away. Policies are not discontinued; we simply add new ones. (p. 38)
- There will be no net growth in our workforce for a long time coming from native-born Americans. All the net growth will come from immigrants. (p. 41)

Step 6: Provide Strong Support to Disadvantaged Students

We would use what was left from the dividend produced by the change in student progression through the system—a little over $18 billion—to "top up" school funding statewide in all the states. This would make it possible to equalize school funding without raiding wealthier districts, which is the only way school funding will ever be made equitable in the United States. It would result in greatly increased funding for schools serving the most disadvantaged students, enabling such schools to operate extended days; provide extensive diagnostic screening and interventions; offer support for students with physical and learning disabilities; and furnish such crucial supports as mentors, tutors, and social and family services. Implementing these measures, along with having high-quality teachers and a strong early childhood education system, would transform the opportunities available to disadvantaged children.

Step 7: Rebuild Standards, Assessment, and Curriculum to Reflect Today's Needs and Tomorrow's Requirements

We have described a highly efficient, highly performance-oriented education system in which competent, entrepreneurial educators have great freedom to chart their own courses as long as they produce solid gains in student achievement. But in such systems, everything depends on how we measure student achievement. We must improve the quality and reduce the quantity of tests that our current accountability system requires. Good examinations exist, such as the advanced placement tests, the International Baccalaureate exams, and the Cambridge University International General Certificate of Secondary Education examinations (which are used in 120 countries).

What do good examinations look like? They are framed by sound, logically ordered curriculum frameworks. They are based on syllabi describing a high-quality curriculum that is intellectually coherent and compelling. They demand broad and deep knowledge. No amount of test preparation will improve a student's performance on these kinds of exams. Students succeed only if they can read and write well across content areas; have a sound grasp of the concepts on which a discipline is based (mathematics and science, for example); or can exhibit called-for performances (in the case of music or art). In all cases, good exams make it possible for students to show what they can do in the form of extended student work samples (like a substantial essay or research project) as well as a written test. They also give students opportunities to creatively answer questions that may not have occurred to those who assembled the exam.

Unfortunately, exams like these cost between $80 and $100 per subject per student tested, which is far more than we currently spend. Only exams of this sort, however, will enable us to properly measure whether our students have successfully mastered key ideas, concepts, facts, and procedures and whether they have the capacity for creativity and innovation crucial for their and the economy's success.

A Nation Still at Risk

Will it be tough to implement a program like this? Sure. Do we have a choice? No. We plan to begin by offering assistance to a small group of states that appear to be most committed to the framework described. We hope that as other states see what such a plan can accomplish, they will follow.

Notes

1. According to OECD's most recent report, the United States ranks third in per-pupil spending for primary education (behind Denmark and Norway). However, the United States ranks first in spending for postsecondary education. Taken together, the United States is second in per-pupil spending in comparison to the other 29 OECD countries. The United States is also second to Korea in terms of per-pupil spending as a percentage of gross domestic product.

References

Burr, J., & Guinewald, R. (2006). *Lessons learned: A review of early childhood development studies.* . . .

King, J. (2006). *Closing the achievement gap through expanded access to quality early education.* Washington, DC: New America Foundation.

Kolderie, T. (2002). *Teacher ownership as entrepreneurship in public education.* St. Paul, MN: Center for Policy Studies.

National Center for Children in Poverty. (2004). *Low-income children in the United States.* New York: Columbia University.

National Center for Education Statistics. (2005). *Digest of education statistics, tables and figures.* . . .

Organisation for Economic Co-operation and Development. (2006a). Table A1.2a. In *Education at a glance.* Paris: Author.

Organisation for Economic Co-operation and Development. (2006b). Table A1.3a. In *Education at a glance.* Paris: Author.

Sacks, L., & Ruzzi, B. (2005). *Early childhood education: Lessons from the states and abroad: 2005.* Paper prepared for the New Commission on the Skills of the American Workforce.

Singapore Ministry of Manpower. (2005). *Report of wages in Singapore 2005: Wage data from local universities.* Singapore: Author.

A Subtractive Education

I am a meandering kind of thinker. Something comes up for me, and that reminds me of something else, and then I remember a third thing, and pretty soon I'm talking about something brand new. Let me take you on a little tour of how that works for me.

I'm walking to Albertson's because Ben & Jerry's Frozen Yogurt is on sale—two pints for five dollars. I get to the store, it's about seven o'clock at night, and the parking lot is jammed; people are weaving around with their shopping carts through the stream of incoming cars trying to get their groceries to their own cars and go home.

And I'm looking at all of these hundreds of people and all of these cars, and I suddenly think, "I wonder how many of these people could resolve a trigonometric identity." Honest to God, that's what came into my head. Well, from there, this meandering thinker was off to the races. "I wonder how many of these people could tell you about the origins of the French Revolution. I wonder how many can still diagram a sentence."

And then I thought, "Well, why would I care if they could or not? They all have enough money to afford their cars and their groceries; they're getting by. Would they get by any better if they remembered how to construct the perpendicular bisector of a line segment using only a straightedge and a compass?"

Well, that of course took me right back to the high school that I wrote my book about and to all the kids who ever asked why they should bother learning something. "Why are we doing this?" That was the plaintive cry from the back corners of the room. "Why are we doing this?" It never came from the front: up front were the kids to whom it never occurred to ask that question or who had given up asking it. And the arguments that came back from the teachers were never very compelling to me. They said things like, "There's *lots* of careers that use algebra," though they never offered a specific example. Or, when the question came up with regard to conjugating French verbs, it would be met with, "Well, you might travel to France someday." For these kids from rural Northern California, even the City of Lights was neither a likely nor an especially desirable destination. Their picture of France amounted to the Eiffel Tower, the Arc de Triomphe, and a language that made them say things like, "Hello, I name myself Stacy. How do you name yourself?"

"Why are we doing this?" the kids ask. So let's ask ourselves why we have them doing all of these crazy things. When I think about what high school is for, I remember that John Ogbu, the educational anthropologist, wrote that, "whatever else education may be, from the standpoint of society it is a preparation of children for adult life as adults in their society conceive it."

Well, I don't know, John. Here I am in the Albertson's parking lot, willing to bet my Ben & Jerry's and most of my paycheck that not one of the next three people I see could name the first European to sail around the Cape of Good Hope. "Adult life as adults in our society conceive it" doesn't typically include answering trivia questions like that, unless we're standing on a stage across from Alex Trebek. (By the way, it was Vasco da Gama in 1497, and yes, I had to look it up.)

But let's give John Ogbu another reading and another chance: "Whatever else education may be, from the standpoint of society it is a preparation of children for adult life as adults in their society conceive it." I think that's true, but the problem we have, in our very diverse society, is that Ogbu's phrase "preparation for adulthood" has many different meanings, based on a lot of potential adulthoods. I think we need to make those adulthoods explicit so that we're not working at cross-purposes. So I'm going to do two things here. I'm going to start out by telling you what I think a successful adulthood is, and then I'm going to tell you—based on the evidence of my own and other people's research—what our education system says that a successful adulthood is.

Here's a definition I hold of strong adulthood. I've cast it in the form of a list of my ideal outcome measures for a high school, the characteristics I hope that graduates have as they prepare to move toward adulthood.

- **Graduates of my ideal high school should love to read.** This is not at all the same as saying that they *can* read. There's an enormous middle ground between illiterate and literate, which has sometimes been called aliterate—a term for people who can read but choose not to, who see little value or reward in it. People who *love to* read are people who are open to new ideas, who are engaged in constant reinvention.
- **Graduates of my ideal high school should enjoy numbers.** I'm no mathematician, but I can do arithmetic in my head very well. It's a skill I developed before I was 8 by playing cribbage and rummy and pinochle and by keeping score at bowling. It's a skill that has served me well all the way through calculus and physics, it's a skill that helps me navigate the everyday world of taxes and budgeting, of saving and knowing when I can indulge in an extravagance, and it's a skill that helps me evaluate the accuracy and pertinence of information that's offered to me.
- **Graduates of my ideal high school should enjoy physical exertion and activity.** And that activity should take several forms, from team sports to hiking across town to playing hacky sack. Anything that gets you sweaty is a damn sight better than television, and we should encourage young people to regard physical activity as a lifelong pursuit, rather than as something to look back on fondly once high school football has ended.
- **Graduates of my ideal high school should have some well-developed outlet for their creative desires.** This will also take all kinds of forms, from writing to visual arts to music to physics, but the quest for

putting ideas together in a unique way is part of what makes us really human.

- **Graduates of my ideal high school should know how to work in groups, and they should know how to teach a skill to someone else.** Kids are going to be working with groups for the rest of their lives, from work to marriage and parenthood to community service. We are social animals, and we need to quit pretending that individual performance is the only thing that really matters.
- **Graduates of my ideal high school should be brave and take risks.** This means that they must be exposed to failure and supported through the other side. They need to know that it's possible to fall down and still get up again. They must know that, if a magazine rejects their article, there are hundreds more to try. They need to know that anything really worth doing will be scary and intimidating—and that they have to do it anyway.
- **Graduates of my ideal high school should understand and take an interest in their community.** They should know something about real estate, local government and services, major local industries, and the natural landscape and climate. Even if they move away, knowing *how* to find out about these things is a skill that will serve them wherever they go.
- **Graduates of my ideal high school should be compassionate and care about people they don't know.** They should understand that a lot of what happens in people's lives isn't their fault—and that even things that *are* someone's fault usually are mistakes that can be recovered from rather than a sign of a core moral failing that leaves people irredeemable and so dismissible.

For me, this list presents a compelling model of an attractive adulthood. It is a set of characteristics that I don't encounter all that often in the adults I know. In fact, it is a set of characteristics that I strive for but sometimes fail to live up to myself. The list outlines adulthood as a rigorous, ongoing practice rather than a state to be obtained and then mounted on the wall with the high school diploma. And such an adulthood is one that will serve as the foundation for an infinite number of careers, in an ever-shifting economic world.

Now, this may not be the same definition that *you* would create for an attractive, complete adulthood. And that's fine, so long as you actually go through the exercise and create a definition that you can really stand behind and don't just accept the default version.

And believe me, there is a default version. Our institutions—maintained and shepherded as they are by white-collar people who understand complex organizations—promote as the norm their own white-collar, managerial, hierarchical, certified view of adulthood. That's what schools attempt to perpetuate, and it's the model of adulthood for which they prepare young people. Half a century ago, the sociologist C. Wright Mills had the same impression and described the high school as "the seed-bed of white-collar skills." Like the early Spanish in California and Mexico, the white-collar, information-laden school takes on the missionary role of civilizing the uncivilized and converting the heathens. Even the most benevolent of the conquerors are preparing the natives for what they see as a materially and morally superior way of life. We are "helping," "developing," or "training," or whatever term we might use to mean making someone else be more like us.

This has led to a model of secondary education that I call an "additive education," in which each certified specialist takes an assembly under construction and screws on a particular component and then passes the material along to the next specialist. One person takes 150 kids and screws on some algebra, and another person takes those same kids and screws on some world history, and a third person takes those same kids and screws on some Hemingway. Over the course of four years, each successful kid gets more than 20 components screwed on. And in the end, they're screwed, indeed. They're encased in this educational armor and have no experience in encountering and challenging their own communities, futures, or desires, because all of that has been sublimated to the repetitive and mechanical structures that they endured.

In the high school I've studied most thoroughly, which is a tragically normal high school, I found six underlying principles of the school, principles that were never stated overtly but that were repeated over and over in the rules that were laid, in the spaces that were created, in the furniture that was used, in the lessons that were taught, and in the lessons that were avoided. And these were the six principles:

1. Kids and adults should be physically separated.
2. Teaching should be active, and learning should be passive.
3. Abstraction is beneficial, and uniqueness should be avoided.
4. Economies of scale are necessary and beneficial.
5. Objective evaluation and peer competition are necessary and beneficial.
6. Students should be prepared for a life of geographic and organizational mobility.

And, after all, the world educators endure is governed by these same rules. So let's look at them as educators suffer them.

1. *Kids and adults should be physically separated.* Certainly, teachers, administrators, and education policy makers are all physically (and conceptually) separated from one another.
2. *Teaching should be active, and learning should be passive.* The school that most completely follows the guidelines is considered the best school by those who write the guidelines, which become more prescriptive all the time.
3. *Abstraction is beneficial, and uniqueness should be avoided.* Unique local outcomes and desires are less important than test scores and standings on other indices of achievement—and certainly less important than the number of AP courses offered.
4. *Economies of scale are necessary and beneficial.* Every single school must be immersed in district, state, and federal systems that ensure completeness and correctness and that avoid duplication of services.

5. *Objective evaluation and peer competition are necessary and beneficial.* Schools themselves are forced to compete with one another on grossly abstract terms that have little to do with the life of learning and citizenship.
6. *Students should be prepared for a life of geographic and organizational mobility. Teachers* and administrators, if they are successful, also move upward or outward from their classrooms and into larger communities or educational structures.

So schools, to their credit, don't ask kids to deal with anything that adults don't have to face as well. Our white-collar organizational biases, in our modern economic circumstances, lead toward an education in which kids are trained primarily to endure what educators themselves endure. Remember again Ogbu's quote: "Whatever else education may be, from the standpoint of society it is a preparation of children for adult life as adults in their society conceive it." The main lessons of the "hidden curriculum" are to compete with your peers, to be compliant with your superiors, and to refrain from asking awkward questions. And those lessons are there on purpose! That's what makes the safest economic life in a culture in which capital is mobile and a company can leave Michigan for Georgia and then leave Georgia for Indonesia. In such a world, you have to demonstrate superiority over other workers and unquestioning loyalty to your supervisors and their world view.

This additive education is an education of fear. It's an effort to avoid disaster rather than to reach for a dream, to avoid a career at McDonald's rather than to pursue a deep personal mission. It's an effort to ensure that kids will have the tools necessary to survive in the similarly white-collar colleges and workplaces they will move on to. It's an effort to keep them from being sorted out of the pool for advancement before they ever really get under way. It's a recognition that our modern economic terrain allows employers to use the desperation of labor as a resource anywhere in the world, that every American who might formerly have done physical work is competing with someone in another country who is willing to work for less, in worse conditions, and for longer hours than our nation allows. It's a recognition that we have educated ourselves into a society in which information is the only material we have left to manipulate.

I understand this education of fear, and I think I know why it exists. But I have no patience for it, because I see how cold and empty it leaves its products—both the kids and the adults. They learn to avoid pain instead of to seek love. They learn to avoid commitment, because they might have to leave. They're never asked to engage who they really are, but rather to be more and more like their masters.

When I encounter students in a high school like that—which is to say, almost all the time—my immediate urge is to help them escape, to get them into the lifeboats before they drown. I'm not entirely sure what we'd be moving toward, but that's not a question that you ask in a time of crisis. You just get people out of the wreckage and away from the danger. This is my own fearful response to the education of fear.

When I was talking to the folks at Duke about the possibility of my coming there to teach their first-year students, I told them that I was fascinated by people who were between about 15 and 25 years old, standing on the brink of adulthood, peering over the edge in simultaneous fear and anticipation. I told them that I thought high school was something that had to be recovered from and that I thought I could aid in that recovery.

And I talked about my friend Pete. Pete is a young man; he'll be 29 soon. He's a wonderful writer, a great friend to those of us blessed to know him well, a great son and brother to his family, and, possibly, the best illustrator that I've ever had the chance to watch at work. He draws like an angel.

Pete has no idea what he wants from an adult life. Both of his parents are teachers, and he enjoyed school all the way up through sixth grade. But when he moved from elementary school to junior high school, began to move from one teacher and 25 classmates to six teachers and 150 classmates who shifted all day long, he didn't survive the change. He told me that he could recognize instantly that those adults weren't really there for him, that they didn't even know him. And about halfway through seventh grade, he tested his hypothesis, as any good scientist would. In the middle of an assigned five-page essay, he wrote the third page in an imaginary alphabet that he'd drawn, to see if anyone would read it. No one did, and his hypothesis was confirmed.

Pete had a naturally occurring social life in elementary school; in a class of 25 kids who are together all year long, people make allowances for eccentricity and learn to appreciate one another's gifts. When you're shoved into an anonymous crowd of 600 kids you don't know, you tend to seek out people who are the most like you in order to have some safety and stability. But Pete wasn't in any of those natural safety groups. His eccentricity and artistic mind, assets through sixth grade, became social and academic liabilities three months later.

By the time I met him in high school, Pete had two lives: exuberant and creative with his small circle of friends and in the theater and completely alienated in the classroom and in the larger social life of the school. He maintained his mathematically precise 2.0 grade-point average so that he could graduate, but there was never even one entire course that reliably captured his attention. There were *days*, there were *topics*, there were *moments* when you could see him come alive and watch the gears turn, but mostly Pete was that kid in the back right corner who you'd never guess was six feet tall because he sat so low in his chair. He saw nothing in the adult world that he trusted, that he wanted, or that he was adequately guided toward. And that distrust of and distaste for adult life persist for him to this day.

So I was talking to the folks at Duke about Pete in the context of helping kids recover from high school, and the director of the writing program said, "Our kids don't come here with 2.0s. We help kids recover from getting 4.3s." And then I began to think in a different way about the scars left by our education system. The rebellious get their 40 lashes on a regular basis, but the silent and compliant have wounds of their own, harder to see but no less real and no less deep. We rightfully strive to eliminate a system of schooling in which there are winners and losers, but we don't think to eliminate a system of schooling in which even the winners have lost their curiosity, have lost their passion, have lost the willingness to ask, "Why are we doing this?"

We are deeply familiar with this screwed-on model of high school, this additive education in which each professional adds his or her component onto the raw material that comes down the line. But I've been wondering: What would a subtractive model of education look like? And I'm beginning to think it might look something like what a sculptor does. When Michelangelo wrote about the experience of sculpting, he said that the stone itself told him what to do, that the figure was waiting inside that stone and that his task as an artist was to take away what wasn't essential. "I saw the angel in the marble and carved until I set him free."

And that's what I do with Pete—informally but very purposefully. And it's what I hoped to be able to do with my Duke students. I think I have to sit with a person and be with him or her for quite a while before I can expect to have much of an effect. And then I think I can ask for permission to pick off some of the armor and maybe find out who's under all of those uniform shells. I trust that there is a core person there, and my belief is that it's probably the same person who was there at 10 years old, before the specialists got to him or her. Once I know who that is, I am able to see some things that excite this student, and I can introduce him or her to a wider range of such things. There will be some natural skills, and I can help the student hone and develop and expand and challenge those.

And each person will have his or her own visions of successful adult life, collected by being a part of a family and immersed in the media and knowing a larger group of friends. I can show a young person my own model of adulthood as another potential way of living to examine, but I can't expect that he or she will choose it, and I can't personalize a response—when he or she *doesn't* choose it—as a rejection of me.

I realize that this is a hazy vision. I can't tell you what the structure of a subtractive education looks like on a day-to-day basis. I know that it looks small and attentive, somewhat passive on the part of the educator, slow, inexpert, and out of control, and that it requires the time and the inclination to listen to and believe young people. But I think it also looks different for every practitioner and with every student, and probably on every day.

Even if you agree with me that a subtractive education would be a humane and powerful experience, I cannot offer you a curriculum that you could all follow to get there with every student. That kind of static curriculum would automatically lead us back toward nonresponsive, non-seeing, automatic, additive ways of being. All I can do is tell you what I see in the world, tell you what I think it means, tell you about some of the lives that are hindered by our common practices, and sit together with you to see if there's something different that we can do.

Here's the vision that drives me, and *this* vision is very clear. I'm 48 years old, and I'm optimistically assuming that I have another 35 years or so to work with teenagers and young adults. My dream is that I will live to see the day that the modern high school will be considered the counterpart of the mission, the orphanage, and the poor farm—an institution that was taken for granted and considered beneficial in its time but has since been judged to be inhumane and unthinkable. High school is taken for granted, and it was and is still considered beneficial. But I believe that we have outgrown the institution's usefulness. I believe that we have different ways of service—different ways of *being*—that we can employ on behalf of young people. And I believe that we are fundamentally not the kind of people who want to make our least powerful citizens endure this four-year sentence of disrespect and invisibility.

We are better than our systems. We are better than our structures. We can be brave, help our kids discover who they are, help them go where they want to go, and wish them Godspeed as they leave us behind.

POSTSCRIPT

Should Global Competition Steer School Reform?

In the June 2007 issue of *Phi Delta Kappan,* a number of prominent leaders (Denis P. Doyle, Michael J. Petrilli, Lawrence Mishel, and Richard Rothstein) respond to the proposals put forth by the New Commission on the Skills of the American Workforce. Doyle, co-founder of SchoolNet, Inc. pumps a bit of realism into some of the Commission's recommendations. He feels that the accelerated graduation idea has little chance of enactment unless we would institutionalize serious rewards, as many other nations do. The recommendation to have school boards turn over operation of schools to third parties under performance contracts, he feels, is doomed to failure. And he finds the strategy of using "savings" to fund other aspects of the program is rather naive because when it comes to public expenditures, there have never been any savings.

Petrilli, vice president of the Thomas B. Fordham Foundation, lauds most of the report's ideas but is concerned that too little attention is given to the K-12 curriculum, which is presently being squeezed by the demands of No Child Left Behind. Mishel and Rothstein of the Economic Policy Institute criticize the position that skill shortages require nearly all students to attend college in a time in which some college graduates are being forced to accept jobs requiring only a high school education. In the same issue of *Phi Delta Kappan,* Marc Tucker is given the opportunity to reply to his critics in an article titled "The Economic Case for Education Reform."

Earlier in 2006, the Bush administration launched its "American Competitiveness Initiative" to bolster instruction in math and science to ensure that America's children have the skills to succeed in life, thus ensuring America's success in the world. However, a basic question is posed by Frederick M. Hess and Andrew J. Rotherham in "NCLB and the Competitiveness Agenda: Happy Collaboration or Collision Course?" in *Phi Delta Kappan* (January 2007), namely "Is meeting the 'global competitiveness' challenge to train elite scientists and engineers compatible with No Child Left Behind?"

Further thought on the basic issue can be found in Richard Florida's "The Flight of the Creative Class: The New Global Competition for Talent" *Liberal Education* (Summer 2006); . . . Patricia Albjerg Graham's *Schooling America: How the Public Schools Meet the Nation's Changing Needs* (2005); "Conspiracy Theory: Lessons for Leaders from Two Centuries of School Reform," *Phi Delta Kappan* (February 2007) by James H. Nehring; and Linda Darling-Hammand and Laura McCloskey, "What Would It Mean to Be Internationally Competitive?" *Phi Delta Kappan* (December 2008).

Internet References . . .

Center for the 4ᵗʰ & 5ᵗʰ Rs

Site espousing democratic classrooms features a comprehensive approach to character education.

http://www.cortland.edu/character

National Alliance for Civic Education

Dedicated to ensuring that the next generation understands and values democracy and participates in its processes.

http://www.civnet.net

Center for Education Reform

Pro-voucher organization that features a reform update, reports, and a weekly newswire.

http://www.edreform.com

Rethinking Schools

Site features special reports on voucher failures across the nation as well as other attacks on privatization.

http://www.rethinkingschools.org

No Child Left Behind

U.S. Department of Education site examines implementation of NCLB and provides links for parents and teachers.

http://www.ed.gov./nclb

No Child Left

Site offering multiple reasons why NCLB must go.

http://nochildleft.com

Inner City Education Foundation

California-based organization sponsoring charter schools in poverty areas featuring a college-prep curriculum.

http://www.icefla.org

UNIT 2

Current Fundamental Issues

*T*he issues discussed in this unit cover a number of fundamental social, cultural, and political problems currently under consideration by education experts, social scientists, and politicians, as well as by parents, teachers, and the media. Positions on these issues are expressed by Kristan A. Morrison, Gary K. Clabaugh, Charles L. Glenn, Paul E. Peterson, Sharon L. Nichols, David C. Berliner, Dianne Piché, Ruby Payne, Mistilina Sato, Timothy J. Lensmire, Frederick M. Hess, Linda Nathan, Joe Nathan, Ray Bacchetti, and Evans Clinchy.

- Are Truly Democratic Classrooms Possible?
- Has the Supreme Court Reconfigured American Education?
- Is No Child Left Behind Irretrievably Flawed?
- Does a "Deficit Model" Serve Poor Children Well?
- Should "Public Schooling" Be Redefined?

ISSUE 6

Are Truly Democratic Classrooms Possible?

YES: **Kristan A. Morrison**, from "Democratic Classrooms: Promises and Challenges of Student Voice and Choice, Part One," *Educational Horizons* (Fall 2008)

NO: **Gary K. Clabaugh**, from "Second Thoughts About Democratic Classrooms," *Educational Horizons* (Fall 2008)

ISSUE SUMMARY

YES: Associate professor of education Kristan A. Morrison explores historical and theoretical bases for implementing democratic practices in schools that would make student experience more appealing and productive.

NO: Professor of education Gary K. Clabaugh examines such factors as top-down management, compulsory attendance, business world influences, and federal mandates to declare Morrison's ideas to be "out of touch" with reality.

Certainly everyone would agree that one of the primary aims of education is to produce citizens capable of effectively participating in their society. The controversial aspect of this aim resides in determining the best way of carrying it out. In recent years educators and theorists have renewed a basic question that has been discussed for over a hundred years, namely "Is it possible to produce democratic citizens if the schooling the young are subjected to is clearly undemocratic?"

As Charles C. Haynes, in "Schools of Conscience," *Educational Leadership* (May 2009), states, "We need schools that actually practice what their civics classes are supposed to teach. . . . At a time when the United States faces unprecedented challenges at home and abroad, public schools must do far more to prepare young people to be engaged, ethical advocates of 'liberty and justice for all.'" Haynes contends that education's highest aim is to create moral and civic habits of the heart. This central purpose was articulated by the early leaders of American education. Thomas Jefferson made the principles of democratic government an essential element in the free public education of the general citizenry. Horace Mann's common school was dedicated to producing people able to critically judge the political and social needs of the nation. Waves of European immigrants in the nineteenth century prompted a new emphasis on socialization strategies and the development of patriotism. As Joel Spring has pointed out in his book *Conflict of Interests*, "In a totalitarian society it is possible to teach a single interpretation of the laws and government in the public schools, but in a society such as that of the United States, which fosters a variety of political beliefs . . . , attempts to teach principles of government can result in major political battles."

In "Civic Education and Political Participation," *Phi Delta Kappan* (September 2003), William A. Galston declares that school-based civic education has been in decline over recent decades. He claims that every significant indicator of political engagement among the young has fallen. Community service programs in high schools are on the increase, but there is no evidence that such "mandatory volunteerism" leads to wider civic participation. He states that "the surge of patriotic sentiment among young people in the immediate wake of September 11th has not yielded a comparable surge in engaged, active citizenship."

If the school atmosphere is by design, by tradition, or by habit undemocratic can truly democratic citizens emerge? Haynes states that "to prepare students to be ethical, engaged citizens we must give them . . . meaningful opportunities to practice freedom responsibly in a school culture that encourages shared decision-making. . . . In short we need schools that actually practice . . . freedom and democracy, not censorship and repression."

Similarly, Marion Brady, in "Cover the Material—Or Teach Students to Think?" *Educational Leadership* (February 2008), claims that students need to tackle issues straight out of the complex world in which they live. "A focus on real-world issues . . . enables students and teachers to experience the 'meatiness' of the direct study of reality. . . . It shows respect for students, who become more than mere candidates for the next higher grade. . . . It disregards the arbitrary, artificial boundaries of the academic disciplines."

In "Democracy and Education: Empowering Students to Make Sense of Their World," *Phi Delta Kappan* (January 2008), William H. Garrison contends that the best learning happens under a truly democratic system in which students assume the freedom and responsibility to make choices and direct their learning experiences. His ideas certainly reflect the basic philosophy of John Dewey and the sentiments of John Holt.

In the articles presented here Kristan A. Morrison aligns herself with critical theorists in the field of education who feel that the public schools have been used by societal and political forces to curtail rather than release student freedom. Gary K. Clabaugh thinks that while some of Morrison's points are well-taken she naively ignores the shaping power of numerous internal and external factors.

YES

Kristan A. Morrison

Democratic Classrooms: Promises and Challenges of Student Voice and Choice

Abstract

If we ever hope to have schools that are engaging and that truly embody democracy, then the classes within them must provide opportunities for students to experience autonomy, freedom, and choice in what is studied, when, and how. This article explores both the historical and theoretical framework of democratic freedom-based education and the promises and challenges of implementing democratic practices in schools.

. . .

Introduction

Schools and society are reflections of one another. Certain values and beliefs are dominant in our society and inculcated in school. They include

- a competitive ethos and firm conviction that a meritocracy exists in our society
- a view that instrumental and extrinsic motivations are more important than intrinsic motivations
- an excessive valuing of academics
- A belief in the atomization and fragmentation of subjects of study, people, and nature
- the conviction that the characteristic of obedience (doing as one is told or believing as one is told) is of more value in our society than that of criticality
- the belief that one's worth can be defined by others (as good student or bad student)

Once students become adults, they perpetuate those same dominant values in both society and school.

This cycle is complicated, however, because beyond those dominant values, schools are "terrains of struggle" (Giroux 1988), places where contradictory values and ideals compete for prominence.

Reprinted with permission of *Educational Horizons,* quarterly journal of Pi Lambda Theta Inc., International Honor Society and Professional Association in Education, P O Box 6626, Bloomington, IN 47401, Fall 2008, pp. 50–59.

Critical educational theorists, who include John Dewey and more-contemporary authors such as Henry Giroux, Paulo Freire, Peter McLaren, bell hooks, David Purpel, and Maxine Greene, argue that certain moral, political, and intellectual ideals should take precedence over others in schools. They assert that our schools should emphasize commitment to a democratic system in which each citizen's autonomy and dignity are honored in an open, just, respectful, and pluralistic community, a community that values and encourages a critical approach in the intellectual search for truth and meaning in each individual's life (Purpel 1989).

The community these theorists seek is a delicately balanced synthesis between the individual (thesis) and a collection of individuals (antithesis). In other words, an individual's autonomy is delimited by others' rights to dignity, respect, safety, and the search for truth and meaning to everyone's lives; if person A decides to do something that somehow infringes on person B's rights, then person A is prohibited from taking that action and encouraged to find actions that can both express his or her autonomy and honor the rights of others.

Many of us know from experience that our society's schools often fall far short of fostering the development of people who value diversity, who are both autonomous yet cognizant of others' needs and rights, and who are open-minded yet equipped with critical-thinking skills to analyze contradictory ideas. Instead, many of our schools foster the development of very different sorts of individuals.

Does that indicate that the critical educational theorists are wrong? No, it just means that they and like-minded educators must struggle to actualize their ideals in schools. One way to do that, I would argue, is to institute more democratic and freedom-based practices within our educational system. This article explores the historical and theoretical framework of such practices, and then goes on to detail their promises and challenges.

Definitions and Historical/Theoretical Framework

The term "democratic education" as used in this article is linked with and synonymous with the term "freedom-based education," for just as democracy as a political system is grounded in individual freedoms, democracy as an educational system is also grounded in freedoms. The linkage between the two terms is supported by the self-descriptions of most freedom-based schools in the United States (e.g., "free schools," Sudbury Valley-modeled schools, "unschooling" families, etc.), which also identify themselves as sites of democratic education.

In democratic and freedom-based education, students are free to decide what they study, and how, and when they study it. This form of schooling has a number of historical antecedents, outlined by Bennis (2006). He argues that one genesis of this model of education is the form of learning found in most pre-industrial societies. In these societies (past and present), children are actively engaged in the life of a given society; they learn skills and knowledge by means of imitation, apprenticeship, modeling, and conversation rather than in any formal school setting. Freedom-based education is also rooted in the Western philosophical tradition of the ancient Greeks, in the Romantic thinkers (e.g., Rousseau and Froebel), in the libertarian-anarchist tradition, in the transcendentalist movement of nineteenth-century America, and in the twentieth-century free-school movement (e.g., Summerhill School, led by A. S. Neill, and the many U.S. free schools that cropped up during the countercultural revolution of the 1960s and 1970s) (pp. 23–32).

Democratic and freedom-based education is grounded in the premise that people are naturally curious and have an innate desire to learn and grow. If left un-fettered, un-coerced, and un-manipulated (e.g., by conventional educational practices that often diminish those innate characteristics), people will pursue their interests vigorously and with gusto, and thus learn and make meaning on their own and in concert with others. Individuals honored and respected in this process become socialized to honor and respect the dignity and autonomy of others (Dennison 1969; Hern 1996; Holt 1972, 1989; Illich 1971; Llewellyn 1997; Mercogliano 1998; Neill and Lamb 1992).

Although most contemporary freedom-based education is found in the form of private schools or the home-schooling version, "unschooling" (Morrison 2007b), American public schools could shift more closely to this model by adopting more-democratic practices and organizational structures (Reitzug 2003). Thus, enacting democratic practices within conventional, more-authoritarian and -bureaucratic schools could serve as a steppingstone toward adopting the model of democratic and freedom-based education more fully.

Democratic education can take multiple forms, ranging from the micro level of within-class democracy to the more-ideal macro level of whole-school democracy, and within each level, a number of different democratic practices can be enacted. For example, at the micro level, a teacher can utilize discussion; offer students test and assignment choices that attend to their unique learning preferences; allow students "protest rights" (Shor 1996); practice contract grading (Shor 1996) or self-grading; allow students to call the teacher by first name; and ask students to co-construct the course (have a voice in course content, grading, rubric creation, etc.). At the macro, whole-school level, schools can allow students to construct their entire curricula. (See Morrison 2007a, which examines the Albany Free School, a school where pre-K through eighth-grade students choose what, how, and when they study subjects, or see Goddard College for university-level self-development of curricula.)

Promises of Democratic Education

Proponents of democratic and freedom-based education argue that with autonomy and choice, people experience a much-different, much-better form of education than that offered by the conventional, hierarchical, more-coercive education system present in most public schools.

First, they argue that a democratic education promises much more meaningful learning. If people have choice and freedom to study what interests them, then they become more deeply engaged in, and thus less alienated from, their learning. More engagement leads to better retention and better critical reflection and analysis. For example, Watson wrote in *Summerhill: For and Against* (1970) that "pupils given freedom to decide what they will do, when, and how develop increasing independence, stronger interests, and better quality of work" (p. 177).

Gatto, in *Dumbing Us Down: The Hidden Curriculum of Compulsory Schools* (1992), echoes that argument, stating that our conventional education system infantilizes students by constantly compelling them and that this compulsion "guarantees that they will do [work] poorly, with a bad will, or indifferently" (p. 93). Democratic education, conversely, has no infantilizing effect; instead, it places great trust in the students, and they, more often than not, rise to the challenge. In the process, students become more mature, self-disciplined, and intrinsically motivated, seeing the value of learning above and beyond its usefulness to getting a "good job" (Bhave 1996; Labaree 1997).

Proponents of democratic education further argue that people who are given freedom and choice will ultimately become better democratic citizens because they have learned how to negotiate with others, to name obstacles, and to know themselves (Bhave 1996; Dewey 1916; Gatto 1992; Goodman 1962; Holt 1972; Holzman 1997; Illich 1971; Morrison 2007a; Shor 1996). That ultimately benefits all of society by developing people who are open to change and to listening to others so that all consider themselves vital to society. As Shor argued in *When Students Have Power* (1996): "Power-sharing . . . creates the desire and imagination of change while also creating the experience and skills for it. The critical-democratic class, then, is a context for change that develops the desire and imagination to make change" (p. 176).

Challenges of Democratic Education

Democratic education is, in many ways, antithetical to conventional school practices in our society. Student voice and choice don't fit particularly well into a system characterized by bureaucracy and hierarchical structure (Reitzug 2003). There are three main areas of challenge to instituting democratic practices in classrooms and schools—students, teachers, and the institution as a whole.

Student Challenges

Students educated in conventional schools for the majority of their lives represent one of the biggest challenges to democratic education. Because soliciting student voice and choice in the classroom lies so far outside the educational norm in our society, democratic education practices may be met, initially, by considerable student resistance. Most students are accustomed to being told what to do and to acting passively in the classroom; they are viewed, and may view themselves, as safe-deposit boxes waiting for deposits of knowledge to fill them (Freire 1970). The hidden curriculum trains students to be quiet and docile, to be indifferent to and bored with course content (because they have no say in what it is), and to accept being told what they and their work are worth (Gatto 1992; Giroux 1978; Illich 1971; Vallance 2003).

It should come as no surprise that students who have experienced this training, especially those students who have succeeded in the "game" of schooling, might resist changed rules that ask them to go against all they have been taught. Students who come from conventional education into classrooms or schools employing democratic practices will often feel uncomfortable with or even fearful of jeopardizing the only pattern of life they know (Goodman 1964). They may become "Siberians" (Shor 1996) who gravitate to the periphery of the class, where they sit silent and disconnected from democratic processes. Asked to play a role in content construction (e.g., explain what they are generally interested in studying, or a particular topic), they may be at a loss, for many have never even considered what their own interests might be. Spontaneous initiative, curiosity, and trust in themselves, by and large, may have been drummed out of them; they may have learned to view education as purely instrumental—a means to an end rather than an end in itself (Bhave 1996; Holt 1972; Labaree 1997). Students thus may resent anyone trying to show them differently. This resentment will be connected to a lack of trust and the antagonistic teacher-student relationships that are the norm. Students have been trained to start out viewing most teachers as "the enemy"—people who infringe on their will and their freedoms. To be asked suddenly to change this view is more than many students can handle.

Besides student resistance to democratic education, another challenge that arises is students mistaking positive freedom for negative freedom. Maxine Greene, in *The Dialectic of Freedom* (1988), has defined negative freedom as freedom from constraints. That is the starting point for positive freedom, but positive freedom also encompasses the freedom to work in concert with others to overcome limits. Democratic education is not negative freedom alone; it does not only mean freeing students to do whatever they want. As Dewey wrote in *Experience and Education* (1938): "For freedom from restriction, the negative side, is to be prized only as a means to a freedom which is power: power to frame purposes, to judge wisely;. . . power to select and order means to carry chosen ends into operation" (pp. 63–64). Because conventionally educated students have so little experience of any freedom in school, so little practice with democratic discussion or with assuming authority on their own, they will often mistake democratic, positive freedom practices for negative freedom only. Students may thus see the teacher who asks for democratic input as weak or unprepared, and they may attempt to evade, rather than make, their opportunities (e.g., push for lowered workloads, etc.) (Shor 1996).

Teacher Challenges

Students will not be the only ones who resist changes; teachers will balk as well. Very few teachers have experienced democratic education themselves, so to attempt to institute democratic practices in their classrooms represents a sizable leap into the unknown. Teachers may be fearful of this unknown, fearful that involving students' voices and choices in running a course will produce chaos and an overall lack of learning. Part of this fear stems from lack of trust in students. Teachers have become accustomed to viewing most students as lazy and uninterested, people who must be pushed, prodded, cajoled, and threatened into doing "what's best for them," and thus they fear that students will try to minimize challenges and take the easy way out (Goodman 1962; Gross 1973; Holt 1970, 1972; Rogers 1969; Sheffer 1996; Watson 1970). Another part of this fear of chaos and lack of learning lies in conventional ideas about what learning is. Many teachers, themselves schooled in conventional educational institutions, believe that their role is to fill students with curricular information. They might argue that students, who don't know what they don't know, cannot possibly exercise choice and freedom in curricular content to create real learning.

The idea that knowledge can be stuffed into the individual, as opposed to being constructed and mediated through the individual (Lamm 1972), has led to the conventional educational practices of mandated courses and pre-established syllabi. Teachers are used to coming, and in fact are expected by both students and their administrators to come, to the first class with content ready for delivery to interchangeable students. Teachers may feel that if they arrive without a pre-set syllabus and lesson plans, students and administrators will view them as weak, unprepared, or lacking in authority. The class's disrespect could lead to poor course and teacher evaluations as well as jeopardize their jobs. Besides losing control, teachers might also fear silence and an emptiness if they attempt democratic practices. They might also fear that some students will take over and silence others. Last, inviting student voice and choice might ill prepare students for the "real world," where they will have to learn to bow their wills to others and see their needs go unmet (Guterson 1996).

Conventionally schooled teachers who dare to implement democratic practices must grapple with all these fears. They must be willing to abandon plans and adjust to the process of dialogue; they must learn to listen more than talk, not apply one lesson plan to all sections of the same class, and surrender their authoritarian supports (Shor 1996). They must learn to trust students' innate curiosity, and if this curiosity has been crushed in the past, they must work to bring it back to life. Teachers must take to heart what Rogers wrote in *Freedom to Learn* (1969):

> If I distrust the human being, then I must cram him with information of my own choosing, lest he go his own mistaken way. But if I trust the capacity of the human individual for developing his own potentiality, then I can provide him with many opportunities and permit him to choose his own way and his own direction in his learning. (p. 114)

And teachers need to recognize that democratic educational practices may well lead students to reject the "real world" of hierarchical authority and to work for more true democracy in the larger economic, political, and social systems. Teachers who attempt more-democratic educational practices thus embrace education for the world that might be rather than for the world that is.

Institutional Challenges

The institutional structures of conventional education also represent significant stumbling blocks to enacting more-democratic practices. Unless the entire institution is itself fully democratic, teachers who attempt to bring democracy into heretofore undemocratic spaces will encounter challenges.

The "deep structures" of schools compose one such challenge: those "widely shared assumptions about what schools are for and how they should function" (Tye 1998, paragraph 5). One example of such deep structures is the conventional schools' view that knowledge exists outside and separate from human mediation and construction and that learning equals the transmission of this information from holders of this knowledge (teachers) to empty vessels (students).

This view of knowledge leads to conventional school practices: mandating that all students learn certain subjects; insisting that subjects be fragmented one from the other; and enforcing a certain progression of information that follows an external, discipline-specific logic (e.g., take algebra before geometry). Educational managers who hold this view of knowledge might argue, as mentioned in "Teacher Challenges," above, that students don't know what they don't know, so how could they possibly decide what should be included in a class? The managers also might worry that students who have voice and choice on subject inclusion might choose not to learn what the institution considers vital information.

That concern, a valid one, can be dealt with by establishing institutional structures and practices that allow time to explore the ideas of negative and positive freedom described earlier. Students' resistance to learning certain ideas often stems from feelings of powerlessness rather than from willed ignorance; if educational institutions can set forth rational and personalized arguments for the worth of some topic (beyond stating in a course catalog that the subject will make one liberally educated), students will willingly include that topic in their studies. Certainly this process can become time-consuming, but that is intrinsic to learning democratic habits of mind.

The view of knowledge and learning described above also impacts assumptions about class sizes. If the subject knowledge is simply to be transmitted to students, a high teacher-student ratio is logically efficient. Institutional structures of large classes and mandated, pre-arranged content render attempts to institute democratic practices uncertain. How can a teacher truly get a large number of students' voices and choices heard? Can a teacher stray too far from the mandated content if the teachers around her are working to perpetuate the curricular status quo? Won't a democratic teacher in a required class have a more difficult time breaking through and connecting with the students who resent this limitation of their freedom of choice?

An additional institutional constraint is the conventional system of grading. I have written elsewhere (Morrison 2003a, 2003b) about how grades can deflect students from creating personal meaning and toward simply performing for sought-for ends (e.g., diploma, college acceptance, scholarships, praise, lack of punishment, etc.). This performance orientation complicates the teacher-student relationship: students come to feel less powerful vis-à-vis the teacher and thus act subserviently to earn good grades. Student subservience manifests itself in not questioning or challenging the teacher in any really meaningful way; in essence, students have learned that classroom success often requires that they check their democratic rights at the door. Grading has, perhaps unintentionally, rendered many students voiceless and dependent. (Admittedly, students participate in their own oppression in this regard, but that makes it no less a form of oppression.)

A last major institutional constraint on introducing democratic educational practices to conventional school settings is the use of space and time. The conventional school day is broken into a series of relatively short periods (forty-five to ninety minutes each); school plants are typically divorced from the wider community (separate, often closed, campuses); and there is an extremely high population density. Such use of space and time is inimical to democracy, in which decisions, discussions, and building trust take time (longer than a semester or academic year, or longer than a single class period); connections to and involvement in community activities and spaces are highly valued; and the ability and space necessary to move about freely, and group and regroup, are needed.

Conclusion

Critical educational theorists believe that democratic values—the search for truth and personal meaning, justice, equality, and respect for the thoughts and humanity of others—will rarely result from schools in which students never have an opportunity to practice democratic habits of mind. Thus, these theorists support including democratic practices in school wherever possible. Clearly, though, there are significant roadblocks to instituting such practices, especially the more deeply these practices infiltrate the organizational structures of schools.

Some might argue that our schools were never meant to create democratic citizens because our society is not now and never truly will be a democracy; the undemocratic characteristics of our conventional schools exist by design. Although such cynicism may be warranted, given what we know about how power is used and abused in our society, critical educational theorists would counter that it is our "ontological vocation" (Freire 1970) to struggle for seemingly far-off ideals. Although we might lack a true democracy now, one will never be attained unless people work for it both inside and outside our educational institutions.

References

Bennis, D. M. 2006. "De-Mystifying Freedom-based Education." Master's thesis, Vermont College of Union Institute & University.

Bhave, V. 1996. "The Intimate and the Ultimate." In *Deschooling Our Lives,* ed. M. Hern, 16–22. Gabriola Island, B.C.: New Society Publishers.

Dennison, G. 1969. *The Lives of Children:The Story of the First Street School.* New York: Random House.

Dewey, J. 1916. *Democracy and Education.* New York: Macmillan Company.

———. 1938. *Experience and Education.* New York: Collier Macmillan Publishers.

Freire, P. 1970. *The Pedagogy of the Oppressed.* New York: Herder and Herder.

Gatto, J. T. 1992. *Dumbing Us Down: The Hidden Curriculum of Compulsory Schooling.* Gabriola Island, B.C.: New Society Publishers.

Giroux, H. 1978. "Developing Educational Programs and Overcoming the Hidden Curriculum." Clearing House 52(4): 148–151.

———. 1988. *Teachers as Intellectuals: Toward a Critical Pedagogy of Learning.* Westport, Conn.: Bergin and Garvey.

Goodman, P. 1962. *The Community of Scholars.* New York: Vintage Books.

———. 1964. *Compulsory Miseducation.* New York: Vintage Books.

Greene, M. 1988. *The Dialectic of Freedom.* New York: Teachers College Press.

Gross, R. 1973. "After Deschooling, Free Learning." In *After Deschooling, What?* ed. I. Illich, 148–160. New York: Harper and Row.

Guterson, D. 1996. "Family Matters: Why Home Schooling Makes Sense." In *Deschooling Our Lives,* ed. M. Hern, 16–22.

Hern, M., ed. 1996. *Deschooling Our Lives.* Gabriola Island, B.C.: New Society Publishers.

Holt, J. 1970. In *Summerhill: For and Against,* ed. H. Hart. New York: Hart Publishing Co.

———. 1972. *Freedom and Beyond.* New York: E.P. Dutton and Co.

———. 1989. *Learning All the Time.* New York: Addison-Wesley Publishing.

Holzman, L. 1997. *Schools for Growth.* Mahwah, N.J.: Lawrence Erlbaum Associates.

Illich, I. 1971. *Deschooling Society.* New York: Harper and Row.

Labaree, David E 1997. *How to Succeed in School without Really Learning: The Credentials Race in American Education.* New Haven: Yale University Press.

Lamm, Z. 1972. "The Status of Knowledge in the Radical Concept of Education." In *Curriculum and the Cultural Revolution,* ed. D. Purpel and M. Belanger, 149–168. Berkeley, Calif.: McCutchan.

Llewellyn, G. 1997. *The Teenage Liberation Handbook: How to Quit School and Get a Real Life and Education.* Shaftsbury, Dorset, U.K.: Element Books Limited.

Mercogliano, C. 1998. *Making It Up as We Go Along: The Story of the Albany Free School.* Portsmouth, N.H.: Heinemann.

Morrison, K. 2003a. "Is Grading Doing What We Want It to Do?" *Paths of Learning* 15 (Winter): 20–23.

———. 2003b. "What Else Besides Grading? Looking for Alternatives in All the Right Places." *Paths of Learning* 16 (Spring): 22–28.

———. 2007a. *Free School Teaching: A Journey into Radical Progressive Education.* Albany, N.Y.: SUNY Press.

———. 2007b. "Unschooling: Homeschools Can Provide the Freedom to Learn." *Encounter: Education for Meaning and Social Justice* 20(2): 42–49.

Neill, A. S., and A. Lamb, eds. 1992. *Summerhill School: A New View of Childhood.* New York: St. Martin's Press.

Purpel, D. 1989. *The Moral and Spiritual Crisis in Education.* New York: Bergin and Garvey.

Reitzug, U. 2003. "Bureaucratic and Democratic Ways of Organizing Schools: Implications for Teachers, Principals, Students, Parents, and Community." In *The Institution of Education,* ed. H. S. Shapiro, S. Harden, and A. Pennell, 4th ed., 85–98. Boston: Pearson Custom Publishing.

Rogers, C. 1969. *Freedom to Learn.* Columbus, Ohio: Charles E. Merrill Publishing.

Sheffer, S. 1996. "Doing Something Very Different: Growing without Schooling." In *Deschooling Our Lives,* ed. M. Hern, 16–22.

Shor, Ira. 1996. *When Students Have Power: Negotiating Authority in a Critical Pedagogy.* Chicago: The University of Chicago Press.

Tye, B. B. 1998. "The Deep Structure of Schooling: What It Is and How It Works." *The Clearing House* 71(6): 332–335. Retrieved February 1, 2006, from Info Trac One File database.

Vallance, E. 2003. "Hiding the Hidden Curriculum." In *The Institution of Education,* ed. Shapiro, Harden, and Pennell, 85–98. (Originally published in 1974. *Curriculum Theory Network* 4[1], 5–21.)

Watson, G. 1970. In *Summerhill,* ed. H. Hart. New York: Hart Publishing.

. . . .

Gary K. Clabaugh **NO**

Second Thoughts about Democratic Classrooms

... Kristan A. Morrison's "Democratic Classrooms: Promises and Challenges of Student Voice and Choice" argues that students must experience autonomy, freedom, and choice if schools will ever be appealing and truly embody democracy. Those who found or find school tedious, oppressive, and uninteresting may be quick to agree, but how realistic is this proposal?

Cutting Costs with Mass Production

It has been well over one hundred years since America embarked on the ambitious venture of universal public schooling. The costs of this endeavor quickly became burdensome, and it was decided to model schools on factories and emphasize mass production and cost-effectiveness, rather than democracy or individuality.

For the most part, today's public schools still are factories. Management is top-down all the way. The federal government sets basic rules. State authorities implement the rules while adding many more. School boards make decisions based on federal and state rules plus fiscal and political realities. The superintendent executes the will of the board through his or her principals. They, in turn, tell teachers what to do and when to do it, and the teachers direct the youngsters in similar manner. Knowledge is fragmented and atomized. Children are compared to one another. Social and emotional development is neglected for more measurable outcomes. Economies of scale are sought at the expense of individuality. Teachers and students are managed.

Sometimes this industrial approach produces not only undemocratic, but peculiarly inefficient, results. One superintendent of the School District of Philadelphia, for example, boasted to the press that she could tell them what was happening in any classroom in the city at any given moment. What was actually happening was administratively induced chaos, because her standardized, teacher-proof curriculum was incapable of accommodating individual differences. Second-grade teachers were forbidden to use anything other than second-grade readers and the canned lesson of the day, even if some of the kids still couldn't read. Similarly, seventh-grade math teachers were forced to "teach" algebra to kids who couldn't even do fractions or long division.

Reprinted with permission of *Educational Horizons*, quarterly journal of Pi Lambda Theta Inc., International Honor Society and Professional Association in Education, P O Box 6626, Bloomington, IN 47401, Fall 2008, pp. 20–25.

In this kind of school system, autonomy, freedom, and choice are anathema. The focus is on standardization, teacher proofing, measured outcomes, and the prison shuffle.

Compulsory Freedom?

We should also consider that democratic, freedom-based schooling would be introduced into an institution in which attendance is compulsory. True, if one can afford an alternative, there is no requirement that kids attend public school. But in every state in the union school attendance of some kind, even if it is only home schooling, is required.

"Democratic Classrooms" indicates that democratic and freedom-based education is *grounded in the premise that people are naturally curious and have an innate desire to learn and grow. If left un-fettered, un-coerced and un-manipulated . . . people will pursue their interests vigorously and with gusto. . . .* Trouble is, when people are compelled to go to school they already are fettered, coerced, and manipulated. That's what we mean by compulsion. Wouldn't compulsory education have to be abolished before freedom-based education could be meaningfully initiated?

And why imagine that youngsters' natural curiosity will be directed at constructive things? One can imagine six-year-olds happily burning insects to death with sunlight and a magnifying glass, or sixteen-year-old inner-city gang members fulfilling their urgent desire to learn small-unit military tactics. Besides which, why assume that everyone is naturally curious? I've taught seventh-graders whose curiosity seemed decidedly undersized.

Of course kids of that age are terribly concerned about peer acceptance, and that places a profound limit on their freedom. Do advocates of freedom-based education adequately consider the tyranny of peers?

The Feds Weigh In

Remember too that there is a powerful new restriction on autonomy, freedom, choice, and democracy in schooling. Emphasizing measurable results, quality control, instrumental and extrinsic motivations, and atomization and fragmentation of knowledge, No Child Left Behind represents the near-total triumph of factory-model schooling in contemporary America. The whole weight of the federal government welds the public school as factory in place as never before.

"Democratic Classrooms" offers the happy prospect of dismantling factory schools and refocusing on student voice and choice. But it's not as if the article advocates moving from A to B. Given the present environment, it advocates moving from A to Z. What are the chances?

"The Business of America Is Business"[1]

Another factor militating against the success of the "Democratic Classrooms" prescription is that most Americans spend far more time in the business world than they do where they have a voice and a choice.

What are the work world's characteristics? It's competitive; instrumental and extrinsic motivations dominate, tasks are atomized and fragmented, obedience is required, believing what one is told is valued over criticality, and a person's worth is defined by comparison to others. In short, work-world values are virtually identical to the present school values decried in "Democratic Classsrooms." Surely that is not an accident.

What would happen if business leaders suddenly found themselves confronted with employees who expected a voice and a choice? Would the CEO of General Electric or Macy's, for example, be grateful? And could our lawmakers sleep if the nation's corporate moguls were dissatisfied?

The claim here isn't that the business of America *should* be business. It is that the business of America *is* business, and this reality has to be taken into account in any prescription written for the public schools.

Freedom: A Modern Luxury?

The article comments: *In democratic and freedom-based education, students are free to decide what they study, and how, and when they study it.* The article links that to *the form of learning found in most pre-industrial societies* [in which] *the children are actively engaged in the lives of a given society; they learn skills and knowledge by means of imitation, apprenticeship, modeling and conversation rather than in any formal school setting.*

Pre-industrial education, though, was not all that free and spontaneous. In my youth, for example, I learned barbering by means of an apprenticeship that closely resembled the apprentice system of the pre-industrial guilds; I was most emphatically *not* free to decide what to learn, or how and when to learn it. The master barber decided.

Remember too that in the pre-industrial era most children grew up on farms. And while those youngsters did learn to farm by imitation, modeling, and conversation, they did *not* have the luxury of freely choosing what they wanted to do and how and when they were going to do it. That's not farm life. If you are haying and it looks like rain, you have to work like hell to get the hay in the barn before it gets wet and spoils; otherwise the livestock starves that winter. Similarly, a kid might prefer not to spend hour after hour in the broiling sun picking potato bugs, but he or she still has to do it for the family to eat potatoes.

Perhaps freedom-based education is a luxury reserved for well-fixed modern kids whom harsh reality doesn't require to do tasks of immediate and urgent importance.

The True Secret of Education

John Locke, a philosopher who inspired the nation's founders, observes in *On Education*: "[I]f the mind be curb'd, and humbled too much in children; if their spirits be abas'd and broken much, by too strict an hand over them, they lose all their vigour and industry."

But Locke also cautions that

> He that has not a mastery over his inclinations, he that knows not how to resist the importunity of present pleasure or pain, for the sake of what reason tells him is fit to be done, wants the true principle of virtue and industry, and is in danger never to be good for anything.

Locke, however, does not stop there. He immediately adds:

> To avoid the danger that is on either hand, is the great art; and he that has found a way how to *keep up a child's spirit easy, active, and free, and yet at the same time to restrain him from many things he has a mind to, and to draw him to things that are uneasy to him* [emphasis added]; he, I say, that knows how to reconcile these seeming contradictions, has, in my opinion, got the true secret of education.[2]

The advocates of freedom-based education, then, may have avoided the first error Locke cautions against, only to stumble into the second. They seem to be overlooking the fact that some measure of mastery over one's inclinations is necessary to ever be good at anything. How can anyone learn to accomplish a truly skilled enterprise such as ballet, glass blowing, or engineering in a reasonable time if the initiate, not the expert, decides what to learn and when to learn it?

To be sure, present-day schooling hasn't got the balance right either. Here, in Locke's words, the mind is "curb'd and humbled too much" and the youngsters too frequently "lose all their vigour and industry." That is what "Democratic Classrooms" quite rightly condemns.

The Principle of Correspondence

Historically there has always been a close correspondence between any society's social structure, values, and norms and its schooling practices. In fact, a case can be made that such correspondence is a universal feature of schooling. And "Democratic Classrooms" gets it wrong when it says, "Schools and society are reflections of one another." No, the history of education demonstrates that schooling practices reflect the values and structures of the host society.

That is not to say that alternative schools of a freer, more-democratic nature can't exist in less-free societies. Various forms of them can be found in nations as different as Israel, Japan, New Zealand, Thailand, and the United States; A. S. Neill's Summerhill, perhaps the best-known, is located in Suffolk, England.[3] But these schools owe their uniqueness to the fact that they do not serve the broad masses at public expense. They have a self-selecting clientele and do not depend on public consensus or public funding.

Still, it's instructive to know that in 1999 Summerhill ran into difficulties with the U.K.'s educational bureaucracy. Despite the school's higher-than-national-average exam pass rates and extraordinary parental and pupil satisfaction, the U.K.'s education bureaucracy inspected the school and found it wanting. It called Summerhill's pupils "foul-mouthed" and accused them of "mistaking idleness for personal liberty." In effect, the report called for

Summerhill's closure if the school failed to abandon the key freedoms it afforded its pupils.

Summerhill took the government to court and won the right to continue its practices. The school survived, and in 2007 another government inspection produced entirely different results. *The Guardian* quotes the new report as saying, "Pupils' personal development, including their spiritual, moral, social and cultural development, is outstanding." Students are "courteous, polite and considerate," make "good progress," and are "well-rounded, confident, and mature" when they leave.

Zoe Readhead, the head teacher and daughter of founder A. S. Neill, said: "The government has persistently refused to acknowledge the individual philosophy of the school, such as that children can learn just as well out of the classroom. We feel vindicated." She also added, "It is not the school that changed."[4] Her point, of course, was that it was the U.K. that had changed.[5]

Undemocratic Americans

"Democratic Classrooms" seems at least as out of step with American values in 2008 as Summerhill was to the U.K.'s in 1999. Certainly the values that "Democratic Classrooms" hopes to promote are anything but widespread. Only some Americans "truly value diversity" and are "truly autonomous yet cognizant of others' needs and rights." And only some Americans "are open-minded yet equipped with critical thinking skills to analyze contradictory ideas." Other Americans angrily deny marriage to gay couples; salivate whenever Rush Limbaugh and his ilk ring a bell; and don't have the vaguest understanding of either freedom or democracy. (They eagerly deny the former to anyone who's different and think of American democracy merely as majority rule.)

Individuals of this persuasion pack a political punch. And they will undoubtedly regard as un-American the values "Democratic Classrooms" prescribes for U.S. public schools. Its new freedoms for students would be understood as self-indulgence and an attack on traditional values such as hard work, discipline, and self-denial—none of which are they particularly keen on practicing themselves.

Remember too that day-to-day U.S. public school policy is set locally by some fifteen thousand elected school boards and, except for large urban districts, broadly representative of village values. So America's public schools have achieved their undemocratic condition in a decidedly democratic manner.

Conclusion

History suggests that public schools rarely, if ever, get out ahead of society. Indeed, they generally lag behind. That is why student voice and choice and all that goes with it will have to await a freer, more-democratic America. If and when that societal change happens, the public schools will follow. Until then, support will be lacking. That's not to say that what "Democratic Classrooms" champions is undesirable. But it may be unattainable, and it is certainly unlikely in the near or intermediate future.

Happily, reform need not be all or nothing. One can, with a little luck, quietly introduce more student voice and choice into one's own classroom. And we should all congratulate any teacher who can elevate the importance of intrinsic motivation; emphasize social and emotional development as well as academics; de-emphasize mere obedience; and get kids to define their own worth rather than let others do it for them. But it had better be done without fanfare and well out of sight of the philistines.

Notes

1. A statement made by Calvin Coolidge in the 1920s.
2. John Locke, "Some Thoughts Concerning Education" (sections 41–50), in *The Harvard Classics,* available at. . . .
3. See Summerhill School's Web site: . . . .
4. Jessica Shepherd, *Guardian* (Manchester), December 1, 2007, available at. . . .
5. Summerhill School, available at. . . .

. . . .

POSTSCRIPT

Are Truly Democratic Classrooms Possible?

E. D. Hirsch, Jr., the well-known core knowledge advocate, in his latest book. *The Making of Americans: Democracy and Our Schools* (2009), is clearly at odds with the "truly democratic classrooms produce engaged citizens" ideology. As he has in his past works, Hirsch has no kind words for the followers of John Dewey whose progressive ideas, he claims, led to an abandonment of definite academic studies resulting in the diminishment of Americans' intellectual standing in the world. He sees hope in recent trends toward higher standards and the rise of Advanced Placement and International Baccalaureate programs in high schools. In a review of *The Making of Americans*, titled "I Pledge Allegiance to Core Knowledge" in *The Washington Post* (August 30, 2009), Jay Mathews states that Hirsch will settle for nothing less than "a coherent, content-based, multi-year curriculum right now to save our democracy from factionalism, inequality, and incompetence."

Another group of theorists settle in a middle-ground position between subject matter centeredness and an emphasis on student voice and choice. See, for example, "Disciplining the Mind" by Veronica Boix Mansilla and Howard Gardner in *Educational Leadership* (February 2008). They recommend the teaching of disciplinary thinking so as to prepare students to understand the real world in which they live and equip them for the future.

The following writers are supportive of Kristan A. Morrison's point of view: Dana L. Mitra, "Amplifying Student Voice," *Educational Leadership* (November 2008), who reviews research into student voice initiatives, including student involvement in reform and the professional development of teachers, and Eric B. Freedman, "Is Teaching for Social Justice Undemocratic?" *Harvard Educational Review* (Winter 2007), who examines the "critical consciousness" approaches of Ira Shor and Paulo Freire, addressing the question "When is education democratic?"

Additional interesting sources are Thomas R. Guskey and Eric M. Anderman, "Students at Bat," *Educational Leadership* (November 2008); Deborah Meier, "Democracy at Risk," *Educational Leadership* (May 2009); Chris W. Gallagher, "Democratic Policy Making and the Arts of Engagement," *Phi Delta Kappan* (January 2008); Stephen Macedo, "Crafting Good Citizens," *Education Next* (Spring 2004); Patrick J. Wolfe, "Civics Exam: Schools of Choice Boost Civic Values," *Education Next* (Summer 2007); Peter Levine, "The Civic Opportunity Gap," *Educational Leadership* (May 2009); Joetta Sack-Min, "A Valued Democracy," *American School Board Journal* (January 2009); Richard Neumann, "American Democracy at Risk," *Phi Delta Kappan* (January 2008); and James A. Banks, "Human Rights, Diversity, and Citizenship Education," *The Educational Forum* (April 2009). Exploration of some of these articles will open doors to a number of important related issues.

ISSUE 7

Has the Supreme Court Reconfigured American Education?

YES: Charles L. Glenn, from "Fanatical Secularism," *Education Next* (Winter 2003)

NO: Paul E. Peterson, from "Victory for Vouchers?" *Commentary* (September 2002)

ISSUE SUMMARY

YES: Professor of education Charles L. Glenn argues that the Supreme Court's decision in *Zelman v. Simmons-Harris* is an immediate antidote to the public school's secularist philosophy.

NO: Professor of government Paul E. Peterson, while welcoming the decision, contends that the barricades against widespread use of vouchers in religious schools will postpone any lasting effects.

In June 2002 the U.S. Supreme Court released its decision of *Zelman v. Simmons-Harris,* which dealt with Ohio's Pilot Project Scholarship Program. This program provides tuition vouchers to certain students in the Cleveland Public School District who wish to transfer from their assigned public school to a participating school of their choosing. The available choices include public schools in adjacent school districts, nonreligious private schools, and religious private schools. Controversy over this program stemmed from the fact that in the 1999–2000 school year, 96 percent of the Cleveland students who were receiving vouchers were enrolled in schools with religious affiliations. Ohio taxpayers (Doris Simmons-Harris et al.) sued state school officials (Superintendent Susan Tave Zelman et al.) to enjoin the program on the grounds that it violated the establishment clause of the U.S. Constitution, which mandates separation of church and state.

The Supreme Court found (by a 5–4 vote) that Ohio's voucher program does not offend the establishment clause, thereby reversing lower courts' judgments that the program is unconstitutional. The majority opinion—delivered by Chief Justice William H. Rehnquist—stated that the program was enacted for the valid secular purpose of providing educational assistance to poor children in a demonstrably failing public school system; that government aid reaches religious institutions only by way of the deliberate choices of individual recipients; and that the only preference in the program is for low-income families, who receive greater assistance and have priority for admission. In dissent, Justice John Paul Stevens queried, "Is a law that authorizes the use of public funds to pay for the indoctrination of thousands of children in particular religious faiths a 'law respecting an establishment of religion' within the meaning of the First Amendment?" He stated, "The voluntary character of the private choice to prefer a parochial education over an education in the public school system seems to me quite irrelevant to the question whether the government's choice to pay for religious indoctrination is Constitutionally permissible. Whenever we remove a brick from the wall that we designed to separate religion and government, we increase the risk of religious strife and weaken the foundation of our democracy."

The history of the Cleveland voucher program and the litigation surrounding it is summarized by Joseph P. Viteritti in "Vouchers on Trial," *Education Next* (Summer 2002). Begun in 1995, the program allows about 4,000 low-income students to attend private schools with up to $2,250 in public support. Since parochial schools were the only nonpublic schools with tuition rates low enough to accommodate voucher students, opponents maintained that the program was indeed an incentive to attend these schools.

Dan D. Goldhaber and Eric R. Eide, in "What Do We Know (and Need to Know) About the Impact of School Choice Reforms on Disadvantaged Students?" *Harvard Educational Review* (Summer 2002), examine empirical evidence and find that school choice programs have little clear-cut impact on either students in the programs or those who remain in their assigned public schools. They do cite evidence that there is greater support for vouchers among African Americans, however. Frederick M. Hess and Patrick J. McGuinn, in "Muffled by the Din: Competitive Noneffects of the Cleveland Voucher Program," *Teachers College Record* (June 2002), contend that the political and legal ambiguity about Cleveland's voucher program dampened the willingness of parochial and independent schools to expand their capacity to receive voucher students. These schools saw voucher programs as a minor threat as far as competitive pressure for reform is concerned. Perhaps the *Zelman* decision will convert this symbolic threat into a true reform movement.

In the following selections, Charles L. Glenn portrays the *Zelman* decision as a harbinger of the emergence of faith-based alternatives to the public school establishment's rampant secularism. Paul E. Peterson admits that *Zelman* is a welcome addition to the pro-voucher arsenal, but he expresses concern about establishment backlash and, even more so, governmental encroachment on religious schools' independence.

YES

Charles L. Glenn

Fanatical Secularism

The Supreme Court's majority opinion in the Cleveland voucher case, *Zelman v. Simmons-Harris*, was of course the most newsworthy aspect of the decision, but the dissents were no less revealing. In about 500 words, Justice Stevens managed to use the word "indoctrination" four times and "religious strife" twice. Likewise, Justice Breyer's dissent begins and ends with warnings of "religiously based social conflict" resulting from allowing parents to use public funding to send their children to sectarian schools. Today it is a little startling to encounter these echoes of Justice Black's 1968 dissent in *Board of Education v. Allen*, in which he warned:

> The same powerful sectarian religious propagandists who have succeeded in securing passage of the present law to help religious schools carry on their sectarian religious purposes can and doubtless will continue their propaganda, looking toward complete domination and supremacy of their particular brand of religion. . . . The First Amendment's prohibition against governmental establishment of religion was written on the assumption that state aid to religion and religious schools generates discord, disharmony, hatred, and strife among our people, and that any government that supplies such aids is to that extent a tyranny. . . . The Court's affirmance here bodes nothing but evil to religious peace in this country.

Although the Supreme Court's decision in *Allen* has left no detectable sign of "disharmony, hatred, and strife among our people," the dissenting justices in the Cleveland case seem to believe that the only way to avoid "indoctrination" and religious warfare is to educate children in government-run schools (even though most industrialized countries provide support to religious schools). Concerns over deep entanglements between government and religion have of course haunted the nation from its very beginning. But in the education realm, the sheer hostility toward religious schools is not just a matter of separating church from state. It in part reflects and derives from the self-image of many educators, who like to think of themselves as having been specially anointed to decide what is in the best interest of children. Faith-based schools, they assume, are in the business of "indoctrinating" their pupils, while public schools are by definition committed to critical thinking and to the emancipation of their pupils' minds from the darkness of received opinions, even those of their own parents.

From *Education Next*, Winter 2003, pp. 61–65. Copyright © 2003 by Education Next. Reprinted by permission of Hoover Institution, Stanford University.

What I have elsewhere called "the myth of the common school" is a deeply held view with tremendous political resonance, first articulated in the 1830s by Horace Mann and his allies. This myth insists that enlightenment is the exclusive province of public schools, which are thus the crucible of American life and character in a way that schools independent of government could never be.

The actual working out of this powerful idea in the 19th and early 20th centuries was not altogether benign. It included, for example, systematically denying that there were a number of ways to be a good American. Nor was the common school ideal ever fully realized, even in its New England home. Segregation by social class persisted, and black pupils were unofficially segregated in much of the North and West and officially segregated in all of the South. Even the famed "steamer classes" that served immigrant children in the cities of the East and Midwest often did not keep them in school beyond the first year or two.

Nonetheless, the myth of the "common school" deserves credit for many of the accomplishments of public education in this country. It articulated a coherent vision of the American character and of an America-in-process, and it made both convincingly attractive. In recent decades, however, this hopeful myth has been transmuted into an establishment ideology that borrows much of the language and the positive associations of the common school to serve a bureaucratized, monopolistic system that is increasingly unresponsive to what parents want for their children.

The Enlightenment Mission

In *The Myth of the Common School* (1988), a historical account of how the ideology of state schooling emerged, I traced the myth's development in 19th century France, the Netherlands, and the United States. To a great extent the myth was informed by a bias against orthodox religion, often in the name of what was considered a "higher and purer" form of Christianity stripped of "superstitious" elements such as an emphasis on sin and salvation, in favor of a purified morality and faith in progress. State-sponsored schooling was intended to replace religious particularism (whether Catholic or Calvinist) as well as local loyalties and norms with an emerging national identity and culture.

Enlightenment in this form was experienced by many as oppressive rather than liberating. In place of the convictions that had given meaning and direction, and often color and excitement, to their lives, people were offered a diffuse array of platitudes, a bloodless "secular faith" without power to shape moral obligation or to give direction to a life. The effect was to set people free for a new and more oppressive bondage, unrestrained by the custom and ceremony from which, as the Irish poet William Butler Yeats reminded us, innocence and beauty come to enrich our lives.

This political account of the development of public education continues to be helpful in understanding present-day conflicts in Western democracies. If we recognize that the attempt to achieve a government monopoly on schooling was intended to serve political purposes during a period of nation-building, we can see that this monopoly is no longer appropriate—if it ever was.

The case for charter schools, vouchers, and other forms of "marketized" education rests not only on educational performance but also on the claims of freedom of conscience. Parents have a fundamental right—written into the various international covenants protecting human rights—to choose the schooling that will shape their children's understanding of the world. But a right isn't really a right if it can't be exercised. Families who can't afford tuition at a private school or a move to the suburbs should still be able to make choices regarding their children's education.

There is, in other words, a strong argument against attempts by government to use schooling to achieve political or cultural change—or stability, for that matter. John Stuart Mill gave this argument definitive form in 1859, writing:

> All that has been said of the importance of individuality of character, and diversity in opinions and modes of conduct, involves, as of the same unspeakable importance, diversity of education. A general State education is a mere contrivance for moulding people to be exactly like one another; and as the mould in which it casts them is that which pleases the predominant power in the government . . . in proportion as it is efficient and successful, it establishes a despotism over the mind, leading by natural tendency to one over the body.

The same point was made in a lapidary phrase by the U.S. Supreme Court in its 1925 *Pierce v. Society of Sisters* decision: "the child is not the mere creature of the State."

But does this leave nothing to be said for the role of schools in fostering the qualities of civic virtue on which, all moralists agree, the meaningful exercise of freedom depends? Put another way, does a commitment to limiting government's role in the education realm also require that schools refrain from seeking to form the character and worldview of their pupils? This is one of the central dilemmas of a republican form of government, at least in its contemporary form of limited state power. While republics pledge to respect the freedom of their citizens, they also depend on the voluntary adherence of those citizens to often complex norms of civic life. As a result, as Montesquieu pointed out, "It is in republican government that the full power of education is needed." The citizens of a republic must be virtuous since they govern themselves.

Jean-Jacques Rousseau wrote that the teacher must choose whether he will make a man or a citizen. The choice is not so stark, but it is nevertheless real. The state may seek to mold citizens on a particular pattern, but citizens in a free society surely have a right not to be molded, in their opinions and character, by the state. The child is not the mere creature of the state.

Emancipating the Mind

Any account of the tensions between the educational goals of government and of families must consider the third side of the triangle: how teachers and other educators have understood their mission. It is easy to assume that public school teachers line up on the side of the "state project" in education, while teachers in faith-based and other nonstate schools line up on the side of parents.

But the reality is much more complex. Indeed, the simple state-versus-parents dichotomy fails to do justice to many educators' perception of themselves as emancipators of the minds of their students.

As noted, education theorists have long contrasted the emancipatory role of the public school with the "indoctrination" they attribute to religious schools. This strikes a note with tremendous cultural resonance. "Emancipation," Jacques Barzun tells us, is "the modern theme par excellence." The most influential of contemporary educators like to think of themselves as liberators of the minds of their pupils rather than as conveyors of "dead" information, such as the traditions of Western culture.

As a result, those who set the pace in the world of American education, and those who follow their lead, look down on the teachers, parents, and policymakers who do not share this understanding of the teacher's mission. Leadership for American education has increasingly been provided by big-city and state superintendents, professors of education, and officials of the education associations and teacher unions who see little need to respond to the uninformed views of the general public and of parents. This was illustrated by a 1997 Public Agenda survey of "teachers of teachers," professors in teacher-training institutions. Of the 900 professors surveyed, 79 percent agreed that "the general public has outmoded and mistaken beliefs about what good teaching means." They considered communication with parents important, but not in order to learn what education parents wanted for their children. Parents were to be "educated or reeducated about how learning ought to happen in today's classroom."

The professors of education surveyed were convinced, for example, that "the intellectual process of searching and struggling to learn is far more important . . . than whether or not students ultimately master a particular set of facts." Sixty percent of them called for less memorization in classrooms, with one professor in Boston insisting that it was "politically dangerous . . . when students have to memorize and spout back." By contrast, according to another Public Agenda study, 86 percent of the public and 73 percent of teachers want students to memorize the multiplication tables and to learn to do math by hand before using calculators.

These are not purely technical questions; they reflect assumptions about the very nature of education. The professors are expressing one form of the "cosmopolitan" values that have been promoted by American schooling over the past century. This perspective has made the exclusion of religion from the public schools seem not a matter of political convenience or respect for societal diversity, but essential to the mission of education. It is also a sign of intellectual laziness. Teaching facts requires knowledge, which is acquired through rigorous study and research. All it takes to teach values is the ability to spout your own beliefs and prejudices.

Platonic Education

The marks of this condescension can be found in the various controversies that swirl around public schooling. State-imposed curriculum frameworks and standardized tests are condemned as distractions from the teaching of "critical thinking." Lecturing is rejected as an unsound practice because it wrongly assumes that the teacher holds some authority. Nor should the teacher stress right and wrong solutions to the problems that she poses; what is important is the pupil's engagement with the search for an answer. This self-censorship on the part of teachers is even more important when it comes to sex education, where talk of "character" and "virtue" is deeply suspect.

So much is this set of attitudes—the priority of "liberation" or "emancipation" as the central metaphor for the teacher's work—taken for granted among American educators that the higher performance of pupils in other countries on international tests in math and science is often dismissed as reflecting other countries' inappropriate stress on drill and memorization. The possibility that a stress on rich curriculum content can result in lively, engaged classrooms is seldom credited. American pupils may not know as much, we are told, but they know how to think and to solve problems creatively.

This complacent assumption rests on a fundamental misunderstanding. Mental "emancipation" can be a very good thing, of course, when it removes the chains of misinformation and when it arouses a thirst for the truth that can be satisfied only by hard, honest mental effort. This is the traditional justification for a "liberal" education.

The classic description of such an emancipation is Plato's parable of prisoners in an underground cavern, convinced that the shadows on the wall are the only reality. One of the prisoners, in a process that Plato explicitly calls an analogy for education, is freed from his chains and brought to a state, literally, of enlightenment.

Plato makes it clear, though, that it is not enough to loosen the chains; the prisoner must be forced to turn toward the light and compelled to venture out of the cavern. Only gradually can he bear the light of day, and only after much experience can he look directly at the source of light and truth. Even the gifted youth who are being groomed for leadership, we are told elsewhere in *The Republic*, should not be exposed to the pleasures and rigors of the search for truth through argument until they have mastered the disciplines of music and gymnastics and have matured through responsibility. Otherwise, Plato warns, they will just play with ideas, without any solid foundation or useful result.

While Plato stressed the laborious acquisition of knowledge and understanding as the means to enlightenment, our impatient age has preferred to think of the emancipation to be achieved through education as simply the removal of the chains of illusion (conventional morality and traditional religious worldviews) without the discipline of seeking truth or the confidence that there is truth to be found.

Critical thinking and creative problem-solving are certainly among the primary goals of a good education, but they are not developed casually in the course of an undirected exploration. Nor should we assume that there is an innate human propensity to rise to that challenge. Most of us are intellectually lazy about large spheres of the world around us. For every person who really wants to know how an automobile engine works, there must be a dozen of us who are content if it starts reliably when we turn the key. This is not necessarily bad. Life would be impossible if we could not take much around us for granted, and even new discoveries rest on the discoveries of others that we do not have to repeat.

Deconstructivism

This is the fundamental wrong-headedness of another classic description of education, Rousseau's Emile. Raised in isolation, denied the use of books and of direct instruction by his tutor, Emile is expected to learn by following his natural inclinations and responding to situations that his tutor secretly creates for him. The boy, Rousseau tells us, "instructs himself so much the better because he sees nowhere the intention to instruct him." His tutor "ought to give no precepts at all; he ought to make them be discovered."

Here is the authentic note of much current pedagogical advice. The article of faith widely held among educators, especially those who have themselves benefited from the most sophisticated education, is that the teacher should never impose anything on his students, nor suggest to them that there are fixed truths that are worth learning or seeking to discover. Instead he should closely observe the interests of his students and create situations in which they are challenged to use those interests as opportunities for learning. In responding to these challenges, the students will "construct" solutions and even meanings that are uniquely their own and will thus be more deeply and validly learned than any that might be suggested by the teacher or by the wider culture and tradition. In the process, students will become autonomous human beings, not the mere creatures of their culture, and will develop capacities of critical judgment that will enable them to participate in creating—"constructing"—a better world.

According to a recent account of "constructivism" in the 2000 yearbook of the National Society for the Study of Education:

> There is to be no notion of correct solution, no external standard of right or wrong. As long as a student's solution to a problem achieves a viable goal, it has to be credited. Nor can relevant educational goals be set externally; they are only to be encountered by the student . . . the constructivistic teacher is to make do without any concept of objective truth or falsehood.

"Even if it were possible to educate children in this way," philosopher Roger Scruton has written, "one thing is certain: that each generation would know less than the one before. . . . And that, of course, is Rousseau's underlying intention—not to liberate the child, but to destroy all intellectual authority, apart from that which resides in the self." As a result, Emile "is the least free of children, hampered at every point in his search for information," and "one can read *Emile* not as a treatise on education, but as a treatise against education." Rousseau's pupil could arrive at a quite incorrect understanding of many natural and social phenomena by relying naively on his experience alone.

Why should we concern ourselves with what Rousseau wrote almost two-and-a-half centuries ago—or indeed with what Plato wrote long before that?

Because education is an enterprise, more perhaps than any other religion, that is shaped by how we choose to think about it.

There is another tradition of thinking about education. It is expressed in the Hebrew scriptures and Jewish practice: "Why do we do these things?" The Passover questions are answered with a story about the experience of a people, a story that has sustained them and given moral direction and meaning to their lives. Does being taught a tradition and taught within a tradition prevent questioning? Of course not; it provides the content that makes questioning fruitful. It can also be found in the classical Greek concept of *paideia* as, in Michael Oakeshott's words, a "serious and orderly initiation into an intellectual, imaginative, moral and emotional inheritance."

"The knowledge-centered teacher," Scruton points out, "is in the business of passing on what he knows—ensuring, in other words, that his knowledge does not die with him." The teacher who loves his subject and cares about his students is concerned that the rising generation not know less than the one that preceded it.

Emancipation is among the elements of a good education; it can help to prepare the way for the exercise of freedom by removing barriers, but it does not of itself make a man or woman free. Education that supports individual freedom and a free society is induction into a culture, not as a straitjacket but as the context of meanings and restraints that make the exercise of real freedom possible. As Philip Rieff has noted, "A culture must communicate ideals . . . those distinctions between right actions and wrong that unite men and permit them the fundamental pleasure of agreement. Culture is another name for a design of motives directing the self outward, toward those communal purposes in which alone the self can be realized and satisfied."

It is for this reason that structural reforms supporting freedom and diversity in education are not enough; they must be paired with a willingness to confront the much more difficult issue of the purposes, the means, and the content of a good education. Diversity and choice must be paired with common standards, and the content of these must be rich and meaningful. This will require an effort for which the schooling we have received in recent decades almost unfits us, to rediscover and give new life and conviction to those elements of history and culture, the virtues, achievements, and consolations, that have at all times shaped and sustained civilization. This is not a plea for a narrowly Western nostalgia trip, but rather an insistence that only a recovery of the permanent things, of humanity's highest accomplishments, can serve as the basis for a worthy education.

Such a happy outcome would be helped along if opponents of school vouchers would refrain from scare tactics based on unfounded stereotypes about faith-based schooling. Schools that teach in ways shown to be harmful to children should be shut down, but the debate over how to organize a pluralistic education system is not helped by worst-case scenarios. Many Western democracies have faced this challenge successfully, finding an appropriate balance between the autonomy of schools and public accountability, and we can do so too, now that the Supreme Court majority has decided in favor of educational freedom.

Paul E. Peterson **NO**

Victory for Vouchers?

In the most anticipated decision of its recent term, the Supreme Court ruled, in the case of *Zelman v. Simmons-Harris*, that the school-voucher program in Cleveland, Ohio did not violate the Constitution's ban on the "establishment" of religion. Opponents of vouchers—i.e., the use of public funds to help families pay tuition at private schools, including religious schools—were predictably disappointed, but pledged to fight on. As Senator Edward M. Kennedy declared, "Vouchers may be constitutional," but "that doesn't make them good policy."

The policy's sympathizers, needless to say, saw the ruling in a different light. President Bush used the occasion of the Supreme Court's decision to issue a full-throated endorsement of vouchers. *Zelman*, he told a gathering in Cleveland, did more than remove a constitutional cloud; it was a "historic" turning point in how Americans think about education. In 1954, in *Brown v. Board of Education*, the Court had ruled that the country could not have two sets of schools, "one for African-Americans and one for whites." Now, he continued, in ruling as it did in the Cleveland case, the Court was affirming a similar principle, proclaiming that "our nation will not accept one education system for those who can afford to send their children to a school of their choice and one for those who can't." *Zelman*, according to the President, is *Brown* all over again.

But is it?

⟵⟐⟶

Publicly funded school vouchers got their start in Milwaukee, Wisconsin in 1990. Established at the urging of local black leaders and Wisconsin Governor Tommy Thompson (now the Secretary of Health and Human Services), the program was originally restricted to secular private schools and included fewer than a thousand needy students. To accommodate growing demand, religious schools were later allowed to participate, an arrangement declared constitutional in 1998 by the Wisconsin Supreme Court. The Milwaukee program now provides a voucher worth up to $5,785 to over 10,000 students, amounting to more than 15 percent of the school system's eligible population.

In 1999, at the behest of Governor Jeb Bush, Florida also established a publicly funded voucher program, aimed at students attending public schools that failed to meet state standards. Though just two schools and fewer than a hundred students have participated in the program thus far, ten other schools, with thousands of students, will be eligible to participate this fall. (The Florida program is also noteworthy because it served as a model for the voucher-like federal scholarship program advocated by George W. Bush during the 2000 presidential campaign—a program subsequently abandoned by the administration in its push for an education bill.)

Though the Milwaukee and Florida programs had until recently received the most public attention, it was the program in Cleveland—the country's only other publicly funded voucher program of any size[1]—that won the opponents of vouchers their day before the Supreme Court. The Cleveland program is relatively small, providing a maximum of $2,250 a year to each of roughly 4,000 students. Parents use the vouchers overwhelmingly for religious schools, which in recent years have enrolled over 90 percent of the program's participants. This, according to lawyers for the teachers' unions, the most powerful foe of vouchers, constituted an obvious violation of the separation between church and state. And they prevailed twice in federal court, winning decisions at the trial and appellate level against Susan Zelman, Ohio's superintendent of public instruction and the official responsible for administering the Cleveland program.

But the five more conservative members of the Supreme Court were not persuaded. In his opinion for the majority in *Zelman*, Chief Justice William Rehnquist pointed to three well-known precedents—*Mueller* (1983), *Witters* (1986), and *Zobrest* (1993)—in which the Court had allowed government funds to flow to religious schools. What these cases had in common, he wrote, and what they shared with the Cleveland voucher program, was that public money reached the schools "only as a result of the genuine and independent choices of private individuals." Under Cleveland's program, families were in no way coerced to send their children to religious schools; they had a range of state-funded options, including secular private schools, charter schools, magnet schools, and traditional public schools. Considered in this wider context, the voucher program was, Rehnquist concluded, "entirely neutral with respect to religion."

The dissenters in *Zelman*, led by Justice David Souter, challenged the majority's reading of the relevant precedents—especially of *Nyquist* (1973), a ruling that struck down a New York State program giving aid to religious schools—and suggested that the choice in Cleveland between religion and non-religion was a mere legal fiction. They saved their most pointed objections, however, for what they saw as the likely social consequences of the ruling. The Court, Souter wrote, was promoting "divisiveness" by asking secular taxpayers to support, for example, the teaching of "Muslim views on the differential treatment of the sexes," or by asking Muslim-Americans to pay "for the endorsement of the religious Zionism taught in many religious Jewish schools." Justice Stephen Breyer suggested that the decision would spark "a struggle of sect against sect," and Justice John Paul Stevens wondered if the majority had considered the lessons of other nations' experience around the world, including "the impact of religious strife . . . on the decisions of neighbors in the Balkans, Northern Ireland, and the Middle East to mistrust one another."

If judicial rhetoric is all that counts, the dissenters in *Zelman* had the better of it. In the majority opinion, by contrast, there is very little that rises to the level of *Brown's* often-cited language about the demands of American equality. Even observers pleased by the ruling were disappointed that the majority's opinion did not go much beyond showing how the facts of the case fit past precedents; no ringing declarations are to be found in Chief Justice Rehnquist's cautious prose.

Only in the concurrences written by two of the Justices does one get a sense of the wider issues at stake. Responding to the worries of the dissenters, Justice Sandra Day O'Connor pointed out that taxpayer dollars have long flowed to various religious institutions—through Pell Grants to denominational colleges and universities; through child-care subsidies that can be used at churches, synagogues, and other religious institutions; through direct aid to parochial schools for transportation, textbooks, and other materials; and, indirectly, through the tax code, which gives special breaks to the faithful. If government aid to religious institutions were such a problem, she suggested, wouldn't American society be torn already by sectarian strife?

What Justice O'Connor failed to answer was the dissenters' obvious disquiet—one shared these days by many Americans—at the prospect of public money going to support the teaching of extremist religious creeds. This is a reasonable concern—though it is hardly clear, as the Justices themselves might have argued, that the best tool for conquering intolerance born of religious zeal is for the government to impose secular enlightenment. The U.S. has achieved religious peace not by depending upon school-based indoctrination of any stripe but by ensuring that the members of all creeds have access to the democratic process and a robust private sphere in which to meet their particular needs.

As an educational matter, several well-designed studies have shown that students who attend private schools in the U.S. are not only just as tolerant of others as their public-school peers but are also *more* engaged in political and community life. Catholic schools have a particularly outstanding record, probably because for more than a century American Catholics have felt compelled to teach democratic values as proof of their patriotism. There are obviously extremist outliers among, for instance, some of the American *madrassas* discovered by journalists since September 11, but there is no reason to doubt that most of the country's religious schools are attempting to prove that they, too, can create good citizens.

As for *Brown* itself, only Justice Clarence Thomas, in his own stirring concurrence, pointed to it as an explicit precedent, quoting Frederick Douglass to argue that today's inner-city public-school systems "deny emancipation to urban minority students." As he observed,

> The failure to provide education to poor urban children perpetuates a vicious cycle of poverty, dependence, criminality, and alienation that continues for the remainder of their lives. If society cannot end racial discrimination, at least it can arm minorities with the education to defend themselves from some of discrimination's effects.

For Justice Thomas—as for President Bush, whose own remarks were undoubtedly influenced by these passages—vouchers are a civil-rights issue; they promise not to intensify religious strife, as the Court's dissenters would have it, but to help heal the country's most enduring social divide.

Whether *Zelman* can in fact meet these high expectations remains very much to be seen. *Brown*, in principle, was self-enacting. Neither state legislatures nor local school boards could defy the ruling without running afoul of the law. George Wallace, Bull Connor, and many other Southern politicians were willing to do just that, but in the end, federal authorities imposed the Supreme Court's decision on the vested interests that opposed it.

Zelman is different. Though it keeps existing voucher programs intact, it does not compel the formation of new ones. Here the barricades to change remain extraordinarily high.

Public opinion does not pose the most serious obstacle; indeed, on this issue it is highly uncertain. Pollsters can get either pro-voucher or anti-voucher majorities simply by tinkering with the wording of their questions and the order in which they are asked. Nor, despite greater exposure for the issue, have the public's views evolved much in recent years; questions asked in 1996 generated basically the same results in 2001.

Vouchers suffer from graver problems among members of the political class. Whether in Congress or at the state level, substantial bipartisan support is usually necessary to get a piece of legislation through the various committees, past a vote in two chambers, and signed into law. For vouchers, such support has never materialized. Whatever the private opinions of Democrats, for most of them, it is political suicide to support vouchers publicly. Teachers' unions have long placed vouchers at the top of their legislative kill list, and they are a key Democratic constituency, providing the party with both substantial financing and election-day shock troops.

Nor can voucher proponents rely on whole-hearted support from the GOP. Most Republicans, especially social conservatives and libertarians who have read their Milton Friedman, support vouchers in principle. Still, an idea whose primary appeal is to black Americans, the most faithful of all Democratic voting blocs, is a hard sell among the Republican rank-and-file. Vouchers simply do not have much resonance with well-heeled suburbanites who already have a range of educational choices. When vouchers came up as state ballot questions in both California and Michigan two years ago, most Republican politicians found a way to dodge the issue—and the proposals lost badly.

Even if this political situation were to change, most states have constitutional restrictions of their own that may be invoked to scuttle attempts to provide vouchers for use at religious schools. Many of these provisions are so-called "Blaine" amendments, dating to the 19th century, when James Blaine, a Senator from Maine and a Republican presidential candidate, sought to win the anti-immigrant vote by campaigning to deny public funds to Catholic schools.

(Blaine is perhaps most famous for describing the Democrats as the party of "Rum, Romanism, and Rebellion.") In its classic version, the Blaine amendment read as follows:

> No money raised by taxation for the support of public schools, or derived from any public fund therefore, nor any public lands devoted thereto, shall ever be under the control of any religious sect; nor shall any money so raised or lands so devoted be divided between religious sects or denominations.

In a number of cases, state courts have interpreted Blaine amendments to mean nothing more than what is required, according to the Supreme Court, by the establishment clause of the First Amendment. On this view, vouchers are safe—but not every state judge necessarily shares this view. Such language—may prove to be a hurdle for the voucher program in Florida, where a trial court has now ruled that the law violates the state constitution. Depending on what finally happens at the state level, the Supreme Court may in time be asked to decide whether, on account of their nativist and anti-Catholic origins, the Blaine amendments themselves are unconstitutional.

♦◈♦

However much of these practical differences may separate *Zelman* from *Brown*, one powerful similarity remains: like the Court's famed ruling against segregation in the schools, the decision to allow vouchers means much more for black students and their families than for other Americans.

For decades, and despite a host of compensatory reforms the sizable gap in educational performance between blacks and whites has remained roughly the same. According to the National Assessment of Educational Progress, black eighth graders continue to score about four grade levels below their white peers on standardized tests. Nor is this gap likely to close as long as we have, in President Bush's words, "one education system for those who can afford to send their children to a school of their choice and one for those who can't."

When parents choose a neighborhood or town in which to live, they also select, often quite self-consciously, a school for their children. That is why various Internet services now provide buyers—and real-estate agents—with detailed test-score data and other information about school districts and even individual schools. But there is a catch: the mobility that makes these choices possible costs money. It is no accident that children lucky enough to be born into privilege also attend the nation's best schools.

African-Americans are often the losers in this arrangement. Holding less financial equity, and still facing discrimination in the housing market, they choose from a limited set of housing options. As a result, their children are more likely to attend the worst public schools. Richer, whiter districts rarely extend anything more than a few token slots to low-income minority students outside their communities.

It is thus unsurprising that blacks have benefited most when school choice has been expanded. In multi-year evaluations of private voucher programs in New York City, Washington, D.C., and Dayton, Ohio, my colleagues and I found that African-American students, when given the chance to attend private schools, scored significantly higher on standardized tests than comparable students who remained in the public schools. In New York, where the estimates are most precise, those who switched from public to private schools scored, after three years, roughly 9 percentage points higher on math and reading tests than their public-school peers, a difference of about two grade levels. If reproduced nationwide, this result would cut almost in half the black-white test-score gap. (Interestingly, there is no evidence that vouchers have improved the academic performance of students from other ethnic groups. In my own research, they had no impact, positive or negative, on the test scores of either whites in Dayton or Hispanics in New York City.)

These findings about the especially positive effects of private schools on African-American students are hardly isolated. One review of the literature, conducted by the Princeton economist Cecilia Rouse, concludes that even though (once again) it is difficult to discern positive benefits for white students, "Catholic schools generate higher test scores for African-Americans." Another, done by Jeffrey Grogger and Derek Neal, economists from the University of Wisconsin and the University of Chicago, finds little in the way of detectable gains for whites but concludes that "urban minorities in Catholic schools fare much better than similar students in public schools."

No less important, in light of concerns about the effect of vouchers on students "left behind," is that school choice also seems to improve the performance of students who remain in the *public* schools. The best data from Milwaukee show strong advances in test scores since the voucher program was put into place there ten years ago, especially at public schools in those low-income neighborhoods where the voucher option was available. As observers in Milwaukee have noted, it was only in the wake of the voucher program's expansion that the public-school system there began to adopt a series of apparently successful reforms.

We do not know precisely what accounts for the gains that black students have made by switching to private schools. The answer is certainly not money, since the private schools they attend are usually low-budget, no-frills operations. The most striking difference, according to my own research, lies in the general educational environment: the parents of these students who reported being much more satisfied with everything from the curriculum, homework, and teacher quality to how the schools communicate with the parents themselves. The classes tend to be smaller, they say, and there is less fighting, cheating, racial conflict, or destruction of property.

꩜

That vouchers can produce such results has been known for some time. The question now is whether the ruling in *Zelman* will have any impact on what the public and politicians think about the issue. If nothing else, the Court's authoritative pronouncement on the constitutionality of vouchers has already conferred new legitimacy on them. Newspaper editors and talk-show hosts have been forced to give the idea more respect, and political opponents cannot dismiss it so easily.

Still, the key to change lies within the black community, and especially with parents, who increasingly know that private schools provide a better education for their children. A 1998 poll by Public Agenda, a nonpartisan research group, found that 72 percent of African-American parents supported vouchers, as opposed to just 59 percent of white parents. A poll conducted two years later by the Joint Center for Political and Economic Studies had similar results, with just under half of the overall adult population supporting vouchers but 57 percent of African-American adults favoring the idea. Perhaps more to the point, blacks constituted nearly half of all the applicants for the 40,000 privately funded vouchers offered nationwide by the Children's Scholarship Fund in 1999, even though they comprised only about a quarter of the eligible population.

Even in the face of such numbers, it is too much to expect that men like Jesse Jackson and Al Sharpton will reconsider their virulent opposition to vouchers; their political tendencies are too well defined. But pressure to support school vouchers is building among black parents, and black leaders will have to act. Howard Fuller, the former superintendent of Milwaukee's public-school system, has formed the Black Alliance for Educational Options, a pro-voucher group that has mounted an effective public-relations campaign and is making waves in civil-rights circles. And young politicians like Cory Booker in Newark have begun to challenge their old-line, machine-style elders, using vouchers as a key dividing point. Responding to these currents—and to the decision in *Zelman*—the city council of Camden, composed entirely of black and Hispanic Democrats, passed a unanimous resolution in July urging the state of New Jersey to establish a voucher program for the city's dysfunctional public schools. Such examples are sure to multiply.

Not even the Supreme Court, it should be recognized, can make educational change come quickly in America. Though *Brown* was handed down in 1954, it took more than a decade before major civil-rights legislation was enacted; Southern schools were not substantially desegregated until the 1970's. Anyone writing about *Brown* ten years after its passage might have concluded that the decision was almost meaningless.

The same may be said about *Zelman* on its tenth anniversary. Perhaps the safest prediction is that, in four or five decades, American education will have been altered dramatically, in ways we cannot anticipate, by the parental demand for greater choice—a demand codified in *Zelman*. Many battles will be fought and lost along the way, to be sure, but the victories will accumulate, because choice, once won, is seldom conceded.

Note

1. New York City, Washington, D.C., and numerous other cities have well-developed *private* voucher programs designed to help low-income families; these currently serve over 50,000 students.

POSTSCRIPT

Has the Supreme Court Reconfigured American Education?

In "Privatizing Education: The Politics of Vouchers," *Phi Delta Kappan* (February 2001), Sheila Suess Kennedy identifies the partisans in the voucher wars. Pro-voucher groups include pro-market libertarians, business organizations, the Christian Right, and the Catholic Church. The anti-voucher side includes the education establishment (teachers' unions, in particular), civil libertarians, church/state separationists, and official African American organizations. Regarding this last group, Michael Leo Owens, in "Why Blacks Support Vouchers," *The School Administrator* (June 2002), states that although urban black America favors school vouchers, its leaders do not. He cites a 1999 survey showing that 68 percent of blacks favor vouchers whereas a similar percentage of black state and local officials do not support voucher plans. Apparently, despite their short-comings, vouchers offer hope to poor families whose children are trapped in the nation's worst schools. On the contrary, Benjamin O. Canada, in "Black Leadership and Vouchers," *The School Administrator* (June 2002), contends that vouchers cannot systematically expand educational opportunities for blacks—they are a hoax. Interestingly, the first federally funded voucher program has been initiated in the predominantly black District of Columbia schools.

Clearly, the *Zelman* decision has rekindled the debate about breaking up the government monopoly in schooling and giving parents and children new options. So say Lawrence W. Reed and Joseph P. Overton in "The Future of School Choice," *USA Today* (January 2003), who assert, "The empowerment and transformation of parents into active agents is the foundation of educa-tional choice theory." Reed and Overton further contend that the Supreme Court's momentous decision has opened the door to improving schools through the power of choice and competition. In time, they say, it will be seen as a pivotal ruling in the restoration of American education.

In contrast, Peterson's concerns are echoed in Steven Menashi's "The Church-State Tangle: School Choice and Religious Autonomy," *Policy Review* (August & September 2002), in which the author worries that "if voucher laws saddle private schools with the same regulatory regime that now hampers the public education system, school choice will prove an iatrogenic aggravation of the educational crisis."

For further slants on the issue, see the April 2002 issue of *Educational Leadership* and the Winter 2001 issue of *Education Next.* More recent sources are Benjamin Dowling-Sendor, "Revisiting the Voucher Debate," *American School Board Journal* (July 2006) and "School Choice: A Progress Report" by Dan Lips and Evan Feinberg in *USA Today* magazine (January 2007).

ISSUE 8

Is No Child Left Behind Irretrievably Flawed?

YES: Sharon L. Nichols and David C. Berliner, from "Testing the Joy Out of Learning," *Educational Leadership* (March 2008)

NO: Dianne Piché, from "Basically a Good Model," *Education Next* (Fall 2007)

ISSUE SUMMARY

YES: Education professors Sharon Nichols and David Berliner cite evidence of the negative effects of test-dominated schooling under the influence of No Child Left Behind (NCLB).

NO: Dianne Piché, executive director of the Citizens' Commission on Civil Rights, supports the testing and accountability measures of the federal law as the best way to advance the interests of the poor and minorities.

Congress and executive branch began wrestling with the reauthorization of the No Child Left Behind (NCLB) Act in 2007, and the issue was a central point of argument in the 2008 national, state, and local political campaigns. There are those who want sweeping changes and those who feel that any change would diminish the law's ambitious goal of raising standards of performance in American schools. Some criticize the unreasonableness of the law's specific demands, citing 2007 figures showing more than 4,500 schools serving over 2 million students failing to meet annual progress goals for four years or more. Wade A. Carpenter, in "The Other Side of No Child Left Behind," *Educational Horizons* (Fall 2006), states that he does not blame the Bush administration for its goals but blames it for its method, namely "test-driven minimalism, with the slower and resistant kids monopolizing the time of frustrated and surly teachers and the brighter kids sitting quietly, bored stupid."

The main points of dispute, as outlined in the *American School Board Journal* of January 2007, are the adequacy of federal funding, the mode of measuring yearly progress, the facilitation of school transfers (an option now taken by a very small percentage of parents of eligible students), the act of providing of tutorial services, the recruitment of highly qualified teachers, and the problem of flexibility in dealing with special education students and English language learners. Supporters of NCLB argue that the law's core provisions are sound and point to significant gains in math and reading scores and new levels of achievement by minority students, as reported in the *Congressional Digest* of May 2008. In addition, a "blueprint" for strengthening the reform has been issued by the administration, emphasizing more rigorous coursework, new tools for chronically underperforming schools, and more options for families. Representative George Miller, a co-author of the law, has put forth some key changes, among them giving credit to schools that make progress, bringing employers and colleges together as stakeholders, and increasing attention to middle and secondary schools. U.S. Department of Education Secretary Margaret Spellings has stated that after decades of doling out federal dollars and hoping for the best, we are now expecting and getting results.

A 2007 report by Jennifer McMurrer of the Center on Education Policy, "Choices, Changes, and Challenges," recommends staggering testing requirements to include tests in other academic subjects, encouraging states to give adequate emphasis to art and music, and requiring states to arrange for an independent review of standards and assessments at least once every three years. Other constructive appraisals of NCLB can be found in "Ten Big Effects of No Child Left Behind on Public Schools" by Jack Jennings and Diane Stark Rentner in *Phi Delta Kappan* (October 2006) and in a forum of articles in the Fall 2007 edition of *Education Next*.

Under NCLB, the federal government has taken an increasingly active role in steering the public schools, perhaps more than at any time in the nation's history. Some see this as a federal takeover, a usurpation of local control. Stephen J. Caldas and Carl L. Bankston III, in "Federal Involvement in Local School Districts," *Society* (May/June 2005), state that "If districts are in accord with the goals of NCLB, then perhaps following the federal guidelines is not viewed as sacrificing local initiative for federal money. The sad truth is, however, that most districts cannot even imagine existence without the huge amount of federal aid they receive. Thus, they are rarely in a position to even ask themselves the hard question of whether or not following federal stipulations is what is best for their students or their communities." This problem is explored in depth by Phillip C. Schlechty in "No Community Left Behind," *Phi Delta Kappan* (April 2008). He contends that the most fundamental flaw in NCLB is that decisions regarding what the young should know and be able to do are removed from the hands of parents and local community leaders, and turned over to officials and experts located far from the schoolhouse door. This, Schlechty feels, "destroys one of the greatest resources the nation has in the struggle to maintain a sense of community in an increasingly globalized and impersonal world."

In the following selections, Nichols and Berliner argue that the high-stakes test emphasis of NCLB exacerbates the problems of reluctant learners, making the law untenable, while Dianne Piché defends NCLB as a boon to students historically shortchanged in our public schools.

YES

**Sharon L. Nichols and
David C. Berliner**

Testing the Joy Out of Learning

Since the passage of No Child Left Behind (NCLB), students have been exposed to an unprecedented number of tests. Every year in grades 3–8 and at least once in high school, virtually all public school students take tests in math and reading (and soon science). Students also take regular benchmark tests—supposedly to predict performance on the mandated tests—and district assessments throughout the school year. The time spent talking about, preparing for, and taking tests has increased exponentially.

What has all this testing achieved? Five years after NCLB was enacted, there is no convincing evidence that student learning has increased in any significant way on tests other than the states' own tests. On measures such as the National Assessment of Educational Progress (NAEP), no reliable increases in scores have occurred, nor have achievement gaps between students of higher and lower socioeconomic classes narrowed.

In contrast, a wealth of documentation indicates that the unintended and largely negative effects of high-stakes testing are pervasive and a cause for concern. In our own research, we have documented hundreds of cases in which high-stakes testing has harmed teaching and learning. For example, high-stakes testing has been associated with suspicious forms of data manipulation, as well as outright cheating. The tests undermine teacher–student relationships, lead to a narrowing of the curriculum, demoralize teachers, and bore students.

Research has not fully examined the impact of this test-dominated school environment on students' attitudes and dispositions toward learning. But we suspect that for most students, schooling is less joyful than it was; and for reluctant learners, schooling is worse than ever.

Overvaluing Testing, Undervaluing Learning

From the motivation literature, we know that learners are more likely to enjoy learning when activities are meaningful, fun, or interesting. Yet, again and again, high-stakes testing diminishes the fun and meaning of learning. Under pressure to prepare students to perform well in math and reading, teachers engage in repetitious instruction that boils down content to isolated bits of information, leaving little time to engage in creative interdisciplinary activities or project-based inquiry. One Colorado teacher reports,

> Our district told us to focus on reading, writing, and mathematics. . . . In the past I had hatched out baby chicks in the classroom as part of the science unit. I don't have time to do that. . . . We don't do community outreach like we used to, like visiting the nursing home or cleaning up the park that we had adopted.

We also know that students are more hardworking and persistent when they perceive the purpose of learning as self-improvement or achievement of personal goals. Yet a high-stakes testing climate sends a message that the primary purpose of learning is to score well on the test. Sometimes teaching to the test is blatant, as when teachers assign daily worksheets taken from released older versions of the test. Sometimes it is less obvious, as when instruction is based on the specific information that will be on the test. One teacher explains,

> I'm teaching more test-taking skills and how to use your time wisely. Also what to look for in a piece of literature and how to underline important details. There is a lot more time spent on teaching those kinds of skills. . . . Read questions, restate the question in your answer, write so the person grading the test can read it, etc.

As a result of the overvaluing of test results, the curriculum has narrowed. All across the United States, the time devoted to untested subjects like art, music, and social studies has been reduced or eliminated completely so that schools can teach more math, reading, writing, and now science. For example, in Kansas in 2006, high school freshmen were required to "double dose" their English classes instead of participating in electives. In a California middle school, students were required to take two periods of all core subjects and funding was dropped for music, Spanish, art, and classes in the trades and industrial design.

In 2006, the Bill and Melinda Gates Foundation released a report on the reasons students drop out of school. In this small survey of students who had already dropped out, 47 percent reported that school was "uninteresting." About 70 percent commented that they didn't feel "inspired" at school. For such reluctant learners, the increased test preparation and narrower curriculum resulting from high-stakes testing exacerbates the problem. Faced with an increasingly disjointed, decontextualized curriculum, many become actively disengaged; others simply leave.

I Pledge Allegiance to the Test

A disturbing phenomenon popping up in more and more U.S. schools is the prevalence of schoolwide pep rallies, ice cream socials, and other peculiar events meant to "motivate" students to do well on the state-mandated test. For example, one Texas high school held a rally for parents, teachers, and students during which the principal informed parents of the importance of the Texas

Assessment of Knowledge and Skills (TAKS) and compared it to a marathon, in which "students need endurance." He was not subtle when he said, "This is the test of your lives!" This speech was followed by a class pledge in which students promised to "pass the test and take Parker High School to the top and lead us to exemplary."

This is not an isolated incident. In one New York school, every spring just before test time, the principal brings students together to sing songs that will "inspire" them before and during the test. Some songs included "I'm a Believer" and "I've Been Working on My Writing."

Bulletin boards, posters, and daily mantras constitute additional forms of explicit emphasis on the importance of tests. Clichéd slogans often appear on posters and banners throughout the school. Messages like "Take Us to Exemplary" are pervasive in many Texas schools.

When teachers report that most of their time is spent preparing for the test, when we go into schools and find hundreds of posters related to the upcoming test, when we hear of schools with daily announcements about the "test standard of the day," and when students tell us that not a day goes by without mention of the test, we can be pretty sure that the test has become the primary focus for learning.

Marginalizing Youth

High-stakes testing encourages teachers to view students not in terms of their potential, or what unique or new qualities they bring to the learning environment, but rather as test-score increasers or suppressors. Students quickly pick this up and realize they are defined as winners or losers on the basis of their test scores.

Test-score suppressors receive the clear message that they are not valued as highly as their better-performing peers. Sadly, some teachers and principals have done all sorts of unprofessional things to ensure that test-score suppressors either pass (because of rigorous test-prep activities or even more questionable means) or are dropped from testing altogether. For example, more than 500 low-scoring students in Birmingham, Alabama, were administratively "dropped" from school just days before state testing. Scores rose, principals received substantial bonuses, and hundreds of students had their lives made infinitely more difficult in the process. Such actions help to transform slow learners into reluctant learners, compounding their problems in school.

Issues associated with test score suppressors are exacerbated in states where high school students have to pass a test to receive a diploma. Hundreds of students are dropping out or opting to take the GED route, mainly because passing the test has become an insurmountable obstacle to them. This is especially true for special education students and English language learners (ELLs). Thousands try as hard as they can but cannot pass the test despite meeting all other graduation requirements. Chronic failure is demeaning, causing many otherwise highly engaged students to give up, drop out, or become increasingly cynical about schooling. The high-stakes testing culture communicates to students that their other abilities are of no value. Outstanding talent in dance, welding, art, knowledge of the U.S. Civil War, computer programming, consensus building in small groups, foreign languages, acting, and so forth count for little.

Even students who score high may become less motivated as a result of the high-stakes testing culture. These test-score increasers often feel "used"— for example, when they are pressured to take the test even when they are sick. As a result, they may adopt cynical attitudes about the purpose of being in school. As one student points out,

> The TAKS is a big joke. . . . *This is the easiest test you could ever take.* . . . I mean, forget logarithms and algebra, forget knowing about government and the Bill of Rights. Instead, we read a two-page story and then answer 11 short questions about it such as, "What was the meaning of the word *futile* in paragraph two? A: generous, B: deceptive, C: useless, and D: applesauce."

Learners Weigh In

When many students see education as punitive and uninteresting, and when they have their abilities narrowly defined by a single test score, the potential for irreparable and damaging consequences is high. For students who struggle academically, high-stakes testing can diminish their sense of self worth, leading to decreased motivation to do well in school. And for students who see the tests as an easy rite of passage, a school culture formed around high-stakes testing is boring and unconnected. Thus, high-stakes testing cultures build reluctant learners out of even these academically talented students.

How do we know this? The voices of youth are pretty clear. They understand the exaggerated importance of tests in their lives, and it frustrates them. A 12th grader writes,

> Students (teachers as well) focus on only the TAKS. It's almost as if they have been given an ultimatum: Either pass the test and get the ticket out of there, or pass the test months later and live with the disappointment all your life. It's not fair.

Others find the tests dehumanizing and feel angry about the narrow curriculum being forced on them. They worry that their schooling ignores other aspects of their lives. An 11th grade student writes,

> In Texas many public school districts have found raising their standardized testing averages to be the No. 1 goal of classroom curriculum. Consequently, school is no longer a forum where students can discuss the effects of alcohol, or the best method to achieve a life filled with value and pleasure, or the simple antics of their daily life.

The pressure to achieve is highest in high-poverty schools because they are most likely to be shut down or reconsolidated under NCLB. There, the score suppressors are often force-fed a daily curriculum that includes bits of information devoid of any connection to their real lives. Foster talking with

Latino students attending a high-poverty high school heard, "We learn in isolation. We learn one skill one day or in a week and then we never see it again until test time." Another Latino student in the same school commented,

> I was written up and sent to the office because I didn't want to do a TAKS assignment. I was told in the office that I had to do it because it was important that I pass this test. I am tired of doing TAKS, TAKS, TAKS. I am not learning anything.

Especially revealing are the following excerpts from a transcript of one teacher's attempt to motivate her 16 Latino 11th graders. The teacher had just handed out an essay similar to those that would be on the upcoming state test. Her goal was to motivate and inspire students to perform well on the test. But students were savvy about what was happening.

Teacher: OK, this is last-minute work for TAKS. You can pass the test. You don't want to take it again, right?

Students: *No response.*

Teacher: Please say yes.

Students: *No response.*

Teacher: You are brilliant. . . . The test is not hard. Take your time; in fact take all the time you need.

Students: *No response.*

Teacher: OK, there will be three types of open-ended questions and three types of literary selections. What does "literary" mean?

Students: *No response.*

Teacher: Is it fiction, nonfiction, or biography?

Students: *No response.*

Teacher: Are you going to talk to me or you don't know?

Students: *No response.*

Teacher: (*in an angry voice*) It's fiction, you all. (*pause*) First thing you do is answer the question. It must be insightful and thoughtful. Do not restate the question. You have five lines to fill in. Then you have to support a response. If you summarize in an open-ended question you get a zero. But if you use support for the passage, you get points. Look at this essay. Do you see how this student used textual support?

Students: *No response.*

Teacher: (*in an angry voice*) Come on!

Students: *No response*

And on it goes. Another exciting day at school marked only by passive resistance to what students accurately perceive to be an inferior (and boring) education.

What Can We Do?

High-stakes tests are not likely to go away, but schools can and should try to minimize their harmful effects. Schools should at least refrain from engaging in test-prep rallies, ice cream socials, or social events that focus specifically on the test. Such activities only reinforce the impression that the test is the primary goal of schooling. If schools want to hold such events to create a sense of community, they might simply rename the events to emphasize learning, not testing (for example, a Rally for Learning). Of course, the learning celebrated has to be genuine: completing outstanding science fair projects; presenting classroom projects to the town council; writing poetry, essays, or a play; and so forth. Schools need to reward demonstrations of learning in all its varieties.

Administrators and teachers should work together to reframe the purposes of learning in their school. As a start, eliminate the word "test" from any banner, poster, or encouraging slogan. Instead, use language that focuses on mastering knowledge, improving individual performance, or seeing the value of schooling for enhancing one's future.

In addition, teachers and administrators should strive to create a climate of caring and cooperation, instead of competition. We know that students are more likely to attend school and excel when they feel they belong. Feelings of connection lead to greater effort, greater persistence, and positive attitudes. Feelings of rejection have the opposite effects.

Significant changes in NCLB are unlikely to occur soon. This law has not only exacerbated the problems of reluctant learners already in our schools, but also manufactured additional reluctant learners for the schools to deal with. It is up to administrators and teachers to mitigate the damaging effects of this untenable law on many of our students by proactively working to diminish the importance of high-stakes testing in schools.

Basically a Good Model

No Child Left Behind (NCLB) may be the most vilified act of Congress in modern times. Just about anybody can find something in the law to get worked up over: the testing rules, "highly qualified teachers," funding shortfalls and so on. It's great fodder for presidential candidates, too, one of whom recently went so far as to blame the childhood obesity problem on NCLB and to equate companies providing tutoring to low-income students to Halliburton. Funny thing is NCLB is actually doing some good things for real people, many of them students who historically have been shortchanged in our public schools.

I was an early, proud supporter of the law, and I still am. My civil rights colleagues and I fought for some of its tougher provisions, like accountability for subgroups of students, the 2014 proficiency deadline, requiring states to submit plans for the equitable assignment of teachers, and providing a way out for kids trapped in failing schools. By now, most of the criticism of NCLB—some legitimate but some ginned up by special interests opposed to real accountability—seems pretty old and tiresome.

Let's examine some of the grenades most commonly lobbed at NCLB. First, there is the oft-heard complaint that the measurement system for accountability is all wrong. Why? Because NCLB doesn't call for measuring students' growth from year to year. Instead, the measurement system in the law compares the proficiency levels of this year's 3rd graders to last year's 3rd graders. This is also called the "status model."

Suggesting that NCLB 1.0 is flawed because it did not explicitly provide, back in 2001, for "growth models" is like saying my 2001 desktop was a bad buy because in 2007 it can't run Windows Vista or streaming video. Virtually none of the states had the technology and other capacity to design and implement growth-measurement systems in the early years of this authorization. The fact that Education Secretary Margaret Spellings has approved only seven to date is not because she's not eager to see many states move in this direction. There simply aren't, even today, many states ready, willing, and able to carry out a credible, statistically sound growth-based accountability system.

Since 1994 the "status model" has been the accountability paradigm embedded in Title I, and in many state accountability systems as well. It was based, in part, on public health models that aspire, for example, to increase numbers of annual healthy births and immunized kindergarteners and decrease things like malnutrition, disease, and teen pregnancy. Significantly, it was not until sometime after NCLB's final passage that the noise level about the "status" model and the plea for growth measures became audible. And this was not because states suddenly had vast new capacity to measure growth. They didn't. Instead, increasingly, leaders of the education establishment (i.e., school boards, administrators, and the teacher unions) were doing their Adequate Yearly Progress (AYP) math in the context of the 2014 deadline. They rightly feared that, unlike the Clinton administration, the Bush administration was determined to enforce the law, particularly with regard to assessment and accountability. Simply put, they hoped that with a growth model, they might get credit for *some* amount of improvement in test scores, even if the requisite numbers of students were not actually proficient.

This political background is important context for the debate taking place in Congress. Virtually nobody disputes the merits of allowing states to base their accountability systems on the value a school or teacher adds to a student's knowledge and skills. But when it comes time for Congress to get down to actual legislative language, members will have to choose whether to open the door to all comers, including states with pitifully low standards (compared to those of the National Assessment of Educational Progress), deficient data and student-tracking systems, and a poor track record on including English language learners and students with disabilities. Or they can take the more prudent course, accede to the secretary's good judgment, and limit the "growth" option to those states that can demonstrate both the capacity and the rigor required to bring students to proficiency within a specified period. Thus, simply arguing "growth measures good, current law bad" may in the end not be very helpful to the deliberations on Capitol Hill and could well undermine the efforts of those who favor only those growth systems that can meet tough standards for rigor, reliability, and inclusion of all students.

Then there's the suggestion that the 2014 proficiency deadline is crazy. Says who? Certainly not the parents whose children attend persistently low-performing schools and for whom even one school year is too much time to lose.

Increasingly we are seeing high-poverty, high-minority schools across the country that are achieving outstanding academic success. In high-achieving schools, proficiency for all students is possible *this year*. Let's do what we can with NCLB to drive the dollars and incentives to the schools that are replicating the no-excuses approach to teaching the children of the poor.

Common Ground?

Perhaps surprisingly, my fellow forum authors and I agree on the importance of NCLB's core aspirations:

- Transparency and public reporting of student achievement data
- The need for high standards pegged to postsecondary education and careers
- Regular assessment in reading and math
- Accountability based on assessment results
- Options for parents.

We even agree on some of the more nuanced, yet potentially powerful, improvements Congress and states could enact to strengthen education reform:

- Differentiated consequences
- Continued efforts to measure growth from year to year
- Measuring effectiveness and attaching rewards/consequences for administrators and teachers.

Finally, we may actually agree on the most radical proposal from the standpoint of the more than 40-year history of the Elementary and Secondary Education Act (ESEA): Congress should not continue to subsidize failure after providing years of assistance and the opportunity to improve. There are a variety of ways to remove funding from chronically low-performing schools and transfer it to better schools (including moving the dollars in the figurative "backpacks" of the students) that merit serious consideration.

Our disagreements reflect our fundamentally different beliefs about the role of the federal government itself, particularly with respect to advancing the interests of the poor and minorities. Since when has leaving it all up to the states helped the poor and minorities achieve equality of opportunity? Not when it came to voting rules. Not when it came to public accommodations. Not when it came to desegregating schools in the aftermath of *Brown* v. *Board of Education*. And certainly not now, when the achievement gaps based on race and class are as virulent as ever, with only modest signs of abatement.

Of course, not everything is working perfectly yet. School choice and supplemental educational services were not high on the political priority list under the first Bush administration, but it does not follow that these two vital provisions for parents cannot be made to work. It often takes a period of years (sometimes even a complete authorization cycle) for a controversial new provision to take root. For example, most states did not pay much attention to the "accountability lite" provisions in the Clinton-era Improving America's Schools Act (IASA), nor did that administration do much to signal to states that it would enforce IASA's requirements for "corrective action" and school improvement. It took another authorization and a clear signal from the Bush administration that the federal government was serious about accountability in order for the states to come up with plans to hold their own schools and districts accountable.

Moreover, there are encouraging signs of bipartisan support for proposals to add some real teeth to the public school transfer options in NCLB. Currently, parents may choose a better school when their child's school fails to make AYP, but as the Lawyers' Committee for Civil Rights Under Law has called it, the choice option is "a right without a remedy." School districts implement the provision only halfheartedly and many argue a lack of space in successful schools. The interdistrict provisions in the law are weak, and charter options are not meaningful in states with arbitrary limits on new charter schools.

The Citizens' Commission on Civil Rights, along with the Aspen Institute's NCLB Commission and other proponents, have proposed tough new measures to guarantee public school choice to children who attend persistently low-performing schools. One proposal would deny states that do not provide parents and children with demonstrably better choices their Title I money. States would have the obligation to create and offer those children in the worst schools seats in better-performing schools. To increase seats, states could lift caps on the number of charter schools, expand successful schools, or provide for interdistrict transfers. A second proposal would require an "audit" to determine whether capacity in better schools actually exists and, if so, where. Finally, the Aspen Institute and a number of civil rights organizations favor enabling parents to take legal action when rights conferred under NCLB, like the right to place their child in a better-performing school, are violated. Congress should consider how best to target funding to the schools, leaders, and models that have the best record of success in high-poverty communities. But the bottom line is that unless and until the money is used to leverage dramatic change, there is unlikely to be any marked change. And without dramatic change, achievement gaps are unlikely to close any time soon. The status quo is a powerful player to be reckoned with in the struggle for educational equity.

The Pace of Reform

NCLB is in many respects the latest in a long line of efforts in the policy and legal arenas to promote equity and opportunity in the public schools, including desegregation cases, the Civil Rights Act of 1964, the original ESEA, and school finance and adequacy cases in the states.

How long does it take a cutting-edge civil rights law to "work"? Could a credible argument have been made in 1969, five years after passage of the Civil Rights Act, that the ambitious law was "not working" and therefore ought to be abandoned?

This particular legislation needs to be strengthened by ensuring high state standards, reliable assessments, realistic school-improvement measures, an equitable distribution of effective teachers, and real parental choice. Those of us—on the left, right, and middle—who believe in the transformative power of education need to draw more from the work of the increasing numbers of urban schools that are demonstrating *how* to succeed with large numbers of poor and minority students despite the odds. We need to learn from the contagious successes of outstanding public schools and choice programs like the Amistad Academy in Connecticut, the Green Dot schools in California, and the voluntary interdistrict transfer program in St. Louis.

Abandoning NCLB now would be the height of cynicism. Instead, like the civil rights movement itself, the education reform movement is in dire need of creative thinking, committed education leaders, and informed, involved parents—all united in our belief in the worth and value of every young life and each child's potential to learn and do great things.

POSTSCRIPT

Is No Child Left Behind Irretrievably Flawed?

"**N**CLB is influenced deeply by the market-based philosophies of its prime, neoconservative movers. Markets inherently create winners and losers. The rhetoric of leaving no child behind is belied by a system geared to a narrow standardization of goals that results in a diminished realm of opportunity to demonstrate accomplishment and achievement." These thoughts from Margaret McKenna and David Haselkorn, in "NCLB and the Lessons of Columbine," *USA Today* (May 2005) certainly run counter to the assessment offered by Dianne Piché. McKenna and Haselkorn believe that our national education policies are seriously misguided, based as they are on a long-discredited behaviorist view of human development prompted by extrinsic rewards and consequences rather than intrinsic motivation.

Another critic, Richard Rothstein, in "The Corruption of School Accountability," *The School Administrator* (June 2008), agrees with Nichols and Berliner that under NCLB reliance solely on flawed numerical measures to evaluate performance has corrupted schooling, causing an emphasis on drill, teaching to the test, and manipulating data. Similarly, W. James Popham in *America's Failing Schools: How Parents and Teachers Can Cope with "No Child Left Behind"* (2004) argues that the prescribed achievement goals are altogether unrealistic, that "the establishment of expectations that are unattainable will rarely spur people to perform at new levels of excellence." Other interesting articles on testing and accountability include Mark F. Goldberg, "The Test Mess," *Phi Delta Kappan* (January 2004) and "Test Mess 2: Are We Doing Better a Year Later?" *Phi Delta Kappan* (January 2005); Thomas Toch, "Turmoil in the Testing Industry," *Educational Leadership* (November 2006); Lawrence A. Uzzell, "Cheat Sheets: No Child Left Behind Has Taught Our Nation's Schools One Thing—How to Lie," *The American Spectator* (September 2005); and Richard Rothstein, "The Limits of Testing," *American School Board Journal* (February 2005).

. . . .

Covering some other crucial related issues are these recommended articles: David Mathews, "The Public and the Public Schools: The Coproduction of Education," *Phi Delta Kappan* (April 2008);. . . . Paul D. Houston, "The Seven Deadly Sins of No Child Left Behind," *Phi Delta Kappan* (June 2007); and John Chubb and Diane Ravitch, "The Future of No Child Left Behind: End It? Or Mend It?" *Education Next* (Summer 2009).

ISSUE 9

Does a "Deficit Model" Serve Poor Children Well?

YES: Ruby Payne, from "Nine Powerful Practices," *Educational Leadership* (April 2008)

NO: Mistilina Sato and Timothy J. Lensmire, from "Poverty and Payne: Supporting Teachers to Work with Children of Poverty," *Phi Delta Kappan* (January 2009)

ISSUE SUMMARY

YES: Ruby Payne, president of aha!Process, Inc., a company that offers guidance to educators in poverty-area districts, puts forth specific ideas for overcoming deficits in students' lives.

NO: Assistant professor of education Mistilina Sato and associate professor of education Timothy J. Lensmire find that Payne's approach offers only simplistic solutions based on a grossly overgeneralized, deficit-laden portrayal of poor children.

J onathan Kozol, long involved in documenting the plight of children in the nation's worst poverty areas in books and articles based on first-hand investigations, has recently responded to the growing evidence of racial and ethnic resegregation in the schools. In "Confections of Apartheid: A Stick-and-Carrot Pedagogy for the Children of Our Inner-City Poor," *Phi Delta Kappan* (December 2005), Kozol cites the evidence of an increasingly segregated social order assembled by Gary Orfield and his colleagues at the Civil Rights Project at Harvard University. Kozol's main concern is with what actions are being taken to deal with this situation. He sees an effort by school administrators to create "an architecture of adaptive strategies that promise incremental gains within the limits inequality allows." He is not at all pleased with the introduction of Skinnerian techniques as a way of altering the attitudes and learning styles of black and Latino children. He is most concerned about the effects of scripted lessons and other elements of order and control, often seen as necessary strategies in a "teacher-proof" approach.

The question of how to best serve children of poverty has become even more crucial during the current economic downturn. According to Naomi

Dillon in "No Place to Call Home," *American School Board Journal* (June 2009), one in 50 American children is homeless and up to 3.4 million more Americans will become homeless by the end of 2009, creating a new mountain of challenges for school districts across the nation. A provocative article dealing with the entire spectrum of poverty-related issues is Richard A. Gibboney's "Why an Undemocratic Capitalism Has Brought Public Education to Its Knees: A Manifesto," *Phi Delta Kappan* (September 2008). Gibboney states, "Rather than support policies designed to reduce poverty and its toxic effects on the ability of children to succeed in school, our lawmakers are pursuing the misbegotten path of penalizing schools in poverty-stricken cities and rural areas for their failure to work educational miracles." He urges educators to rise up and fight to protect public education and democracy, which will both collapse if our society refuses to take the steps necessary to eliminate poverty.

Richard Rothstein poses the question "Whose Problem Is Poverty?" in *Educational Leadership* (April 2008) in which he offers an inventory of deficits experienced by the poor. These deficits include a lack of health care, lower birth weight, more lead poisoning, iron-deficiency anemia, family instability, more exposure to crime and drugs, fewer positive adult role models, and less exposure to culturally uplifting experiences. And each of these disadvantages makes a small contribution to the achievement gap. Paul Gorski, in "The Myth of the 'Culture of Poverty,'" *Educational Leadership* (April 2008) contends that deficit theories are "the most destructive tool of the culture of classism: which ignores systemic conditions, such as inequitable access to high-quality schooling, that support the cycle of poverty. He claims, furthermore, that "we ignore the fact that poor people suffer disproportionately the effects of nearly every social ill . . . that limit their abilities to achieve to their full potential." This "socioeconomic opportunity gap can be eliminated only when we stop trying to 'fix' poor students and start addressing the ways in which our schools perpetuate classism," Gorski concludes.

Among the most prominent person to embrace the "culture of poverty" premise is Ruby Payne, whose corporation is dedicated to "fixing" the deficits in the lives of poor children. Payne's popularity is analyzed in "The Class-Consciousness Raiser," *The New York Times* (June 10, 2007) by Paul Tough and "Revisiting Ruby Payne," *Rethinking Schools* (Fall 2007) by Anita Perna Bohn.

In the articles presented here Ruby Payne details some of her strategies for increasing achievement levels among the poor and two education professors, Mistilina Sato and Timothy J. Lensmire, offer a critique of Payne's approach and a set of alternatives.

YES

Ruby Payne

Nine Powerful Practices

Students from families with little formal education often learn rules about how to speak, behave, and acquire knowledge that conflict with how learning happens in school. They also often come to school with less background knowledge and fewer family supports. Formal schooling, therefore, may present challenges to students living in poverty. Teachers need to recognize these challenges and help students overcome them. In my work consulting with schools that serve a large population of students living in poverty, I have found nine interventions particularly helpful in raising achievement for low-income students.

1. Build Relationships of Respect

James Comer (1995) puts it well: "No significant learning occurs without a significant relationship." Building a respectful relationship doesn't mean becoming the student's buddy. It means that teachers both insist on high-quality work and offer support. When my colleagues and I interviewed high school students in 1998 about what actions show that a teacher has respect for them, students identified the following:

- The teacher calls me by my name.
- The teacher answers my questions.
- The teacher talks to me respectfully.
- The teacher notices me and says "Hi."
- The teacher helps me when I need help.

The nonverbal signals a teacher sends are a key part of showing respect. I have found that when students feel they have been "dissed" by a teacher, they almost always point to nonverbals, rather than words, as the sign of disrespect. Nonverbal signals communicate judgment, and students can sense when a teacher's intent is to judge them rather than to offer support. Although it's hard to be conscious of nonverbal signals at times, one way to sense how you're coming across is to deeply question your intent. Your gestures and tone will likely reflect that intent.

From *Educational Leadership*, April 2008, pp. 48–52. Copyright © 2008 by ASCD. Reprinted by permission. The Association for Supervision and Curriculum Development is a worldwide community of educators advocating sound policies and sharing best practices to achieve the success of each learner. To learn more, visit ASCD at www.ascd.org.

2. Make Beginning Learning Relational

When an individual is learning something new, learning should happen in a supportive context. Teachers should help all students feel part of a collaborative culture. Intervene if you see an elementary student always playing alone at recess or a middle or high school student eating lunch alone. Assign any new student a buddy immediately and ensure that each student is involved with at least one extracurricular group at lunch or after school. Whenever possible, introduce new learning through paired assignments or cooperative groups.

3. Teach Students to Speak in Formal Register

Dutch linguist Martin Joos (1972) found that every language in the world includes five registers, or levels of formality: frozen, formal, consultative, casual, and intimate. . . . Both school and work operate at the consultative level (which mixes formal and casual speech) and the formal level (which uses precise word choice and syntax). All people use the casual and intimate registers with friends, but students from families with little formal education may default to these registers. Researchers have found that the more generations a person lives in poverty, the less formal the register that person uses, with the exception of people from a strong religious background, who frequently encounter formal religious texts (Montana-Harmon, 1991). Hart and Risley's (1995) study of 42 families indicated that children living in families receiving welfare heard approximately 10 million words by age three, whereas children in families in which parents were classified as professional heard approximately 30 million words in the same period. Teachers conduct most tests through formal register, which puts poor students at a disadvantage. Teachers should address this issue openly and help students learn to communicate through consultative and formal registers. Some students may object that formal register is "white talk"; we tell them it's "money talk."

Have students practice translating phrases from casual into formal register. For example, a student I worked with was sent to the office because he had told his teacher that something "sucked." When I asked him to translate that phrase into formal register, he said, "There is no longer joy in this activity." Teachers should use consultative language (a mix of formal and casual) to build relationships and use formal register to teach content, providing additional explanation in consultative register.

4. Assess Each Student's Resources

One way to define poverty and wealth is in terms of the degree to which we have access to the following eight resources.

- Financial: Money to purchase goods and services.
- Emotional: The ability to control emotional responses, particularly to negative situations, without engaging in self-destructive behavior. This internal resource shows itself through stamina, perseverance, and good decision making.

- Mental: The mental abilities and acquired skills (such as reading, writing, and computing) needed for daily life.
- Spiritual: Some belief in a divine purpose and guidance.
- Physical: Good physical health and mobility.
- Support systems: Friends, family, and resource people who are available in times of need.
- Relationships and role models: Frequent contact with adults who are appropriate role models, who nurture the child, and who do not engage in self-destructive behavior.
- Knowledge of unspoken rules: Knowing the unspoken norms and habits of a group.

School success, as it's currently defined, requires a huge amount of resources that schools don't necessarily provide. Teachers need to be aware that many students identified as "at risk" lack these outside resources. Interventions that require students to draw on resources they do not possess will not work. For example, many students in households characterized by generational poverty have a very limited support system. If such a student isn't completing homework, telling that student's parent, who is working two jobs, to make sure the student does his or her homework isn't going to be effective. But if the school provides a time and place before school, after school, or during lunch for the student to complete homework, that intervention will be more successful.

5. Teach the Hidden Rules of School

People need to know different rules and behaviors to survive in different environments. The actions and attitudes that help a student learn and thrive in a low-income community often clash with those that help one get ahead in school. For example, when adult family members have little formal schooling, the student's environment may be unpredictable. Having reactive skills might be particularly important. These skills may be counterproductive in school, where a learner must plan ahead, rather than react, to succeed. If laughter is often used to lessen conflict in a student's community, that student may laugh when being disciplined. Such behavior is considered disrespectful in school and may anger teachers and administrators.

Educators often tell students that the rules they come to school with aren't valuable anywhere. That isn't true, and students know it. For example, to survive in many high-poverty neighborhoods, young people have to be able to fight physically if challenged—or have someone fight for them. But if you fight in school, you're usually told to leave.

The simple way to deal with this clash of norms is to teach students two sets of rules. I frequently say to students,

> You don't use the same set of rules in basketball that you use in football. It's the same with school and other parts of your life. The rules in school are different from the rules out of school. So let's make a list of the rules in school so we're sure we know them.

6. Monitor Progress and Plan Interventions

One teacher alone cannot address all students' achievement issues. Monitoring and intervening with at-risk kids must be a schoolwide process. Take the following steps:

- Chart student performance and disaggregate this data by subgroups and individuals.
- Keeping in mind your district's learning standards, determine which content you need to spend the most time on. Bloom (1976) found that the amount of time devoted to a content area makes a substantial difference in how well students learn that content. Set up a collaborative process for teachers to discuss learning standards and make these determinations.
- Plan to use the instructional strategies that have the highest payoff for the amount of time needed to do the activity. For example, teaching students to develop questions has a much higher payoff for achievement than completing worksheets.
- Use rubrics and benchmark tests to identify how well students are mastering standards; discuss the results.
- Identify learning gaps and choose appropriate interventions. Interventions can include scheduling extra instruction time, providing a supportive relationship, and helping students use mental models.
- Schedule these activities on the school calendar regularly.

7. Translate the Concrete into the Abstract

To succeed in school, students need to move easily from the concrete to the abstract. For example, a kindergarten teacher may hold up a real apple and tell students to find a drawing of an apple on a given page. Even though the two-dimensional apple on the page doesn't look like the real apple, students come to understand that the drawing represents the apple. In math, students need to understand that a numeral represents a specific number of items.

Teachers can help students become comfortable with the abstract representations characteristic of school by giving them *mental models*—stories, analogies, or visual representations. Mental models enable the student to make a connection between something concrete he or she understands and a representational idea. For example, in math, one can physically form a square with the number of items represented by any square number. We can teach students this concept quickly by drawing a box with nine Xs in it. The student can visually see that 3 is the square root of 9, because no matter how the student looks at the model, there are 3 Xs on each side.

Excellent teachers use mental models all the time, although they may not call them that. I have found that using mental models decreases the amount of time needed to teach and learn a concept.

8. Teach Students How to Ask Questions

When you have asked a student what part of a lesson he or she didn't understand, have you heard the reply, "All of it"? This response may indicate that the student has trouble formulating a specific question. Questions are a principal tool to gain access to information, and knowing how to ask questions yields a huge payoff in achievement (Marzano, 2007). In their research on reading, Palincsar and Brown (1984) found that students who couldn't ask good questions had many academic struggles.

To teach students how to ask questions, I assign pairs of students to read a text and compose multiple-choice questions about it. I give them sentence stems, such as "When _____ happened, why did _____ do _____?" Students develop questions using the stems, then come up with four answers to each question, only one of which they consider correct and one of which has to be funny.

9. Forge Relationships with Parents

Many low-income parents are so overwhelmed with surviving daily life that they can't devote time to their children's schooling. Even when time is available, the parent may not know how to support the child's learning.

It is essential to create a welcoming atmosphere at school for parents. Ask yourself these questions about the kind of experience parents have when they enter your building:

- How are parents usually greeted? With a smile, a command, a look, or the parents name?
- What is the ratio of educators to parent in meetings? Six educators to one parent? Many parents experience such a situation as being "ganged up on." To avoid this perception, designate a person to greet the parent five minutes before the meeting starts and tell him or her who will be present and what is likely to happen. This is much better than having the parent walk into the room cold. When the meeting is over, have all the educators leave the room (and don't have another obvious consultation in the parking lot). The person who met the parent ahead of time should walk the parent out of the building, ask how he or she is feeling, and find out whether the parent has more questions.
- Is the language used in parent meetings understandable, or is it "educationese"?
- Are parents often asked to make interventions they do not have the resources to make?
- Do parents realize that people at the school care about their children? Parents want to know first whether the school cares about and respects their child. Communicate this message early in the conference. It also helps to say, "We know that you care about your child, or you wouldn't be here."

I recommend doing home visits. Arrange to have a substitute for a particular day and send a letter home to a few parents saying that because teachers always ask parents to come to school, a pair of teachers would like to come by their house, say hello, and bring a gift. The gift should be something small, such as a magnet listing the school's name, phone number, and hours. If a parent wants to have an in-depth talk about the child, schedule a time that's good for both parties to talk further. Schools that have taken this approach, such as

East Alien County Schools in Fort Wayne, Indiana, have strengthened the rapport between parents and teachers and lessened discipline referrals.

The Gift of Education

Educators can be a huge gift to students living in poverty. In many instances, education is *the* tool that gives a child life choices. A teacher or administrator who establishes mutual respect, cares enough to make sure a student knows how to survive school, and gives that student the necessary skills is providing a gift that will keep affecting lives from one generation to the next. Never has it been more important to give students living in poverty this gift.

References

Bloom, B. (1976). *Human characteristics and school learning*. New York: McGraw-Hill.

Comer, J. (1995). Lecture given at Education Service Center, Region IV. Houston, TX.

Hart, B., & Risley, T. R. (1995). *Meaningful differences in the everyday experience of young American children*. Baltimore: Paul H. Brookes.

Joos, M. (1972). The styles of the five clocks. In R. D. Abrahams & R. C. Troike (Eds.), *Language and cultural diversity in American education* (pp. 145–149). Englewood Cliffs, NJ: Prentice-Hall.

Marzano, R. J. (2007). *The art and science of teaching. A comprehensive framework for effective instruction*. Alexandria, VA: ASCD.

Montana-Harmon, M. R. (1991). Discourse features of written Mexican Spanish: Current research in contrastive rhetoric and its implications. *Hispania, 74*(2), 417–425.

Palincsar, A. S., & Brown, A. L. (1984). The reciprocal teaching of comprehension-fostering and comprehension-monitoring activities. *Cognition and Instruction, 1*(2), 117–175.

Mistilina Sato
and Timothy J. Lensmire

 NO

Poverty and Payne

As conversations about students who live in poverty begin to become more commonplace, we are seeing two things. First, on a positive note, teachers and administrators are awakening to the reality that not all students embody white, middle-class values, experiences, and cultural norms. This is leading schools and districts to seek professional development experiences for teachers to help them grapple with yet another form of diversity in their classrooms. There seems to be agreement on many fronts that teachers need better models, practices, and frameworks for teaching students from a multitude of backgrounds, especially if the students represent cultures and social classes that are different from the teacher's.

Second, children from poverty are being identified and labeled with grossly overgeneralized, deficit-laden characteristics that put them at risk of being viewed as less capable, less cultured, and less worthy as learners. While we do not want to underplay the stresses on some children who live in poverty, we do want to advocate for a perspective that sees these children and their families as historied and cultural beings, full persons with dreams and aspirations of success, with abilities to use language with sophistication, and with intelligences that may be underappreciated in schools as institutions.

If we want to help teachers develop awareness and pedagogies that are sensitive to children who live in poverty, we must first challenge the misinformation that is being disseminated and set a new course. This new direction should have three key features: 1) an emphasis on children's competency, 2) a focus on the teacher's cultural identity, and 3) a professional development model based in ongoing collaborative work among teachers.

Rejecting Stereotypes of the Poor

Ruby Payne (with her company, aha! Process Inc.) is perhaps the most visible educator providing materials and workshops about poverty for teachers and principals. Payne has been featured in high-profile news outlets, including the *New York Times* (Tough 2007) and *Education Week* (Keller 2006), and her materials are used in teacher education programs across the country (Osei-Kofi 2005). According to her web site, Payne and her certified trainers, consultants, and employees conduct 800 to 1,000 workshops and seminars a year in the U.S. and Canada; and the book with which she launched her business, *A Framework for Understanding Poverty* (2005; hereafter, *Framework*), now in its 4th edition, has sold over a million copies.

Reviewers of Payne's *Framework* have noted the ways that she stereotypes people living in poverty (Gorski 2006; Ng and Rury 2006; Osei-Kofi 2005). In their recent, painstaking content analysis of *Framework*, Bomer et al. (2008) found that Payne's claims about the poor are unsubstantiated in her text and contradicted by mountains of research in education, anthropology, sociology, and related fields. They conclude that Payne's work is a classic example of "deficit thinking," where "students who struggle or fail in school do so because of their own internal deficits or deficiencies"(Discussion section, para. 1).

To give you a sense of this stereotyping, we share the complete list of what Payne calls "behaviors related to poverty." According to Payne, poor children:

- Laugh when disciplined as a "way to save face in matriarchal poverty";
- Argue loudly with the teacher;
- Make angry responses;
- Make inappropriate or vulgar comments;
- Physically fight because they "do not have language or belief system to use conflict resolution";
- Always have their hands on someone else;
- Cannot follow directions because "little procedural memory is used in poverty" and "sequence is not used or valued";
- Are extremely disorganized because "planning, scheduling, or prioritizing skills" are "not taught in poverty";
- Complete only part of a task because they have "no procedural self-talk" and "do not 'see' the whole task";
- Are disrespectful to the teacher because they "may not know any adults worthy of respect";
- Harm other students, verbally or physically;
- Cheat or steal because of "weak support system, weak role models/emotional resources"; and
- Talk incessantly because "poverty is very participatory" (pp. 79–80).

Gorski (2006) argues that Payne is participating in what Herbert Gans (1995) has called the "war against the poor." That is, even as Payne advertises herself as seeking to help people living in poverty, she actually contributes to the larger effort to persuade society that the poor are undeserving of society's help. In this list and elsewhere, Payne evokes the Reagan-era "black welfare queen," she asserts that poor people cheat and steal, and she claims the poor just are not organized enough to make things work out for themselves or their children. As Bomer et al. put it:

> Payne repeatedly selects elements of daily life that represent the lives of the poor as characterized by violence, depravity, and criminality. Payne's selective representations are negative stereotypes that essentialize poor people as immoral, violent, and socially deficient. These representations do not account for the majority of low-income people, who work hard, obey the law, and do not exhibit the behaviors and

attitudes that Payne has described. (2008, Immediate Environment of Poor Children section, para. 4)

Finally, even as we read Payne against the backdrop of the current "war against the poor," we must also recognize that she is dredging up older stereotypes. According to Payne, the poor have inadequate language and inadequate brains, they fight, they're loud. In the Western tradition, to be human is to use your head. Payne is defining the poor in terms of their body and lack of cognitive power.

Children's Competence

But, if not Payne's *Framework,* then what? How can school districts address issues of poverty? Based on the prevailing recommendations of the best minds in teacher development, we begin with the assumption that professional development opportunities should allow teachers sustained time to work together on substantive and important issues. Rather than dwelling on children's perceived deficits, we believe teachers should be encouraged to focus instead on children's competence as cultural and intellectual people.

If, indeed, we recognize students who have lived a life in poverty as having different cultural norms (through language, custom, tradition, and experience) than those expected in a school classroom, then drawing on well-theorized and empirically grounded work that investigates culture can be particularly helpful to classroom teachers. Several scholars have written about culturally relevant pedagogy. This work can be foundational to helping educators understand the cultural mismatches that happen in classrooms every day whether the cultural issues are associated with race, ethnicity, life in urban or rural settings, or social class including poverty.

Research on the role of cultural relevance in classroom teaching identifies how students' culture—the values, beliefs, practices, and experiences they bring with them from their homes, communities, and heritage—can be an integral part of a student's successful academic experience when teachers know how to relevantly build on them (Delpit 1995; Ladson-Billings 1994, 1995a, 1995b; Lee 1995). Geneva Gay has argued that "a very different pedagogical paradigm is needed to improve the performance of underachieving students from various ethnic groups—one that teaches *to and through* their personal and cultural strengths . . ." (2000, p. 24). According to Gay, dimensions of culturally responsive teaching include:

- Acknowledging the legitimacy of the cultural heritages of different ethnic groups as content to be taught in the formal curriculum;
- Bridging home and school experiences;
- Finding meaningful connections between academic abstractions and lived sociocultural realities;
- Using a variety of instructional strategies aligned with student learning styles; and
- Incorporating multicultural information, resources, and materials in all the subjects and skills routinely taught in schools.

Within these principles, we see a complex treatment of culture that speaks to the variety of individual realities, rather than viewing culture as a monolithic and static feature of groups of people because they share the same skin color, social class, or country of origin. We also see a complex pedagogy that attends to students' home life, their everyday lived experiences, and the relationship of understanding built between the teacher and students. Culturally responsive teaching is a mindset and way of being in the classroom, rather than a list of techniques and strategies.

For example, work done within a "funds of knowledge" framework (Gonzalez, Moll, and Amanti 2005) offers a practical model for developing professional practice that is culturally relevant and socially responsible to the students' home communities. The approach to professional learning in this work is grounded in action research in the local community. Teachers conduct home visits in quest of understanding and appreciating the lives of the families they serve. By putting the teacher in the position of learner (researcher), the family and community are viewed as resources and assets who have "funds of knowledge" that are integral to the lives of the students but that may not be readily apparent when the child is in the classroom and not surrounded by the family or home culture. Viewing a student's home culture as robust, historical, and worthy stands in stark contrast to deficit models.

When we believe there is value in what a child brings into the classroom from their home culture, we listen for that value and build formal educational experiences on what the student brings with them. Carol Lee (1995) demonstrated how listening to students with a mind toward recognizing intellect and thoughtfulness can translate into productive classroom interactions between teacher and student and among students. In her work, she used a cognitive apprenticeship model in which the invisible complex processes of thinking, comprehension, and problem solving were made visible (Collins, Brown, and Newman 1989). A variety of teaching strategies can be used within a cognitive apprenticeship environment, such as reciprocal teaching, think-alouds during a cognitively demanding task, constructing heuristics, and creating criteria to judge the quality of work with students.

Lee combined the cognitive apprenticeship pedagogies with curriculum materials grounded in the home cultures of students. By doing this, she found that students engaged in sophisticated analyses of the texts they were reading, articulated their understanding in both the academic discourses of the classroom and the traditional styles of their home culture, and attended to each others' ideas.

Teachers' Cultural Identity

Study around such concepts as funds of knowledge will enable teachers to rewrite their often stereotyped views of poor students. But if this is going to work, educators will also need to put themselves under the microscope. What do we, as educators, bring to our work with students living in poverty? What role do we imagine for ourselves?

Usually, when we are concerned about stereotyping, we worry about the functions and effects of stereotypes in relation to those being stereotyped.

Osei-Kofi (2005) thinks that Payne's stereotypes provide the well-meaning educator with a certain "guilty voyeuristic pleasure" as they get to affirm their own normalcy against the "comfortably familiar" image of the poor as pathological. Payne plays on our sense of ourselves as normal, the norm, as well as on our sense of the poor as different, other. Furthermore:

> Based on this depiction of the poor, educators become perfectly situated to take on the role of *middle-class, primarily white, saviors of children in poverty* by being "good" role models, and teaching these children the so-called hidden rules of middle-class. Through the objectification of the poor, educators are implicitly positioned as the true historical subjects with ability to act in creating social change. (Osei-Kofi 2005, p. 370; emphasis added)

Payne offers educators the role of savior. It is an offer we need to reject, and to reject it, we need to bring the same sorts of assumptions and concepts to bear in relation to ourselves that we bring to our rewriting of who we imagine the poor to be. That is, we need to imagine and examine ourselves, as educators and citizens; as complex, cultural, and historical beings; as human actors born into a web of meanings and values of which we are only partially aware and not in complete control.

The current teaching population in the U.S. comprises mostly white, middle-class women. An important starting point for making sense of who we are as educators of students living in poverty is an engagement with the emerging body of work called *critical whiteness studies*. The white historian David Roediger, with his book *The Wages of Whiteness: Race and the Making of the American Working Class* (1991), is often credited with beginning this work. But Roediger always defers and points to people of color as the "nation's keenest students of white consciousness and white behavior" (1998, p. 4). Teacher study groups could begin an important journey of cultural understanding by taking up Roediger's edited volume, *Black on White: Black Writers on What It Means to Be White* (1998).

A second, powerful way into critical whiteness studies is through the work of the Rev. Thandeka, in her *Learning to Be White: Money, Race, and God in America* (2001). Thandeka is interested in making better sense of how white racial identify develops, because she sees religious, educational, and political efforts meant to mobilize white people for social justice failing—failing over and over again. She believes these programs are failing, in part, because they are based on an inadequate concept of who white people are and how they got that way. Thandeka presents a fascinating account of the development of white racial identity as grounded in how both race and social class have played out and continue to play out in U.S. society. Hers is a story both devastating and hopeful—and generative. We have used Thandeka's work in our education courses, and it has enabled amazing examinations of self in relation to others by future and practicing teachers and activists.

If, as Gramsci thought, the "starting point of critical elaboration is . . . 'knowing thyself' as a product of the historical process to date which has deposited in you an infinity of traces, without leaving an inventory" (1971,

p. 324), then we need to create inventories, understand traces, so that we might do critical and creative work on ourselves, in preparation for and as part of our critical and creative work with our students. The engagement with critical whiteness studies by teacher study groups is an important component of re-imagining ourselves as educators and our relationships to students living in poverty.

Becoming Teachers of Children from Poverty

Living in poverty lies far outside of the realm of most teachers' experience. Our best guess as to why Payne's work is so popular is that she is comforting to white people, to white educators. She offers simple and simplistic solutions to complex problems; she allows white educators to think of themselves as normal and even saviors of poor pathological children and their parents. When we think about America and its sacred belief that all people are created equal, and then we are perhaps troubled by the massive and increasing inequalities we see all around us, Payne comforts us with her soothing repetitions of centuries-old stereotypes of the poor. We can then get on with being white and privileged and free from responsibility for the well-being of our neighbors and fellow citizens.

While we know teachers crave new ideas for teaching and want access to "ideas that work," we also know teaching is a complex and uncertain endeavor. To imagine that we can create a list of strategies and assign them to whole groups of children because of who their parents are or where they live is a gross over-simplification of what it means to teach or to be a teacher. As teachers begin to embrace issues of social class differences among their students and themselves, pedagogical shifts will need to be more than the addition of a few technical strategies.

Teachers will need support in developing a better understanding of themselves and their own worldviews in order to better engage with children who bring different experiences, cultures, values, and ways of understanding the world into the classroom. New ways of being in the classroom must be taken up by teachers. Part of that being is to be present in the moment with students, while listening to them and respecting their ideas. Part of that being is a willingness to ask students questions, to get to know them as thinkers, as children, and as people. And part of that being is patience and grace in response to uncertainty, in response to the everyday classroom's pervasive demands for wise decisions and action.

References

Bomer, Randy, Joel E. Dworin, Laura May, and Peggy Semingson. "Miseducating Teachers About the Poor: A Critical Analysis of Ruby Payne's Claims About Poverty." *Teachers College Record* 110, no. 12 (2008), ... ID Number: 14591.

Collins, Allan, John S. Brown, and Susan E. Newman. "Cognitive Apprenticeship: Teaching the Crafts of Reading, Writing, and Mathematics." In *Knowing, Learning, and Instruction: Essays in Honor of Robert Glaser,* ed. Robert Glaser and Lauren. B. Resnick. Hillsdale, N.J.: Lawrence Erlbaum Associates, 1989.

Delpit, Lisa. *Other People's Children.* New York: New Press, 1995.

Gans, Herbert. *The War Against the Poor: The Underclass and Antipoverty Policy.* New York: Basic Books, 1995.

Gay, Geneva. *Culturally Responsive Teaching: Theory, Research, and Practice.* New York: Teachers College Press, 2000.

Gonzalez, Norma, Luis C. Moll, and Cathy Amanti, eds. *Funds of Knowledge: Theorizing Practices in Households, Communities, and Classrooms.* Mahwah, N.J.: Lawrence Erlbaum Associates, 2005.

Gorski, Paul. "Savage Unrealities." *Rethinking Schools* 21, no. 2 (2006): 16–19.

Gramsci, Antonio. *Selections from the Prison Notebooks.* New York: International Publishers, 1971.

Keller, Bess. "Payne's Pursuit." *Education Week,* May 3, 2006, pp. 30–32.

Ladson-Billings, Gloria. *The Dreamkeepers: Successful Teaching for African American Students.* San Francisco: Jossey-Bass, 1994.

Ladson-Billings, Gloria. "But That's Just Good Teaching! The Case for Culturally Relevant Pedagogy." *Theory into Practice* 34 (Summer 1995): 159–165. a

Ladson-Billings, Gloria. "Toward a Theory of Culturally Relevant Pedagogy." *American Educational Research Journal* 32 (Autumn 1995): 465–491. b

Lee, Carol D. "A Culturally Based Cognitive Apprenticeship: Teaching African American High School Students Skills in Literary Interpretation." *Reading Research Quarterly* 30, no. 4 (1995): 608–630.

Ng, Jennifer C., and John Rury. "Poverty and Education: A Critical Analysis of the Ruby Payne Phenomenon." *Teachers College Record* (July 2006). . . .

Osei-Kofi, Nana. "Pathologizing the Poor: A Framework for Understanding Ruby Payne's Work." *Equity and Excellence in Education* 38 (2005): 367–375.

Payne, Ruby. *A Framework for Understanding Poverty,* 4th ed. Highlands, Texas: aha! Process, 2005.

Roediger, David R. *The Wages of Whiteness: Race and the Making of the American Working Class.* London: Verso, 1991.

Roediger, David R., ed. *Black on White: Black Writers on What It Means to Be White.* New York: Random House, 1998.

Thandeka. *Learning to Be White: Money, Race, and God in America.* New York: Continuum, 2001.

Tough, Paul. "The Class-Consciousness Raiser." *New York Times Magazine,* June 10, 2007. . . .

POSTSCRIPT

Does a "Deficit Model" Serve Poor Children Well?

Closing the achievement gaps among racial, ethnic, and socioeconomic groups in America remains a major problem in education and in society in general. In their 2003 book, *No Excuses: Closing the Racial Gap in Learning*, Abigail and Stephan Thernstrom claim that the essence of disadvantage has little to do with poverty or class or school funding. The real problem, they suggest, lies in a combination of school inertia, a lack of high standards, and the learning-resistant cultures that some students come from. Psychiatrist James P. Comer puts another slant on the problem in *Leave No Child Behind* (2004), stating that because many poor children are not "immersed in positive and protective family and community networks many will embrace harmful non-mainstream habits and styles as 'our culture.' And because the habits do not promote school and life success, their involvement is not just an adolescent interlude but often a one-way ticket to marginality."

David Whitman, author of *Sweating the Small Stuff: Inner-City Schools and the New Paternalism* (2008), links current efforts to the historical attempt to "civilize" Native Americans and "Americanize" immigrants. In his article, "An Appeal to Authority" in *Education Next* (Fall 2008), Whitman examines urban schools dominated by paternalistic policies, including those of the KIPP and SEED programs, which assume that disadvantaged students do best when structure and expectations are crystal clear and consistent. A contrasting view is put forth by Stanley Pogrow in "Accelerate the Learning of 4th and 5th Graders Born into Poverty," *Phi Delta Kappan* (February 2009). He suggests that disadvantaged students need to develop a sense of understanding and a heightened level of engagement to enable them to fully participate in the learning process.

In "Get Real: Here's the Boost That Poor Children, Their Teachers, and Their Schools Really Need," *American Educator* (Spring 2007), Antonia Cortese advocates a sweeping program that includes emphasis on teacher quality in poverty areas, developing a culture of respectful student behavior, providing a knowledge-rich core curriculum, and delivering additional supports and resources to the neediest students.

Further perspectives may be found in "Class and the Classroom," *American School Board Journal* (October 2004) by Richard Rothstein; Janice E. Hale's "How Schools Shortchange African-American Children," *Educational Leadership* (November 2004); and in a hard-hitting 2006 book by journalist Juan Williams titled *Enough: The Phony Leaders, Dead-end Movements, and Culture of Failure That Are Undermining Black America—And What We Can Do About It.*

ISSUE 10

Should "Public Schooling" Be Redefined?

YES: Frederick M. Hess, from "What Is a 'Public School?' Principles for a New Century," *Phi Delta Kappan* (February 2004)

NO: Linda Nathan et al., from "A Response to Frederick Hess," *Phi Delta Kappan* (February 2004)

ISSUE SUMMARY

YES: Frederick M. Hess, a resident scholar at the American Enterprise Institute, advocates a broadening of the definition of "public schooling" in light of recent developments such as vouchers, charter schools, and home schooling.

NO: Linda Nathan, Joe Nathan, Ray Bacchetti, and Evans Clinchy express a variety of concerns about the conceptual expansion that Hess proposes.

The original public school crusade, led by Massachusetts education official Horace Mann (1796–1859) and other activists, built on the growing sentiment among citizens, politicians, and business leaders that public schools were needed to deal with the increase in immigration, urbanization, and industrialism, as well as to bind together the American population and to prepare everyone for participatory democracy. For the most part, the right of the government to compel school attendance, dating from Massachusetts legislation in 1852, went unchallenged, although Catholics formed their own private school system in reaction to the predominant Protestantism of public schools in certain areas. In the 1920s there were efforts to eliminate all alternatives to government-run public schools to ensure attendance compliance and curricular standardization. Such an effort in Oregon was challenged in court, and the U.S. Supreme Court ultimately ruled, in *Pierce v. Society of Sisters* (1925), that such legislation unreasonably interferes with parental rights. While this ruling preserved the private school option, it did not alter the governmental prerogative to compel school attendance.

This governmental authority met with sharp criticism from liberal writers in the 1950s and beyond, in works such as Paul Goodman's *Compulsory*

Mis-education (1964), Ivan Illich's *Deschooling Society* (1971), John Holt's *Instead of Education* (1976), and John Taylor Gatto's *Dumbing Us Down: The Hidden Curriculum of Compulsory Schooling* (1992). Gatto condemned the public school system for its emphasis on obedience and subordination rather than the unleashing of the intellectual and creative powers of the individual. Since the 1980s, a parallel attack has come from conservatives, such as William J. Bennett, E. D. Hirsch, Jr., Chester E. Finn, Jr., Charles J. Sykes, Grover Norquist, and Cal Thomas, and conservative groups, such as Parents for School Choice, the Cato Institute, and the Alliance for Separation of School and State. Building on the findings of the 1983 *A Nation at Risk* report, a significant segment of the American population continues to express disdain for the public education "establishment" (the U. S. Department of Education, the National Education Association, and teacher-training institutions) for its inability or unwillingness to improve public school performance. Their basic contention is that only choice-driven competition will bring about lasting improvement. William J. Bennett, in "A Nation Still at Risk," *Policy Review* (July/August 1998), has stated that although choices are spreading, charter schools are proliferating, privately managed public schools have long waiting lists, and home schooling is expanding, "the elephant still has most of the power." He concludes that "we must never again assume that the education system will respond to good advice. It will change only when power relationships change, particularly when all parents gain the power to decide where their children go to school."

Educator-reformer Deborah Meier, in "The Road to Trust," *American School Board Journal* (September 2003), argues that we must make public education feel like a public enterprise again. Hers is a call for the rebuilding of trust between public schools and the communities they directly serve. "Our school boards need to turn their eyes to their constituencies—not just to following the dictates of state and federal government micromanagers."

In the following articles, Frederick M. Hess makes the case that the time has come for a reconception of "public schooling" while four prominent educators challenge what they perceive to be an unproductive assault on public schooling.

YES

Frederick M. Hess

What Is a 'Public School?' Principles for a New Century

The phrase "public schooling" has become more a rhetorical device than a useful guide to policy. As our world evolves, so too must our conception of what "public" means. James Coleman eloquently made this point more than two decades ago, implying a responsibility to periodically reappraise our assumptions as to what constitutes "public schooling."[1] In a world where charter schooling, distance education, tuition tax credits, and other recent developments no longer fit neatly into our conventional mental boxes, it is clearly time for such an effort. Nonetheless, rather than receiving the requisite consideration, "public schooling" has served as a flag around which critics of these various reforms can rally. It is because the phrase resonates so powerfully that critics of proposals like charter schooling, voucher programs, and rethinking teacher licensure have at times abandoned substantive debate in order to attack such measures as "anti-public schooling."[2]

Those of us committed to the promise of public education are obliged to see that the ideal does not become a tool of vested interests. The perception that public schooling has strayed from its purpose and been captured by self-interested parties has fueled lacerating critiques in recent years. Such critics as Andrew Coulson and Douglas Dewey find a growing audience when they suggest that the ideal of public schooling itself is nothing more than a call to publicly subsidize the private agendas of bureaucrats, education school professors, union officials, and leftist activists.[3] While I believe such attacks are misguided, answering them effectively demands that we discern what it is that makes schooling public and accept diverse arrangements that are consistent with those tenets. Otherwise, growing numbers of reformers may come to regard public schooling as a politicized obstacle rather than a shared ideal.

While I do not aim to provide a precise answer as to what public schooling should mean in the early 21st century, I will argue that public schools are broadly defined by their commitment to preparing students to be productive members of a social order, aware of their societal responsibilities, and respectful of constitutional strictures; that such schools cannot deny access to students for reasons unrelated to their educational focus; and that the system of public schools available in any community must provide an appropriate placement for each student. In short, I suggest that it is appropriate to adopt a much more

From *Phi Delta Kappan,* February 2004, pp. 584–590. Copyright © 2004 by Phi Delta Kappan. Reprinted by permission of Phi Delta Kappan and Frederick M. Hess.

expansive notion of public schooling than the one the education community holds today.

What Isn't Public?

Traditionally, "public schools" are deemed to be those directly accountable to elected officials or funded by tax dollars.[4] As a practical matter, such definitions are not very useful, largely because there are conventional "public" schools that do not fit within these definitions, while there are "private" providers that do.

We generally regard as "public schools" those in which policy making and oversight are the responsibility of governmental bodies, such as a local school board. Nongovernmental providers of educational services, such as independent schools or educational management organizations (EMOs), are labeled "nonpublic." The distinction is whether a formal political body is in charge, since these officials are accountable by election or appointment to the larger voting "public."

There are two particular problems here. First, how "hands on" must the government be for us to regard a service as publicly provided? The National Aeronautics and Space Administration, the Environmental Protection Agency, the U.S. Department of Education, and most other state, federal, and local government agencies contract with for-profit firms for support, to provide services, and to evaluate service delivery. Yet we tend to regard the services as "public" because they were initiated in response to a public directive and are monitored by public officials. It is not clear when government-directed activity ceases to be public. For instance, if a for-profit company manages a district school, is the school less public than it was when it purchased its texts from a for-profit textbook publisher and its professional development from a private consultant?

A second approach to defining "public" focuses on inputs. By this metric, any activity that involves government funds is public because it involves the expenditure of tax dollars. However, this distinction is more nebulous than we sometimes suppose. For instance, schools in the Milwaukee voucher program receive Wisconsin tax dollars. Does this mean that voucher schools ought to be regarded as de facto public schools? Similarly, Wisconsin dairy farmers receive federal subsidies. Does this make their farms public enterprises?

A particular complication is that many traditional public schools charge families money. For instance, during 2002–03, the families of more than 2,300 Indiana students were paying tuition of as much as $6,000 to enroll their children in a public school in another district. Public schools routinely charge fees to families that participate in interdistrict public choice plans, and they frequently charge families fees if a child participates in extracurricular activities. Would proponents of a revenue-based definition suggest that such practices mean that these schools are no longer "public"?

A third approach, famously advanced by John Dewey, the esteemed champion of "public" education, recognizes that private institutions may serve public ends and that public institutions may fail to do so.[5] Such a recognition suggests that public schools are those that serve public ends, regardless of the monitoring arrangements or revenue sources. This approach is ultimately problematic, however, because we do *not* have clear agreement on appropriate public purposes. I'll have more to say on this point shortly.

What Is Public Schooling?

Previously, I have posed five questions to guide our efforts to bring more precision to our understanding of "public schooling."[6] Here, I offer these questions as a way to sketch principles that may help shape a contemporary conception of "public schooling."

What are the purposes of public schooling? Schooling entails both public and private purposes, though we often fail to note the degree to which the private benefits may serve the public interest. In particular, academic learning serves the individual and also the needs of the state. Successful democratic communities require a high level of literacy and numeracy and are anchored by the knowledge and the good sense of the population. Citizens who lack these skills are less likely to contribute effectively to the well-being of their communities and more likely to be a drain on public resources. Therefore, in a real sense, any school that helps children master reading, writing, mathematics, and other essential content is already advancing some significant public purposes.[7] It is troubling that prominent educational thinkers, including Frank Smith, Susan Ohanian, Deborah Meier, and Alfie Kohn, have rejected this fundamental premise and encouraged "public schools" to promote preferred social values even at the expense of basic academic mastery.[8]

More fundamentally, there are two distinct ways to comprehend the larger public purposes of education. One suggests that schools serve a public interest that transcends the needs of individuals. This line of thought, understood by Rousseau as the "general will," can be traced to Plato's conviction that nations need a far-sighted leader to determine their true interests, despite the shortsighted preferences of the mob. A second way of thinking about the public purposes of education accepts the classically "liberal" understanding of the public interest as the sum of the interests of individual citizens and rejects the idea of a transcendent general will. This pragmatic stance helped shape American public institutions that protect citizens from tyrannical majorities and overreaching public officials.

While neither perspective is necessarily "correct," our government of limited powers and separate branches leans heavily toward the more modest dictates of liberalism. Despite our tendency to suffuse education with the sweeping rhetoric of a disembodied national interest, our freedoms are secured by a system designed to resist such imperial visions.

The "public" components of schooling include the responsibility for teaching the principles, habits, and obligations of citizenship. While schools of education typically interpret this to mean that educators should preach "tolerance" or affirm "diversity," a firmer foundation for citizenship education would focus on respect for law, process, and individual rights. The problem with phrases like "tolerance" and "diversity" is that they are umbrella terms with multiple interpretations. When we try to define them more precisely—in policy or practice—it becomes clear that we must privilege some values at the expense of others. For instance, one can plausibly argue that tolerant citizens should respectfully hear out a radical Muslim calling for jihad against the U.S. or that tolerance extends only to legalistic protection and leaves one free to express social opprobrium. If educators promote the former, as their professional community generally advises, they have adopted a particular normative view that is at odds with that held by a large segment of the public.

Promoting any one particular conception of tolerance does not make schools more "public." In a liberal society, uniformly teaching students to accept teen pregnancy or homosexuality as normal and morally unobjectionable represents a jarring absolutism amidst profound moral disagreement.

Nonetheless, many traditional "public" schools (such as members of the Coalition of Essential Schools) today explicitly promote a particular world view and endorse a particular social ethos. In advancing "meaningful questions," for instance, faculty members at these schools often promote partisan attitudes toward American foreign policy, the propriety of affirmative action, or the morality of redistributive social policies. Faculty members in these schools can protest that they have no agenda other than cultivating critical inquiry, but observation of classrooms or perusal of curricular materials makes clear that most of these schools are not neutral on the larger substantive questions. This poses an ethical problem in a pluralist society where the parents of many students may reject the public educators' beliefs and where the educators have never been clearly empowered to stamp out "improper" thoughts.

Public schools should teach children the essential skills and knowledge that make for productive citizens, teach them to respect our constitutional order, and instruct them in the framework of rights and obligations that secure our democracy and protect our liberty. Any school that does so should be regarded as serving public purposes.

How should we apportion responsibility between families and public schools? The notion that schools can or should serve as a "corrective" against the family was first promulgated in the early 19th century by reformers who viewed the influx of immigrants as a threat to democratic processes and American norms. In the years since, encouraged by such thinkers as George Counts, Paulo Freire, Michael Apple, Peter McLaren, and Amy Gutmann, educational thinkers have unapologetically called for schooling to free students from the yoke of their family's provincial understandings.

The problem is that this conception of the "public interest" rests uneasily alongside America's pluralist traditions. American political thought, dating back to Madison's pragmatic embrace of "faction," has presumed that our various prejudices and biases can constructively counter one another, so long as the larger constitutional order and its attendant protections check our worst impulses.

The notion that schools are more "public" when they work harder to stamp out familial views and impress children with socially approved beliefs is one that ought to give pause to any civil libertarian or pluralist. Such schools are more attuned to the public purposes of a totalitarian regime than those of a democratic one. While a democratic nation can reasonably settle upon a range of state/family relationships, there is no reason to imagine that a regime that more heavily privileges the state is more "public." The relative "publicness" of education is not enhanced by having schools intrude more forcefully into the familial sphere.

Who should be permitted to provide public schooling? Given publicly determined purposes, it is not clear that public schooling needs to impose restrictions on who may provide services. There is no reason why for-profit or religious providers, in particular, ought to be regarded as suspect.

While traditional public schools have always dealt with for-profit providers of textbooks, teaching supplies, professional development, and so on, profit-seeking ventures have recently emerged as increasingly significant players in reform efforts. For instance, the for-profit, publicly held company Edison Schools is today managing scores of traditional district schools across the nation. Yet these are still regarded as "public" schools. In fact, Edison is managing the summer school programs, including curricula and personnel, for more than 70 public school *districts*. Yet those communities continue to regard summer school as public schooling.

Such arrangements seem to run afoul of our conventional use of the term "public," but the conflict is readily resolved when we recognize that all public agencies, including public hospitals and public transit systems, routinely harness the services of for-profit firms. Just as a public university is not thought to lose its public status merely because portions of it enter into for-profit ventures with regard to patents or athletics, so the entry of for-profit providers into a K–12 public school does not necessarily change the institution's fundamental nature. What matters in public higher education is whether the for-profit unit is controlled and overseen by those entrusted with the university's larger public mission. What matters in public schooling is whether profit seekers are hired to serve public ends and are monitored by public officials.

The status of religious providers has raised great concern among such groups as People for the American Way and the Center on Education Policy. However, the nation's early efforts to provide public education relied heavily upon local church officials to manage public funds, to provide a school facility, and to arrange the logistics of local schooling. It was not until the anti-Catholic fervor of the mid- and late-19th century that states distanced themselves from religious schooling. It was not until the mid-20th century that advocacy groups such as the American Civil Liberties Union pushed the remnants of religion out of state-run schools.

In recent decades, the U.S. Supreme Court has made clear that the push for a "wall of separation" had overreached and run afoul of First Amendment language protecting the "free exercise" of religion. Moreover, contemporary America has continued to evolve since the anti-Catholic zeal of the 19th century and the anti-religious intellectualism of the mid-20th century. Those conflicts were of a particular time and place. Today, church officials have less local sway and lack the unquestioned authority they once held, while they are more integrated into secular society. Just as some onetime opponents of single-sex schools can now, because of changes in the larger social order, imagine such schools serving the public interest, so too we should not reflexively shrink from viewing religious schools in a similar light. In most industrial democracies, including such nations as Canada, France, and the Netherlands, religious schools operate as part of the public system and are funded and regulated accordingly.

What obligations should public schools have to ensure opportunity for all students? We have never imagined that providing opportunity to all students means treating all students identically. The existence of magnet schools, special education, gifted classes, and exam schools makes it clear that we deem it appropriate for schools to select some children and exclude others in order to provide desirable academic environments. Our traditional school districts have never sought to ensure that every school or classroom should serve a random cross-section of children, only that systems as a whole should appropriately serve all children.

Given the tension between families who want their child schooled in an optimal environment and public officials who must construct systems that address competing needs, the principle that individual schools can exclude children but that systems cannot is both sensible and morally sound. That said, this principle does mean that some children will not attend school with the peers their parents might prefer.

The dilemma this presents is that no solitary good school can serve all the children who might wish to attend and that randomly admitting students may impede a school's effectiveness. Demanding that a science magnet school accept students with minimal science accomplishments or that any traditional school accept a habitually violent student threatens the ability of each school to accomplish its basic purposes. This is clearly not in the public interest. The same is true when a constructivist school is required to admit students from families who staunchly prefer back-to-basics instruction and will agitate for the curricula and pedagogy they prefer. In such cases, allowing schools to selectively admit students is consistent with the public interest—so long as the process furthers a legitimate educational purpose and the student has access to an appropriate alternative setting. Such publicly acceptable exclusion must be pursued for some reasonable educational purpose, and this creates a gray area that must be monitored. However, the need to patrol this area does not require that the practice be preemptively prohibited.

Moreover, self-selected or homogeneous communities are not necessarily less public than others. For instance, no one suggests that the University of Wyoming is less public than the University of Texas, though it is less geographically and ethnically representative of the nation. It has never been suggested that elections in San Francisco or Gopher Springs, West Virginia, would be more public if the communities included more residents who had not chosen to live there or whose views better reflected national norms. Nor has it been suggested that selective public institutions, such as the University of Michigan, are less public than are community colleges, even though they are selective about whom they admit. Moreover, there is always greater homogeneity in self-selected communities, such as magnet schools, as they attract educators and families who share certain views. None of this has been thought to undermine their essential "publicness."

Even champions of "public education," such as Deborah Meier and Ted Sizer, argue that this shared sense of commitment helps cultivate a participatory and democratic ethos in self-selected schools. In other words, heightened familial involvement tends to make self-selected schools more participatory and democratic. Kneeling before the false gods of heterogeneity or nonselectivity undermines our ability to forge participatory or effective schools without making schools commensurately more "public."

Nowhere, after all, does the availability of a "public service" imply that we get to choose our fellow users. In every field—whether public medicine, public transportation, or public higher education—the term "public" implies our right to a service, not our right to have buses serve a particular route or to have a university cohort configured to our preferences. Even though such considerations influence the quality of the service, the need for public providers to juggle the requirements of all the individuals they must serve necessarily means that each member of the public cannot necessarily receive the service in the manner he or she would ultimately prefer. "Public schooling" implies an obligation to ensure that all students are appropriately served, not that every school is open to all comers.

What parts of public schooling are public? Debates about publicness focus on the classroom teaching and learning that is central to all schools. Maintenance, accounting, payroll, and food services are quite removed from the public purposes of education discussed above. Even though these peripheral services may take place in the same facility as teaching and learning, their execution does not meaningfully affect the "publicness" of schooling. Rather, we understand that it is sufficient to have ancillary services provided in a manner that is consistent with the wishes of a public education provider. For example, federal courts and state legislatures are indisputably public institutions, yet they frequently procure supplies, services, and personnel from privately run, for-profit enterprises. We properly regard these institutions as public because of their core purposes, not because of the manner in which they arrange their logistics.

Today's 'Public' Schools Often Aren't

Given the haphazard notion of public schooling that predominates today, it comes as little surprise that we offer contemporary educators little guidance in serving the public interest. This poses obvious problems, given that employment as an educator doesn't necessarily grant enhanced moral wisdom or personal virtue. If schools are to serve as places where educators advance purposes and cultivate virtues that they happen to prefer, it is not clear in what sense schools are serving "public purposes."

Blindly hoping that educators have internalized shared public purposes, we empower individuals to proselytize under the banner of "public schooling." This state of affairs has long been endorsed by influential educational theorists like George Counts, Paulo Freire, Henry Giroux, and Nel Noddings, who argue that teachers have a charge to use their classrooms to promote personal visions of social change, regardless of the broader public's beliefs. For these thinkers, "public schooling" ironically implies a community obligation to support schools for the private purposes of educators. The problem is that public institutions are not personal playthings. Just as it is unethical for a judge to disregard the law and instead rule on the basis of personal whimsy, so it is inappropriate for public school teachers to use their office to impose personal views upon a captive audience.

One appropriate public response is to specify public purposes and to demand that teachers reflect them, though we are reasonably cautious about adopting such an intrusive course. To the extent that explicit direction is absent, however, educators are left to their own devices. In such a case, our liberal tradition would recommend that we not subject children to the views of educators at an assigned school but allow families to avail themselves of a range of schools with diverse perspectives, so long as each teaches respect for our democratic and liberal tradition.

Conclusion

Today, our system of "public schooling" does little to ensure that our schools serve public purposes, while permitting some educators to use a publicly provided forum to promote their personal beliefs. Meanwhile, hiding behind the phrase's hallowed skirts are partisans who furiously attack any innovation that threatens their interests or beliefs.

There are many ways to provide legitimate public education. A restrictive state might tightly regulate school assignment, operations, and content, while another state might impose little regulation. However, there is no reason to regard the schools in the one state as more "public" than those in the other. The "publicness" of a school does not depend on class size, the use of certified teachers, rules governing employee termination, or the rest of the procedural apparatus that ensnares traditional district schools. The fact that public officials have the right to require public schools to comply with certain standards does not mean that schools subjected to more intrusive standards are somehow more public. The inclusion of religious schools in European systems, for instance, has been accompanied by intensive regulation of curricula and policy. Regulation on that order is not desirable, nor is it necessary for schools to operate as part of a public system; it is merely an operational choice made by officials in these relatively bureaucratic nations.

As opportunities to deliver, structure, and practice education evolve, it is periodically necessary to revisit assumptions about what constitutes public schooling. The ideology and institutional self-interest that infuse the dominant current conception have fueled withering attacks on the very legitimacy of public schooling itself. Failure to address this impoverished status quo will increasingly offer critics cause to challenge the purpose and justification of public education. Maintaining and strengthening our commitment to public schooling requires that we rededicate ourselves to essential principles of opportunity, liberal democracy, and public benefit, while freeing ourselves from political demands and historic happenstance.

In an age when social and technological change have made possible new approaches to teaching and learning, pinched renderings of "public schooling" have grown untenable and counterproductive. They stifle creative efforts, confuse debates, and divert attention from more useful questions. A more expansive conception is truer to our traditions, more likely to foster shared values, and better suited to the challenges of the new century.

Notes

1. James Coleman, "Public Schools, Private Schools, and the Public Interest," *Public Interest,* Summer 1981, pp. 19–30. See also idem, "Quality and Equality in American Education," *Phi Delta Kappan,* November 1981, pp. 159–64.

2. For the best empirical examination of the scope and nature of the "public school ideology," see Terry Moe, *Schools, Vouchers, and the American Public* (Washington, D.C.: Brookings, 2001).

3. See Andrew Coulson, *Market Education: The Unknown History* (New Brunswick, N.J.: Transaction Publishers, 1999); and Douglas Dewey, "An Echo, Not a Choice: School Vouchers Repeat the Error of Public Education," *Policy Review,* November/December 1996. . . .

4. See Frederick M. Hess, "Making Sense of the 'Public' in Public Education," unpublished paper, Progressive Policy Institute, Washington, D.C., 2002.

5. John Dewey, *The Public and Its Problems* (1927; reprint, Athens: Ohio University Press, 1954).

6. See Frederick M. Hess, "What Is 'Public' About Public Education?," *Education Week,* 8 January 2003, p. 56.

7. An extended discussion of this point can be found in Paul T. Hill, "What Is Public About Public Education?," in Terry Moe, ed., *A Primer on America's Schools* (Stanford, Calif.: Hoover Institution, 2001), pp. 285–316.

8. Frank Smith, "Overselling Literacy," *Phi Delta Kappan,* January 1989, pp. 353–59; Alfie Kohn, *No Contest: The Case Against Competition* (Boston: Houghton Mifflin, 1986); Susan Ohanian, "Capitalism, Calculus, and Conscience," *Phi Delta Kappan,* June 2003, pp. 736–47; and Deborah Meier, "Educating a Democracy," in idem, ed., *Will Standards Save Public Education?* (Boston: Beacon Press, 2000).

A Response to Frederick Hess

Linda Nathan, The Larger Purpose of Public Schools

At times I want to cheer for Frederick Hess's words in "What Is a 'Public School'? Principles for a New Century." How true it is that many reformers "regard public schooling as a politicized obstacle rather than a shared ideal." How true that "those of us committed to the promise of public education are obliged to see that the idea does not become a tool of vested interests."

Yet there is also something chilling about his article that stops the cheer in my throat. His use of innuendo in place of evidence, his sloppy logic, and his attacks on some of the most effective public school reformers—painting them as the enemy—suggest that his real agenda is not strengthening public education but privatizing it through vouchers and for-profit takeover schemes.

Hess's labored analysis obscures a simple fact: public schools have a larger and more democratic purpose than private and parochial schools (although this is not to say that these schools contribute nothing to public life). Public school systems are open to everyone regardless of disability, wealth, status, race, or religion. Private and parochial schools are not. While some are more open than others, they can have entrance exams and can explicitly exclude students with disabilities or those who otherwise don't fit a preferred profile. And of course they can also exclude those who can't pay. They can expel students who cause trouble, at their sole discretion, without recourse.

Hess himself acknowledges this core principle of universal access, conceding that public schooling "implies an obligation to ensure that all students are appropriately served." But he seems indifferent to the inequities inherent in his "more expansive" notion of what makes a school public.

Hess makes a false analogy when he equates schools that buy textbooks from for-profit companies with schools that are managed by for-profit firms. Basic educational decisions should be made by citizens of the local school community—not by distant shareholders looking only at a corporate balance sheet. (It's ironic that Hess picks as his exemplar Edison Schools, Inc., which sold off the textbooks, computers, lab supplies, and musical instruments of the Philadelphia public schools it had been hired to manage just days before school was to open in 2002 in order to pay down the company's mounting debt.)

Hess objects to teaching "tolerance" and affirming "diversity" because, he says, these words are open to multiple interpretations. Then he states that "public schools should teach children the essential skills and knowledge that make for productive citizens" and "teach them to respect our constitutional order," as if these were absolute truths *not* open to interpretation. The example of tolerance he cites, wherein a radical Muslim is calling for jihad, slyly exploits a hot-button issue to imply that the "professional community" of educators condones terrorism. Similarly, he smears the notion of defending tolerance as "uniformly teaching students to accept teen pregnancy as normal" and implies that liberals equate these activities with their definition of "public schooling." Nonsense.

His attack on Deborah Meier, Alfie Kohn, and others is equally baseless. It's the classic straw man fallacy: he attributes a position to them—that they oppose the teaching of basic academic mastery in favor of promoting "preferred social values"—that they have in fact never espoused. Meier's argument, with which Hess is surely familiar, is that such a tradeoff is unnecessary and that strong academic habits and mastery of literacy are essential and are furthered by an intellectually open and challenging spirit of inquiry.

The Coalition of Essential Schools, another of Hess's targets, gets similar treatment. Without offering a single example or other evidence of any kind, he asserts that faculty members at Coalition schools routinely promote partisan political views and are determined to "stamp out 'improper' thoughts." Of course, he's right that some teachers and schools—including many private and religious schools—do have a "party line," whether they're conscious of it or not. But he wants to have it both ways. While he attacks Coalition teachers for promoting values he dislikes, he argues at the same time that there should be choice in education so that parents can select schools that reflect their values.

Hess's argument with regard to the personal views and political leanings of educators is simply a red herring. The underlying issue is his fear that his own preferred values are being "stamped out." He uses that phrase again in making the absurd claim that the goal of liberal educators is to subvert the influence of families on their children. If he were serious about the rights of parents, Hess would be attacking the idea of a federalized education system—with or without vouchers—in which the *state* defines which values, priorities, intellectual habits, and performance standards will dominate and in which schools must accept intrusive guidelines to receive a stamp of approval and public funding. It seems to me that his scorn should fall not on Deborah Meier and Ted Sizer but on George W. Bush and the other proponents of top-down standardization.

Hess wants teachers to promote respect for the law—unless the laws in question are those that guarantee equal rights to people regardless of sexual orientation. When I began teaching in the late 1970s, it was dangerous for a teacher to be homosexual, not because of students' or parents' reactions but because of administrative reprisals. And it was dangerous in those days to talk about the threat of nuclear war or to suggest that the U.S.-sponsored war in El Salvador was unjust or even to imply that there was another view of these issues than the government's. My colleagues daily taught their students that might was right and homosexuality was a sin. I had my tires slashed by colleagues who felt that desegregation had ruined the Boston Public Schools. That we have created schools in which more open dialogue is possible indeed represents progress.

In calling for more innovation and choice in public education, Hess is absolutely right. In diversity, after all, there is strength. The U.S. has tried many experiments in public schooling over the past two centuries. We are in the midst of yet another experiment with our charter schools. In many ways, this kind of exploration is healthy. It allows us to look at different models and seek out best practices. Yet the charter school experiment has largely ignored issues of equity. In Boston and many other districts, charter schools often make no provision for accepting students who require special educational services or facilities, while traditional public schools are required to do so. This is one reason that some see charter schools as less "public" than other public schools. The same inequities exist in many parochial schools.

We need schools that help young people and adults learn and practice the skills necessary to be participants in a vibrant democracy. Such schools will be messy places that must balance the public interest with America's pluralist tradition. In their classrooms everyone learns to ask probing questions, to use evidence well, to make legitimate arguments, and to recognize fallacies and lies. I invite Frederick Hess to come to the Boston Arts Academy, where we will be happy to give him the opportunity to practice these skills with our students.

Joe Nathan, Some Questions for Advocates of Public Education

Three very specific questions for advocates of public education came to my mind as I read Frederick Hess's argument that we need to "reappraise our assumptions as to what constitutes 'public schooling.'" Let me pose them to *Kappan* readers, who no doubt are advocates for public education.

What is public about a suburban district in which the price of admission to the local public schools is the ability to purchase a home for more than one million dollars (and to pay tax-deductible property taxes on that home)?

What is public about an inner-city school with an admissions test that screens out all students with mental disabilities and more than 95% of the students in the surrounding district and so proclaims that it serves only the "cream of the crop"?

What is public about preventing some inner-city students from attending a magnet school just a few blocks from their homes that receives $1,500 per pupil more than the neighborhood school they attend? At the same time, in the name of integration, white students from wealthy suburbs are transported to this school—some via taxi.

These three questions form the basis for two larger questions that continue to trouble me even after being involved with public education for 33 years. I don't have definitive answers to these larger questions. But I share them with readers in the hope that they, too, will find them worth pondering. . . .

⋅⟨⊙⟩⋅

. . . 1. *Since all public schools are not open to all kinds of students, what admissions standards should be acceptable for schools supported by public funds?* When my teachers in the Wichita public schools talked about public education, they stressed that a key difference between public and private schools was that public schools were open to all. Many of the authorities I read while I was at Carleton College, preparing to become a teacher, said the same thing.

This idea of "open to all" makes great sense to me. It seems like the right and just way to operate. Hess writes that he thinks it "appropriate" for some public schools to select some children and exclude others. I've disagreed with this position for more than 30 years. But lately, I'm not so sure.

When I began teaching I learned that many public schools were *not* open to all students. As I traveled the country, I learned that there were more than a thousand magnet schools and programs that have admissions tests. A study some years ago found that more than half of the nation's secondary magnet schools have admissions tests, as do about a quarter of the elementary magnets.[1]

Wisconsin Rep. Polly Williams, a Democrat and an African American state legislator, was enraged because most of the youngsters in her inner-city Milwaukee district were not able to get into exclusive magnet schools in the neighborhood, which brought in affluent, white, suburban students. Her frustration led her to fight successfully for the nation's first formal voucher plan.

Some opponents of vouchers insist that a level playing field isn't available when private schools can cherry-pick their students. I agree. But many educators, including me, have the same frustration about elite magnet schools: they have an unfair advantage over neighborhood public schools that are open to all in that they can screen out students with whom they don't wish to work.

I also learned that the country's single biggest choice system is called the suburbs. Millions of youngsters attend schools in the suburbs, and these schools clearly are *not* open to all students. They are open only to those whose families can afford to live in suburban communities.

A few years ago, I visited a school district on the northern coast of Long Island. Administrators there told me that the least expensive home in the district sold for $1,000,000. None of the district's teachers could afford to live there.

Today, some people argue that there should be publicly funded schools that are open only to young women. Two such schools have opened—one in New York, the other in Chicago. Even though I was not fond of this type of school, I visited the New York City district school, Young Women's Leadership Academy. I was impressed. The young women reported that, without boys around, they felt much more comfortable raising their hands in class and much more comfortable doing well on tests.

Should public funds go to some schools of choice that are only open to women? Or only to men? Five years ago, I would have said emphatically not. Today, I don't know.

2. *Shouldn't schools we describe as public accept and use some of the country's basic ideas to help improve education?* Americans generally endorse a number of ideas:

- choice of religion, job, neighborhood, places to obtain services, and so on;
- the provision of opportunities to try new ideas and approaches;
- the shared belief that this is a country not just of rights, but of responsibilities; and
- the notions that our cherished freedoms are not unlimited.

However, for three decades I've watched major public education groups vigorously oppose school choice programs, including public school choice programs, that are built on these principles. For example, there was intense opposition from educators in 1970 to the creation of the St. Paul Open School.

These organized groups ignore the professional and pedagogical rationales for public school choice, expressed best by veteran educator Deborah Meier:

> Choice is an essential tool in the effort to create . . . good public education. . . . We'll have to allow those most involved (teachers, administrators, parents) to exercise greater on-site power to put their collective wisdom into practice. Once we do all this, however, school X and school Y are going to start doing things differently. . . . Creating a school different from what any of those who work in the system are familiar with, one that runs counter to the experiences of most families, is possible only if teachers, parents, and students have time to agree on changes and a choice on whether or not they want to go along with them.[2]

Colleagues involved in other efforts to create new options over the last three decades have had similar experiences. During his tenure as president of the American Federation of Teachers, Al Shanker described what happened to teachers who proposed schools-within-schools:

> Many schools-within-schools were or are treated like traitors or outlaws for daring to move out of the lockstep and do something different. Their initiators had to move Heaven and Earth to get school officials to authorize them, and if they managed that, often they could look forward to insecurity, obscurity, or outright hostility.[3]

Over the past decade, with help from the Gates, Blandin, and Annenberg Foundations, the Center for School Change at the University of Minnesota has tried to help educators create new schools-within-schools in a number of communities. Shanker's words have often proved to be very accurate. The most intense, vigorous critics of offering a different kind of school—whether in a single building or in a district—have often been other educators.

Many educators have argued over the past 30 years that public, district schools serving racial minorities and students from low-income families are doing the best job they can with existing funds. According to the most recent

Phi Delta Kappa/Gallup poll, 80% of the public thinks the achievement gap between white children and minority children is mostly related to factors other than the quality of schooling.[4]

Perhaps in part because some educators have helped to convince the public that inner-city schools are mostly not responsible for the achievement gap, 58% of the nation and 62% of public school parents think it is possible to narrow the achievement gap *without* spending more money than is currently being spent on these students.[5] Unfortunately, many state legislators are opting not to raise taxes and not to give more to schools serving low-income, limited-English-speaking students.

Some of us vigorously disagree with these legislative actions and think that both more public school choice and more funding would help reduce the achievement gap. We have seen—and in some cases have worked in—schools that have served the public interest by helping all youngsters achieve their potential and have done much to close the gap between students of different races.

Despite encouragement from such strong public school supporters as former President Bill Clinton, former Secretary of Education Richard Riley, and the late Sen. Paul Wellstone (D-Minn.), efforts to create independent charter public schools still face huge opposition from state teacher, school board, and superintendent groups. The opposition uses the same arguments used in 1970 against the St. Paul Open School: new options take away our money.

But it isn't their money. Legislatures allocate money for the education of children, not for the preservation of a system. If 50 students move from a city to a suburb or from a suburb to a city, the dollars follow them. The money doesn't belong to "the system."

Thousands of parents and educators are voting with their feet. The number of states with a charter law has gone from one in 1991 to 40 in 2003. The number of charter schools has gone from one school in 1991 to more than 3,000 in 2003. Federal statistics show that low-income students and racial minorities are overrepresented in charter schools. While the evidence is mixed—and almost certainly will be so when charter and district schools are compared—some charters are clearly producing major achievement gains. Shouldn't we learn from and replicate their best practices?

Starting new schools is extremely difficult work. But whether it's a Pilot School in the Boston Public Schools or a New Visions option in New York City or a charter school in any of 40 states, the opportunity to try new approaches is as vital for education as it is for medicine, business, or technology.

Some Tentative Conclusions

So Frederick Hess wants to "discern what . . . makes schooling public and accept diverse arrangements that are consistent with those tenets." I'm not sure what standards all publicly supported schools should meet. But after 33 years, I offer these as minimum requirements for schools that serve the public interest and are thus eligible to receive public funds. Public schools should:

- be open to all kinds of students and not use admissions tests;
- follow due process procedures with regard to students and educators;

- use state-approved, standardized, and other measures to help monitor student progress or lack thereof;
- have closing the achievement gap between white students and racial minority and low-income students as an explicit, measurable goal;[6] and
- be actively chosen by faculty, families, and students.

Thanks to Hess and to the *Kappan* for urging a timely reconsideration of the basic principles of public education. As social justice activist Leonard Fein states it:

> The future is not something we discover around the next corner. It is something we shape, we create, we invent. To hold otherwise would be to view ourselves as an audience to history, and not its authors. History, and even our own lives, cannot always be turned and twisted to make them go exactly where we should like. But there is, for people of energy and purpose, more freedom of movement than most ever exercise.[7]

Notes

1. Lauri Steel and Roger Levine, *Educational Innovation in Multiracial Contexts: The Growth of Magnet Schools in American Education* (Palo Alto, Calif.: American Institutes for Research, 1994). This study was prepared for the U.S. Department of Education under Contract No. LC 90043001.
2. Deborah Meier, "Choice Can Save Public Education," *The Nation,* 4 March 1991.
3. Al Shanker, "Where We Stand: Convention Plots New Course—A Charter for Change," *New York Times* (paid advertisement), 10 July 1988, p. E-7.
4. Lowell C. Rose and Alec M. Gallup, "The 35th Annual Phi Delta Kappa/Gallup Poll of the Public's Attitudes Toward the Public Schools," *Phi Delta Kappan,* September 2003, p. 48.
5. Ibid.
6. Student progress should be monitored using various measures, not just standardized tests. If there is not major improvement in narrowing the achievement gap in most areas over a five-year period, the school should be "reconstituted."
7. Leonard Fein et al., *Reform Is a Verb: Notes on Reform and Reforming Jews* (New York: Union of American Hebrew Congregations, 1972), p. 152.

Ray Bacchetti, An Ongoing Conversation

We don't look at the big issues of the principles and purposes of public schools often or carefully enough. Sadly, the political and philosophical conversation seems increasingly polarized. In Venn diagram terms, the two circles—

labeled right/left, basics/constructivist, academic/child-centered, etc.—reveal at best a vanishingly thin region of overlap. When the true believers on either side look in the mirror, they see Dumbledore. Over their shoulders and gaining, they see Voldemort.

Frederick Hess's beefy rhetoric stakes out a position that reflects a more conservative world view than my own. In essence, he argues that the purposes of public education will be better served if we narrow the number of principles that define its publicness and expand the number of ways those principles can be implemented. In that expanded universe, religious schools, vouchers, for-profit ventures, and other alternatives would be welcome.

The principles advertised in Hess's title are woven through his essay, making it difficult to distinguish his main point from his subsidiary concerns. Here is what I take to be the core of his definition of what makes a school public. In addition to teaching skills and content, public schools should:

- prepare students to be "productive members of the social order";
- enable students to "become aware of their societal responsibilities," including the "principles, habits, and obligations of citizenship"; and
- educate students to be "respectful of constitutional strictures," including laws, process, and individual rights.

In carrying out these functions, public school systems should also:

- not "deny access to students for reasons unrelated to [a school's] educational focus"; and
- "provide an appropriate placement for each student" in every community.

Asserting by implication that the meanings of his key terms are inherently obvious, Hess goes on to argue that the terms others might use to set forth other principles are not. For example, he observes that "diversity" and "tolerance" are "umbrella terms with multiple interpretations." Therefore, they lie outside his cluster of principles because, when we try to define them more precisely, "it becomes clear that we must privilege some values at the expense of others." If he believes that a similar privileging of certain values might color his own key terms, such as "obligations of citizenship," "productive members of the social order," "societal responsibilities," "individual rights," and the like, he gives no indication.

Hess seems to arrive at his position partly for affirmative reasons (e.g., an emphasis on academic learning) and partly because of a surprisingly bitter view of educators (some of whom he names, but most of whom he only characterizes). In his view, these educators:

- "explicitly promote a particular world view and endorse a particular social ethos";
- "promote partisan attitudes toward American foreign policy, the propriety of affirmative action, or the morality of redistributive social policies";

- teach students to "accept teen pregnancy or homosexuality as normal and morally unobjectionable";
- attempt to "stamp out familial views and impress children with socially approved beliefs"; and
- treat public institutions as their personal playthings.

To illustrate his more general points, Hess portrays the "meaningful questions" asked in the classrooms of the Coalition of Essential Schools as a herd of Trojan ponies surreptitiously unloading the teachers' agendas. It's not clear what "meaningful questions" might be in the classrooms he approves of, though readers might infer that they would be limited to the rational analysis of topics that arise from well-developed and authoritatively taught subject matter. There is nothing wrong with such questions, of course. But anyone who thinks that they—or the answers to them—would be value-free is likely to have slept through his or her undergraduate philosophy classes.

More to the point, however, a narrow and academic definition of such questions would exclude from the public school universe those who think students should also wrestle with forming habits of the heart as well as the mind, should learn to use critical inquiry to amend and expand values and understandings as well as to confirm them, and should go beyond "my country, right or wrong" to embrace the rest of Carl Schurz's famous phrase, "if right, to be kept right; and if wrong, to be set right."

I have spent a fair amount of time in schools of late, witnessing heroic efforts of underfinanced and overregulated teachers to enact both the academic preparation *and* the democracy-building ethos that our schools were meant to embody. If Hess is suggesting that generally left-leaning personal agendas have dominated public school instruction for a generation or more, then we should be able to see around us a widely shared value system that reflects those views. However, when I survey newspapers, polls, elections, and even school reform debates at national and local levels, I see instead an enormous variety of values and priorities. Some may find that diversity of views troubling. What troubles me is not that people disagree but that we seem increasingly incapable of working through our differences to embed public school policies and practices in a conception of the common good that can transcend political perspectives without disrespecting them.

The sort of public conversations about public education that would open minds to a critical look at new ideas would be, as I'm sure Hess would agree, tough to structure and to conduct. Where he and I are likely to disagree is on whether the topic of those conversations will ever be settled and, more important, whether it ever should be. Teaching skills and developing in each generation the social cohesion on which so much else depends will be easier (though never easy) to approach than will matters of values, educational philosophies, social goals, and civic priorities. Moreover, balancing the relative claims of the student, family, community, nation, and the wider world on how and what schools teach is a democratic journey, not a settled destination.

From the start, Hess acknowledges the powerful resonance of the concept of public education. What seems to make him impatient, even exasperated, is that the people who lead what he and some others pejoratively call "government-run schools" aren't listening to him. Not listening can be a stance or a reaction. Seeing it as a *stance,* I join him in his exasperation. The habit of "reflexively shrinking" from a consideration of alternatives hardens the democratic arteries. Seeing it as a *reaction,* I worry that world views (a term I prefer to "ideology") too often appear as righteous opposites, leaving all but the most robust listeners wondering what's the point.

Finding areas of overlap in our views under such conditions isn't easy. Developing the skills of measured and thoughtful dialogue needed to create such overlap is even harder. The challenge of doing so, however, demonstrates why a free nation needs public schools that are set up to make public decision making meaningful at the daily, close-to-home levels, as well as at higher levels. Such deliberative procedures force us to ask not only what we want our own children to learn but also what we want all children to learn. Children are, after all, collectively as well as individually the next generation, and the education we bequeath to them is communal as well as personal.

We need to talk and listen our way into more overlap in our political/ philosophical Venn diagrams. Having that running conversation looms large in my definition of what makes the public schools public. Hess seems to argue that, through a few principles and a multitude of entities all claiming the mantle of public education, we can make the need for that conversation go away. I would argue instead that getting better at it should be our number-one priority.

Evans Clinchy, Reimagining Public Education

I heartily agree with Frederick Hess that we need to rethink and reimagine our antiquated American system of public education. But not for the reasons he sets forth.

I also agree with his broad definition of the purposes of public schooling: "that public schools are . . . defined by their commitment to preparing students to be productive members of the social order" (and therefore active citizens of a democratic society) who are able to think and use their minds well and are "aware of their societal responsibilities and respectful of constitutional strictures" (including an understanding of the Constitution and especially the Bill of Rights); "that such schools cannot deny access to students for reasons unrelated to their educational focus" (i.e., no racially, ethnically, or economically segregated schools); "and that the system of public schools available in any community must provide an appropriate placement for each student" (all students and their parents must be offered the kind of schooling they believe is most suitable). But I do not agree that we should seek to create the kind of reimagined system Hess appears to be proposing.

Questions of Definition, Control, and Funding

Throughout most of the history of the U.S., a public school has been defined as a school created, operated, and largely paid for by the citizens of each community through a locally elected board of education. While the Constitution leaves the basic authority for education in the hands of the individual states, and even though such locally controlled schools have, over the past century, received increased funding from both state and federal sources, this tradition of local control has managed to endure more or less intact—at least until the past 25 or so years.

The continued importance of this tradition was underscored in 1973 by the U.S. Supreme Court in its *Rodriguez* decision. The majority opinion put the matter this way:

> In an era that has witnessed a consistent trend toward centralization of the functions of government, local sharing of responsibility for public education has survived. The merit of local control was recognized in both the majority and dissenting opinions in *Wright v. Council of the City of Emporia*. Mr. Justice Stewart stated there that "direct control over decisions vitally affecting the education of one's children is a need that is strongly felt in our society." The Chief Justice in his dissent agreed that local control is not only vital to continued public support of the schools, but it is of overriding importance from an educational standpoint as well.
>
> The persistence of attachment to government at its lowest level where education is concerned reflects the depth of commitment of its supporters. In part local control means . . . the freedom to devote more money to the education of one's children. Equally important, however, is the opportunity it offers for participation in the decision-making process that determines how those local dollars will be spent. Each locality is free to tailor local programs to local needs. Pluralism also affords some opportunity for experimentation, innovation, and a healthy competition for educational excellence. An analogy to the Nation-State relationship in our federal system seems uniquely appropriate. Mr. Justice Brandeis identified as one of the peculiar strengths of our form of government each state's freedom to "serve as a laboratory; to try novel social and economic experiments." No area of social concern stands to profit more from a multiplicity of viewpoints and from a diversity of approaches than does public education.
>
> Further, Justice William Brennan found in his dissent that "Here, there can be no doubt that education is inextricably linked to the right to participate in the electoral process and to the rights of free speech and association guaranteed by the First Amendment."[1]

During the past quarter century, however, the "consistent trend toward centralization of the functions of government" has run rampant in the field of public schooling. In the name of public school "reform," the states have usurped local control by imposing uniform, authoritarian, "high," "rigorous," one-size-fits-all academic standards and punitive high-stakes standardized testing on all students, all schools, and all school systems.

The federal education establishment, through its No Child Left Behind Act, has carried this intrusive, antidemocratic curricular control and standardized testing program to ludicrous extremes, requiring the testing of all students in grades 3 through 8 and insisting on annual progress in test scores with severe sanctions for schools that fail to show such progress. However, neither the federal government nor the states have provided the financial resources to pay for all this "reform" or to remedy the gross inequities that exist between those school systems that serve the wealthy and those that serve our poor and minority students and parents. I find these events distressing, but none of them appear to worry Hess very much.

If the powerful democratic tradition of local control is to be maintained and if we are to genuinely reimagine our public education system, we will need to do several things. First, we will have to abandon the authoritarian standards and high-stakes testing agenda that currently afflict our public schools and return to the citizens of our local communities the control over what is taught, how it will be taught, and who will teach it. State and federal interference should be limited to ensuring minimum competency in the basic skills of reading, writing, and mathematics.

Second, we will simultaneously need both state and federal governments to guarantee that all of the nation's public schools are fully and equitably funded and that the civil rights of all students and parents—but especially our poor and minority students and parents—are fully protected. Hess does not appear to recommend any of these policies.

The Threat of Vouchers and Privatization

We will also have to erect strong safeguards against the threat of vouchers and any further encroachment of the private corporate sector into the field of public schooling. Now that the Supreme Court has permitted the use of public funds to finance vouchers that can be used to pay tuition at nonpublic, including religious, schools, Hess appears to be saying that we should aim to create a system of public education similar to that of many European countries, where public funding is given directly to all nonpublic schools. Such a proposal would still violate both the First Amendment's separation of church and state and the democratic commitment to local public citizen control.

In addition, Hess proposes that we permit the private, for-profit sector to run both schools and school systems so long as those schools are monitored by some public body—despite the fact that the track record of Edison and other corporate EMOs (education management organizations) is educationally and economically dismal. Hess appears to believe that it is morally legitimate for private corporations to profit from the education of children, rather than being required to plow "profits" back into our chronically underfunded public schools. This thinking parallels the already-established view that it is somehow morally legitimate for corporate HMOs to make a profit out of caring for the sick, rather than being required to plow that money back into the health-care system. Neither of these policies is morally acceptable in any fair, just, and equitable system of democratic government.

A Truly Reimagined, Genuinely Democratic Public System of Diversity and Choice

Hess does raise an issue of fundamental importance when he points out that "there are many ways to provide legitimate public education." I assume that he means that there is no single kind of school—be it rigidly "traditional," wildly "progressive," or something in between—that could possibly serve the diverse educational beliefs of this nation's parents, the equally diverse professional philosophies of our public school educators, and most especially the enormously varied educational needs of our children and young people.

Strangely, however, Hess believes that many "prominent educational thinkers" (among others, he names Frank Smith, Susan Ohanian, Deborah Meier, and Alfie Kohn) have encouraged the public schools to promote "preferred social values" to the American public rather than advocating that all public schools limit themselves to teaching children "the essential skills and knowledge that make for productive citizens." He asserts that the "public schools should teach children . . . to respect our constitutional order and instruct them in the framework of rights and obligations that secure our democracy and protect our liberty." He argues this point as if this educational prescription were not itself an ideology—even if it is one that may be widely shared and one that in its main outlines is most certainly shared by his list of misguided thinkers.

Hess then goes on to advocate not just his own ideological prescription but the basic rule of what I would see as that truly reimagined public system we should be attempting to create. In order to encompass those diverse educational beliefs of parents and professional educators and to meet the varied educational needs of our children and young people, he says that we should "allow families to avail themselves of a range of schools with diverse perspectives, so long as each teaches respect for our democratic and liberal tradition." Thus we need that wide diversity of public schools—ranging from traditional to progressive—from which parents, teachers, administrators, and older students can choose the type of schooling they believe will most benefit each child and young person. As Hess puts it, such strictly public school choice would create "heightened family involvement" and produce "a shared sense of commitment" that would tend to make such "self-selected schools more participatory and democratic."

It is, I believe, the job of our local public school systems, assisted and encouraged by state and federal governments, to provide that diversity of options. But the basic control of what goes on in all of our public schools must always remain solely in the public domain and solidly anchored in the will of the citizens of our local communities.

Note

1. *San Antonio Independent School District* v. *Rodriguez*, U.S. Supreme Court, 411 U.S. 1 (1973).

POSTSCRIPT

Should "Public Schooling" Be Redefined?

In the February 2004 issue of *Phi Delta Kappan*, Frederick M. Hess put forth a rejoinder to his four critics in an article titled "Debating Principles for Public Schooling in a New Century." He lists some significant points of agreement, including that it is necessary and useful to reconsider the essence of "public schooling" in an age marked by radical changes in how education is being provided. However, these critics, Hess contends, attack reforms as "anti-public education" for permitting the same practices that some "public schools" already engage in—for example, schools that are not open to all students when located in an affluent community. He feels that some critics allow the notion of public schooling to become a rhetorical banner for bolstering partisan positions and delegitimatizing opposing ideas. Hess further states that "there is a real danger to the rhetorical strategy of branding objectionable reforms as de facto 'assaults on public schooling.' This device is fruitless and divisive. Perhaps more forebodingly, it excommunicates many who honor public education because they fail to endorse the 'right kind' of public schooling."

John C. Lundt, a professor of educational leadership, says that education is leaving the schoolhouse as technology increasingly makes it an anytime-anywhere activity. In a provocative article in the December 2004 issue of *The Futurist* titled "Learning for Ourselves: A New Paradigm for Education," Lundt concludes that the antiquated structure of today's school was designed to meet the needs of a world that no longer exists, that public schools will not change as long as they monopolize educational funding, and that growing numbers of parents find the activities and values of public schools inappropriate for their children. This basic concern about funding is echoed by reporter Joe Williams in his book *Cheating Our Kids: How Politics and Greed Ruin Education* (2005). Williams examines the impact of special-interest groups on local public school systems (specifically in New York and Milwaukee), finding that most "reform" money only expands already bloated district bureaucracies. He calls for a concerted effort by concerned parents to reclaim power.

Additional challenging ideas may be found in Paul A. Zoch's *Doomed to Fail: The Built-in Defects of American Education* (2004); Susan Ohanian's "Refrains of the School Critics," *The School Administrator* (August 2005); Hannah Lobel's "Putting the Public Back in Public Education," *Utne* (January–February 2009); and Ross Hubbard's "Tinkering Change vs. System Change," *Phi Delta Kappan* (June 2009).

Internet References . . .

Federation for American Immigration Reform (FAIR)

Offers materials concerning school overcrowding, budget straining, and other effects of policies favoring undocumented immigrants.

http://www.fairus.org

About.com

Discusses rights of undocumented immigrants from a supportive stance.

http://civilliberty.about.com

Pre-K Now

Offers reports and fact sheets on the universal preschool movement.

http://preknow.org

Privatization Approaches

Covers controversies over privatization, vouchers, and charter schools.

http://hypertextbook.com

Circle of Inclusion

Offers materials and methods for serving learners with disabilities in inclusive school settings.

http://www.circleofinclusion.org

Silent Epidemic

Source for date on the dropout problem, with possible solutions and a catalog of resources for dealing with it.

http://www.silentepidemic.org

Americans United

Organization that has worked since 1947 to protect the principle of church-state separation in schools and elsewhere.

http://www.au.org

National Association for Single-Sex Public Education

Advocacy group presenting the case for single-sex schools and classes.

http://singlesexschools.org

Current Specific Issues

*T*his unit probes specific questions currently being discussed by educators, policy-makers, and parents. In most cases these issues are grounded in the more basic questions explored in Units 1 and 2. Views are expressed by a wide variety of writers, including Supreme Court Justices Brennan, Burger, Souter, and Thomas, David L. Kirp, Douglas J. Besharov, Chris Whittle, Henry Levin, Mara Sapon-Shevin, Wade A. Carpenter, Thomas Toch, Robert Epstein, Mark Terry, Dan Peterson, Peter Meyer, Vincent A. Anfara, Jr., Lowell Monke, Robert Holland, and Linda Darling-Hammond.

- Are Undocumented Immigrants Entitled to Public Education?
- Has the Time Arrived for Universal Preschool?
- Is Privatization the Hope of the Future?
- Is the Inclusive Classroom Model Workable?
- Can Current High School Reform Curtail Dropouts?
- Is "Intelligent Design" a Threat to the Curriculum?
- Are Single-Sex Schools and Classes Effective?
- Can Zero Tolerance Violate Student Rights?
- Do Computers Negatively Affect Student Growth?
- Should Alternative Teacher Training Be Encouraged?
- Can Merit Pay Accelerate School Improvement?

ISSUE 11

Are Undocumented Immigrants Entitled to Public Education?

YES: William J. Brennan, Jr., from Majority Opinion in *Plyler v. Doe* (June 15, 1982)

NO: Warren Burger, from Dissenting Opinion in *Plyler v. Doe* (June 15, 1982)

ISSUE SUMMARY

YES: Justice William Brennan argues that the action of the Texas state legislature to authorize local school districts to deny enrollment in public schools to children not "legally admitted" to the country violates the Fourteenth Amendment.

NO: Chief Justice Warren Burger, in dissent, counters that the Court has no business assuming a policymaking role simply because the legislative branches of government fail to act appropriately.

$\mathbf{T}$he situation regarding the treatment of immigrants who are not authorized to be here has deteriorated in the last few years. The period has been marked by congressional inaction on immigration policy, acceleration of authorities' raids on businesses harboring undocumented workers, actions of local governments seeking to reverse the impact of immigrants, and the increase in fearfulness in immigrant communities. According to some sources, about 70 percent of the undocumented immigrants have been residing here for at least five years and identify themselves as Americans, making the sudden enforcement of existing laws rather problematic. Approximately 5 percent of the American workforce consists of undocumented immigrants, and only 66,000 visas are currently available for immigrant unskilled workers, a number considered laughable by some.

There are those who want to arrest and deport all these people. There are those who want to work out some sort of amnesty program. Tom Bethell, in "Freedom of Immigration Acts: A Special Report," *The American Spectator* (September 2007) states "My sense is that ending the contribution of the illegals to the U.S. economy would have an effect comparable to that of a major tax increase. Possibly there would be a real economic contraction. Without an expanding, dynamic economy, America would soon be in a great mess." Beyond such broad economic concerns lies the situation of the children of undocumented immigrants who may or may not be availing education and other social services during their stay in the United States.

The National Association for Bilingual Education has estimated that over one million children, aged 5–19, are the offspring of parents who are undocumented immigrants. Some groups have pressured schools to turn away such children in spite of the Supreme Court's decision in *Plyler v. Doe* that protected them from exclusion. Since that 5-4 decision, public schools across the nation have been obligated to enroll children regardless of their immigration status. Mary Ann Zehr, in "Amid Immigration Debate, Settled Ground: High Court's School Access Ruling Endures as a Quiet Fact of Life," *Education Week* (June 12–13, 2007), cites a number of attempts to counteract the Court's ruling. In 1994, California voters tried to deny a K–12 education and other public services to undocumented immigrants in Proposition 187, which stipulated that "no public elementary or secondary school shall admit, or permit the attendance of, any child who is not a citizen of the United States, an alien lawfully admitted as a permanent resident, or a person who is otherwise authorized under federal law to be present in the United States." The Proposition was thrown out by a federal court and the appeal process fizzled. In 1996, there was an unsuccessful attempt by a California congressman to attach an amendment to federal legislation that would allow states to pass laws similar to that disallowed by *Plyler v. Doe*. In 2004, an Arizona ballot measure denied adults the opportunity to get a free K–12 education, thus partially diminishing the impact of the *Plyler v. Doe* ruling.

In an article commemorating the 25th anniversary of *Plyler,* Sarah Karlin, in "The Invisible Class," *American School Board Journal* (November 2007), says that challenges still persist for undocumented students who secure a high school diploma. They cannot receive federal financial aid for higher education, and most are not offered in-state tuition. A 2007 National Survey of Latinos by the Pew Hispanic Center shows that they are "feeling a range of negative effects from the increased public attention and stepped-up enforcement measures that have accompanied the growing national debate over illegal immigration." Federal policies to strictly enforce laws by workplace crackdowns could certainly have a long-term impact on children whose family life may be compromised.

The landmark case, *Plyler, Superintendent, Tyler Independent School District, et al. v. Doe, Guardian, et al.* involved a Texas statute that withheld from local school districts any state funds for the education of children who were not "legally admitted" into the United States and that authorized local school districts, like that in Tyler, to deny enrollment to such children. The majority and dissenting opinions in that case are herein presented.

YES

William J. Brennan, Jr.

Undocumented Children Deserve Equal Protection

J USTICE BRENNAN delivered the opinion of the Court.

The question presented by these cases is whether, consistent with the Equal Protection Clause of the Fourteenth Amendment, Texas may deny to undocumented school-age children the free public education that it provides to children who are citizens of the United States or legally admitted aliens.

I

Since the late 19th century, the United States has restricted immigration into this country. Unsanctioned entry into the United States is a crime, and those who have entered unlawfully are subject to deportation. But despite the existence of these legal restrictions, a substantial number of persons have succeeded in unlawfully entering the United States, and now live within various States, including the State of Texas.

In May, 1975, the Texas Legislature revised its education laws to withhold from local school districts any state funds for the education of children who were not "legally admitted" into the United States. The 1975 revision also authorized local school districts to deny enrollment in their public schools to children not "legally admitted" to the country. These cases involve constitutional challenges to those provisions.

Plyler v. Doe

This is a class action, filed in the United States District Court for the Eastern District of Texas in September 1977, on behalf of certain school-age children of Mexican origin residing in Smith County, Texas, who could not establish that they had been legally admitted into the United States. The action complained of the exclusion of plaintiff children from the public schools of the Tyler Independent School District. The Superintendent and members of the Board of Trustees of the School District were named as defendants; the State of Texas intervened as a party-defendant. After certifying a class consisting of all undocumented school-age children of Mexican origin residing within the School District, the District Court preliminarily enjoined defendants from denying a free education to members of the plaintiff class. In December 1977, the court conducted an extensive hearing on plaintiffs' motion for permanent injunctive relief.

From Supreme Court of the United States, June 15, 1982, parts I–VI.

In considering this motion, the District Court made extensive findings of fact. The court found that neither 21.031 nor the School District policy implementing it had "either the purpose or effect of keeping illegal aliens out of the State of Texas." Respecting defendants' further claim that 21.031 was simply a financial measure designed to avoid a drain on the State's fisc [treasury], the court recognized that the increases in population resulting from the immigration of Mexican nationals into the United States had created problems for the public schools of the State, and that these problems were exacerbated by the special educational needs of immigrant Mexican children. The court noted, however, that the increase in school enrollment was primarily attributable to the admission of children who were legal residents. It also found that while the "exclusion of all undocumented children from the public schools in Texas would eventually result in economies at some level," funding from both the State and Federal Governments was based primarily on the number of children enrolled. In net effect then, barring undocumented children from the schools would save money, but it would "not necessarily" improve "the quality of education." The court further observed that the impact of 21.031 was borne primarily by a very small subclass of illegal aliens, "entire families who have migrated illegally and—for all practical purposes—permanently to the United States." Finally, the court noted that, under current laws and practices, "the illegal alien of today may well be the legal alien of tomorrow," and that without an education, these undocumented children, [a]lready disadvantaged as a result of poverty, lack of English-speaking ability, and undeniable racial prejudices, . . . will become permanently locked into the lowest socio-economic class.

The District Court held that illegal aliens were entitled to the protection of the Equal Protection Clause of the Fourteenth Amendment, and that 21.031 violated that Clause. Suggesting that "the state's exclusion of undocumented children from its public schools . . . may well be the type of invidiously motivated state action for which the suspect classification doctrine was designed," the court held that it was unnecessary to decide whether the statute would survive a "strict scrutiny" analysis because, in any event, the discrimination embodied in the statute was not supported by a rational basis. The District Court also concluded that the Texas statute violated the Supremacy Clause.

The Court of Appeals for the Fifth Circuit upheld the District Court's injunction. The Court of Appeals held that the District Court had erred in finding the Texas statute pre-empted by federal law. With respect to equal protection, however, the Court of Appeals affirmed in all essential respects the analysis of the District Court, concluding that 21.031 was "constitutionally infirm regardless of whether it was tested using the mere rational basis standard or some more stringent test."

In re Alien Children Education Litigation

During 1978 and 1979, suits challenging the constitutionality of 21.031 and various local practices undertaken on the authority of that provision were filed in the United States District Courts for the Southern, Western, and Northern Districts of Texas. Each suit named the State of Texas and the Texas Education

Agency as defendants, along with local officials. In November 1979, the Judicial Panel on Multi-district Litigation, on motion of the State, consolidated the claims against the state officials into a single action to be heard in the District Court for the Southern District of Texas. A hearing was conducted in February and March 1980. In July 1980, the court entered an opinion and order holding that 21.031 violated the Equal Protection Clause of the Fourteenth Amendment. The court held that "the absolute deprivation of education should trigger strict judicial scrutiny, particularly when the absolute deprivation is the result of complete inability to pay for the desired benefit." The court determined that the State's concern for fiscal integrity was not a compelling state interest; that exclusion of these children had not been shown to be necessary to improve education within the State; and that the educational needs of the children statutorily excluded were not different from the needs of children not excluded. The court therefore concluded that 21.031 was not carefully tailored to advance the asserted state interest in an acceptable manner. While appeal of the District Court's decision was pending, the Court of Appeals rendered its decision in No. 80-1538. Apparently on the strength of that opinion, the Court of Appeals, on February 23, 1981, summarily affirmed the decision of the Southern District. We noted probable jurisdiction, and consolidated this case with No. 80-1538 for briefing and argument.

II

The Fourteenth Amendment provides that "[n]o State shall . . . deprive any person of life, liberty, or property, without due process of law; nor deny to any person within its jurisdiction the equal protection of the laws." Appellants argue at the outset that undocumented aliens, because of their immigration status, are not "persons within the jurisdiction" of the State of Texas, and that they therefore have no right to the equal protection of Texas law. We reject this argument. Whatever his status under the immigration laws, an alien is surely a "person" in any ordinary sense of that term. Aliens, even aliens whose presence in this country is unlawful, have long been recognized as "persons" guaranteed due process of law by the Fifth and Fourteenth Amendment. Indeed, we have clearly held that the Fifth Amendment protects aliens whose presence in this country is unlawful from invidious discrimination by the Federal Government.

Appellants seek to distinguish our prior cases, emphasizing that the Equal Protection Clause directs a State to afford its protection to persons within its jurisdiction while the Due Process Clauses of the Fifth and Fourteenth Amendments contain no such assertedly limiting phrase. In appellants' view, persons who have entered the United States illegally are not "within the jurisdiction" of a State even if they are present within a State's boundaries and subject to its laws. Neither our cases nor the logic of the Fourteenth Amendment supports that constricting construction of the phrase "within its jurisdiction." We have never suggested that the class of persons who might avail themselves of the equal protection guarantee is less than coextensive with that entitled to due process. To the contrary, we have recognized that both provisions were fashioned to protect an identical class of persons, and to reach every exercise of state authority. . . .

In concluding that "all persons within the territory of the United States," including aliens unlawfully present, may invoke the Fifth and Sixth Amendments to challenge actions of the Federal Government, we reasoned from the understanding that the Fourteenth Amendment was designed to afford its protection to all within the boundaries of a State. Our cases applying the Equal Protection Clause reflect the same territorial theme . . .

There is simply no support for appellants' suggestion that "due process" is somehow of greater stature than "equal protection" and therefore available to a larger class of persons. To the contrary, each aspect of the Fourteenth Amendment reflects an elementary limitation on state power. To permit a State to employ the phrase "within its jurisdiction" in order to identify subclasses of persons whom it would define as beyond its jurisdiction, thereby relieving itself of the obligation to assure that its laws are designed and applied equally to those persons, would undermine the principal purpose for which the Equal Protection Clause was incorporated in the Fourteenth Amendment. The Equal Protection Clause was intended to work nothing less than the abolition of all caste-based and invidious class-based legislation. That objective is fundamentally at odds with the power the State asserts here to classify persons subject to its laws as nonetheless excepted from its protection.

Use of the phrase "within its jurisdiction" thus does not detract from, but rather confirms, the understanding that the protection of the Fourteenth Amendment extends to anyone, citizen or stranger, who is subject to the laws of a State, and reaches into every corner of a State's territory. That a person's initial entry into a State, or into the United States, was unlawful, and that he may for that reason be expelled, cannot negate the simple fact of his presence within the State's territorial perimeter. Given such presence, he is subject to the full range of obligations imposed by the State's civil and criminal laws. And until he leaves the jurisdiction—either voluntarily, or involuntarily in accordance with the Constitution and laws of the United States—he is entitled to the equal protection of the laws that a State may choose to establish.

Our conclusion that the illegal aliens who are plaintiffs in these cases may claim the benefit of the Fourteenth Amendment's guarantee of equal protection only begins the inquiry. The more difficult question is whether the Equal Protection Clause has been violated by the refusal of the State of Texas to reimburse local school boards for the education of children who cannot demonstrate that their presence within the United States is lawful, or by the imposition by those school boards of the burden of tuition on those children. It is to this question that we now turn.

III

The Equal Protection Clause directs that "all persons similarly circumstanced shall be treated alike." But so too, "[t]he Constitution does not require things which are different in fact or opinion to be treated in law as though they were the same." The initial discretion to determine what is "different" and what is "the same" resides in the legislatures of the States. A legislature must have substantial latitude to establish classifications that roughly approximate the nature of the problem perceived, that accommodate competing concerns both public and private, and that account for limitations on the practical ability of the State to remedy every ill. In applying the Equal Protection Clause to most forms of state action, we thus seek only the assurance that the classification at issue bears some fair relationship to a legitimate public purpose.

But we would not be faithful to our obligations under the Fourteenth Amendment if we applied so deferential a standard to every classification. The Equal Protection Clause was intended as a restriction on state legislative action inconsistent with elemental constitutional premises. Thus we have treated as presumptively invidious those classifications that disadvantage a "suspect class," or that impinge upon the exercise of a "fundamental right." With respect to such classifications, it is appropriate to enforce the mandate of equal protection by requiring the State to demonstrate that its classification has been precisely tailored to serve a compelling governmental interest. In addition, we have recognized that certain forms of legislative classification, while not facially invidious, nonetheless give rise to recurring constitutional difficulties; in these limited circumstances we have sought the assurance that the classification reflects a reasoned judgment consistent with the ideal of equal protection by inquiring whether it may fairly be viewed as furthering a substantial interest of the State. We turn to a consideration of the standard appropriate for the evaluation of 21.031.

A

Sheer incapability or lax enforcement of the laws barring entry into this country, coupled with the failure to establish an effective bar to the employment of undocumented aliens, has resulted in the creation of a substantial "shadow population" of illegal migrants—numbering in the millions—within our borders. This situation raises the specter of a permanent caste of undocumented resident aliens, encouraged by some to remain here as a source of cheap labor, but nevertheless denied the benefits that our society makes available to citizens and lawful residents. The existence of such an underclass presents most difficult problems for a Nation that prides itself on adherence to principles of equality under law.

The children who are plaintiffs in these cases are special members of this underclass. Persuasive arguments support the view that a State may withhold its beneficence from those whose very presence within the United States is the product of their own unlawful conduct. These arguments do not apply with the same force to classifications imposing disabilities on the minor children of such illegal entrants. At the least, those who elect to enter our territory by stealth and in violation of our law should be prepared to bear the consequences, including, but not limited to, deportation. But the children of those illegal entrants are not comparably situated. Their "parents have the ability to conform their conduct to societal norms," and presumably the ability to remove themselves from the State's jurisdiction; but the children who are plaintiffs in these cases "can affect neither their parents' conduct nor their own status." Even if the State found it expedient to control the conduct of adults by acting against their children, legislation directing the onus of a parent's misconduct against his children does not comport with fundamental conceptions of justice.

Of course, undocumented status is not irrelevant to any proper legislative goal. Nor is undocumented status an absolutely immutable characteristic since it is the product of conscious, indeed unlawful, action. But 21.031 is directed against children, and imposes its discriminatory burden on the basis of a legal characteristic over which children can have little control. It is thus difficult to conceive of a rational justification for penalizing these children for their presence within the United States. Yet that appears to be precisely the effect of 21.031.

Public education is not a "right" granted to individuals by the Constitution. But neither is it merely some governmental "benefit" indistinguishable from other forms of social welfare legislation. Both the importance of education in maintaining our basic institutions, and the lasting impact of its deprivation on the life of the child, mark the distinction. The "American people have always regarded education and [the] acquisition of knowledge as matters of supreme importance." We have recognized "the public schools as a most vital civic institution for the preservation of a democratic system of government," and as the primary vehicle for transmitting "the values on which our society rests." "[A]s . . . pointed out early in our history, . . . some degree of education is necessary to prepare citizens to participate effectively and intelligently in our open political system if we are to preserve freedom and independence." And these historic "perceptions of the public schools as inculcating fundamental values necessary to the maintenance of a democratic political system have been confirmed by the observations of social scientists." In addition, education provides the basic tools by which individuals might lead economically productive lives to the benefit of us all. In sum, education has a fundamental role in maintaining the fabric of our society. We cannot ignore the significant social costs borne by our Nation when select groups are denied the means to absorb the values and skills upon which our social order rests.

In addition to the pivotal role of education in sustaining our political and cultural heritage, denial of education to some isolated group of children poses an affront to one of the goals of the Equal Protection Clause: the abolition of governmental barriers presenting unreasonable obstacles to advancement on the basis of individual merit. Paradoxically, by depriving the children of any disfavored group of an education, we foreclose the means by which that group might raise the level of esteem in which it is held by the majority. But more directly, "education prepares individuals to be self-reliant and self-sufficient participants in society." Illiteracy is an enduring disability. The inability to read and write will handicap the individual deprived of a basic education each and every day of his life. The inestimable toll of that deprivation on the social, economic, intellectual, and psychological well-being of the individual, and the obstacle it poses to individual achievement, make it most difficult to reconcile the cost or the principle of a status-based denial of basic education with the framework of equality embodied in the Equal Protection Clause. What we said 28 years ago in Brown v. Board of Education (1954), still holds true:

> Today, education is perhaps the most important function of state and local governments. Compulsory school attendance laws and the great expenditures for education both demonstrate our recognition of the importance of education to our democratic society. It is required in the performance of our most basic public responsibilities, even service in the armed forces. It is the very foundation of good citizenship. Today it is a principal instrument in awakening the child to cultural values, in preparing him for later professional training, and in helping him to adjust normally to his environment. In these days, it is doubtful that any child may reasonably be expected to succeed in life if he is denied the opportunity of an education. Such an opportunity, where the state has undertaken to provide it, is a right which must be made available to all on equal terms.

B

These well-settled principles allow us to determine the proper level of deference to be afforded 21.031. Undocumented aliens cannot be treated as a suspect class because their presence in this country in violation of federal law is not a "constitutional irrelevancy." Nor is education a fundamental right; a State need not justify by compelling necessity every variation in the manner in which education is provided to its population. But more is involved in these cases than the abstract question whether 21.031 discriminates against a suspect class, or whether education is a fundamental right. Section 21.031 imposes a lifetime hardship on a discrete class of children not accountable for their disabling status. The stigma of illiteracy will mark them for the rest of their lives. By denying these children a basic education, we deny them the ability to live within the structure of our civic institutions, and foreclose any realistic possibility that they will contribute in even the smallest way to the progress of our Nation. In determining the rationality of 21.031, we may appropriately take into account its costs to the Nation and to the innocent children who are its victims. In light of these countervailing costs, the discrimination contained in 21.031 can hardly be considered rational unless it furthers some substantial goal of the State.

IV

It is the State's principal argument, and apparently the view of the dissenting Justices, that the undocumented status of these children vel non establishes a sufficient rational basis for denying them benefits that a State might choose to afford other residents. The State notes that while other aliens are admitted "on an equality of legal privileges with all citizens under nondiscriminatory laws," the asserted right of these children to an education can claim no implicit congressional imprimatur. Indeed, in the State's view, Congress' apparent disapproval of the presence of these children within the United States, and the evasion of the federal regulatory program that is the mark of undocumented status, provides authority for its decision to impose upon them special disabilities. Faced with an equal protection challenge respecting the treatment of aliens, we agree that the courts must be attentive to congressional policy; the exercise of congressional power might well affect the State's prerogatives to afford differential treatment to a particular class of aliens. But we are unable to find in the congressional immigration scheme any statement of policy that might weigh significantly in arriving at an equal protection balance concerning the State's authority to deprive these children of an education.

⋅⟨⊙⟩⋅

We are reluctant to impute to Congress the intention to withhold from these children, for so long as they are present in this country through no fault of their own, access to a basic education. In other contexts, undocumented status, coupled with some articulable federal policy, might enhance state authority with respect to the treatment of undocumented aliens. But in the area of special constitutional sensitivity presented by these cases, and in the absence of any contrary indication fairly discernible in the present legislative record, we perceive no national policy that supports the State in denying these children an elementary education. The State may borrow the federal classification. But to justify its use as a criterion for its own discriminatory policy, the State must demonstrate that the classification is reasonably adapted to "the purposes for which the state desires to use it." We therefore turn to the state objectives that are said to support 21.031.

V

Appellants argue that the classification at issue furthers an interest in the "preservation of the state's limited resources for the education of its lawful residents." Of course, a concern for the preservation of resources standing alone can hardly justify the classification used in allocating those resources. The State must do more than justify its classification with a concise expression of an intention to discriminate. Apart from the asserted state prerogative to act against undocumented children solely on the basis of their undocumented status—an asserted prerogative that carries only minimal force in the circumstances of these cases—we discern three colorable state interests that might support 21.031.

First, appellants appear to suggest that the State may seek to protect itself from an influx of illegal immigrants. While a State might have an interest in mitigating the potentially harsh economic effects of sudden shifts in population, 21.031 hardly offers an effective method of dealing with an urgent demographic or economic problem. There is no evidence in the record suggesting that illegal entrants impose any significant burden on the State's economy. To the contrary, the available evidence suggests that illegal aliens underutilize public services, while contributing their labor to the local economy and tax money to the state fisc [treasury]. The dominant incentive for illegal entry into the State of Texas is the availability of employment; few if any illegal immigrants come to this country, or presumably to the State of Texas, in order to avail themselves of a free education. Thus, even making the doubtful assumption that the net impact of illegal aliens on the economy of the State is negative, we think it clear that "[c]harging tuition to undocumented children constitutes a ludicrously ineffectual attempt to stem the tide of illegal immigration," at least when compared with the alternative of prohibiting the employment of illegal aliens.

Second, while it is apparent that a State may "not . . . reduce expenditures for education by barring [some arbitrarily chosen class of] children from its schools," appellants suggest that undocumented children are appropriately singled out for exclusion because of the special burdens they impose on the State's ability to provide high-quality public education. But the record in no way supports the claim that exclusion of undocumented children is likely to improve the overall quality of education in the State. As the District Court in No. 80-1934 noted, the State failed to offer any "credible supporting evidence that a proportionately small diminution of the funds spent on each child [which might result from devoting some state funds to the education of the excluded group] will have a grave impact on the quality of education." And, after reviewing the State's school financing mechanism, the District Court in No. 80-1538 concluded that barring undocumented children from local schools would not necessarily improve the quality of education provided in those schools. Of course, even if improvement in the quality of education were a likely result of barring some number of children from the schools of the State, the State must support its selection of this group as the appropriate target for exclusion. In terms of educational cost and need, however, undocumented children are "basically indistinguishable" from legally resident alien children.

Finally, appellants suggest that undocumented children are appropriately singled out because their unlawful presence within the United States renders them less likely than other children to remain within the boundaries of the State, and to put their education to productive social or political use within the State. Even assuming that such an interest is legitimate, it is an interest that is most difficult to quantify. The State has no assurance that any child, citizen or not, will employ the education provided by the State within the confines of the State's borders. In any event, the record is clear that many of the undocumented children disabled by this classification will remain in this country indefinitely, and that some will become lawful residents or citizens of the United States. It is difficult to understand precisely what the State hopes to achieve by promoting the creation and perpetuation of a subclass of illiterates within our boundaries, surely adding to the problems and costs of unemployment, welfare, and crime. It is thus clear that whatever savings might be achieved by denying these children an education, they are wholly insubstantial in light of the costs involved to these children, the State, and the Nation.

VI

If the State is to deny a discrete group of innocent children the free public education that it offers to other children residing within its borders, that denial must be justified by a showing that it furthers some substantial state interest. No such showing was made here. Accordingly, the judgment of the Court of Appeals in each of these cases is Affirmed.

NO

The Decision Distorts the Function of the Court

CHIEF JUSTICE BURGER, with whom JUSTICE WHITE, JUSTICE REHNQUIST, and JUSTICE O'CONNOR join, dissenting.

Were it our business to set the Nation's social policy, I would agree without hesitation that it is senseless for an enlightened society to deprive any children—including illegal aliens—of an elementary education. I fully agree that it would be folly—and wrong—to tolerate creation of a segment of society made up of illiterate persons, many having a limited or no command of our language. However, the Constitution does not constitute us as "Platonic Guardians" nor does it vest in this Court the authority to strike down laws because they do not meet our standards of desirable social policy, "wisdom," or "common sense." We trespass on the assigned function of the political branches under our structure of limited and separated powers when we assume a policymaking role as the Court does today.

The Court makes no attempt to disguise that it is acting to make up for Congress' lack of "effective leadership" in dealing with the serious national problems caused by the influx of uncountable millions of illegal aliens across our borders. The failure of enforcement of the immigration laws over more than a decade and the inherent difficulty and expense of sealing our vast borders have combined to create a grave socioeconomic dilemma. It is a dilemma that has not yet even been fully assessed, let alone addressed. However, it is not the function of the Judiciary to provide "effective leadership" simply because the political branches of government fail to do so.

The Court's holding today manifests the justly criticized judicial tendency to attempt speedy and wholesale formulation of "remedies" for the failures—or simply the laggard pace—of the political processes of our system of government. The Court employs, and in my view abuses, the Fourteenth Amendment in an effort to become an omnipotent and omniscient problem solver. That the motives for doing so are noble and compassionate does not alter the fact that the Court distorts our constitutional function to make amends for the defaults of others.

I

In a sense, the Court's opinion rests on such a unique confluence of theories and rationales that it will likely stand for little beyond the results in these

From Supreme Court of the United States, June 15, 1982, parts I–II.

particular cases. Yet the extent to which the Court departs from principled constitutional adjudication is nonetheless disturbing.

I have no quarrel with the conclusion that the Equal Protection Clause of the Fourteenth Amendment applies to aliens who, after their illegal entry into this country, are indeed physically "within the jurisdiction" of a state. However, as the Court concedes, this "only begins the inquiry." The Equal Protection Clause does not mandate identical treatment of different categories of persons.

The dispositive issue in these cases, simply put, is whether, for purposes of allocating its finite resources, a state has a legitimate reason to differentiate between persons who are lawfully within the state and those who are unlawfully there. The distinction the State of Texas has drawn—based not only upon its own legitimate interests but on classifications established by the Federal Government in its immigration laws and policies—is not unconstitutional.

A

The Court acknowledges that, except in those cases when state classifications disadvantage a "suspect class" or impinge upon a "fundamental right," the Equal Protection Clause permits a state "substantial latitude" in distinguishing between different groups of persons. Moreover, the Court expressly—and correctly—rejects any suggestion that illegal aliens are a suspect class, or that education is a fundamental right. Yet by patching together bits and pieces of what might be termed quasi-suspect-class and quasi-fundamental-rights analysis, the Court spins out a theory custom-tailored to the facts of these cases.

In the end, we are told little more than that the level of scrutiny employed to strike down the Texas law applies only when illegal alien children are deprived of a public education. If ever a court was guilty of an unabashedly result-oriented approach, this case is a prime example.

(1)

The Court first suggests that these illegal alien children, although not a suspect class, are entitled to special solicitude under the Equal Protection Clause because they lack "control" over or "responsibility" for their unlawful entry into this country. Similarly, the Court appears to take the position that 21.031 is presumptively "irrational" because it has the effect of imposing "penalties" on "innocent" children. However, the Equal Protection Clause does not preclude legislators from classifying among persons on the basis of factors and characteristics over which individuals may be said to lack "control." Indeed, in some circumstances persons generally, and children in particular, may have little control over or responsibility for such things as their ill health, need for public assistance, or place of residence. Yet a state legislature is not barred from considering, for example, relevant differences between the mentally healthy and the mentally ill, or between the residents of different counties, simply because these may be factors unrelated to individual choice or to any "wrongdoing." The Equal Protection Clause protects against arbitrary and irrational classifications, and against invidious discrimination stemming from prejudice and hostility; it is not an all-encompassing "equalizer" designed to eradicate every distinction for which persons are not "responsible."

The Court does not presume to suggest that appellees' purported lack of culpability for their illegal status prevents them from being deported or otherwise "penalized" under federal law. Yet would deportation be any less a "penalty" than denial of privileges provided to legal residents? Illegality of presence in the United States does not—and need not—depend on some amorphous concept of "guilt" or "innocence" concerning an alien's entry. Similarly, a state's use of federal immigration status as a basis for legislative classification is not necessarily rendered suspect for its failure to take such factors into account.

The Court's analogy to cases involving discrimination against illegitimate children is grossly misleading. The State has not thrust any disabilities upon appellees due to their "status of birth." Rather, appellees' status is predicated upon the circumstances of their concededly illegal presence in this country, and is a direct result of Congress' obviously valid exercise of its "broad constitutional powers" in the field of immigration and naturalization. This Court has recognized that in allocating governmental benefits to a given class of aliens, one "may take into account the character of the relationship between the alien and this country." When that "relationship" is a federally prohibited one, there can, of course, be no presumption that a state has a constitutional duty to include illegal aliens among the recipients of its governmental benefits.

(2)

The second strand of the Court's analysis rests on the premise that, although public education is not a constitutionally guaranteed right, "neither is it merely some governmental 'benefit' indistinguishable from other forms of social welfare legislation." Whatever meaning or relevance this opaque observation might have in some other context, it simply has no bearing on the issues at hand. Indeed, it is never made clear what the Court's opinion means on this score.

The importance of education is beyond dispute. Yet we have held repeatedly that the importance of a governmental service does not elevate it to the status of a "fundamental right" for purposes of equal protection analysis. In San Antonio Independent School Dist. v. Rodriguez (1973), JUSTICE POWELL, speaking for the Court, expressly rejected the proposition that state laws dealing with public education are subject to special scrutiny under the Equal Protection Clause. Moreover, the Court points to no meaningful way to distinguish between education and other governmental benefits in this context. Is the Court suggesting that education is more "fundamental" than food, shelter, or medical care?

The Equal Protection Clause guarantees similar treatment of similarly situated persons, but it does not mandate a constitutional hierarchy of governmental services. JUSTICE POWELL, speaking for the Court in San Antonio Independent School Dist., put it well in stating that to the extent this Court raises or lowers the degree of "judicial scrutiny" in equal protection cases according to a transient Court majority's view of the societal importance of the interest affected, we "assum[e] a legislative role and one for which the Court lacks both authority and competence." Yet that is precisely what the Court does today.

The central question in these cases, as in every equal protection case not involving truly fundamental rights "explicitly or implicitly guaranteed by the Constitution," is whether there is some legitimate basis for a legislative distinction between different classes of persons. The fact that the distinction is drawn in legislation affecting access to public education—as opposed to legislation allocating other important governmental benefits, such as public assistance, health care, or housing—cannot make a difference in the level of scrutiny applied.

B

Once it is conceded—as the Court does—that illegal aliens are not a suspect class, and that education is not a fundamental right, our inquiry should focus on and be limited to whether the legislative classification at issue bears a rational relationship to a legitimate state purpose.

The State contends primarily that 21.031 serves to prevent undue depletion of its limited revenues available for education, and to preserve the fiscal integrity of the State's school-financing system against an ever-increasing flood of illegal aliens—aliens over whose entry or continued presence it has no control. Of course such fiscal concerns alone could not justify discrimination against a suspect class or an arbitrary and irrational denial of benefits to a particular group of persons. Yet I assume no Member of this Court would argue that prudent conservation of finite state revenues is per se an illegitimate goal. Indeed, the numerous classifications this Court has sustained in social welfare legislation were invariably related to the limited amount of revenues available to spend on any given program or set of programs. The significant question here is whether the requirement of tuition from illegal aliens who attend the public schools—as well as from residents of other states, for example—is a rational and reasonable means of furthering the State's legitimate fiscal ends.

Without laboring what will undoubtedly seem obvious to many, it simply is not "irrational" for a state to conclude that it does not have the same responsibility to provide benefits for persons whose very presence in the state and this country is illegal as it does to provide for persons lawfully present. By definition, illegal aliens have no right whatever to be here, and the state may reasonably, and constitutionally, elect not to provide them with governmental services at the expense of those who are lawfully in the state. In De Canas v. Bica (1976) we held that a State may protect its "fiscal interests and lawfully resident labor force from the deleterious effects on its economy resulting from the employment of illegal aliens." And only recently this Court made clear that a State has a legitimate interest in protecting and preserving the quality of its schools and "the right of its own bona fide residents to attend such institutions on a preferential tuition basis." The Court has failed to offer even a plausible explanation why illegality of residence in this country is not a factor that may legitimately bear upon the bona fides of state residence and entitlement to the benefits of lawful residence.

It is significant that the Federal Government has seen fit to exclude illegal aliens from numerous social welfare programs, such as the food stamp program, the old-age assistance, aid to families with dependent children, aid to the blind, aid to the permanently and totally disabled, supplemental security income programs, the Medicare hospital insurance benefits program, and the Medicaid hospital insurance benefits for the aged and disabled program. Although these exclusions do not conclusively demonstrate the constitutionality of the State's use of the same classification for comparable purposes, at the very least they tend to support the rationality of excluding illegal alien residents of a state from such programs so as to preserve the state's finite revenues for the benefit of lawful residents.

The Court maintains—as if this were the issue—that "barring undocumented children from local schools would not necessarily improve the quality of education provided in those schools." However, the legitimacy of barring illegal aliens from programs such as Medicare or Medicaid does not depend on a showing that the barrier would "improve the quality" of medical care given to persons lawfully entitled to participate in such programs. Modern education, like medical care, is enormously expensive, and there can be no doubt that very large added costs will fall on the State or its local school districts as a result of the inclusion of illegal aliens in the tuition-free public schools. The State may, in its discretion, use any savings resulting from its tuition requirement to "improve the quality of education" in the public school system, or to enhance the funds available for other social programs, or to reduce the tax burden placed on its residents; each of these ends is "legitimate." The State need not show, as the Court implies, that the incremental cost of educating illegal aliens will send it into bankruptcy, or have a "grave impact on the quality of education"; that is not dispositive under a "rational basis" scrutiny. In the absence of a constitutional imperative to provide for the education of illegal aliens, the State may "rationally" choose to take advantage of whatever savings will accrue from limiting access to the tuition-free public schools to its own lawful residents, excluding even citizens of neighboring States.

Denying a free education to illegal alien children is not a choice I would make were I a legislator. Apart from compassionate considerations, the long-range costs of excluding any children from the public schools may well outweigh the costs of educating them. But that is not the issue; the fact that there are sound policy arguments against the Texas Legislature's choice does not render that choice an unconstitutional one.

II

The Constitution does not provide a cure for every social ill, nor does it vest judges with a mandate to try to remedy every social problem. Moreover, when this Court rushes in to remedy what it perceives to be the failings of the political processes, it deprives those processes of an opportunity to function. When the political institutions are not forced to exercise constitutionally allocated powers and responsibilities, those powers, like muscles not used, tend to atrophy. Today's cases, I regret to say, present yet another example of unwarranted judicial action which in the long run tends to contribute to the weakening of our political processes.

Congress, "vested by the Constitution with the responsibility of protecting our borders and legislating with respect to aliens," bears primary responsibility for addressing the problems occasioned by the millions of illegal aliens flooding across our southern border. Similarly, it is for Congress, and not this Court, to assess the "social costs borne by our Nation when select groups are denied the means to absorb the values and skills upon which our social order rests." While the "specter of a permanent caste" of illegal Mexican residents of the United States is indeed a disturbing one, it is but one segment of a larger problem, which is for the political branches to solve. I find it difficult to believe that Congress would long tolerate such a self-destructive result—that it would fail to deport these illegal alien families or to provide for the education of their children. Yet instead of allowing the political processes to run their course—albeit with some delay—the Court seeks to do Congress' job for it, compensating for congressional inaction. It is not unreasonable to think that this encourages the political branches to pass their problems to the Judiciary.

The solution to this seemingly intractable problem is to defer to the political processes, unpalatable as that may be to some.

POSTSCRIPT

Are Undocumented Immigrants Entitled to Public Education

The provocative Web site of illegal immigrants (. . .) proclaims that calling an illegal immigrant an "undocumented worker" is like calling a burglar an uninvited houseguest. Hostile attitudes such as this seem to be on the rise as the impact of increasing numbers of immigrants in a broad spectrum of American communities is being felt. In her 1997 book, *Made in America: Immigrant Students in Our Public Schools,* Laurie Olsen candidly discussed situations faced by most of the immigrants. She concluded that "few immigrants get the preparation they need academically . . . that they are largely precluded from access to the curriculum that their English-fluent and U.S.-born schoolmates receive. And as they begin to develop some fluency in English, they learn that it is not the only requirement for being accepted in their new land. They begin to see that to become American is to take one's place on the 'racial map' of our nation." The book chronicles life in a richly multicultural school environment that, ironically, does not produce wider choices and "more appreciation and support for multiple human identities."

This exploration of the deeper problems of immigrants, documented and undocumented alike, can be found in the Winter 2008 issue of *Theory into Practice* featuring articles on the theme "Immigrant Families and U.S. Schools." Included are "Beyond a 'Culture Clash' Understanding of Immigrant Experiences" by Bic Ngo, "Listening to Hyphenated Americans: Hybrid Identities of Youth from Immigrant Families" by Nina Asher, and "Demographic Data and Immigrant Student Achievement" by Lesa M. Clarkson. Another source of facts and figures is Lawrence Hardy's *Education Vital Signs 2007,* published by the National School Boards Association, especially the chapter on "The New Americans: Educating All Children—Regardless of Status."

"Anti-Immigration Legislation, Social Justice, and the Right to Equal Educational Opportunity" by Loucas Petronicolos and William S. New in the *American Educational Research Journal* (Fall 1999) offers a conceptual analysis of policies that seek to exclude undocumented youths from public education. Also of special interest are "Build Fences or Open Doors?" by John Kavanagh and Martin Lancaster in *Community College Journal* (April/May 2008) and "Fighting for Immigrant Rights" by Scott LaFee in *The School Administrator* (November 2007). . . .

Journal theme issues of special note are "Immigration and Diversity," *American School Board Journal* (September 2008) and "The Politics of Immigrant Education," *Theory into Practice* (Autumn 2009).

ISSUE 12

Has the Time Arrived for Universal Preschool?

YES: David L. Kirp, from *Big Ideas for Children: Investing in Our Nation's Future* (First Focus, 2008)

NO: Douglas J. Besharov and Douglas M. Call, from "The New Kindergarten," *The Wilson Quarterly* (Autumn 2008)

ISSUE SUMMARY

YES: David L. Kirp, a professor of public policy and author of *The Sandbox Investment,* calls for expansion of federal support for universal preschool and other child care services.

NO: Professor Douglas J. Besharov and research associate Douglas M. Call of the University of Maryland School of Public Policy examine the development of child care programs and conclude that the case for universal preschool is not as strong as it seems.

In an article titled "Preschool Education: A Concept Whose Time Has Come," *Principal* (September/October 2005), W. Steven Barnett, director of the National Institute for Early Education Research, states that "no area in education has grown like preschool in recent decades." Preschool education received a powerful boost when the federal Head Start program was launched in 1964, but major barriers in affordability and accessibility for those not eligible for Head Start have slowed the movement.

Individual states have moved toward providing preschool programs in recent years. Oklahoma and Georgia have led the country in offering voluntary programs for four-year-olds. Florida, New York, North Carolina, and Massachusetts have moved toward universally available programs. However, neither Georgia or Oklahoma has experienced significant improvement in students' academic performance. According to The Heritage Foundation's *Backgrounder* (May 14, 2009), 80% of children in preschool are in programs run by private providers and who would likely be displaced or burdened with heavy regulation if federal support is vastly expanded.

But the Obama administration has pushed for major increases in federal subsidies, with some commentators saying that this effort is second only to universal health care on the liberal policy agenda. In "Protect Our Kids from Preschool," *The Wall Street Journal* (August 22, 2008), Shikha Dalmia and Lisa Snell of the Reason Foundation claim that our understanding of preschool effects is in its infancy, that kids with attentive parents might well be better off spending more time at home during their formative years, and that "the last thing that public policy should do is spend vast new sums of taxpayer dollars to incentivize a premature separation between toddlers and parents." In agreement with this position, Lindsey Burke of the Heritage Foundation states, "While proponents of universal preschool often cite the findings of small, high intervention programs, it is unlikely that any large-scale implementation of universal preschool could mimic their conditions and would thus fail to produce the results promised by proponents."

Among the advocates of universal preschool is the Pew Center of the States with its Pre-K Now campaign. This organization monitors progress in all states and makes recommendations for strengthening the movement. In spite of recent growth, less than 30 percent of three- and four-year-olds are served in publicly funded early education, according to a 2009 report by the Pew Center. The report calls for a new strategy of collaboration with community-based partners (child care centers, Head Start programs, and faith-based organizations, for example) to enhance access and choice. Sara Mead of the New America Foundation is concerned that a major spike in federal funding may get ahead of the capacity to deliver high-quality programs. She calls for expedited alternative routes to Pre-K teaching, creation of research-based Early Education Academies in neighborhoods now served by low-performing schools, and improvement of articulation between Pre-K programs and the elementary school curriculum. Mead, in "A Case for Pre-K," *The American Prospect Online* (July 18, 2007), states that David L. Kirp and other advocates of universal preschool see it "not as an end in itself but as the groundwork for a more ambitious effort to expand public and social services for children."

In an article in *The Washington Post* (May 15, 2009), "Slow the Preschool Bandwagon," Chester E. Finn, Jr. warns that everybody should pause before embracing universal preschool since "it dumps 5-year-olds, ready or not, into public school classrooms that today are unable even to make and sustain their own achievement gains, much less to capitalize on any advances these youngsters bring from preschool. He concludes that "done right, preschool programs can help America address its urgent education challenges, but today's push for universalism gets it almost entirely wrong."

In the following articles Kirp makes a case for both universal preschool and expanded child development action, while Besharov and Call sound cautionary warnings.

YES

David L. Kirp

The Kids-First Agenda

To say that, when it comes to children's issues, Washington has been asleep at the switch, is much too kind.

Since 2004, as First Focus's 2008 report on the children's budget shows, kids have been losing out to seniors, wealthy taxpayers, and everyone else. A single penny out of every new nondefense dollar is being spent on children's programs; the overall share of federal nondefense spending on kids has dropped by 10 percent; and while other discretionary spending on social initiatives has grown 8 percent, children's programs have been cut by 6 percent. What makes this malign neglect especially infuriating is the impeccable evidence that kids are the best social investment the government can make.

Washington's dereliction is not only a matter of dollars and cents, but the fact that the government has not figured out how to spend its money wisely. The Bush administration's signature initiative, the No Child Left Behind Act, has been a debacle. The promised increased in education funding never materialized, and neither did the predicted improvement in reading and math test scores. What is more, the narrow-gauge, high-stakes testing regimen has distorted educational priorities, giving an entirely new meaning to the practice of teaching to the test.

The lion's share of federal dollars pays for child care, and if that money were well-spent it could make a huge difference. The most famous example, the Abecedarian Program, delivered intensive support to poor children starting a few months after birth. A study done a generation later showed that Abecedarian participants had higher IQs, stayed in school longer and held down better jobs. The annual rate of return over the course of those children's lives is an impressive 7 percent.

Federal policy-makers have ignored such evidence—the rationale for funding child care is not helping kids but expanding the workforce. Child care, as conceived in Washington, is simply a cheap way to park infants and toddlers while their mothers are on the job. There is no Abecedarian—and precious few slots in the considerably less expensive Early Head Start program, despite solid evidence of its success. What is available, whether at child care centers or from the kindly lady down the block, is usually mediocre—and one out of every eight licensed child care centers has been rated "unsafe." Kids do benefit from the sense of self-sufficiency that their parents gain when they are working. But these ill-conceived, on-the-cheap ventures do not help kids. In fact, the worst of them can do harm. Some youngsters who spend long days in impoverished environments become more aggressive.

In the impoverished world into which these children have been dumped, aggression becomes a *Lord of the Flies* survival tactic.

Washington operates too many mini-programs, mostly well-intentioned, but few of them demonstrably effective. The laundry list—everything from educating homeless children to making schools safe and drug-free—has grown haphazardly, with little understanding of what will have the biggest impact. Early Head Start limps along with barely half a billion dollars—essentially a rounding error in the federal budget—and can serve just 2.4 percent of poor children. Meanwhile programs such as teacher quality grants, on which $3 billion is being spent, prosper despite a lack of evidence that, as currently structured, they are worth the investment.

Since the mid-1990s, all the action has taken place outside the Beltway. Forty-one states now support prekindergarten. Public-private partnerships such as Ounce of Prevention have devised exemplary models for infant and toddler care. Foundations have underwritten promising experiments such as the Harlem Children's Zone and the Nurse-Family Partnership. But among Washington lawmakers there is little discussion of which programs need to be overhauled (whether, for instance, Head Start can learn something from the best state-funded preschools), which initiatives should be merged to streamline bureaucracy, and which ought to be dropped. A top-to-bottom rethink of what Washington is doing seems, well, unthinkable.

The public is miles ahead of the politicians. "Overwhelmingly, Americans care about meeting the needs of children," Democratic pollster Geoff Garin has written. And because of their "strong sense of obligation to give children a good start in life" many citizens see the un-benign neglect of children as a "crisis." A new poll commissioned by Every Child Matters, a Washington advocacy group, finds that a sizeable percentage of voters—notably the swing voters—rank increasing the Head Start budget and guaranteeing health care to all children above paying more for homeland security or farm support. The belief that child-rearing ought to be left entirely to parents is being replaced by an ethic of empathy—an acknowledgement that, while parents play a pivotal role, the polity must become a "good steward."

The old saw that children don't matter because they don't vote and don't consume no longer holds true. Governors from both sides of the political aisle—among them Tim Kaine (Virginia), Bobby Jindal (Louisiana), Phil Bredesen (Tennessee), Richard Riley (Alabama), Ted Strickland (Ohio), and Rod Blagojevich (Illinois)—have made children's needs a priority. Politically, they have done well by doing good. The kids-first agenda is the proverbial $20 bill that economists insist cannot be—but is—lying on the sidewalk, awaiting a politician on the national scene to pick it up. Imagine the impact of a kids-first presidential address, delivered with even a fraction of the eloquence of Barack Obama's meditation on race.

The Kids-First Agenda

- Offer help to families from the start.
- Give families the opportunity for top-quality zero-to-five care and education.
- Promote safe and strong communities, with schools as their hub.
- Provide kids the support of a stable, caring adult.
- Support families that save for their children's future.

What is needed in 2008 is not utopian dreaming but "pragmatopia"—a doable agenda that carries the promise of benefiting all children while narrowing race and class gaps. With a new administration in place, Washington is likely to address the basics—guaranteeing health care to all children (which requires only a modest expansion of the overwhelmingly popular Children's Health Insurance Program); liberalizing the child tax credit to reach the poorest 10 million children whose families pay no taxes and so get nothing, and the 10 million youngsters whose families do not earn enough to benefit from the full credit; rewriting the No Child Left Behind Act to make its testing regimen more attentive to thinking and emotional well-being than to parroting; and improving public education with matching grants for states that couple higher salaries with more rigorous training and greater accountability.

The kids-first agenda builds on these basics. It specifies five powerful ideas that, taken together, confront an array of children's needs from birth through adolescence. These ideas, a few of which show good promise of success, are based on solid research. That is crucial, since at present, a host of untested ideas—as well as a goodly number of demonstrably failed ideas—compete with known successes for scarce dollars and attention. The result is Gresham's Law in action: bad initiatives, usually inexpensive and slickly promoted, drive out the good. The kids-first agenda does not focus on K-12 education, since ideas for revamping—or blowing up—the public schools are already thick on the ground. Instead, it specifies what is needed to pull off what University of Chicago economist James Heckman calls "a policy of equality of opportunity in access to home environments *(or their substitutes)."*

Modest expectations are in order, since new ideas, however carefully thought through and faithfully put in place, cannot guarantee that lives turn out well. But the kids-first agenda goes a long way toward assuring that all children, whatever their social circumstances, are treated decently. While that may sound like mommy-state-ism run amok, it makes good economic sense. Not only does the kids-first agenda promote the cognitive skills that can lead to decent jobs and effective membership in the society, it also encourages the acquisition of "soft" skills—perseverance, dependability, consistency, and the ability to keep one's emotions in check—that report cards used to call "working and playing well with others." These non-cognitive abilities have a powerful effect on which teenagers can find jobs, avoid cigarettes and drugs, keep from becoming pregnant, and stay out of jail.

Anticipating a new political regime, the children's advocacy groups are dusting off their wish lists. The most predictable objection to the Kids-First agenda is that it does not include x or y or z initiative. No short list can hope to cover everything, and there is room for full-throated debate about what should be on it. But the pragmatopia agenda must be short because a flood of competing proposals only assures failure. And it must be based on what is best, not for the politicians, bureaucrats, or professionals, but for the kids.

1. Offer Help to Families from the Start

As every parent appreciates, raising kids is hard work. Its importance in shaping children's lives cannot be exaggerated, because parents are youngsters' first and most influential teachers and their emotional buttress—what sociologist Christopher Lasch memorably called a "haven in a heartless world." This is complicated stuff, and many mothers and fathers will value help that begins during pregnancy and continues through the first years of an infant's life. This used to be the province of mothers and grandmothers, but with so many splintering families and single-family households, as well as a deeper understanding of all that is involved in being a good parent, such support can be invaluable.

First-time, poor mothers, especially teenage moms, are likely to be under the greatest stress and the least equipped to cope. They can benefit particularly from a top-notch program, the best of which is the Nurse-Family Partnership. Beginning with home visits during pregnancy, the intention is to build long-term, trusting relationships between these new young moms and highly-trained nurses. (It is considerably harder to get fathers involved.) Mothers who participate are less likely to need social services such as Medicaid and food stamps, less likely to expose their children to abuse, and less likely to have additional children during their teen years. Their children pick up language more quickly, do better in school and, as teenagers, are less likely to get in trouble with the law. Those positive outcomes translate into $5.70 in benefits for every $1 invested. The Nurse-Family Partnership is a good illustration of why quality, though expensive, is what makes the critical difference: The identical program did not have any impact when carried out by paraprofessionals. What began three decades ago as a three-city experiment now operates in 22 states, and within a decade it will expand to reach 150,000 mothers and their children. While that is impressive, the Nurse-Family Partnership only reaches 3 percent of the target population. There is a political lesson to be gleaned from the success of the pre-K movement: Good ideas need powerful advocates.

Many mothers, not just those who are poor, will fare better if they do not have to go it alone. Second and third children often pose new challenges, and middle class moms can be just as ill-prepared as their poorer sisters. We would do well to follow Vermont's lead and make sure that every new mother receives least one home nurse visit. Promising and widely-used initiatives such as Parents as Teachers, which combines group support with one-on-one relationships, have a broader reach. The effect of such programs is likely to be cumulative: As more parents become actively engaged, more children become better off; as good parenting becomes the norm, a critical mass of knowledgeable parents makes for a better community.

The essential bond between a parent and a child would be stronger if the parent with primary child-rearing responsibility didn't have to return to work soon after giving birth. Even though unpaid leave is guaranteed by federal law, few parents have been able to take advantage of the opportunity, since most cannot do without a salary. Logically, four to eight weeks of paid leave is an idea that should appeal to conservatives as well as liberals because it enables parents to raise their infants. At-home care during the first months significantly lowers the rate of infant mortality, and that adds to its moral and economic appeal. California offers workers up to eight weeks to care for a newborn or a sick relative. The federal government should give incentives to states that do the same.

2. Give Families the Opportunity for Top-Quality, Zero-Five Care and Education

Oceans of ink have been spilled addressing the issue of reforming schools—understandably so, since children spend so many hours of their lives there—but what transpires before kids enter kindergarten makes a bigger difference. By their fourth birthday, children from professional families have heard 30 million more words than youngsters whose mothers are on welfare, while the four year old from a professional family has a bigger vocabulary than the mother who is on welfare.

In a kids-first society, every child would have access to good care and education from birth to the age of five. Infants and toddlers are natural explorers whose brains are developing at a phenomenal rate, and in the right setting they can flourish. And they are social beings who learn from example. Geneticists report that while the genetic potential of well-off children has been maxed out, IQ differences among poor children overwhelmingly depend on whether they have grown up in a world that is stable or chaotic, nurturing or punishing.

The best-studied early education program, Abecedarian, which began at infancy and extended through the first years of school, cost about $14,000 a year for each child. That amount is not surprising when you consider that the infant-adult ratio was three-to-one. But it is not necessary to spend that much money to make a meaningful difference.

Early Head Start delivers an array of services, including health care, as well as play-centered education and parent outreach. It costs about $9,000, and the research finds a significant impact.

Even if Washington expands Early Head Start so that all eligible children can participate, millions of youngsters who are not living in dire poverty, but whose parents cannot afford decent early education, are still left out. North Carolina's Smart Start has the right idea, one that other states are picking up: Spend public dollars to underwrite higher-quality early education, explain to parents why quality makes a difference, give them options, and let the market do the rest. Instead of building something brand new, that is the approach that Washington should underwrite with incentive grants.

Preschool for three- and especially four-year-olds has lately become popular. No wonder. The landmark studies report returns on investment as unbelievably high at 17:1 for Perry Preschool. While a scaled-up venture of a high-quality pre-K would yield a considerably lower return—RAND Corporation estimated a 2.7:1 return for a statewide preschool initiative in California—that is still impressive, as are new data from Tulsa, Oklahoma's pre-K program. Those returns signify better lives: more children graduating from high school, going to college, getting decent jobs, remaining healthy, and staying out of jail.

Put pre-K together with nurse-family partnerships and care that is as good as Early Head Start and the cumulative effects logically multiply. In Minneapolis, Federal Reserve economist Art Rolnick is testing this approach. High-quality nurse home visiting for poor mothers and scholarships for carefully vetted pre-K programs make a powerful dose of two proven strategies. Give poor kids access to decent elementary schools, with good teachers and a proven curriculum, and there will be still greater gains to report.

As with every kids-first initiative, pre-K will succeed only if it is top-notch. Studies show what "quality" means: engaged parents and small classes so that well-trained teachers can pay attention to each kid. The best teaching uses kids' play as its starting point. It concentrates less on drilling children in the alphabet than on engaging their social and emotional lives: learning to wait in line, to share, to keep their tempers in check, letting them tell their stories. That quality does not come cheap. Perry Preschool cost about $12,000, and despite the benefits such an investment would yield, that is more money than the government is likely to commit. The Chicago Child-Parent Centers, which have been running for 40 years with remarkable success, cost $8,500, about $2,000 more than Head Start, but less than what many public schools spend on elementary school students.

The federal government should not pick a single winner. Instead, it should follow the same approach as in early education: Help states that offer incentives to strengthen pre-K programs and give parents information that makes them informed consumers.

3. Promote Safe and Strong Communities, with Schools as Their Hub

A decade ago, Judith Harris made headlines with her claim in *The Nurture Assumption* that children's peers, not their parents, shape how they grow up. Like so many single-factor explanations, this one proves too simple. But Harris is onto something important. Community characteristics can affect children's health, their readiness for school, and the likelihood that they will commit crimes. What factors other than sheer poverty make the biggest difference is a conundrum with which researchers have long grappled. But when Harvard sociologist Robert Sampson compared the lives of black children growing up in "concentrated disadvantage" with those who lived in more stable neighborhoods, he found the impact of that experience—the cumulative effect of neighborhood conditions on parenting and school quality as well as children's levels of distrust and fear for their own safety—is equal to an entire year of school.

One response that has been tested with mixed success is to take children out of the places that produce bad outcomes and put them and their families in environments that produce better ones. But the moving van is not a solution, since poor neighborhoods are not going to disappear. A kids-first agenda needs to reach kids where they live and to develop place-based solutions.

In most communities, the school makes a natural hub that has the potential to go far beyond teaching the three Rs, as mandated by the No Child Left Behind Act, or even nurturing the growth of the mind. It can bring together parents, kids, and the child-serving agencies and everything from sports clubs to health clinics. That is the strategy of the Schools of the 21st Century, a model devised by Edward Zigler, Head Start's first director. Those schools house child care, health care, after-school and summer programs under one roof. More than 1,000 of these schools are operating across the country. The evidence suggests that they work. Not only do kids do better on standardized tests, they are also physically and emotionally better off.

The Harlem Children's Zone, the brainchild of charismatic educator Geoffrey Canada, has a bolder vision: to build a cocoon for children from birth to age 20 in one of the country's toughest neighborhoods. It has seeded a 97-block area with an array of initiatives that would be the envy of most places. There is something for almost every child and young adult, including pre-K with a 4:1 adult-child ratio, a "Baby College" for young parents, a charter school for elementary and middle school youngsters, an arts program, after-school tutoring and an investment club for high school students, and tech training for young adults.

Canada would like to see similar ventures in other beleaguered cities, and several places, among them Los Angeles and Baltimore, are giving consideration to emulating the model. While the complexity of the enterprise and the character of its force-of-nature founder make replication especially challenging, the reach of its ambition—the commitment to turn a mean-streets neighborhood into one that is truly kids-first—is what makes the Harlem Children's Zone so exciting. Other place-based models deserve a look. Britain's Sure Start, which began a decade ago in the poorest neighborhoods, offering everything from child care to medical check-ups for young children, has gone nationwide because of parent demand. Similarly, Best Start LA, now getting off the ground in Los Angeles, aims to bring together an array of services for parents, infants, and toddlers.

While these community-building ideas are promising, there is no solid evidence of their long-term effects, no Nurse-Family Partnership studies for neighborhood ventures. Still, it is not too early for Washington to become a partner in underwriting and studying promising initiatives—funding 20 "children's zones," perhaps, as Barack Obama has proposed, as well as assisting school districts that operate "Schools of the 21st Century." The dream is powerful and the logic persuasive. Children start forming ties based on love and trust at home. Child care and preschool, and later the school and the neighborhood, build on that foundation. At each of those critical stages, government can help out.

4. Provide Kids the Support of a Stable, Caring Adult

Ask anyone who works with kids what they need most and the answer is almost always the same: a mentor, a stable and caring adult, someone with the know-how to help a youngster navigate the twisting and sometimes treacherous pathway from early childhood to adulthood. As Generations United, a Washington, DC nonprofit, points out, many baby-boomer retirees do not want to spend their retirement on the golf course.

The century-old Big Brother-Big Sister program has shown that it can boost school attendance and achievement and reduce juvenile crime. There are 250,000 adults in the program. It merits public support so that it can expand. The Senior Grandparents Program, a federal enterprise established in 1965, offers services that range from caring for premature infants to mentoring troubled teens. Its current budget, just $68 million, supports 168,000 children, or less than $500 per child, and there is a waiting list of youngsters needing such help.

In San Diego, a more ambitious model is a work in progress. There, bridging the generational divide is not a one or two hour-a-week activity, but is woven into the fabric of government. Kids' impact is the watchword: Housing for seniors is built on the grounds of an elementary school, Alzheimer's patients are spending time with toddlers in child care centers, and public space is being designed to be child-friendly. The government is looking at the world through kids-first lenses—that is an approach worth replicating with federal support.

5. Support Families that Save for Their Children's Future

The income gap between rich and poor is sizeable and growing. The asset gap, the amount of money that is in the piggybank, is far larger. It also matters more, because it is nearly impossible to spend one's way out of poverty. One way to narrow that gap is for the government to start savings accounts for America's 4.2 million newborns. A kids' saving account plan would give families and children a kick-start in preparing for what is down the road. It is a nest egg built on compound interest that can help to pay for college or job training.

The children's savings account not only puts dollars and cents behind society's commitment to the well-being of the next generation, it also encourages families—especially poor families—to see the payoff from investing in their children's well-being. The best evidence that it works comes from Britain, where 3.2 million accounts have been established since the program was launched in 2001. Three-quarters of these accounts have been invested in stock market funds, and one out of four families has added its own money to the kitty. To encourage parents, as well as neighbors, church, and community groups to chip in, Washington should match additional contributions made by families with limited means.

When Hilary Clinton floated this plan last fall, she was pilloried and quickly backed down. But there is no reason why, as in Britain, the idea's appeal should not transcend party lines. For liberals, it is a step toward equity. Conservatives should find it attractive because it fosters a new generation of capitalists.

From the Kids-First Agenda to Facts on the Ground: Holding Government Accountable

"End child poverty by 2020" was British Prime Minister Tony Blair's bold pledge in 1997, renewed by Gordon Brown this year. Not only did this become the metric that drove policy, it also became a measure of accountability. The press continues to scrutinize the government's success in meeting interim goals, and that oversight by the Fourth Estate has kept the pressure on.

In this country, the Annie E. Casey Foundation's "Kids Count" report highlights differences among the states on a number of measures including child poverty, infant mortality, premature births, teen births, and high school dropouts, while the Education Trust plays a similar role with respect to public education. These foundations are performing a great service, but this is really a job for the government. A national Kids-First Commission would collect information on key indicators, expanding the Casey Foundation's list to include such items as the percentage of children enrolled in prekindergarten, performance on the National Assessment of Educational Progress, and juvenile crime rates. An annual report could spur competition among the states. That is what has happened when states receive grades on "report cards" issued by Pre-K Now, a Washington advocacy group, and are rated by the National Institute for Early Education Research. In Oklahoma, after that state received high marks and flattering national media attention, preschool became a source of state pride, even among conservatives who had strongly opposed it. The same thing happened this year in Alabama, when the state, not usually known as socially progressive, received kudos. A federal seal of approval—or a failing grade—would have an even bigger effect.

The Kids-First Commission would also be charged with seeking out initiatives that have a profound payoff, such as assuring that all children who need them have a pair of glasses; that good dental treatment be made universally available; that pregnant women be screened for HIV (if an expectant mother is treated during the last few weeks of pregnancy with an antiviral drug her child will likely not carry the virus); and that youngsters in the inner cities, where asthma is endemic, receive needed attention.

A "kids' impact" statement also warrants testing. Its purpose is not to add another layer of paperwork, but to encourage agencies to view their programs in a new light. It might encourage HUD to underwrite more cross-generation housing, for instance, or prompt the Health and Human Services Department to join forces with the Education Department in supporting school-based health programs.

For too long, Washington has been an idea-free zone when it comes to children. Thinking "kids first" would change that—and it could change the arc of children's lives as well.

Douglas J. Besharov
and Douglas M. Call

 NO

The New Kindergarten

In her Christmas 2007 campaign AD, Hillary Clinton was shown arranging presents labeled "Universal Health Care," "Alternative Energy," "Bring Troops Home," and "Middle-Class Tax Breaks." She then paused, looking somewhat puzzled, before delivering the punch line: "Where did I put universal pre-K?"

"Universal pre-K" has become a politically popular campaign cause. Clinton is no longer a candidate, of course, but Barack Obama has promised an ambitious pre-kindergarten agenda; John McCain's advisers have hinted that he will do the same. And why not? The rhetoric surrounding pre-K programs is quite extraordinary: They close the achievement gap between low-income children and their more affluent peers; they prepare all children, including middle-income children, for school; and they provide financial relief to working mothers who have been paying for child care.

Yet as the Clinton TV spot unwittingly suggested, universal pre-K programs do not have an obvious place in today's crowded child-care world. Sometimes called "the new kindergarten," pre-K is in most cases just what its name implies: a year of publicly funded half-day school before kindergarten—for all children, regardless of whether their mothers work and regardless of family income. Pre-K has hardly enjoyed a universal embrace. Twice in recent history, attempts to create similar national programs foundered on controversy and went down to defeat. In California, voters recently turned their backs on a statewide plan.

In a 2006 referendum, the Golden State's voters rejected universal "free" preschool by a margin of three to two. Proposition 82, "Preschool for All," was backed by the activist actor-director Rob Reiner and the California Teachers Association; it would have given all California four-year-olds "equal access to quality preschool programs" for three hours a day for about eight months a year—to be paid for by a 1.7 percentage-point increase in the tax rate for single individuals making more than $400,000 and couples making more than $800,000 (almost a 20 percent tax increase, by the way). Although attendance was theoretically voluntary, the proposition would have effectively withdrawn government subsidies from other forms of care, so that families needing or wanting a free or subsidized program would have had no choice but to use their local school's pre-K.

The referendum sparked a statewide debate that went beyond the typical mix of platitudes, generalizations, and exaggerations. Yes on 82, the prime sponsor of the referendum, repeated the oddly precise claim of RAND researchers that "every dollar California invests in a quality, universal preschool program will return $2.62 to society because of savings from reduced remedial education costs, lower high school dropout rates, and the economic benefits of a better-educated work force."

Opponents pointed out, however, that more than 60 percent of California four-year-olds were already in a child-care center, a nursery school, or Head Start, and that the new program would have subsidized the middle-class families now paying for child care while, in the words of a *Los Angeles Times* editorial, establishing "a cumbersome bureaucracy . . . under the state Department of Education, which has done a disappointing job with K–12 schools."

Strangely, the overwhelming rejection of universal pre-K by the voters of our largest state has had no discernible impact on the national debate. It's not that California just happened to have more preschool programs than the rest of the country. Nationwide, about 74 percent of four-year-olds now spend time in some form of organized child care.

⋅⟨☉⟩⋅

To understand what is going on, a little history will help. Beginning in the 1950s, a steadily higher proportion of married women with children took jobs outside the home. Between 1950 and 1970, the proportion of *married* mothers in the work force doubled, rising from about 20 percent to about 40 percent. (Single mothers have always had little choice but to work, or go on welfare.) In 1971, spurred by this change, as well as the emerging women's movement, a group of liberal Democrats led by Walter Mondale (D.-Minn.) in the Senate and John Brademas (D.-Ind.) in the House pushed the Child Development Act through Congress. It was an expansive measure, designed to create a federalized system of child development services. Children were to be enrolled regardless of whether their mothers worked and needed child care, on the ground that all children would benefit from a government-supervised child development effort.

Initially, key senior officials in the Nixon administration supported the measure, seeing child care as an important component of their approach to welfare reform. But after some uncertainty, President Richard M. Nixon vetoed the bill, famously criticizing its "communal approaches to child rearing over [and] against the family-centered approach." His veto—and the specter of "communal" child rearing—not only killed the bill but took the political wind out of the child-care issue for a decade. Mondale himself became alarmed by the backlash even in his politically liberal home state.

Most liberal commentators have seen only conservative politics in the Nixon veto, but even many supporters of a federal child-care program thought the bill was deeply flawed, in ways that its congressional backers may not have understood. The legislation would have jumped past the states to fund hundreds if not thousands of "prime sponsors" (mostly local governments and nonprofit organizations)—all to be selected by officials of the U.S. Department of Health, Education, and Welfare. The prime sponsors were, in turn, supposed to establish local "child development councils" composed of parents, children's services specialists, and community activists. These local entities would then fund as many as 40,000 individual providers.

If this web of federally administered, community-based programs sounds like an echo of the War on Poverty, that's because it sprang from the same social agenda—and many of the same activists. They distrusted state and local governments and wanted "community groups" in control. The bill's supporters boasted that this nationwide cadre of well-funded organizations would be a strong political force for their favored causes. Maurien McKinley of the Black Child Development Institute explained: "It is to the advantage of the entire nation to view the provision of day care/child development services within the context of the need for a readjustment of societal power relationships. . . . As day care centers are utilized to catalyze development in black and other communities, the enhanced political and economic power that results can provide effective leverage for the improvement of the overall social and economic condition of the nation."

In the next three-plus decades, child-care advocates struggled to come up with a formula that would be more attractive to voters, but they repeatedly overestimated support for government-provided child care for middle-class children and underestimated the desire of parents for choice and flexibility.

In the years after Nixon's veto, tens of millions of American mothers entered the labor force. By the 1990s, about 70 percent of married mothers had left full-time child rearing for jobs outside the home, and child-care options had proliferated. According to the National Institute for Early Education Research (NIEER), about 74 percent of all four-year-olds are in "formal" child-care centers for at least part of the day, while the remainder are in "informal" arrangements, a category that includes care by anybody from their parents or relatives to the lady down the street.

Married mothers entered the labor force in waves. First came married women with older children, who were in school anyway and often could take care of themselves after school. Then came those with young children, who needed someone else to care for them. In 1975, only 34 percent of mothers with a child under age three worked outside the home; by 1990, 54 percent did. Moreover, new mothers are quick to return to work. About seven percent do so within one month of their child's birth, and about 41 percent within three months.

Some think that American mothers are in the process of completely abandoning their traditional child-rearing role, but the picture is more mixed. The influx of married women with children into the labor force largely came to a halt in the 1990s. About 30 percent of all mothers today still do not work outside the home. Include those who work only part time—most often less than 20 hours a week—and you will find that almost 50 percent of all mothers, and almost 60 percent of those with a child under three, are not in the full-time labor force.

Although some of these women might take full-time jobs if child care were free, most have decided to delay returning to the labor force until their children are older. In fact, even though they do not "need" child care, about half of stay-at-home mothers place their children in a preschool or nursery school (for at least a year) because they want them to be with other children in a structured learning environment. For these mothers, government-funded pre-K might be a welcome financial break, but it would have little or no educational effect.

Except among women on welfare, the great increase in working mothers had taken place by the late 1980s, when child-care advocates made their second major push for a universal program. In 1987, the Act for Better Child Care Services, or the "ABC bill," as its supporters happily dubbed it, was introduced in Congress. Like the legislation Nixon had vetoed 15 years earlier, the ABC bill sought to create a nationwide system of child development services.

This time, however, there was no Great Society model; the states would administer the program, although they were to be guided by local advisory councils. Each year, the states would distribute $4.6 billion as grants to child-care centers or, in some circumstances, as vouchers to eligible families. Families would be eligible to receive assistance on a sliding scale if their income did "not exceed 115 percent of the State median income for a family of the same size." In high-income states such as Connecticut and New Jersey, that meant a family of four with an income of more than $100,000 would have been eligible. Nationally, the average income cutoff for eligibility for a family of four was about $79,000. (Unless otherwise indicated, all dollar amounts in this essay are in 2007 dollars.)

The ABC bill seemed headed for easy passage until controversy broke out among its liberal backers over a new provision barring the states from expending child-care money for "sectarian purposes or activities." In other words, no money for child care by religiously oriented organizations—even though 28 percent of all center-based programs in 1990 were operated by religious groups—unless they removed all elements of religiosity from their premises.

That provision was a late addition to the bill, apparently at the urging of the National Education Association and the National Parent Teacher Association. These organizations were interested less in the theory of church-state relations than in maximizing the money available for public schools and their employees. And they worried that by using vouchers (thus avoiding strictures against federal aid to religious institutions), the bill would create a precedent for vouchers in K–12 education. Many of the advocacy groups that originally supported the ABC bill—especially those representing religiously based providers, such as the U.S. Catholic Conference and its allies—were incensed.

While the fight over aid to sectarian programs festered for almost two years, another, and ultimately more significant, rift developed among the Democrats who controlled Congress. Key leaders in the House, led by Thomas Downey (D.-N.Y.) and George Miller (D.-Calif.), decided that any new child-care bill should provide greater assistance to low-income families rather than attempt to start a universal child development system, as the ABC bill would. It is unclear whether they opposed a universal federal program in principle—as Marian Wright Edelman of the Children's Defense Fund charged—or were simply being pragmatic. Their own explanation was that a universal system was unlikely to be funded (at least in any meaningful way) and that, in the meantime, low-income families needed help.

Meanwhile, Congress had passed legislation that encouraged mothers to leave welfare for work. Downey, Miller, and their allies wanted to "make work pay" for these mothers—by providing government-funded child care and by supplementing low earnings through an expanded Earned Income Tax Credit (EITC).

In 1990, Congress and President George H. W. Bush finally agreed on a law, much different from the original 1987 ABC bill, that created a $1.3 billion annual program called the Child Care and Development Block Grant and a new half-billion–dollar entitlement for families "at risk" of becoming welfare recipients. It also doubled the EITC, from $11.9 billion in 1990 to $24.6 billion in 1993.

It is difficult to judge what would have happened had the original ABC bill become law, but the narrower Downey-Miller approach was a boon to low-income families. The EITC is now a $45 billion-a-year program, providing financial assistance to more than 23 million families. And the administrative structure it created—especially child-care vouchers—became the basis of the massive expansion of child-care funding six years later under President Bill Clinton's 1996 welfare reform law. That year, the Republican Congress—pushed hard by the Clinton administration—decided that if mothers were expected to work, the government should help pay for child care—the same argument that had appealed to Republicans as far back as the Nixon administration. In only five years, from 1996 to 2000, federal and related state child-care spending almost doubled, rising from $7 billion to $13.6 billion. Add in funding for Head Start, and the total rose from $11.7 billion to $19.9 billion. Spending has remained relatively flat since then.

The result has been an unprecedented increase in the number of children in government-subsidized child care. But more needs to be done. Only half of all eligible four-year-olds with low-income working mothers (and only 18 percent of those under age two) receive child-care aid.

Both the Child Development Act of 1971 and the ABC bill of 1987 foundered, in part, on the seemingly wide political opposition to a universal child-care program that ignores the immediate needs of low-income families. But rather than learn from this lesson, advocates are pushing yet again for a universal program. This time, the selling point is "school readiness" rather than child development, and the focus is only on placing four-year-olds in public schools. But the result is the same: a middle-class–oriented program that does not meet the needs of low-income families.

Advocates claim that pre-K programs do not have to be in schools, and that they would be happy to see existing child-care centers improved with pre-K funds (though that would leave out sectarian programs). But the "quality" requirements these programs impose, such as college degrees and specialized credentials for teachers, are, in the words of *The Los Angeles Times*, "written in such a way to favor programs at public schools."

In any event, given the strong political support for universal pre-K from teachers' unions and the allied educational establishment, it should not be surprising that most state pre-K money has gone to new programs in public schools. In the 2003–04 school year, about 90 percent of children supported by pre-K funds were enrolled in public schools.

Why add a new, school-based program for four-year-olds when, as we have seen, about 70 percent of all three- and four-year-olds nationwide *already* spend at least some time in some form of center-based child care or Head Start? Wasn't this goal of universality the political and programmatic hurdle that brought down California's Proposition 82? Would it not be sounder policy to expand the programs that already exist?

Perhaps the politicians supporting universal pre-K do not know the extent of existing preschool services. (That seems to have been the case in California.) After all, like the rest of us, they are constantly exposed to a barrage of complaints about the inadequacy of child-care services. And some governors seem to have been persuaded that a pre-K program would raise test scores, thus helping to prevent the financial penalties for failing to meet the standards of the No Child Left Behind Act.

The advocates of universal pre-K, however, know exactly what they are doing. In public, they justify creating a new program by claiming—often with some hyperbole—that existing programs are of such poor quality that displacing them will be a net good. Thus, Nathan James, a spokesman for Rob Reiner, asserted that as few as 25 percent of the four-year-olds in day care were in quality programs. Care for the others "could be baby-sitting or throwing a kid in front of a TV set," he said.

That kind of exaggeration—with its remarkable suggestion that the majority of parents hand their children over to dreadful caregivers—distracts attention from the real question: Would it not make more sense to improve the existing programs than to start up a fresh group of efforts whose quality is far from guaranteed? For example, "Project Upgrade" (funded by the U.S. Department of Health and Human Services) used rigorous evaluation techniques to test a revised curriculum for child-care centers in Florida. It raised test scores on at least some elements of cognitive development as much as the best state pre-K programs—at a much lower cost. (Because pre-K pays teacher-level salaries, on an hourly basis it costs about 50 percent more than center-based care.)

In private, advocates give a more plausible explanation. They say that the phrases "universal preschool" and "universal pre-K" are meant to suggest the extension of public education. The idea is to finesse the major reasons why past efforts to enact a universal child-care program failed. If pre-K is just adding another year to schooling, then it is not taking over child rearing (a prerogative carefully guarded by American parents). And if it is an education program, it might attract the children of stay-at-home mothers and would certainly justify taxpayer spending on middle-class and more affluent families. (After all, schools are free to all, regardless of income.)

Justifying free pre-K is politically important because, contrary to what the news media imply, two-parent families in which the mother works are actually much wealthier than those with stay-at-home mothers. As *The Los Angeles Times* complained, universal pre-K makes a "taxpayer-funded preschool available to middle-class and rich families, which can easily afford it." Although other factors are involved, consider that in 2006 the median income for households with two earners was $76,635, almost 40 percent more than that for married-couple households with only one earner ($55,372).

The key to this "pre-K is just another year of school" argument is the claim that, unlike Head Start, pre-K programs provide educational benefits to all children, not just the disadvantaged. "All children make phenomenal gains" in pre-K, claims Libby Doggett, executive director of the advocacy group Pre-K Now. Rob Reiner told the National Governors' Association that pre-K programs produce a "huger impact" on how all children do "in school and later on in life."

At first glance, the idea that starting school a year earlier would boost the learning of middle-class children might make sense. (Let's pass on the worry that many experts have about the negative impact of starting formal education too soon.) We want our children to do the best they can in school, so, presumably, the earlier they start preparing for school, the better.

Unfortunately, no scientifically rigorous evidence supports the claims of pre-K's impact on middle-class children. James Heckman, a University of Chicago Nobel laureate in economics, is one of the strongest voices in favor of early education for low-income children, but here is what he says about applying the model to the middle class: "Advocates and supporters of universal preschool often use existing research for purely political purposes. But the solid evidence for the effectiveness of early interventions is limited to those conducted on disadvantaged populations." As Bruce Fuller, an education professor at the University of California, Berkeley, and author of *Standardized Childhood* (2007), explains, "For middle-class kids the quality of preschool centers would have to approach a nirvana-like condition to present radically richer environments than the majority of middle-class homes, or home-based caregivers."

It's not that knowledgeable pre-K backers don't know this. Fuller reports on a conversation he had with one of the key foundation funders of the pre-K movement: "When I asked [universal pre-K] benefactor Sue Urahn of the Pew Charitable Trusts why government should subsidize preschools for all families, rich or poor, she acknowledged that 'you probably won't get the degree of benefit for middle-class children that you would for poor kids.' But, she added, universality may bolster the political will to widen children's access to, and to improve the quality of, preschool."

So that's the strategy: promise the middle class a free lunch. Thus far, it seems to be working. Each year sees an increase in the number of children in pre-K programs. In the 2006–07 school year, the NIEER reports, 14 states had 25 percent or more of all four-year-olds in pre-K, and three states had reached 50 percent.

In most places, pre-K programs are simply being added to the mix of pre-school programs, with little or no attempt to coordinate them with existing child-care programs or Head Start. The eventual goal, apparently, is to have universal pre-K programs substitute for all programs that now serve four-year-olds.

But is it the right strategy? What about the nearly 500,000 four-year-olds in Head Start? And what about the almost 1.6 million four-year-old children of full-time working women—children who need more than part-time care while their mothers are on the job?

◦◦◦

Pre-K is already eating into Head Start enrollments. Last year, Congress responded to what was called "underenrollment" by allowing Head Start grantees to enroll more infants and toddlers, and to raise income eligibility ceilings. This is, at best, a temporary fix to a long-term problem.

Nonprofit and for-profit child-care centers face a subtler threat. Full-time working mothers who use pre-K (whether because of its presumed quality or because it is free) no longer need their services. And because pre-K fills only a few hours of each day, these mothers tend to patch together some combination of before– and after–pre-K activities for their children. Because they generally cannot use child-care centers for this purpose, children are more likely to wind up in informal care, provided by neighbors, relatives, and others—the very care that pre-K advocates criticize most.

When researchers studying New York State's universal pre-K program raised the possibility that pre-K programs "could negatively impact the enrollment of four-year-olds at nonpublic child-care centers and preschools," a pre-K advocate asked, "Is this necessarily an all-negative outcome?"

Or perhaps advocates would prefer the Oklahoma solution. Using mostly federal funds, the state simply pays child-care centers for a full day for each child, even if the child is only present for four hours. (This practice is documented in government reports, but the folks in Washington either don't know or don't care about it.)

Another troubling aspect of the pre-K movement is that it is a retreat from parental choice in early childhood arrangements, an approach that has been nurtured since the passage of the block grant bill in 1990. Since then, more than $100 billion in child-care subsidies has been distributed through vouchers—with nary a problem—while low-income parents have had the freedom to choose the providers they want, largely without government constraints. (Even unlicensed providers can be used in most states.) But parents in neighborhoods served by pre-K have only one choice: send their children to the public program or dig into their pockets to send them to one of their own choosing.

Vouchers are controversial for K–12 education, but they have been widely accepted in the child-care world—because the context is so different. Remember, the children involved are three-year-olds and four-year-olds. Even some strong critics of vouchers for the schools, such as John Witte, a political scientist at the University of Wisconsin, Madison, have concluded that *for preschool programs* a "voucher system seems to be the best choice to maximize opportunity and equity and educational efficiency."

Besides encouraging responsive programming and service improvement, vouchers provide a high degree of flexibility needed to accommodate the disparate needs of families. Some parents want, or need, only half-day care; some need evening or after-hours care; others need full-day care, perhaps with extended hours. Some parents want their children cared for by other family members; some want to use neighbors; others want a nursery school; still others prefer a care center, perhaps in a church. Some parents may want all their children of different ages in one place; others may not care. Some parents will want their children close to home; others will want them close to work. The variations are almost infinite. Accommodating such variation is all but impossible in a top-down, pre-K regime.

Perhaps most troubling, universal pre-K does little, if anything, to solve the most vexing educational problem facing America: the achievement gap that puts low-income, mostly minority children so far behind more fortunate children. On a host of important developmental measures, low-income children suffer large and troubling social and cognitive deficits compared with others. This translates into a lifelong achievement gap that curtails the educational attainment, employment opportunities, and earnings potential of large numbers of children—especially among African Americans, Latinos, and other disadvantaged minorities.

⋅⟨⊙⟩⋅

The achievement gap has many causes, from the poverty stemming from a history of discrimination and restricted opportunity to the child-rearing styles of many disadvantaged families. Cause and effect are intermingled in multiple and controversial ways. Early childhood education is a potentially important remedy to some of these problems, but the plain fact is that the family is the primary teacher of young children—and compensatory programs face a much larger challenge than pre-K advocates' rhetoric commonly suggests. What parents do (and do not do) counts much more than any early education program.

Debate rages about how best to close the achievement gap, but all specialists agree that to be successful, programs must be focused on the children's deep needs and be intense enough to make a difference. That means multiple years of educational and support services for the parents as well as the children—and that simply is not something pre-K and its three or four hours of school-based services will provide.

Some observers think that, if pre-K programs really worked for the middle class, they would widen the achievement gap. Bruce Fuller points out, "The well-orchestrated universal preschool campaign at once says their silver bullet will help all kids and close early achievement gaps. That's pretty difficult to pull off. It means that children from middle-class and wealthy families will accelerate in their development, AND then poor kids will accelerate even more."

Perhaps sometime in the future all American children will be in free child care, at least by the time they are four years old. But we seem far from that goal. One research group estimates that a universal pre-K system would cost roughly $55 billion a year, more than six times the roughly $9 billion the federal and state governments now spend on four-year-olds. If past estimates for the costs of other social programs are any guide, it would not be unreasonable to double that forecast.

Universal pre-K might be a boon to the middle class—depending on whether, in the end, it is their tax dollars that pay for it—but it would still leave unmet the much more serious needs of low-income children. Half of all eligible low-income working mothers still do not receive child-care subsidies. Would it not be wiser policy to help them purchase better child care than to channel more funding into pre-K programs that serve higher-income children whose parents do not necessarily work?

Twice before, efforts to create a universal program stalled in Washington. But this round's education-based strategy may work. Although it failed with the voters of California, special interests hold much greater sway in the nation's capital. So, to answer Hillary Clinton's question: Universal pre-K is caught in the midst of middle-class and interest-group politics. As usual, the most disadvantaged children may lose out.

POSTSCRIPT

Has the Time Arrived for Universal Preschool?

Lisa Snell, in an October 31, 2008 web posting, "Preschool's Failures: Where Are the Long-term Benefits?" cites evidence that the high-quality preschool program in Tennessee produced no statistical achievement difference between those who attended preschool and those who did not. In Oklahoma, where preschool had been in place for 18 years, math and reading scores are still below the national average. In his recently published book, *Reroute the Preschool Juggernaut* (2009), Chester E. Finn, Jr. attempts to stifle the momentum of the universal preschool campaign spearheaded by secretary of education Arne Duncan, David L. Kirp, Libby Doggett of Pre-K Now, W. Steven Barnett, and others. Precisely as these strategists intend, he claims, "many Americans are coming to believe that pre-kindergarten is a good and necessary thing for government to provide; indeed that not providing it will cruelly deprive our youngest residents of their birthrights, blight their educational futures, and dim their life prospects." The result, he contends, has been strong public support for the movement with little consideration of how it will be paid for.

Further expansion of Douglas Besharov's concerns about the movement can be found in "Preschool Puzzle: As State After State Expands Pre-K Schooling, Questions Remain," *Education Next* (Fall 2008) and in his testimony of June 27, 2007 before the Joint Economic Committee of the U.S. Congress. In these documents Besharov addresses the problem of whether a preschool program can reduce the racial/ethnic achievement gap and the issue of who should receive expanded funding for early care and education.

An even-handed appraisal of the issue can be found in "Invest in Early Childhood Education," *Phi Delta Kappan* (April 2009) by Sharon Lynn Kagan and Jeanne L. Reid and in "Preparing for Change: A Case Study of Successful Alignment Between a Pre-K Program and K-12 Education," *Childhood Education* (Spring 2009) by Christopher Brown and Brian Mowry. Other worthwhile sources on the topic are "Pre-K 101," *Education Next* (Summer 2007) by Stephen Goldsmith and Nina S. Rees, which argues for parental choice; "Preschool Is School, Sometimes," *Education Next* (Winter 2007) by Robert C. Pianta; "Changing the Odds," *Educational Leadership* (October 2007) by Susan B. Neuman; and Bruce Fuller's book, *Standardized Childhood* (2007).

ISSUE 13

Is Privatization the Hope of the Future?

YES: Chris Whittle, from "Dramatic Growth Is Possible," *Education Next* (Spring 2006)

NO: Henry Levin, from "Déjà Vu All Over Again," *Education Next* (Spring 2006)

ISSUE SUMMARY

YES: Chris Whittle, founder and CEO of Edison Schools, contends that public school systems still operate in an eighteenth-century mindset and offers an "independent learning" model as a replacement.

NO: Professor of economics and education Henry Levin criticizes the assumptions on which Whittle bases his prediction of successful operation of schools by for-profit management organizations such as Edison.

Nobel prize–winning economist Milton Friedman, in an article appearing in *The Washington Post* on February 19, 1995, put forth the idea that the American system of public education needs to be radically reconstructed. Specifically, he stated that this could be achieved "only by privatizing a major segment of the educational system—i.e. by enabling a private, for-profit industry to develop that will provide a wide variety of learning opportunities and offer effective competition to public schools." He conceded that this reconstruction must be gradual, that it cannot come overnight.

This theoretical base provided a springboard for a number of entrepreneurial ventures. Chris Whittle has led two major efforts to participate in such a reconstruction: Channel One and the Edison Project. The former places computer networks in schools to provide news programs accompanied by targeted advertising. The service now reaches about one-sixth of public school students. The Edison Project, as of the 2006–07 school year, reaches about 285,000 students in 19 states, the District of Columbia, and the UK, according to its Web site.

Meanwhile, the National Education Association (NEA) has taken a firm stance in regard to such inroads in the public domain. Their position on the matter is clear: "In public schools today, little is safe from commercialization and privatization." For many decades, private companies have contracted to perform various support functions in transportation, maintenance, and food services. In recent years, there has been a growth in private sector involvement in administrative and instructional functions for individual schools and entire school districts. The NEA fears that these movements, combined with a steady growth of corporate commercial activities within public schools, amount to an attempted private sector takeover of the entire system.

Edison Schools, Inc. has become the nation's largest for-profit manager of public schools. These schools place a heavy emphasis on teamwork and employ a "distributive leadership" model, dividing teachers into teams, each with a lead teacher who runs staff meetings, holds demonstrations, and handles discipline problems. Edison principals are supervised by a regional manager, are often guided by a mentor, and are assisted by a financial manager. In a January 1997 article in *The School Administrator*, "The Edison Project Founder's Musings on American School," Chris Whittle optimistically predicted "the merging of public education and entrepreneurism, the convergence of caring and capital, and the coming together of local control and national resources" that may reward shareholders and will definitely benefit children, teachers, parents, and the nation. In the years following this statement, the enterprise fell on hard times as contracts were lost and its stock price plummeted. In 2003, however, Edison was bailed out by an investment firm representing the Florida pension fund that, perhaps ironically, serves teachers who are mostly opposed to privatization, according to an article by David Moberg, "How Edison Survived," *The Nation* (March 15, 2004). That influx of capital and some successes in Philadelphia breathed new life into Edison.

The February 2007 issue of *Phi Delta Kappan* features a lively exchange on private educational management organizations between Peter Campbell, Missouri state coordinator for the Assessment Reform Network, and John E. Chubb, chief education officer of Edison. In his article, "Edison Is the Symptom, NCLB Is the Disease," Campbell contends that Edison Schools, operating primarily in inner-city poverty areas, are characterized by harsh discipline, a rigid basic curriculum paced by tests, and the use of non-unionized teachers. Chubb's point-by-point refutation emphasizes that Edison brings scientific research and nationwide experience to otherwise failing schools.

In the articles paired here, Chris Whittle expresses hope that private ventures will radically reform America's schools, while Henry Levin argues that Whittle's scenario ignores contrary evidence about the complexities of school reform.

YES

Dramatic Growth Is Possible

Until Thomas Friedman recently discovered otherwise, we believed the world was round. We also thought that phone calls had to travel through Ma Bell wires, and that your operator would be in Des Moines, not in New Delhi. Remember when we had just three daily television news programs, one with father Walter, and all at precisely the time when only our grandmothers could watch? And are you bothered that now anyone can see what's on your rooftop or in your driveway, anytime, via Google Earth? Does all this change, turmoil, even progress, concern you? Is your world being rocked?

Don't worry; if you need a fetal-like retreat to times gone by, there is a place you can find respite: *your childhood school is still here.* Even if the old buildings are gone, your old daily routine within them has been superbly, if unconsciously, preserved to a degree that would make King Tut beam brighter than the gold in his tomb. And not only can *you* return to your school-day experience just by visiting your children's schools; at the rate change is occurring in education, your great-grandchildren will attend the same ones!

The point is simple: how we educate our children today is remarkably similar to how we educated them decades ago. Perhaps more than any other modern-day institution, schooling is nearly impervious to change. If our "old school design" was working with a high degree of consistency and reliability, such inflexibility might be fine. But decades of facts say that it isn't fine. Results from the most recent National Assessment of Educational Progress (NAEP) show that roughly 15 million American children—more children than reside in all of England—are achieving below basic levels of literacy and numeracy. If the scale of this number concerns you, you should find it even more troubling that it has been that way for decades. And our problems don't stop with the children most in need. Even our best students are falling behind, in international comparisons and at home. Among the "talented tenth," those in the top 10 percent of NAEP test-takers, reading scores have dropped four points since 1971, and math scores have not budged since they were first measured in 1978.

Simply put, we are not making the grade *at the bottom or the top.*

From *Education Next,* Spring 2006, pp. 14–19. Copyright © 2006 by Education Next. Reprinted by permission of Hoover Institution, Stanford University.

Why Things Stay the Same

Why does America seem so unresponsive? Let me suggest three reasons.

First, because "numb" is the root word of numbers. We have lost our outrage (if indeed we ever had it) about the deplorable statistics . . . Education inadequacy is not sexy. Illiteracy is not sudden in its cause nor quick with its solution and thus lacks the "production values" highly desired by our ratings-craved media. Illiteracy can't compete with Katrina, 9/11, Iraq, or even a good Supreme Court nomination fight. Sure, there's the obligatory annual story in most news vehicles about "our education crisis," but contrast that to, say, round-the-clock, multiple-week coverage of a devastating hurricane. Our sound bite-oriented media find it far too complex to connect what is going on in our schools with the possibility of a 21st-century, full-eclipse of the American economy, imported from the Pacific Rim. Let C-SPAN or PBS do that kind of dull coverage.

A second reason is the colossal, $400 billion per year status quo that makes the military-industrial complex look nimble by comparison.

The third reason for our inaction is even more important: *America does not believe there is a "next" generation of schools.* What, we think, could be *that* different in schools of the future? We might change the calendar around, pay teachers a little more, update the curriculum, but none of those things is that big a deal. After all, schools are schools are schools.

A Failure of Imagination

I've now been involved in the world of public education for 15 years, as the founder and CEO of Edison Schools, one of the country's first private companies to take on the challenge of improving public schools. If Edison, which now works in various ways in nearly 1,000 schools and serves more than 300,000 students, were a public school district, I would be one of the longest-serving heads of a major school system in the United States (average tenure for the superintendent of a major system is less than four years). I've seen and heard a lot. And one of the things I've seen is stunningly uncharacteristic of America, earth's creative capital. We've had a national failure of imagination when it comes to what our schools can and should be. We don't *believe* there is anything particularly new to discover in schooling, so, as a society, we don't set out to find it. Columbus believed. NASA believed. When it comes to schools, we don't. For sure, there are pioneers here and there, but our national mindset does not embrace the possibility that our schools could be and should be radically different.

Instead, because "the way school is" was imprinted on all of us with Intel-like precision by our own 12 years of schooling, America believes that schools are governed by a set of immutable, almost physical, laws, which include:

1. In schools, adults must supervise children virtually all of the time (Dickens would feel right at home).

2. The school day must be rigidly organized, generally chopped up into 45-minute or one-hour blocks (changing this to longer periods of time was, some years back, viewed as a grand breakthrough).
3. The smaller the number of children in a class, the better the education results (never mind if a smaller class might mean a teacher who is paid less and is less prepared).
4. Adults must run all aspects of the school—and do all the work within it (that many teenagers now work after school and on weekends is a fact to ignore).
5. There are no efficiencies, economies, or new qualities to be found in "design breakthroughs"; greater spending is the only way to improve education (disregard more or less flat education results after two decades of real-dollar annual spending increases).

What if *all* of the above "truths" are incorrect—truths that we will some day regard as myths, artifacts of a forgotten era? What if we approached the organization of a school *without* any of these "truths" as cornerstones? Where might simple logic and our own real-life experiences take us?

Let me suggest what some of the new truths of school design might be:

1. Learning accomplished through individual effort, or through working in small teams, is as "sticky" (well retained) as that served up in a classroom group, no matter what its size.
2. Learning can come in many forms, and the size of the learning group can vary greatly without any penalization of effect.
3. Children are capable of tremendous focus and responsibility, and they can be taught these traits at a much younger age than many people might think.
4. Variety matters in learning; too much of any one thing, like sitting passively in a classroom for 12 years, has rapidly diminishing returns; and lack of variety negatively affects teachers as much as children.
5. Students can teach as well as learn. Has your child ever taught you anything? Has one of your older children ever taught something to one of your younger ones?

The Future

Working from these potential new "truths," let's imagine what a school of the future might look like. In fact, in key respects, the best school of the future might share some aspects of the school of the past, the 19th-century past that existed in many places of America up to the 1920s: the schoolhouse where older students were instructors, teaching under the guidance of a highly qualified adult. Indeed, we can reconstruct a school of the past that is appropriate to the modern era, where teachers' salaries are competitive with other professions, where students are taught by older peers under the supervision of master teachers who can use technology for pedagogical purposes.

Suppose, for example, that beginning in the 1st grade children spent an hour a day learning on their own, not under the direct supervision of a teacher (although perhaps watched over by an older peer). Let's presume that by the

3rd grade, the amount of time students were "on their own" increased to two hours per day. By the 6th grade and throughout middle school, let's assume that only half of a student's time was spent in what we now think of as a classroom. Finally, imagine that by high school only one-third of a student's time was in a traditional classroom setting. If this sounds overly radical, consider that many college students are in class fewer than 15 hours a week, half the time of a high-school senior. College freshmen are only 90 days older than high-school seniors. Did something magical occur in that short period to make them more capable of independent learning? Remember that fully half of all high-school seniors enter college.

If students are not in a classroom, where are they? Sleeping at their desks? Playing video games on school computers? Well, the answer is that they are learning—just not at that very moment with a teacher, just not in a class, but still "in school." More often than not, they will be reading! Educators believe deeply that students should read, but there is very little time in the school day for that to happen. And after a long day at school and with other homework and important activities, how much time is realistically available in the evening? They also will be working with a small group of other students. And they might be on their computers, writing, researching, exploring, mining that almost endless, great new ethereal library—the Internet. All the while, they will be monitored by their somewhat older peers, just as graduate students supervise and aid undergraduates in college environments. Though they will not be in class half of their day, they will be in a school building all of it.

On the Henry Levin Commentary

Editors' note: Since Henry Levin considered, in some detail, the record of Edison Schools in his essay on the future, Chris Whittle responds here to Levin's essay.

Henry Levin's essay criticizes the involvement of the private sector in public education, Edison Schools, and my vision of public education's future. These responses to selected points are intended to provoke thought on the overall thrust of his argument.

Economies of Scale. Superintendents struggling with the *loss of scale* resulting from enrollment declines would strongly disagree with Levin's contention that there are few economies of scale in education. Economies of scale occur at the *system* level—not the school level. As in well-run, large, public-school systems, Edison's central costs have improved significantly, in percentages, over time, which is a key reason Edison is now profitable.

Academic Results. Levin calls Edison's academic results "mediocre" and cites a recent RAND report and his view of results in Baltimore and Philadelphia. Readers can draw their own conclusions with data in hand, but this much we know: In the fall of 2002, Edison was assigned to manage 20 schools in Philadelphia with an average proficiency of only 6 percent. Proficiency has nearly *quadrupled* in 36 months. These schools—among the district's most challenging—have kept pace with a district achieving the highest gains among America's major urban systems. Edison was recently asked to manage two additional schools in Philadelphia.

Since the fall of 2000, Edison has managed three schools in Baltimore. The average ranking of those schools in 2000 was 101 out of 117 district schools. Today, their average ranking is *57 out of 115 schools,* with one school going from 107th to 24th. Our contract there was recently extended.

The RAND report says, "From 2002 to 2004, average proficiency rates in currently operating Edison schools increased by 11 percentage points in reading and 17 percentage points in math. Meanwhile, average proficiency rates in a matched set of comparison schools increased by lesser amounts, 9 percentage points in reading and 13 percentage points in math (although the Edison advantage is statistically significant only in math)."

Greater Funding. Levin incorrectly says that Edison receives more funding than typical public schools. Edison on average receives resources *below* those of public schools in the cities where it works. Exceptions are rare. An excellent report from the Thomas B. Fordham Foundation Institute shows charter-school funding well below comparable public school funding.

The Model. Levin uses a 40-year-old study to support his view that our current education model cannot be changed. However, a miraculous technological leap occurred on the way to the 21st century: the invention of the Internet and the PC. Levin correctly states that early uses of such technologies in classrooms have not worked well, but Wright's first flight did not go very far either.

Hope vs. Pessimism. Mr. Levin foresees the "struggle of incremental reforms in a system designed to conserve rather than transform society." While America's public educators want to conserve democracy and freedom, they do *not* want an education design that dooms 15 million children to near illiteracy. We *can* change this outcome by transforming a model that may have once served us well but is now out of date.

—Chris Whittle

Many educators reading this are probably saying, perhaps in less kindly terms, "This idea is hopelessly naive. Students cannot be entrusted with their own education; they cannot be expected to manage their own time. Students don't understand the importance of education and, therefore, can't be expected to manage it."

My response: schools have failed to make students the masters of their own learning, and we have the results to show for it. We are still operating in an 18th-century mindset, believing that these young, half-civilized things called children must be literally whipped into shape, if not with a stick then with a never-ending schedule. If students don't understand the importance of education enough to take charge of their own, it is because the schools we have designed don't spend any real time helping them understand this.

A huge side benefit of this "independent learning" model—and I am talking here mainly about middle- and high-school programs—is that it would *double* teachers' compensation in the United States. If students spent half as much time in class, then half as many teachers would be needed. And we could pay those remaining twice as much—without increasing taxes by one cent.

I introduce the concept of large-scale, independent learning in America's middle- and high-school communities and the corresponding increase in teachers' pay to suggest that there may be a more powerful school design "out there" that is radically different from what we now know. My example is only one idea of what education might be like. There are many more concepts worthy of serious consideration and development. However, most of these will never achieve meaningful scale unless America takes a fundamentally different approach to how it brings about change in its schools.

Focus on Education

This year, the federal government will spend $27 billion on healthcare research and development (R&D) through the National Institutes of Health. The Department of Defense recently invested $9 billion just on the prototype of the next generation of fighter planes. These investments are precisely why we have one of the finest health-care systems on the globe (providing our citizens one of the longest life spans of any country) and an unparalleled military. We have exceptional health care and national security because we constantly *invest in change*—above and beyond what we spend to merely operate our military and health-care systems. Our health care and national security may not be perfect, but there is little question about our international placement in these fields.

By contrast, we invest virtually nothing in changing our schools. Education research-and-development spending at the federal government level is 1/100th of what we spend in health care. Why, then, are we surprised when our K–12 schools are far from the envy of the world? We spend a staggering sum, $400 billion a year, to run the schools we inherited from one hundred years ago. At the same time, we are investing, by modern R&D standards, only a pittance ($260 million) to design and test the next generation of schools. As a result, we get exactly what we pay for—out-of-date school designs.

Our local school districts don't have the scale to take on these R&D initiatives. The private sector of K–12 education, which is still in a fledgling stage, does not have the resources, either. And if you expect philanthropy to come to the rescue, think again. The endowment of just one Ivy League college is more than ten times all the annual giving to our public schools. Only one institution in America has the scale required to fund the invention of our next generation of public schools: our federal government. If 15,000,000 less-than-literate students are not enough to move it to action, let's hope, for the sake of our children, that the looming threat of second-class economic citizenry in the 21st century does the trick.

Déjà Vu All Over Again?

My vision of where education will be—and where it must be—overlaps with Chris Whittle's to some extent. But it also differs in significant ways. Whittle's essay, drawn from his cheerful book (*Crash Course*), tells us that most of our education troubles will be over in just a quarter century. I disagree. His assumptions often differ markedly from the available evidence on what works and ignore the complexity of the witches' brew of politics, unions, bureaucracies, immigration, economics, and the social sciences. He implies that his vision is inexorable when it is merely wishful.

Chris Whittle's projection for 2030 is an elaborated echo of the 1990s, when for-profit education-management organizations (EMOs) proposed a mission and rationale for transforming American education. The standard fare promoted by those EMOs and their venture-capital sources was that the education industry was the next big opportunity for private capital, following the profitable example of the earlier HMO transformation of health care.

The lead financial actor at the beginning of that EMO era was Merrill Lynch, advisor to Whittle's company, Edison Schools. Merrill Lynch published *The Book of Knowledge*, a 193-page report on the $740 billion education and training market. Distributed widely to potential investors, *The Book* identified five "Big Ideas" that would transform the education and training industry over the next decade. But the book's story begins with the ostensible failure of public education and its rapidly rising costs, mediocre student achievement results, poor high-school graduation rates, and limp international rankings. The reason given for this miserable showing was the inefficiency of government.

Business enterprise efficiency would rescue the schools through organizational improvements; selection, training, assessing, and rewarding of principals and teachers on the basis of performance; and adoption of promising education technologies. Sophisticated business projections were conjured to assure potential investors that these enterprises would be highly profitable (doing well) while serving society (doing good).

The Wrong Assumptions

Not all has gone well, and Edison is a good case study, having lost more than six hundred million dollars of its investors' funding. Edison has one of the most complete models among the EMOs. It has truly attempted to deliver a quality school, but the evidence on raising student achievement shows no

From *Education Next*, Spring 2006, pp. 21–24. Copyright © 2006 by Education Next. Reprinted by permission of Hoover Institution, Stanford University.

revolution in results. According to a recent evaluation by the RAND Corporation and comparisons in Philadelphia and Baltimore, Edison's record is not very different from that of similar public schools, though it has received greater funding than its public counterparts.

Somehow, in projecting to the future, Whittle posits a large number of changes in the basic institutions for delivering education, education research, and education personnel, based on the "success" of the EMOs, especially Edison. And despite the financial losses and mediocre achievement results, he believes that schools should be turned over to large businesses—with "economies of scale." Teachers' salaries would be double those of today to obtain the best professional talent; new training institutions for principals would arise through collaborative efforts of top business and education schools to churn out exemplary leadership; and government would increase funding for education research by a factor of ten or more.

The Whittle scenario also assumes that school districts would retain only a tiny percentage of federal, state, and local revenues, perhaps 1 percent, and limit themselves to "monitoring and quality-control" oversight of schools; private contractors would receive the other 99 percent. National and international education firms will compete for these contracts, and their retention by the district will depend on their performance. Teachers will be chosen by contracted schools, but will be employees of both districts and contractors (opening up districts to liability for personnel whom they neither select nor supervise). Teachers' salaries will reach numbers like $130,000 (adjusted for inflation) at the highest ranks. Principals will earn up to $250,000 with a base of 60 percent of this amount and the remainder in bonuses.

Back to the Future

The complete shift of schools to for-profit contractors seems to be based on the old business claims of the 1990s and Whittle's selective interpretation of Edison's record. It is also based on the argument that the contracting firms will benefit from economies of scale that are unavailable to the average school district in the United States. This is a strange and stubborn argument for Edison, which persistently claimed that annual losses in the tens of millions of dollars were due to insufficient numbers of schools. Subsequent expansions led only to larger losses.

Research has shown that beyond very small schools and school districts, there are few opportunities for economies of scale in education because most of the costs increase with enrollments and are not fixed costs that decline with additional clients. In fact, the number of teachers and other employees per student has increased in recent decades. Further, size tends to depersonalize education. As a consequence, the leading edge of school reform is the promotion of smaller rather than larger units.

Whittle supports his assertion on scale economies with a table (page 180 in his book) that contrives the appearance of economies of scale by comparing a school district spending $28 million in 2030 with a hypothetical contractor receiving $25 billion in revenues. The table purports to show where contractors would experience scale economies and how they would yield a profit of

10 percent of revenues. As Yogi Berra would say, It's *déjà vu* all over again. It hasn't worked in the past; there's no reason to believe it will work in 2030.

Even more puzzling is how schools would prosper with half the teaching personnel. According to Whittle, this would be done largely through replacing teachers with student labor. Educators have long argued for greater participation of students in the education process, but not as a way of reducing costs. Four decades ago, noted economist William Baumol argued that the idea of reducing costs in education and similar labor-intensive industries by substituting capital for labor or less-skilled labor for higher-paid professionals was impractical, at best. According to Baumol, education, by its very nature and its intransigence to change (whether public or private), is a teacher-intensive activity and so cannot benefit from standard approaches to increasing productivity. Equally, it is not possible to eliminate half of the opera singers in a classical opera or to replace two members of a string quartet with music synthesizers as a cost-effective way of improving quality. To this point no one has succeeded in disproving Baumol's thesis, nor has anyone discovered methods of providing the same education with half the number of teachers.

What Else Won't Work

Whittle's prime example of assigning students to peer tutoring is already used widely in public schools. I don't know a single situation where this method has reduced teachers' responsibilities. It is a form of supplementary instruction for selected students who are far behind other students (particularly for those with learning disabilities), not a substitute for regular teachers. And peer tutoring is not "free." The cost of effective peer tutoring is higher than alternatives, such as computer-assisted instruction or smaller class sizes or longer school days, because of the needs for adult personnel to coordinate, train, and monitor the student tutors. If peer tutoring has the capability of replacing half of our teachers, why wait until 2030?

Whittle suggests that charters and EMOs would do well to establish demonstration schools to show how we can use student chores to reduce the teachers by half. But it is remarkable that at present he can promise a sweeping future based on this phenomenon without dredging up even a single example as a proof of its existence.

Whittle also assumes (in his book) that the "wireless revolution" will contribute to independent learning and a reduction in the need for teachers. But even if this claim were supported by evidence, the record shows that technology did not reduce teacher cost significantly enough to make Edison profitable or to create superior student achievement. Larry Cuban's history of the overblown promises of education technology (in his 2001 book *Oversold and Underused: Computers in the Classroom*) provides a concrete picture of why we cannot count on technology. Of course, even as astute an observer as Bertrand Russell got this wrong in predicting in 1933 that instruction by motion pictures would require only large auditoriums with low-paid classroom monitors. Whittle is in good company in his zeal for a strategy that has always generated more vision than reality.

In his infomercial on behalf of for-profit education enterprises, there is a technological determinism that assumes no opposition from or conflict with special interests such as teacher unions, administrators, and education bureaucracies. Every projected change is in the interest of all groups, a harmonious solution to what ails the schools. Even teacher organizations that would lose half of their membership and half of their collegial help at the school site will capitulate to the siren song of higher salaries. And new approaches to teacher training will enable them to get better results with half of the labor force and student assistance.

What Can and Should Be Done?

Whittle's assertion of the dominant role of for-profit firms in 2030 and the feasibility of halving the teaching force are not demonstrated to be feasible or desirable. Of course, the education system will be pressed to improve, especially on behalf of children from families in poverty, minorities, and immigrants, who will eventually compose a key component of the labor force. We will also need to find ways to ensure that all students master basic skills and that a substantial portion master the thinking skills and collaborative methods that will ensure a productive polity and prosperous economy. It should be noted that there has never been a golden age in education in which these goals were met, and the future will represent a struggle of incremental reforms in a system designed to "conserve" rather than transform society.

What types of reforms?

I agree completely with Whittle that we must improve the selection and training of teachers and principals, and increase funding for education research. Raising teachers' salaries is absolutely necessary to get the best talent into teaching. At the same time, the system needs better career ladders for teachers and far more effective approaches to selection, mentoring, and evaluation in order to enlist such talent productively. Teacher turnover, a high-cost item, must be reduced. Almost half of the teachers in Ohio's charter schools quit their schools in the four-year period between 2000 and 2004, in comparison with about 8 percent in conventional public schools and 12 percent in high-poverty, urban public schools, suggesting that new organizations are not a magic formula for school stability. Although technology is unlikely to replace many teachers, it is still a powerful tool for raising education quality by providing a vehicle for topic enrichment, student research, more challenging student projects, and greater student engagement. At the same time, the education community must be open to new forms of enterprise wherever it can make a contribution, such as contracting of specific instructional services, teacher cooperatives, and information technologies that enhance evaluation of students' knowledge and capabilities.

If present evidence is to be used, two potent contributions to raising student achievement will be widespread: effective preschool programs for all children and intensive interventions that build capacities of families to support the education of their children. I believe that both of these will be prevalent by 2030 because they show evidence of great promise even today. If I had my druthers, I would also add that education of at-risk students will shift from remediation and "drill and kill" to enrichment and acceleration, as we have tried to accomplish with the Accelerated Schools Project over the past two decades. The instructional approaches used in the best gifted and talented programs, with their emphasis on engagement, depth, and real-world applications, reinforce both basic skill development and more advanced learning. And the implementation of powerful and widespread approaches to building parents' capacity to support out-of-school learning will gain support from community organizations.

Where will the money come from? By recouping funds that are "lost" to society because of poor education we can easily fund the improvements. Recent work by economists and other academic researchers—some of it presented at a recent symposium at Columbia University ("The Social Costs of Inadequate Education")—concluded that such investments have large payoffs in raising national income and tax revenues and reducing the cost of public services. For example, improvements in the availability and quality of preschool education would save large expenditures on special education and grade retention and improve high-school graduation rates and college attendance, especially among the poor, minorities, and immigrants. Just the loss in state and federal tax revenues from the 23 million high-school dropouts has been estimated at $50 billion a year. High-school dropouts pay about one-half the taxes of high-school graduates, and about one-third the taxes of those with more than a high-school diploma. Public health costs for the estimated 600,000 high-school dropouts in 2004 totaled about $58 billion. Some $10 billion could be saved each year in public assistance through universal high-school graduation; a mere 10 percent increase in the high-school completion rate would shave about $14 billion from the cost of crime. By investing in more productive educational practices, we can recoup magnitudes of investment that can easily fund the improvements set out above. And we don't have to wait until 2030.

POSTSCRIPT

Is Privatization the Hope of the Future?

Which is more "democratic": a public school system serving all equally but controlled by a governmental and professional bureaucracy, or a privatized system offering choice and variety but controlled by business interests seeking profits? This question is addressed by Randy Hewitt in "Human Capital as the *Summum Bonum* of Public Education: Past and Present," *The Educational Forum* (Winter 2007); by Kenneth J. Saltman in his 2007 book *Capitalizing on Disaster: Taking and Breaking Public Schools*; in John E. Chubb's "Privatization: A Solution for School Inequities?" *Reason* (October 2001); and in *Educational Entrepreneurship: Realities, Challenges, Possibilities* (2006) by Frederick M. Hess.

The largest-scale privatization of public school management undertaken to date has been in Philadelphia where, as of 2005, seven private companies, including Edison, were operating 45 previously poorly performing schools. Analyses of this endeavor may be found in Lauren Morando Rhim's "School Restructuring in Philadelphia: Management Lessons from 2002 to 2005," an Education Commission of the States case study (2005), and Suzanne Blanc and Elaine Simon's "Public Education in Philadelphia: The Crucial Need for Civic Capacity in a Privatized Environment," *Phi Delta Kappan* (March 2007).

Another aspect of the privatization issue is the increasing encroachment of commercial interests in a wide range of school activities. April Moore, in "A Balancing Act," *American School Board Journal* (May 2007), examines corporate support and commercial infringement. She finds that there are many examples of successful school-business partnerships, but she expresses concern that a recent study found that corporate advertising is part of daily life in more than 80 percent of the nation's public schools. Alex Molnar of Arizona State University's Commercialization in Education Research Unit has identified and monitored eight categories of corporate involvement: sponsorship of programs and activities, exclusive agreements, incentive programs, appropriation of space, sponsored educational materials, electronic marketing, privatization, and fund-raising. His concerns have been documented in *Giving Kids the Business: The Commercialization of America's Schools* (1996), *Virtually Everywhere: Marketing to Children in America's Schools* (2004), and "The Commercial Transformation of Public Education" in the *Journal of Education Policy* (September 2006).

[Of special note on the basic topic are Andy Smarick's "Wave of the Future: Why Charter Schools Should Replace Failing Urban Schools," *Education Next* (Winter 2008) and Paul E. Peterson and Matthew M. Chingos, For-Profit and Nonprofit Management in Philadelphia Schools," *Education Next* (Spring 2009).]

ISSUE 14

Is the Inclusive Classroom Model Workable?

YES: Mara Sapon-Shevin, from "Learning in an Inclusive Community," *Educational Leadership* (September 2008)

NO: Wade A. Carpenter, from "The Other Side of Inclusion," *Educational Horizons* (Spring 2008)

ISSUE SUMMARY

YES: Professor of inclusive education Mara Sapon-Shevin presents a redefinition of the inclusive classroom and offers specific strategies for bringing it about in practice.

NO: Associate professor of education Wade A. Carpenter expresses concerns about the inclusive ideology's uncritical infatuation with socialization.

The Education for All Handicapped Children Act of 1975 (Public Law 94-142), which mandated that schools provide free public education to all students with disabilities, is an excellent example of how federal influence can translate social policy into practical alterations of public school procedures at the local level. With this act, the general social policy of equalizing educational opportunity and the specific social policy of ensuring that young people with various physical, mental, and emotional disabilities are constructively served by tax dollars were brought together in a law designed to provide persons with disabilities the same services and opportunities as nondisabled individuals. Legislation of such delicate matters does not ensure success, however. Although most people applaud the intentions of the act, some people find the expense ill-proportioned and others feel that the federal mandate is unnecessary, heavy-handed, and ill-funded.

Some of the main elements of the 1975 law were that all learners between the ages of 3 and 21 with handicaps—defined as students who are hearing impaired, visually impaired, physically disabled, emotionally disturbed, mentally retarded, or have special learning disabilities—would be provided a free public education that each would have an individualized program jointly developed by the school and parents, that each student would be placed in the least restrictive learning environment possible, and that parents would have approval rights in placement decisions.

The 1990 version of the law, the Individuals with Disabilities Education Act (IDEA), has spawned an "inclusive schools" movement whose supporters recommend that no students be assigned to special classrooms or segregated wings of the school. According to advocates of this view, "the inclusion option signifies the end of labeling and separate classes but not the end of necessary supports and services" for all students needing them.

The primary justification for inclusion has traditionally resided in the belief that disabled children have a right to and can benefit from inclusion in a regular educational environment whenever possible. French sociologist Emile Durkheim felt that attachment and belonging were essential to human development. If this is the case, then integration of young people with disabilities into regular classrooms and into other areas of social intercourse would seem to be highly desirable.

According to Richard A. Villa and Jacqueline S. Thousand in "Making Inclusive Education Work," *Educational Leadership* (October 2003), in some schools inclusion means the mere physical presence or social inclusion in regular classrooms of students with disabilities while in others it means modification of content, instruction, and assessments to enable these students to engage in core academic experiences. Villa and Thousand see inclusion as a general education initiative, not just a add-on unrelated school reform. Karen Agne, in "The Dismantling of the Great American Public School," *Educational Horizons* (Spring 1998), takes a dim view of inclusion and cites examples of classroom disruption, frazzled teachers, and disproportionate expenditures of time and money (citing, for example, a single disabled child being granted over $140,000 per year to meet his special needs). She is especially concerned with disregard of gifted students and the fact that disabled students do not get appropriate academic development in regular classrooms.

In a 2007 book, *Widening the Circle: The Power of Inclusive Classrooms*, Mara Sapon-Shevin puts forth the proposition that the entire classroom, viewed as a learning community, will benefit from a welcoming approach to all students assumed to be full members of the community, perhaps with modifications, adaptations, and extensive support. She frames inclusion in terms of social justice, an excellent idea sometimes badly implemented.

In the articles presented here Mara Sapon-Shevin offers details of her expanded theory of inclusion which develops students who are comfortable with differences, skilled at confronting challenging situations, and aware of human interconnectedness and Wade A. Carpenter offers a pungent, mostly negative, appraisal of the inclusion effort, drawing parallels with another "right-thing-to-do" campaign, desegregation.

YES

Mara Sapon-Shevin

Learning in an Inclusive Community

Schools are increasingly acknowledging the heterogeneity of their student populations and the need to respond thoughtfully and responsibly to differences in the classroom. It's understandable that educators often feel overwhelmed by growing demands for inclusion, multicultural education, multiple intelligences, and differentiated instruction to deal with the growing diversity.

But what if including all students and attending thoughtfully to diversity were part of the solution rather than part of the task overload? What if we put community building and the emotional climate of the classroom back at the center of our organizing values? What if we realized that only inclusive classrooms can fully support the goal of creating thoughtful, engaged citizens for our democratic society?

Redefining the Inclusive Classroom

Alter years of struggle about the politics and practice of inclusion and multicultural education, it's time we understand that inclusive, diverse classrooms are here to stay. But inclusion is not about disability, and it's not only about schools. Inclusion is about creating a society in which all children and their families feel welcomed and valued.

In truly inclusive classrooms, teachers acknowledge the myriad ways in which students differ from one another (class, gender, ethnicity, family background, sexual orientation, language, abilities, size, religion, and so on); value this diversity; and design and implement productive, sensitive responses. Defining inclusion in this way requires us to redefine other classroom practices. For example, *access* can mean, Is there a ramp? But it can also mean, Will letters home to parents be written in a language they can understand?

Differentiated instruction can mean allowing a nonreader to listen to a book on tape. But it can also mean organizing the language arts curriculum using principles of universal design, assuming and planning for diversity from the beginning rather than retrofitting accommodations after the initial design.

Positive behavior management can be a system of providing support to students with diagnosed emotional problems. But it can also mean ongoing community building, classroom meetings, cooperative games, and a culture of appreciation and celebration for all students.

What does it mean to think inclusively, and how can this framework enhance the learning of all children? There are many lessons that inclusive education settings can teach us. Here are just a few.

Comfort with Diversity

In our increasingly diverse world, all people need to be comfortable with diversity. Inclusion benefits all students by helping them understand and appreciate that the world is big, that people are different, and that we can work together to find solutions that work for everyone.

Inclusion teaches us to think about *we* rather than *I*—not to ask, Will there be anything for me to eat? but rather to wonder, How can we make sure there's a snack for everyone? Not, Will I have friends? but rather, How can I be aware of the children here who don't have anyone to play with? When we are surrounded by people who are different from us, we are forced to ask questions that go beyond the individual and address the community. When we have friends who use wheel-chairs, we notice that there are steep stairs and no ramps. When we have friends who wear hearing aids, we listen differently to comments like "What are you, deaf or something?" When we have friends with different skin colors, we become more alert to racist and exclusionary comments. When we have friends from different religious backgrounds, we are more aware that the decorations in the mall are about only one religion.

In the absence of diversity, it's hard to learn to be comfortable with difference. The white college-age students I teach are often confounded about how to talk about people of color: "Is the right term *African American* or *black*? What if the person is from Jamaica or Haiti? How do I describe people?" Similarly, many adults are nervous about interacting with people with disabilities, unsure whether they should offer help or refrain, mention the person's disability or not.

The only way to gain fluency, comfort, and ease is through genuine relationships in which we learn how to talk to and about people whom we perceive as different, often learning that many of our initial assumptions or judgments were, in fact, erroneous. The goal is not to make differences invisible ("I don't see color"; "It's such a good inclusive classroom, you can't tell who the kids with disabilities are") but to develop the language and skill to negotiate diversity. Classrooms cannot feel safe to anyone if discussions of difference are avoided, discouraged, or considered inappropriate.

I am always delighted, and a bit stunned, when I see young people easily negotiating conversations about difference that would have been impossible a decade ago and that are still out of reach for many of us. I recently witnessed a discussion of different kinds of families during which children from ages 5 to 8 spoke of adoption, same-sex parents, known and unknown donors, and the many ways they had come to be members of their family. These students, growing up in an inclusive, diverse community, will not need a book that says,

"There are many kinds of families." That understanding is already part of their lived experience.

As a teacher, you can successfully facilitate discussions like this by doing the following:

- Familiarize yourself with the current terminology and debates about what people are called: Do Puerto Ricans call themselves *Latino*? Why is the term *hearing impaired* preferred by some but not all "deaf" people? If there are disagreements about terms—for example, some people prefer the term *Native American* and some *Indian*—find out what that conversation is about. Model appropriate language when discussing differences in the classroom.
- Provide multiple opportunities for talking about diversity When a news story is about a hurricane in Haiti, pull down the map: Where is that country? What languages do the people there speak? Do we have anyone at our school from Haiti?
- If you hear teasing or inappropriate language being used to discuss differences, don't respond punitively ("I don't ever want to hear that word again!"), but don't let it go. As soon as possible, engage students in a discussion of the power of their language and their assumptions. Teach students the words *stereotype, prejudice,* and *discrimination* and encourage them to identify examples when they see them: "On the commercial on TV last night, I noticed that all the people they identified as 'beautiful' were white."

Inclusion is not a favor we do for students with disabilities, any more than a commitment to multicultural education benefits only students of color. Inclusion is a gift we give ourselves: the gift of understanding, the gift of knowing that we are all members of the human race and that joy comes in building genuine relationships with a wide range of other people.

Honesty About Hard Topics

Inclusion not only makes students better educated about individual differences, but also provides a place to learn about challenging topics. In inclusive classrooms, teachers and students learn to talk about the uncomfortable and the painful.

Often, as adults, we don't know what to do when we are confronted by people and situations that frighten, surprise, or confound us. Children, through their eagerness to engage with the world and seek answers to their questions, can learn important repertoires of communication and interaction in inclusive settings: How can I find out why Michelle wears that scarf on her head without hurting her feelings? How can I play with Jasper if he doesn't talk? Learning how to ask questions respectfully and how to listen well to the answers are skills that will provide a smoother entry into the complexities of adulthood.

In one school, a young boy who required tube feeding provided the opportunity for all the students to learn not only about the digestive system but also about ways to help people while preserving their dignity and autonomy. In another school, a child whose religion kept him from celebrating birthdays and holidays gave other students the opportunity to not only learn about different religions but also brainstorm ways of keeping Jonah a valued and supported member of the classroom. And when a young Muslim child was harassed on the way home from school in the months after the attack on the World Trade Center, the whole class was able to engage in an important discussion of racism and being allies to those experiencing prejudice and oppression.

A student in one classroom was dying of cancer. The teachers, rather than excluding the student and avoiding the subsequent questions, helped all the other students stay informed and involved in his life (and eventually, in his death). With close communication with parents, the teachers talked to students about what was happening to Trevor and how they could support him: "Of course we would miss you if you died." "Yes, it's very, very sad." "No, it's not fair for a 6-year-old to die; it doesn't happen very often." On days when Trevor was in school and feeling weak, the students took turns reading to him. On days when he was not able to come to school, they wrote him notes and made cards. When he died, many of them went to the funeral. Tears were welcomed and tissues were widely used; the teachers were able to show their sadness as well. Teachers had to be thoughtful about discussions of religious beliefs in order to be inclusive: "Yes, some people believe in heaven, and they think that's where Trevor is going."

Although no parents would want their children to have to deal with the death of a classmate, the sensitivity and tenderness of the experience helped bond the class and enabled students to connect to both the fragility and the sacredness of life. When they experience death again later in their lives, they will have some understanding of what it means to offer and receive support and will be able to seek the information and caring they need for their own journeys.

In inclusive classrooms, I have seen students learn to support a classmate with cerebral palsy, become allies in the face of homophobic bullying, and help a peer struggling with academic work. All of these were possible because the teachers were willing and able to talk to the students honestly about what was going on, creating a caring, supportive community for all students rather than marginalizing those who were experiencing difficulty.

Mutual Support

Sadly, teasing and exclusion are a typical part of many students' school experience. Bullying is so common that it can become virtually invisible. But inclusive classrooms foster a climate in which individual students know they will not be abandoned when they experience injustice. Inclusion means that we pay careful attention to issues of social justice and inequity, whether they appear at the individual, classroom, or school level or extend into the larger community.

I have used Peggy Moss's wonderful children's book *Say Something* (Tilbury House, 2004) to engage students and teachers in discussions about what we do when we see someone being picked on. In the book, a young girl goes from witnessing and lamenting the mistreatment of her classmates to taking action to change the patterns she observes.

Ten Strategies for Creating a Positive, Inclusive Classroom

1. Make time for community building throughout the year. Time spent building community is never wasted.
2. Proactively teach positive social skills: how to make friends, how to give compliments, what to do if someone teases you or hurts your feelings. Don't wait for negative things to happen.
3. Be explicit in explaining to your students why treating one another well and building a community is important. Use key terms: *community, inclusion, friends, support, caring, kindness.* Don't let those words become empty slogans; give lots of examples of positive behaviors.
4. Adopt a zero-indifference policy. Don't ignore bullying in the hope that it will go away. Don't punish the participants, but be clear about what is acceptable. Say, "I don't want that word used in my classroom. It hurts people's feelings and it's not kind."
5. Share your own learning around issues of diversity and inclusion. When students see that you are also learning (and struggling), they can share their own journeys more easily. Tell them, "You know, when I was growing up, there were some words I heard and used that I don't use anymore, and here's why." "You know, sometimes I'm still a little uncomfortable when I see people with significant physical differences, but here's what I've been learning."
6. Think about what messages you're communicating about community and differences in everything you do, including the books you read to your students, the songs you sing, what you put on the walls, and how you talk about different families and world events.
7. Seize teachable moments for social justice. When students say, "That's so gay," talk about the power of words to hurt people and where such oppressive language can lead. When a student makes fun of another student, talk about different cultures, norms, and experiences.
8. Provide lots of opportunities for students to work together, and teach them how to help one another. End activities with appreciation circles: "What's something you did well today?" "How did Carlos help you today?"
9. Don't set students up to compete with one another. Create an atmosphere in which each student knows that he or she is valued for something.
10. Keep in mind that your students will remember only some of what you taught them but everything about how they felt in your classroom.

This book and similar materials encourage students to talk about the concept of courage, about opportunities to be brave in both small and large ways, and about how they can make a difference.

Inclusive classrooms give us many opportunities to be our best selves, reaching across our personal borders to ask, Do you want to play? or Can I help you with that? Our lessons about how we treat one another extend beyond the specificity of rules (Don't tease children with disabilities) to broader, more inclusive discussions: How would you like to be treated? What do you think others feel when they're left out? How could we change this activity so more kids could play? How do you want others to deal with your challenges and triumphs, and what would that look like in our classroom?

Teachers in inclusive classrooms consider helping essential. The classroom becomes a more positive place for everyone when multiple forms of peer support—such as peer mentoring and collaborative learning—are ongoing, consistent, and valued. Rather than saying, "I want to know what you can do, not what your neighbor can do," inclusive teachers say, "Molly, why don't you ask Luis to show you how to do that," or "Make sure everyone at your table understands how to color the map code."

Inclusive settings provide multiple opportunities to explore what it means to help one another. By challenging the notion that there are two kinds of people in the world—those who need help and those who give help—we teach all students to see themselves as both givers and receivers. We recognize and honor multiple forms of intelligence and many gifts.

Courage to Change the World

When students develop fluency in addressing differences, are exposed to challenging issues, and view themselves as interconnected, teachers can more easily engage them in discussions about how to improve things.

Having a personal connection profoundly shifts one's perception about who has the problem and who should do something about it. When students have a classmate who comes from Mexico and is undocumented, discussions of immigration rights, border patrols, and fair employment practices become much more real. When students have learned to communicate with a classmate with autism, they understand at a deep level that being unable to talk is not the same as having nothing to say. When a classmate comes from a family with two mothers, reports of gay bashing or debates about marriage rights become more tangible.

A powerful way to combat political apathy is by helping young people make connections between their lives and those of others and giving them opportunities to make a difference in whatever ways they can. Although it's certainly possible to teach a social-justice curriculum in a fairly homogeneous school, inclusive classrooms give us the opportunity to put social-justice principles into action. In inclusive classrooms, students can *live* a social-justice curriculum rather than just study it.

Inclusive classrooms that pay careful attention to issues of fairness and justice bring to the surface questions that have the potential to shift students' consciousness now and in the future: Who gets into the gifted program, and how are they chosen? How can we find a part in the school play for a classmate who doesn't talk? Why do people make fun of Brian because he likes art and doesn't like sports? How can we make sure everyone gets to go on the field trip that costs $20?

Inclusive classrooms put a premium on how people treat one another. Learning to live together in a democratic society is one of the most important goals and outcomes of inclusive classrooms. How could we want anything less for our children?

Wade A. Carpenter

 NO

The Other Side of Inclusion

According to the big shot running the meeting the other day, anyone who questions inclusion is a candidate for commitment. Our special education textbook is almost as supercilious: "Inclusion is a belief system shared by every member of a school as a learning community . . . about the responsibility of educating all students so they reach their potential." It is precisely this kind of simplistic triumphalism that makes it next to impossible to improve practices that are sadly insufficient. So yes, I question it.

Unlike the aforementioned true believer, the textbook goes on to admit that the real world is not quite so tidy and to cite a few sources that show problems:

> In today's schools, what is considered inclusive practice varies widely depending on the clarity of state and local policies related to inclusion, the resources available to foster such practices, teacher and administrative understanding and commitment, and parent and community support.[1]

Ya' think?

If inclusion means on one hand the latest good-willed attempt to solve the problem of what to do for our extreme cases—our privileged, our victims, our victimizers, and our unfortunate—by careful placement and enhanced resources, then I'm for it. But let's acknowledge the reports indicating that this problem is still pretty intractable, and try to do something sensible about it.[2]

If, on the other hand, inclusion means that every kid should be confined for the greater part of the day with students requiring extraordinary attention (much less every psycho, free rider, and drug dealer), then no, I'm not for it, *and the law does not require it.*[3] Our textbook finally acknowledges that inclusion

> does not mean that every student is educated with peers at all times, but it does mean that the responsibility of discovering effective means for all students to learn together is taken very seriously and deviations from this approach are made with reluctance and only after careful deliberation.[4]

With that caveat I have no quarrel. We know that the old special education models did not work adequately, and I'm glad they have been discarded. I believe full inclusion is the right thing to do. Nonetheless, in nearly every conversation I have with practicing teachers, they express frustration and sadness, usually without prompting of any sort, over students questionably included or included in large classes with inadequate support. In nearly every observation I conduct, I see other kids bored stiff; they could have been challenged and could excel or even come to love learning, except that the teacher is pressured to focus on the "bubble kids" most likely to show substantial improvement on test scores. I also see far too many kids who think they can get by with insubstantial and careless work, and they are probably right. If inclusion for students with disabilities is combined with weak administrative support on behavior problems and modest intellectual goals for everyone, the process is unlikely to work. Making this right-thing-to-do even more problematic is that we are trying to include an extraordinary range of abilities, advantages, disadvantages, and handicaps while also trying to keep the criminals and those who hate school (for no matter how good a reason) in school.

I've seen this situation before, in my generation's struggles with another right-thing-to-do that has, until now, been sacrosanct: desegregation. If by desegregation one meant the morally necessary attempt to resolve three hundred years of racial injustice, to promote domestic tranquility, and to guarantee a decent chance at the American dream to decent people of all races, then I'm for it. In fact, I spent the greater part of my career working awfully hard to make it work, occasionally putting myself at considerable physical risk. By the twentieth century our society had been so morally corrupted and impoverished by generations of racism and discriminatory schooling that we rightly put freedom of association in abeyance, or at least reduced it considerably. But how far can we take that reduction in the twenty-first century and still call ourselves "the land of the free"?

Leveling downward is not compatible with education, either, by any definition of the word to which I care to subscribe. If by desegregation we mean the socially toxic result of miseducating kids of whatever race to the level of the street-corner hustler or the semiliterate Ku Kluxer, then no, I'm not for it at all. I did my high school teaching in Charlotte, North Carolina, the "home" of busing, in the 1970s and '80s, and I witnessed firsthand the results of doing the right thing badly; now I read that just about everything we accomplished for desegregation back then has been undone.[5] For many years I was a good soldier and kept my mouth shut. I'm too old for that stuff now.

Part of the problem, I think, was that we were desegregating without any regard whatsoever for whether or not that particular child belonged in that particular class. I well remember the sweet little old lady from downstairs coming into my classroom at the beginning of every semester with her clipboard, and moving kids—lots of them—to and from advanced and low-level classes *simply to comply with the court order.* You, you, and you are now slow learners. Sorry. You, you, and you are now advanced. Congratulations.

I believe the other problem with desegregation, and now inclusion, lies in an uncritical infatuation with socialization, resulting in a seduction pulled off with an awful cynicism.[6] To quote British philosopher Michael Oakeshott:

> Modern governments are not interested in education: they are concerned only to impose "socialization" of one kind or another upon the surviving fragments of a once considerable educational engagement. . . . [This is] the alternative to education, invented for the poor as something instead of virtually nothing.[7]

While the rationale for both desegregation and inclusion is multi-faceted, nuanced, and intellectually and morally compelling, most of the evidence for their effectiveness has been built around socialization, and socialization done poorly, at that. Discrimination may or may not be an evil, depending on how it's done, but indiscriminate inclusion may bring with it an evil far worse, and I fear it will hurt the kids with disabilities, probably even worse than their nondisabled classmates.

"Socialization" is important, but it is not unproblematic. A facile "They're all equal in God's sight" from developmentally delayed social gospelers just won't do, nor will an equally facile "They all have to learn to get along with all kinds of people" from historically bypassed egalitarians. Most children are perfectly capable of learning about a sewer without having to roll around in one, so it stands to reason that they can also learn about felons without having to sit beside them eight hours per day, one hundred eighty days per year, for twelve (or more) years. Our society has not yet provided enough support or alternatives for exceptional kids, nor has it learned how to discriminate *well*.[8] To make inclusion work beyond the merely "adequate," we need to provide more attractive alternatives for those kids who don't want to be in schools and who detract from the education of those who do. We need to give teachers more support and give the kids more teachers—I would suggest no more than fifteen kids per class in inclusive settings. Blithely asserting that "individualization," "inclusive practices," or a bigger "bag of tricks" will solve the problem of extreme cases applies methodological Band-Aids to political diseases, places undue burdens (including a deeply unfair load of guilt) on conscientious and overloaded teachers, and ultimately hurts far too many kids.[9] As with segregation, this is not a methods problem; it is a policy problem. "Best practices" should never be a bureaucratic placebo for bad policy. A naive notion of equality and socialization is no more helpful than is a bigoted attitude toward diversity and social mobility. Contrary to some egalitarians, a good society rightly honors those who through intelligent good will, artistic talent, athletic prowess, or plain honest hard work make our lives better. Conversely, a good society shelters *all* children from being held down by conservative elitists, held back by liberal egalitarians, or held up by criminals. Benjamin Barber elegantly describes a kinder view of equality:

> When democratic citizenship insists on leveling, it demands that slaves be emancipated, not that masters be enslaved; that suffrage be granted to the dispossessed, not taken from the powerful; that I win the exercise of my rights, not that you lose the exercise of yours.[10]

Contrary to some devotees of socialization, schools are not likely to fix every kid, and not every kid belongs in a school. Unless we figure that out, we will find ourselves increasingly burdened by schools in which nobody belongs, and as usual, the exceptional will be victimized even more savagely, because they are more vulnerable. The thrust of this column is simple: *inclusion is not likely to work if we insist on including the victimizers with the victims.*

Equality and socialization should accompany—not replace—judgment and education. To substitute the former for the latter, or vice versa, is an unsafe practice, pure and simple. No child should be denied the benefits of our education, but many do not deserve the burdens of our schooling—as it is currently practiced.

Notes

1. Marilyn Friend, *Special Education: Contemporary Perspectives for School Professionals.* 2nd ed. (Boston: Pearson/Allyn Bacon, 2008), pp. 20, 21.

2. Start with Friend, then go to the USDOE's site and take up with . . ., and then surf from there. Be forewarned, however: although the research is pretty solid that inclusion seldom hurts and often helps students with disabilities, and may have affective and social benefits for all, the research "suggesting" that it doesn't hurt "the other kids" academically is dated, limited, and unconvincing. Those who even think about it generally finesse the issue. And even its most enthusiastic proponents do not approve of inclusion without adequate support systems—including alternative systems for those who resist schooling and make it difficult for others. And that is my beef. See also Debbie Staub, *Inclusion and the Other Kids* (Newton, Mass.: National Institute for Urban School Improvement, 1999), ERIC ED 439206.

3. "All children have the right to learn together"; "[t]here are no legitimate reasons to separate children for their education. Children belong together—with advantages and benefits for everyone. They do not need to be protected from each other" (Organization for Inclusion, Acceptance, and Respect, "Questions and Answers about Inclusion" . . .). Such statements are sentimentalist rubbish. Ask any cop, social worker, or even bullying victim whether protection from *some* children is needed. And that kind of bogus "rights talk" just trivializes worthy and weighty matters: one could just as easily invent a "right" to learn separately, a "right" to attend the college or university of one's choice, or even a "right" to live in a smoke-free city. I found it interesting to hear not long ago that Estonia has declared Internet access a "fundamental human right." It may indeed be very desirable, but compared to life, liberty, and the pursuit of happiness . . . c'mon, folks, get a grip.

4. Friend, *Special Education,* 21.

5. My own experience gives me enough lamentable war stories from "back then," and Ann Doss Helms's articles in my hometown *Charlotte Observer* about post-desegregation outcomes are depressing reading. For broader perspectives and some precise figures, see the NAEP reports on the racial gaps at . . .; the Uniform Crime Statistics published yearly by the FBI at . . .; the drug-abuse figures and the teenage-pregnancy figures released by the

U.S. Department of Health and Human Services at . . .; and the findings of the Guttmacher Institute at . . .. Maybe I have to confess that although my generation of teachers did a good job with a lot of individual kids, societally we may have been a disaster.

6. Most of us are probably aware that St. Peter left half the statement unsaid: Love may indeed cover a multitude of sins, but infatuation can lead to a lot more. I Peter 4:8.

7. Timothy Fuller, ed. *Michael Oakeshott on Education* (New Haven:Yale, 1989), p. 86.

8. "Enough support or alternatives": my best suggestion at this point is in Wade A. Carpenter (2007): "For Those We Won't Reach: An Alternative" in *Educational Horizons* 85 (3): 146–155.

9. "Methodological Band-Aids . . . political diseases": an intentional mixed metaphor. I'm not disputing the need for better teaching methods for intellectually challenged and behaviorally challenging children; I am asserting that they may be necessary, but they are unlikely to be sufficient.

10. Benjamin R. Barber, *An Aristocracy of Everyone: The Politics of Education and the Future of America* (New York: Oxford University Press, 1992), p. 6. Allow me to add the suggestion that an aristocracy of everyone is the only democracy worth living in.

POSTSCRIPT

Is the Inclusive Classroom Model Workable?

One wit has stated that P.L. 94-142 was really a "full employment act for lawyers." Indeed, there has been much litigation regarding the identification, classification, placement, and specialized treatment of disabled children since the introduction of the 1975 act. The 1992 ruling in *Greer v. Rome City School District* permitted the parents to place their child, who has Down syndrome, in a regular classroom with supplementary services. Also, the decision in *Sacramento City Unified School District v. Holland* (1994) allowed a girl with an IQ of 44 to be placed in a regular classroom full time, in accordance with her parents' wishes (the school system had wanted the student to split her time equally between regular and special education classes). These cases demonstrate that although the aspect of the law stipulating parental involvement in the development of individual educational programs can invite cooperation, it can also lead to conflict.

Teacher attitude becomes a crucial component in the success or failure of placements of disabled students in regular classrooms. Teacher training institutions have tried to incorporate "special education" material into the preparation of regular classroom teachers, but many of these teachers find themselves at a loss when it comes to dealing with and assisting children with special needs. Some articles dealing with this and related problems are "Disruptive Disabled Kids: Inclusion Confusion," *School Board News* (October 1994) by Diane Brockett and "Discipline Procedures with Students with Disabilities," *The Clearing House* (January/February 2000), by Jean Mueth Dayton.

Of special interest are "The Oppression of Inclusion," *Educational Horizons* (Fall 2000), by David Aloyzy Zera and Roy Maynard Seitsinger; "Americans with Disabilities: Are They Losing Ground?" *The Clearing House* (January/February 2002), by Nathan L. Essex; "More Choices for Disabled Kids," *Policy Review* (April & May 2002), by Lewis M. Andrews; and Lisa Snell's "Special Education Confidential," *Reason* (December 2002).

More recent material may be found in Thomas Hehir, "Confronting Ableism," *Educational Leadership* (February 2007); Joetta Sack-Min, "The Issues of IDEA," *American School Board Journal* (March 2007); Cynthia G. Simpson, Rebecca McBride, Vicky G. Spencer, John Lowdermilk, and Sharon Lynch, "Assistive Technology: Supporting Learners in Inclusive Classrooms," *Kappa Delta Pi Record* (Summer 2009); and Rachel Hughes, "Learning Disabilities and Social Inclusion," *Journal of Intellectual Disability Research* (June 2009).

ISSUE 15

Can Current High School Reform Curtail Dropouts?

YES: Thomas Toch, Craig D. Jerald, and Erin Dillon, from "Surprise— High School Reform Is Working," *Phi Delta Kappan* (February 2007)

NO: Robert Epstein, from "Why High School Must Go: An Interview with Leon Botstein," *Phi Delta Kappan* (May 2007)

ISSUE SUMMARY

YES: Thomas Toch, Craig D. Jerald, and Erin Dillon, think-tank researchers at Education Sector, review recent efforts at high school reform by the Gates Foundation, the National Governors Association, and other groups, identifying many signs of progress.

NO: Scholar, author, and editor Robert Epstein, interviewing college president Leon Botstein, explores the abolition of high school as it now exists.

The growing demands for high school reform have emphasized the need for higher achievement levels for students who graduate from high school so they are prepared to either succeed in college or go directly into academically demanding jobs. Although such efforts are important, any reform initiatives that do not also make inroads on the dropout situation can hardly be considered successful. We face a hard battle on two fronts—one to make high school more rigorous, and the other to keep more students in high school through graduation.

So says Paul E. Barton in "The Dropout Problem: Losing Ground," *Educational Leadership* (February 2006). Determining the depth of the dropout crisis has been problematic. The National Governors Association claims that almost a third of our students fail to graduate from high school on time, with a dropout rate for African-American and Hispanic students of close to 50 percent. Much higher completion rates are displayed by experts using other data sources (such as the Current Population Survey, the American Community Survey, or the National Education Longitudinal Study), according to Lawrence Mishel and Joydeep Roy in "Accurately Assessing High School Graduation Rates," *Phi Delta Kappan* (December 2006). These authors conclude that "it is primarily a crisis of youths at the bottom of the socioeconomic scale, regardless of race. To address these children's problems, we need comprehensive efforts to improve their schools, including offering alternative programs and developing second-chance systems." At a recent summit held in Washington, D.C. titled "America's Silent Epidemic," Education Secretary Margaret Spellings accused state and local education officials of masking the problem by manipulating data. "It's hard to believe such a pervasive problem has remained in the shadows for so long," she stated.

The complexities of high school reform are laid out by Chester E. Finn, Jr. in "Things Are Falling Apart," *Education Next* (Winter 2006) in which he poses the following questions:

> Is the problem with high school that it is not engaging students or that it is not academically challenging enough? Can we *simultaneously* reduce dropouts and beef up academic achievement? Will stiffer graduation requirements and more high-stakes testing cause even more young people to quit? Are these complementary goals or are they trade-offs? Are these even the right questions?

Finn details the specific problems to be faced: (1) achievement is too low, (2) students aren't working hard enough, taking the right courses, or learning enough, (3) high school is a lockstep bore, and consequently too many kids turn off, tune out, and quit, (4) the circa-1950s one-size-fits-all comprehensive high school is itself dysfunctional, an inefficient, outmoded vehicle for teaching young people what they need to learn, (5) the courses are too easy, pointless, and ill-matched to the demands of the real world, and (6) academic work and intellectual activity are no way to the adolescent heart.

The central question is, What should be in the curriculum to ensure that all students gain the knowledge and skills to prepare them for a life of employment and social engagement? Dave F. Brown, in "It's the Curriculum, Stupid: There's Something Wrong With It," *Phi Delta Kappan* (June 2006), prioritized a list based on surveys of employers, educators, and parents: (1) critical-thinking skills, (2) problem-solving strategies and decision-making skills, (3) creative-thinking processes, (4) effective oral and written communication skills, (5) basic reading, mathematics, and writing abilities, (6) knowledge of how to use research to solve problems, (7) effective interpersonal skills, (8) technology skills, (9) knowledge of good health and hygiene habits, (10) understanding diverse cultures and ethnicities, (11) knowledge of money management, and (12) willingness and ability to continue learning.

The traditional curriculum, Brown assets, is too fragmented to productively engage learners in activities that will prepare them to meet most of life's challenging circumstances. He suggests an integrated curriculum designed by the students themselves.

The following articles offer a positive appraisal of recent efforts in high school reform by Thomas Toch and associates and a radical proposal regarding secondary education from a college professor's perspective.

YES

Thomas Toch, Craig D. Jerald, and Erin Dillon

Surprise—High School Reform Is Working

Those who would reform America's education system have focused tremendous energy on improving the nation's high schools in the last half-decade. And the high schools have proved less impervious to change than many believed they would be.

Spurred by sobering reports of ill-prepared students and a billion dollars in funding from the Bill & Melinda Gates Foundation, policy makers nationwide have embraced the issue. Political, business, and education leaders convened at a National Education Summit on High Schools in Washington, D.C., in 2005. Later that year, the National Governors Association (NGA) awarded the first of nearly $24 million in grants to more than two dozen states to develop comprehensive high school improvement plans, and every governor has signed an unprecedented NGA pact to measure high school graduation rates more accurately.

Commission reports, conferences, and research briefs have made a compelling case for reform. Only 68 percent of the nation's high school freshmen—and only about half of African American and Hispanic students—graduate on time.[1] Just 57 percent of high school graduates take the core academic courses proposed by a national commission two decades ago.[2] As a result, only one-third of high school freshmen graduate on time with the academic preparation necessary to succeed in college.[3]

The Gates Foundation put high school reform on the national agenda when in 2000 it launched a five-year high school initiative. The Gates initiative focused on addressing the anonymity and resulting apathy and alienation that earlier reform proponents—among them Theodore Sizer in *Horace's Compromise*, his influential 1984 study of public high schools; Ernest Boyer in his 1983 report *High School*; and John Goodlad in his 1984 book *A Place Called School*—had identified as so detrimental to the productivity of public high schools. The Gates Foundation has captured the major underlying principles of today's high school reform movement—and the movement's ambitiousness—with a new version of the Three R's: rigor, relevance, and relationships. Reforms, Gates and others have argued, need to focus on raising academic standards, connecting students' studies to their lives outside of school, and addressing the anonymity of the nation's many large, comprehensive high schools.

The high school reform movement resembles a sprawling nineteenth-century Russian novel, with dozens of actors and innumerable initiatives. But

From *Phi Delta Kappan* by Thomas Toch et al., February 2007, pp. 433–437. Copyright © 2007 by Thomas Toch, Craig D. Jerald, and Erin Dillon. Reprinted by permission of the authors.

reformers are focusing primarily on five strategies—improving school climate, strengthening curriculum and instruction, raising graduation requirements, helping freshmen get up to speed academically, and preventing students from dropping out.

At the same time, these reform efforts have been accompanied by an equally ambitious effort to gauge the effectiveness of the reforms. Researchers have conducted a range of studies on the high school reforms of the last half-decade. The results are just now starting to emerge, and they are more promising than many would expect.

Personal, Challenging, Engaging

Over the past seven years, the Gates Foundation alone has invested more than $1 billion to create more than 1,500 "small learning communities" of, optimally, fewer than 400 students each. Some were built from scratch while others were created by "redesigning" existing high schools and breaking them up into smaller, semi-autonomous units. The new (from-scratch) schools are replications of promising "model schools" that the foundation had identified throughout the country, such as High Tech High in San Diego.

The foundation also invested $5 million in a major, multi-year evaluation of the initiative, conducted by two independent research organizations, the American Institutes for Research (AIR) and SRI International. Evaluators judged how well the schools were doing in the following areas: personally tailored learning, relationships based on mutual respect and responsibility, high expectations, a shared focus, and teacher collaboration.[4] In a report of the results, released by the foundation in November 2005, evaluators found that the new schools resembled the models on which they were based and that "most have the 'relationships' piece of the foundation's vision firmly in place."[5] While the redesigned schools made less progress toward that vision than the new ones, evaluators still found marked improvements in school culture, especially in creating a more personalized, caring climate.

A similar study, released in mid-2006, was conducted by Policy Studies Associates to evaluate the New Century High Schools initiative, which has created 75 small high schools in New York City through a funding partnership that includes the Gates Foundation, the Carnegie Corporation of New York, and the Open Society Institute. Researchers found that the majority of schools succeeded in establishing a safe, academically focused, and socially supportive environment. They also concluded that "NCHS schools contributed importantly to the educational achievement of enrolled students."[6]

Though early results are generally positive, other recent research on efforts to create "schools-within-schools" has sounded a note of caution: significant differences in personalization and academic expectations among small learning communities could lead to students sorting themselves, in effect re-creating the school-initiated system of "tracking" students of different backgrounds into different academic programs, a vestige of a practice that the Gates reforms were intended to eliminate.[7]

Strengthening Curriculum and Instruction

Gates conducted a second study to determine whether a more supportive learning climate translates into stronger curriculum and instruction in the classroom. During 2002–03 and 2003–04, evaluators asked experienced teachers to assess the intellectual rigor of classroom assignments and student work from 12 new high schools and 12 traditional, comprehensive high schools that had yet to be redesigned.

The findings were mixed. On the positive side, English teachers in the new high schools gave assignments that were much more demanding and relevant. But math teachers in new schools were no more likely than those in conventional schools to assign intellectually demanding class work.[8] Thus it is not surprising that test results in the Gates-funded schools generally have been no better than in traditional schools, except for a slightly more positive trend in reading scores.[9]

The Gates Foundation began modifying its high school reform strategy as the results of the AIR/SRI evaluation emerged. While not abandoning the belief that high schools can change largely on their own, the foundation has now embraced a "tighter" approach, designed to ensure that the schools it supports have rigorous standards and challenging classroom instruction. Says Tom Vander Ark, former executive director of the foundation's education initiatives: "With many of our early grants, I encouraged people to fix the architecture. Several years later, many of those same folks are stuck in architectural arguments and never got to the heart of the issue—teaching and learning."[10]

Reform, it is increasingly clear, depends on improving both school climate and the quality and rigor of classroom instruction.

Raising Academic Graduation Requirements

Since 2001, 11 states and Los Angeles, the second-largest school district in the nation, have decided to begin requiring students to complete a full college-prep course sequence. Twenty-two states currently require graduation exams.

Many educators are concerned that raising graduation standards will increase dropout rates because low-performing students might be "pushed out" in order to pump up schoolwide passing rates or might become disengaged from a curriculum that is focused on academics rather than personal relevance.

As counterintuitive as it may be, low-achieving students do not appear to suffer from taking tough, college-prep courses. The evidence indicates that a combination of rigor, relevance, and good instruction can lead to higher student achievement. Researchers at Johns Hopkins University recently found that enrollment in career and technical education is positively associated with higher graduation rates, but *only* when the tech courses are taken along with more challenging academic courses. The ideal ratio appears to be roughly one career or technical course to every two academic courses.[11]

Perhaps the most compelling evidence on the question of graduation requirements and graduation rates comes from Chicago. In 1997, Chicago raised its graduation standards to well above Illinois' statewide standards. Beginning with entering freshmen in 1997–98, students were required to complete the courses necessary for entry to competitive state universities.[12] Over the next few years, graduation rates *improved*.

An analysis by the Consortium on Chicago School Research found that most of the improvement was attributable to higher levels of preparation among entering ninth-graders—the result of K–8 reforms. But a small part was driven by the new graduation requirements themselves. The graduation requirements encouraged freshmen and sophomores to take and complete more courses, and students who accumulated more credits early in high school were more likely to earn on-time diplomas.[13]

Chicago's experience also adds an important caveat to the wholesale embrace of higher graduation requirements. Despite the city's 1997 decree that students must take high-level courses to graduate from high school, in 2005 the *Chicago Tribune* published a devastating article on the dismal preparation of the city's public school students who were entering area colleges. The paper found that more than 60 percent of freshmen failed the placement test in English and had to take a remedial course in the subject. About 70 percent failed the writing test, and more than 90 percent failed the math test.[14] In other words, "college-prep" courses prepare students for college only when the courses are taught by capable teachers who provide a challenging curriculum and motivate students to master the material.

Getting Students Ready for Rigor

The push for rigorous classroom curricula and tougher graduation requirements has generated increasing concern about the poor academic preparation of many entering ninth-graders. Students who enter ninth grade poorly prepared are more likely to fail ninth grade, and students who fail ninth grade are more likely to drop out. In a study of nonselective neighborhood high schools in Philadelphia, researchers Ruth Curran Neild and Robert Balfanz found that only one in four freshmen had reading skills appropriate for his or her age; roughly half read at the sixth-grade level or below.[15] In response to students' poor preparation, foundations, the federal government, and many organizations have invested in "accelerated" instruction that quickly catches students up and helps them handle challenging college-prep coursework.

So far, the only large-scale evaluation of accelerated "catch-up" courses in both reading and math appears to be one conducted by Johns Hopkins University researchers affiliated with the university's Talent Development high school model. Ninth-graders in Talent Development high schools spend double the amount of time in math and English courses for the entire year— 90 minutes in each. During the first semester, they take classes designed to give them the academic and study skills necessary to handle college-prep courses later on; during the second semester, teachers follow the district's regular curricula for English and algebra, supplemented with special materials developed by Johns Hopkins University.

Researchers found that students taking the Talent Development catch-up courses significantly outperformed their peers in comparison schools, taking into consideration the students' previous achievement levels and their attendance over the course of the school year. Interestingly, students who started out with higher-than-average achievement seemed to benefit from the courses, too, which led the researchers to conclude that high-poverty urban high schools should consider making such courses standard for all entering freshmen.[16]

Preventing Students from Dropping Out

Research on the dropout problem clearly suggests that graduation rates should improve if reformers are successful in implementing several of the strategies discussed above. But most researchers contend that only intensive, pervasive *institutional* reforms can significantly improve graduation rates in the nation's most troubled high schools.

It is important to note that the dropout problem is very unevenly distributed across the nation's high schools. Robert Balfanz and Nettie Legters, researchers at Johns Hopkins University, report that 2,000 high schools—about 15 percent of the nation's total—produce half of the nation's dropouts.[17]

Results from a rigorous evaluation of the Talent Development model, released in 2005 by MDRC, a nonprofit social policy research organization based in New York City, suggest that even such severely challenged high-poverty schools can improve ninth-grade promotion and on-time graduation rates if they "layer on" overlapping reform strategies. Evaluators noted that Talent Development's strong positive impacts seem to come from implementing prescriptive strategies for upgrading curricula and improving teaching at the same time that high schools are broken into smaller, more personal learning communities.[18]

In 2006 MDRC released a review of three comprehensive high school reform initiatives: the Talent Development model; Career Academies, a school-within-a-school model that emphasizes a career-oriented curriculum; and First Things First, a small-learning-communities model that was initially, and very successfully, implemented in Kansas City, Kansas. After assessing the successes and failures of each model, the researchers concluded that "structural changes to improve personalization and instructional improvement are the twin pillars of high school reform."[19]

Valuable Combinations

The current research on high school reform suggests two very powerful conclusions. First, the American high school is not as impervious to change as many thought it to be. Both real change and real progress are possible, slow and difficult though they may be. Second, the most significant improvements in high schools come from *combining* strategies and solutions long thought to be ideologically disparate or even mutually exclusive. Though limited, the research cited here suggests that more rigorous curricula and tougher graduation standards might *not* hurt graduation rates and might even help improve them. Rigor and relevance are not engaged in a zero-sum tradeoff, but can actually work best in combination. Helping educators become more supportive of students is critical, but doing so produces more significant improvements in student learning when combined with high expectations and rigorous instruction.

The challenge now becomes how to create the conditions that allow such solutions to flourish together and how to get them into the communities and high schools that need them the most. High school reform is achievable. But if reformers are to be successful, they must leave very little to chance.

References

1. Jay P. Greene and Marcus A. Winters, *Public High School Graduation and College Readiness Rates: 1991–2002* (New York: Manhattan Institute for Policy Research, Education Working Paper No. 8, February 2005). The rate does not include students who graduate later than expected or who earn a nonstandard diploma, such as the GED (General Education Development) diploma.

2. National Center for Education Statistics, *Digest of Education Statistics 2004*. . . .

3. Greene and Winters, op. cit.

4. Brand-new schools based on specific designs were compared both with their original "model schools" and with traditional, comprehensive high schools. High schools that had been "redesigned" into clusters of small learning communities were compared with a sample of schools that had been surveyed prior to being redesigned.

5. Linda Shear et al., *Creating Cultures for Learning: Supportive Relationships in New and Redesigned High Schools* (Washington, D.C.: American Institutes for Research and SRI International, April 2005), p. 42.

6. *Evaluation of the New Century High Schools Initiative, Report on the Third Year* (Washington, D.C.: Policy Studies Associates, June 2006), p. v.

7. See, for example, Douglas D. Ready, Valerie E. Lee, and Kevin G. Welner, "Educational Equity and School Structure: School Size, Overcrowding, and Schools-Within-Schools," *Teachers College Record*, October 2004, p. 10. The authors found that "to varying degrees subunit choice permitted students to sort themselves based on their race, social class, academic backgrounds, and aspirations. Parallels to the stratification common to tracked high school curricula were striking. Academically motivated students tended to select subunits with reputations for academic rigor, while struggling students often chose subunits they thought had low academic and behavioral expectations. Moreover, some subunits were designed to attract certain types of students, including those with math or science themes and those with traditional vocational themes" (p. 27).

8. Karen Mitchell et al., *Rigor, Relevance, and Results: The Quality of Teacher Assignments and Student Work in New and Conventional High Schools* (Washington, D.C.: American Institutes for Research and SRI International, 2005), p. 43.

9. American Institutes for Research and SRI International, *Executive Summary: Evaluation of the Bill & Melinda Gates Foundation's High School Grants, 2001–2004* (Washington, D.C., April 2005), p. 8.

10. Quote is from Vander Ark's foreword to Tony Wagner et al., *Change Leadership: A Practical Guide to Transforming Our Schools* (San Francisco: Jossey-Bass, 2006), p. xiii.

11. Stephen Plank, Stefanie DeLuca, and Angela Estacion, *Dropping Out of High School and the Place of Career and Technical Education: A Survival Analysis of Surviving High School* (Minneapolis: National Research Center for Career and Technical Education, University of Minnesota, 2005).

12. That course sequence is a somewhat stricter version of the one recommended in *A Nation at Risk*, minus the half-credit in computer science.

13. Melissa Roderick, Elaine Allensworth, and Jenny Nagaoka, "How Do We Get Large Urban High Schools to Care About Dropout Rates and Will No Child Left Behind Help or Hurt?," paper prepared for the Developmental, Economic, and Policy Perspectives on the Federal No Child Left Behind Act Conference, Center for Human Potential and Public Policy, Harris School of Public Policy, University of Chicago, 6 May 2004, pp. 37–38.

14. Jodi S. Cohen, "Colleges Find Many Lacking: Students Fall Short in Math, English and Put in Remedial Courses," *Chicago Tribune*, 20 November 2005.

15. Ruth Curran Neild and Robert Balfanz, "An Extreme Degree of Difficulty: The Demographics of the Ninth Grade in Non-Selective High Schools in Philadelphia," paper presented at the annual meeting of the American Sociological Association, Anaheim, Calif., 2001.

16. Robert Balfanz, Nettie Legters, and Will Jordan, "Catching Up: Impact of the Talent Development Ninth Grade Instructional Interventions in Reading and Mathematics in High-Poverty High Schools," Johns Hopkins University, April 2004, ERIC ED 484524.

17. Robert Balfanz and Nettie Legters, "Locating the Dropout Crisis: Which High Schools Produce the Nation's Dropouts?," in Gary Orfield, ed., *Dropouts in America: Confronting the Graduation Rate Crisis* (Cambridge, Mass.: Harvard Education Press, 2004), p. 72.

18. James J. Kemple, Corinne M. Herlihy, and Thomas J. Smith, *Making Progress Toward Graduation: Evidence from the Talent Development High School Model* (New York: MDRC, May 2005), p. ES-8.

19. Janet Quint, *Meeting Five Critical Challenges of High School Reform: Lessons from Research on Three Reform Models* (New York: MDRC, May 2006), p. ES-10.

Robert Epstein

NO

Why High School Must Go: An Interview with Leon Botstein

Whenever there's a new school shooting, journalists looking for experts dust off their copies of a book called *Jefferson's Children: Education and the Promise of American Culture*, by Leon Botstein, longtime president of Bard College and music director and conductor of the American and Jerusalem symphony orchestras. Published in 1997 and thus predating the tragedies at Jonesboro, Arkansas, and Littleton, Colorado, this rambling collection of occasional lectures seems to help explain the carnage.

Botstein's views on teens are far from the mainstream. The public believes that the teen years are necessarily a time of "storm and stress"—a perspective etched into the American consciousness in 1904 by psychologist G. Stanley Hall in a book that defined, and perhaps even invented, modern adolescence. Teens, most people would insist, are inherently incompetent and irresponsible, desperately in need of protection and indoctrination. That's why part-time cashiering is practically the only work we let them do, and that's why we force them to attend school even if they're not ready to learn. That's also why we don't let them sign contracts, own property, start businesses, marry, drink alcohol, or smoke cigarettes—or, in some states, visit malls without chaperones, get tattoos without parental permission, use cell phones while driving, or even enter tanning salons without a physician's prescription.

But Botstein says that teens are as capable as adults in many respects and that they are certainly capable of learning important and interesting things—as opposed to all that "crap" we learned in high school (to borrow singer Paul Simon's word, not Botstein's). High school should, in fact, Botstein says, be abolished. It demeans our young, wastes their time, traps them in the vacuous world of teen culture, turns them off to learning, and isolates them from and makes them hostile toward the very people they're about to become: adults.

Botstein knows whereof he speaks. The youngest college president in American history (Franconia College, age 23), he's a living reminder of the extraordinary capabilities of young people, and Bard College has further proved the point by recently creating a thriving college for high school-age teens in New York City, as well as by taking over and running another successful college for teens, Simon's Rock College in Great Barrington, Massachusetts.

Jefferson's Children came to my attention in connection with survey research I was conducting with a doctoral student, Diane Dumas. We developed a

From *Phi Delta Kappan*, May 2007, pp. 659–663. Copyright © 2007 by Robert Epstein. Reprinted by permission of the author.

wide-ranging test of adult competencies and compared the scores of adults and teens. To the surprise of many, there was little or no difference. Other research shows that teens are actually far superior to adults in some areas: memory, reasoning ability, reaction time, and sensory abilities, in particular. What's more, in countries where teens are integrated into adult society at an early age, there is no sign whatsoever of teen turmoil. Could it be, as Botstein suggested, that our culture was creating the horrendous problems of American teens—the high rates of depression, suicide, crime, drug abuse, and pregnancy—by infantilizing them? I eventually began working on a book, *The Case Against Adolescence: Rediscovering the Adult in Every Teen*, summarizing the relevant psychological, historical, biological, and multicultural evidence to support this idea.

Unfortunately, Botstein's perspective garners media attention mainly while the blood is still wet, and it's almost never considered as part of the solution. Once a crisis is over, the view that teens are needy children prevails, and the typical response is not to reconnect teens with adults, or to give them more responsibility, or to treat them with greater respect, but rather to place more powerful metal detectors in the high school doorways and more video cameras in the hallways and bathrooms—in other words, to infantilize teens even more.

Somehow, Botstein remains optimistic about our ability to see teens in a more realistic and constructive light. Here are his current views about teens and high schools in America.

Epstein: Where did *Jefferson's Children* come from?

Botstein: One of the unattractive requirements of being a college president is that you have to say something in public and presumably about education. You end up developing unvarnished opinions without knowing much about a wide range of subjects, and usually those opinions are relatively bland. In my case, having been a college president for a long time and having been asked to say what I think about a variety of issues that I know nothing about, I ended up giving a variety of talks, and an enterprising editor heard one of these and approached me about putting all my unvarnished prejudices on the subject of education into one volume. But the book fell flat until the shootings at Columbine. Then the press began to look for people who had something to say about the Columbine event but who hadn't waited to say it until after the fact. After the shooting, everybody had an opinion. As my father, who was a great physician, used to say, the most important medical instrument is the "retro-spectroscope." But some journalists wanted more predictive wisdom.

Epstein: What did your book say that was so relevant to the Columbine shooting?

Botstein: There's a chapter which argues for the abolition of the high school and argues that the high school is an infantilizing structure. I wrote that we hadn't paid attention to adolescents properly as young adults and that we fail miserably when puberty meets education; we fail to nurture young people when they have the greatest capacity to learn. As a result, we fail to produce people with any real ambition to learn. College is too late, and the arrogance of college educators is unbelievable. Having criticized the high school environment as a way we treat adolescents, the book seemed to overlap with some of the observations about the Columbine event. A journalist asked to interview me about this, and then I did a couple of op-ed pieces for leading newspapers. Then Oprah Winfrey got wind of this, and the book suddenly had a magical revival from the moribund.

Epstein: I understand that officials in New York took your ideas about teens quite seriously. What happened?

Botstein: The mayor of New York and then the governor of the state supported the idea of our creating an early college in the public sector, which would take young people out of the eighth grade and give them a real college education. By the time they finished the year that they would normally have received a high school diploma, they would have finished an AA degree. So we developed the Bard High School Early College, which is a public school on the Lower East Side of New York that mirrors the demography of the city. It's a fantastic success, and it proves the point. The Gates Foundation has now jumped in behind it and has put about $40 million into trying to replicate versions of this early college idea.

Epstein: In Chapter 3 of *Jefferson's Children*, you say, quite simply, that "the American high school is obsolete." What is the basis for this idea?

Botstein: There are two types of warriors: those trained at West Point and Annapolis, who know about war mainly by studying it, and those of us who rise through the ranks by having fought a lot of wars in the trenches. I discovered this idea through years of observing entering first-year college students—from observing what they thought education was, what they thought reading was, and what they thought interpretation was. Choose your poison. That, and the huge disparity between what they wanted to do or were motivated to do and what they were actually capable of doing. They were sexually active, they appeared to be adults, and they had mannerisms of adulthood, but they were horrifically at odds with their own adulthood when it came to the use of their minds. And this disparity cut across lines of race and class.

Epstein: But why did you notice these disparities when virtually no other prominent educators have expressed concern about them?

Botstein: When people go into a profession, they become socialized, and their training is internalized; it's self-replicating. If you become a teacher or an educational administrator, you are trained to adopt the norms, and you are rewarded to the extent to which you vindicate those norms. I have always been an outsider. I was never trained in those norms. And so I looked at the high school with a kind of shockingly simple-minded common sense.

Take curiosity. Every parent knows that a child wants to know things about the natural world. They're not worried about who Thomas Jefferson was. They're worried about why the sun rises, why it snows, why the stars glitter in the sky. Every child wants to know. Their most important question is why. But our worst pursuit in schooling is the teaching of science, even though it should be our most popular subject. This has to be because of the way science is institutionalized and transmitted. There isn't something in our development that shuts off our curiosity about the natural universe.

Epstein: You have 24 maxims in *Jefferson's Children*, one for each hour of the day. I find one of them particularly interesting. It is to "reflect on the exercise of authority." What does this mean?

Botstein: It's advice to parents, and it extends to school administrators as well. Authority is terribly important. Everybody wants to feel that they're in charge of their own lives. But if you observe patrons in a restaurant, you find that people like restaurants in part because they can order somebody around. Some people send the wine back; some people are upset about the service. Ask anyone who works for an airline or in the service professions, where someone has paid for the right to be the boss. Many, many people revel in being the boss. Parenting is often motivated by such desires. Some people have children in order to create pets whom they can order around.

Authority is legitimate when you're causing something to be done that is essential. Sometimes people—teachers, for example—exercise legitimate authority simply by knowing something. But the base of authority should be as transparent as possible, and students, and even young children, should be able to distinguish between legitimate and illegitimate authority. Sometimes the best thing you can do for a child is to tell the child you don't know something—to tell the child that you yourself are self-critical and that you don't wield authority arbitrarily. So if my son asks me a question and I don't know the answer, I say, "I really don't know. I've got to find out." He observes that I'm uncomfortable with not being able to answer his question, and I try to figure out the answer.

Epstein: You're talking about creating a kind of connection between adults and young people that is pretty rare these days. You're talking about creating a much more substantive type of connection.

Botstein: Yes, much more substantive. One of the reasons adults don't like adolescents—why adults are so hostile and seek to restrict adolescents so much—is that they are envious. We define adulthood in a way that is not actually true. We say adulthood is all about circumspection and self-denial and responsibility—all high-minded moral talk. It's not the way we actually behave, and in that sense we hold teens to impossible standards.

But one of the things that we do know—one area where we can truly help young people—is to teach them not to dissipate an enormously important part of their lives. This is the ideal time for them to learn, to shape their interests, to develop self-confidence and characteristics which we may not have developed adequately ourselves. Unfortunately, because we secretly envy adolescents, many of us—even educators—react terribly toward teens without realizing what we're doing. I'm always struck when I see how little entering college students appreciate the joy of their own youth—probably because of the way they've been treated by adults.

Epstein: Perhaps teens have no point of comparison. They know nothing about adulthood, after all. They've been completely isolated from it, and everything they've learned, they've learned from peers—probably the last people on Earth from whom they should be learning.

Botstein: Exactly right. This is the problem of age segregation. I'm strongly opposed to the institutionalization and segregation of young people, which is much worse now because we don't have extended families living together at home anymore. We don't introduce our children early enough to the real criteria by which life is measured, and we allow them to develop hothouse criteria of their own that turn out to be totally irrelevant in life. We don't teach them that the real rules of life are not the rules of Hollywood, not the rules of pop culture, and not the rules of high school. And we certainly don't teach them to develop their mental faculties.

Epstein: You mentioned the early college program that you've established with the city of New York, and since 1979 Bard has also run Simon's Rock College in Massachusetts, which is a college program for young people. What happens when you provide higher education for young people? Does it work?

Botstein: Yes, quite well. We made our share of mistakes, particularly during the early years of Simon's Rock, but we've learned a great deal. We've learned that young people—ages 14 and 15—are capable of an enormous amount of absorption of and response to serious information. They're ready to be taught serious science, serious mathematics, serious history, serious reading, as well as philosophy, literature, foreign languages, and mathematics.

And it's not only the gifted. It's hypocritical, in my view, to reserve such experiences for the elite. Adulthood has the potential to begin much earlier than we think, and it cuts across everyone, not just those we call gifted. The young people who drop out of the inner-city schools are doing the right thing because there's nothing there for them to learn, and the curriculum that is mandated by the state is ridiculous and trivial in terms of what a young person can do. We've learned that people right in the middle of the proverbial bell-shaped curve respond very well to college material, and their expectations and performance rates change beyond predicted patterns—if they're treated properly. However, we also learned that you need a new kind of teacher, a kind of cross between the college teacher and the high school teacher. The college teacher brings real love of subject and real competence in the subject area and membership in a community that's defined by liking to do certain things.

Epstein: But perhaps not competence in teaching?

Botstein: Yes, teaching is not necessarily where they excel; they may like teaching, but only because they like the subject and they're active in their subject area. High school teachers, on the other hand, tend to enjoy both teaching and teens. Consequently, you can't simply throw young people into what we now know as college. You have to create a different kind of environment in which you combine the best of college, which is intellectual ambition and competence, with a willingness to spend time with young people and deal with the age group with the kind of attention and caring that's sometimes characteristic of high school teachers.

Epstein: Can we really abolish the American high school?

Botstein: Absolutely. In fact, there's a tremendous upward pressure from below to do so, from both ends of the spectrum of students. Good students who are college-bound are restless and bored, and there's a huge dropout rate at the bottom end—the people who are least well served. We don't have a clue how to deal with them, and they can't wait to get out of the system that doesn't serve them. And they're right.

Epstein: There are more than half a million dropouts a year right now, and in some minority groups in major cities, the dropout rate is about 50 percent.

Botstein: Because the system is broken. No one would keep a fleet flying if half of the planes crashed. So, the country is derelict, the President is derelict, his predecessor Mr. Clinton was derelict, the Congress is derelict, the state legislators are derelict, and the education establishment is routinely committing a kind of crime.

The solution is simple, and it's a solution which should appeal to both the conservative and the liberal. The conservative will like that fact that you can get more done in fewer years with less cost, and the liberal will like the fact that young people will have fewer problems and more opportunities. We need a compulsory education system from K through 10, with two levels, elementary and secondary; we can get rid of the middle school entirely. The middle school is nothing but a reflection of the American puritanical discomfort with early puberty. We wanted to separate the early adolescents from the children and the grown adolescents. So we created the middle school, which is to me an idiotic notion. It's idiotic because, again, it increases age segregation. Younger and older role models are absent. We need a two-level system that ends in the 10th grade, after which we can offer a variety of interesting options: work, national service, education in specialty areas, and, of course, college.

To make this happen, colleges will have to adapt. The real resistance to making this practical is not the high school or the legislature or the public; the public can be sold on the idea. Real resistance will come from the colleges. It's disappointing how few colleges have stepped up to take over the responsibility for secondary education, which is in their interest, actually. And the reason is that college faculty members have gotten used to having no responsibility for the well-being of students.

Epstein: Is there hope for our colleges?

Botstein: The quality of teaching in undergraduate colleges—universities particularly—is not high. We've created a kind of sink-or-swim situation where faculty members are much more concerned about their professional status and their graduate students than about undergraduates. We have a bizarre hierarchy in our education system by which the most rewarded person ends up at the Institute for Advanced Studies and doesn't have to do any teaching at all. In my view, that is the undoing of real scholarship.

POSTSCRIPT

Can Current High School Reform Curtail Dropouts?

A major effort to improve America's high schools in recent years has been launched by the Bill & Melinda Gates Foundation, which has invested about a billion dollars in the redesign of this institution. So far those involved with this effort have tried to incorporate ideas associated with progressive education, have developed and tested a small-school strategy, have supported various charter school programs, and have attempted to develop a portfolio-based public school system. There have been successes and failures and, according to Paul T. Hill in "Bill and Melinda Gates Shift from Computers in Libraries to Reform in High Schools," *Education Next* (Winter 2006), "the Gates Foundation is still looking for the breakthrough education program—the instructional method, the way of organizing a school, the way of using money—that will lead to dramatic improvement in outcomes for the most disadvantaged children in America."

Can any set of strategies work? Jay P. Greene, in "A 'Comprehensive' Problem: The Disconnect Between Fantasy and Reality," *Education Next* (Winter 2006), insists that despite reform efforts, American high school performance has hardly budged over the past three decades, and he offers data to make his point. "The problems with our high schools," he contends, "are chronic, widespread, and painfully obvious." From his point of view, the problem is that we lump high schools in with elementary schools as part of a K–12 system, rather than with colleges with which they have much more in common. In this respect, he lends support to the Botstein position presented above.

In some school districts, students who are at risk of dropping out are placed in a school populated by similar students. This, however, is often seen as a "dumping ground" strategy. Montgomery County (MD) is in the process of closing its "Evening High School," which had grown to over 2100 students (four-fifths minority students), and sending the students back to their regularly assigned locations where a "High School Plus" program will give them special attention and help.

Further perspectives can be gained from *Dropouts in America* (2004), edited by Gary Orfield, Nathan Thornburgh's "Dropout Nation," *Time* (April 17, 2006); Paul D. Houston's "Intelligent Redesign," *The School Administrator* (January 2006); . . . [Bob Wise's "High Schools at the Tipping Point," *Educational Leadership* (Summer 2008); and "Dropping the Ball on Dropouts" by Richard P. Phelps in *Educational Horizons* (Spring 2009).]

ISSUE 16

Is "Intelligent Design" a Threat to the Curriculum?

YES: Mark Terry, from "One Nation, Under the Designer," *Phi Delta Kappan* (December 2004)

NO: Dan Peterson, from "The Little Engine That Could . . . Undo Darwinism," *The American Spectator* (June 2005)

ISSUE SUMMARY

YES: Biology teacher and science department administrator Mark Terry warns of the so-called Wedge Strategy being employed by the Discovery Institute to incorporate the "intelligent design" approach into the public school science curriculum.

NO: Attorney Dan Peterson presents fact-based arguments that separate "intelligent design" from previous campaigns for inclusion of "creation science" in the biology curriculum and cause evolution theorists to possibly adjust their standard positions.

For the past few years, fresh challenges in the old debate over the teaching of evolution in America's schools have emerged. Most of these challenges have been orchestrated by proponents of "intelligent design" who desire, at a minimum, the inclusion of supernatural explanations of biological origins to be added to the science curriculum as a companion to instruction about the theory of evolution.

Much of the impetus for this renewed campaign comes from early 1980s' concerns by religious fundamentalists about the domination of secular humanism in the public school curriculum. Members of organizations such as Rev. Jerry Falwell's Moral Majority expressed the view that humanism and naturalism indoctrinate the young with ideas and attitudes that are contrary to traditional religious teachings. A focal point of the campaign against secular humanist influences was an effort to include "creation science" in the curriculum and its textbooks. George E. Hahn, in "Creation-Science and Education," *Phi Delta Kappan* (April 1982), claimed that nearly 1,500 scientists felt that creationism was not only scientifically legitimate but actually superior to the evolution-science perspective. Legislative efforts were initiated at the state and local levels to bring science instruction into a more balanced format by injecting religious interpretations of data examined. Such efforts in California, Arkansas, Louisiana, and other locales, however, were curtailed by adverse judicial rulings.

In the 1990s, religious leaders such as Ralph E. Reed, Jr. of the Christian Coalition and Robert L. Simonds of Citizens for Excellence in Education rekindled public concern about the unquestioned acceptance of the theory of evolution and the exclusion of religion in public schools. In the political arena, support for the ideas of these and like groups came from the Heritage Foundation and luminaries such as Newt Gingrich, William J. Bennett, and Rush Limbaugh. On the other side, in this phase of the so-called culture wars, stood the National Education Association, People for the American Way, and various organizations championing the separation of church and state. By the early 2000s, the strategy of the Christian right had switched from creation science, which had been consistently prohibited by the courts, to arguments grounded in the concept of "intelligent design," which suggests that some organisms in the natural world are far too complex to have developed by evolutionary processes alone. Charles Haynes of the Freedom Forum believes that intelligent design has the best chance of making inroads into the curriculum and that the majority of Americans want to see a reasonable alternative to evolution in science courses.

Spearheading recent attempts to get public schools to move away from teaching evolution as an incontrovertible "truth" are scientists affiliated with the Seattle-based Discovery Institute. It is their contention that teachers should learn the scientific arguments for, and against, modern evolutionary theory. These scientific arguments against Darwinism are presented without specific religious underpinnings, but in December 2005 the federal judge presiding in *Kitzmiller v. Dover Area School District* in Pennsylvania disallowed the intelligent design alternative, stating that it is a religious rather than scientific view, "an extension of the Fundamentalists' view that one must either accept the literal interpretation of Genesis or else believe in the godless system of evolution." This judicial setback, however, will not diminish the contentious disputes likely to persist at state and local levels of policymaking.

In the following selections, Mark Terry warns of religious incursions into the science curriculum, while Dan Peterson pleads for a widening of the science curriculum to include "design" theories and evidence.

YES

Mark Terry

One Nation, Under the Designer

If you're not a high school biology teacher, you may be missing some of the current excitement in American education. There has been a sea change in the tactics of the anti-evolution forces, whose efforts have waxed and waned ever since the Scopes Trial. Before you dismiss this topic as of no interest to you as a history, English, or social studies teacher or as an administrator, watch out for the Wedge. For the Wedge is looking for you, too. Evolution is simply the initial target of opportunity, and there is a special emotional attachment to rooting it out. But make no mistake: if the first dangerous weed, modern science, can be removed from the garden, your area will be ripe for replanting as well.

Back to the Future

The sea change is taking us back to mid-19th-century Europe, a period whose intellectual history I love but never expected to relive. Pre-Darwin, or one might better say pre-Huxley, English secondary and university education, with all of its advancements, was still in the hands of clerics. The Church of England provided the lion's share of instructors and professors, and the colleges were built physically and philosophically around religious centers, a logical extension of the origin of the universities in the Middle Ages.

But a rigid scholasticism had also been retained, and this became particularly obvious in the sciences. Geology and, in its very infancy, biology were busy discovering phenomena and hazarding theories that seemed to have no relationship to scripture. Yet most of the early researchers and thinkers were religious and would often base part of their teaching on religious texts. Tensions grew. And it began to appear that, for science and other educational enterprises to progress, to admit to unknowns and to explore those unknowns, references to Christian scriptures would have to take a back seat. It was not a question of abandoning Christianity itself, but rather any limiting hold it had over the study of the natural world.[1]

Enter T. H. Huxley. A commoner, Huxley was practical and down-to-earth, but he nonetheless remained somewhat idealistic and saw one arena in which change was essential: science teaching. A wonderfully complex fellow, he saw that the teaching of science was lagging far behind developments in science itself and even farther behind the promise and potential of science. Something had to be done. This meant schools had to have labs where students could gain direct experience. From direct experience, real learning would come; from real learning would spring new questions and, ultimately, greater progress. Scriptural limitations on the understanding of the natural world must be left behind. And for all of this to happen, new instructors, themselves practically trained scientists, not clerics, needed to be placed in charge of those new science classrooms.

Huxley is known as Darwin's bulldog because he was such a great popularizer of the idea of evolution. But perhaps his most important and lasting legacy was a revolution in science education. After publication of *On the Origin of Species*, while Darwin was at Down House quietly pursuing further evolutionary questions, Huxley was politicking on the London School Board. Great institutions, and great expectations, were initiated throughout British education in the pursuit of free and open inquiry into the processes of science and the study of history. The hold of the Church of England was loosened. Science was to be pursued for science's sake and for the sake of improving the lot of humankind, without constant reference to a deity or to scripture. And the same was to hold true for education in general.[2]

In the century and a half since Huxley, we have assumed that both science and education should be pursued in this way. Of course, it's fine if members of a religiously committed group wish to pursue science and education within the confines of their beliefs, doctrines, or scriptures in their own institutions. That's what religious schools are for. But, given the separation of church and state that Huxley promoted and that the U.S. is founded upon, public education and public science must be free of religious orientation.

Back to the Present

I've been teaching biology for over 30 years, and I always used to enjoy the creationist/evolutionist tension. Each decade's version of the controversy allowed me to say to my biology students, "See, this topic is not buried on some 19th-century shelf. It's here, and it's vital to those folks in Arkansas or Louisiana." And each time, as the courts ruled against creationism—then against creation science—it all seemed instructive and worth discussing in the classroom. It was not in the least threatening.[3] I used to think my colleagues who taught physics or chemistry must be jealous. What wouldn't they give for a headline-generating controversy to put an edge on, say, the periodic table or the wave-particle nature of light? But there are no religio-political factions—at least none that I'm aware of—willing to lobby state legislatures or to stack school boards with arguments either for or against the role of electrons or photons. Only in biology and earth science can we count on one of our core concepts being labeled controversial, even dangerous.

For most of my career I've been teaching about evolution in an integrated curriculum that joins biology and the humanities. It has been a delight to be able to place evolution in a historical and cultural context, while at the same time studying its scientific content and its current application. My colleagues and I have made sure that students see their humanities teachers grappling with the science and their biology teachers working to interpret the cultural scene. The history of the public's perception of evolution and the controversies that continue to swirl around it have themselves arrested our attention. Students and teachers of all sorts of religious or nonreligious persuasions have enjoyed and benefited from this study, which has never been aimed at challenging anyone's religious beliefs, though we have examined the fact that some people feel that their beliefs are challenged by the very idea of evolution itself.

These days, I teach in an independent school, where the freedom to develop and carry out such a curriculum is a tremendous asset. But I know of plenty of public school biology teachers who have also done excellent work over the years. Evolution became a strong component of a terrific group of high school textbooks in the 1960s, and there have been many fine additions to that list in the decades since.[4]

But a couple of years ago I began to sense something new in the air. The school where I work is just a couple of blocks up the hill from downtown Seattle, and, in one of the nearby high-rises, a great searchlight seemed to be scanning the country. If only it had been a light designed to illumine and promote great science teaching! But no. I began to see that the search was for efforts to revise statewide science standards, so that the forces of the Discovery Institute might weigh in on the side of weakening or eliminating evolution and substituting something called "Intelligent Design." This was not restricted to Arkansas or Louisiana; this was a national campaign, directed from the home of Starbucks, Microsoft, and a highly sophisticated biomedical research complex.

Creation science always sounded a little foolish, trying to establish the scientific basis for religious writings that are thousands of years old. Intelligent Design (ID), however, is not about Biblical literalism. In fact, in their public battles ID proponents try to shift the entire discussion away from religion. Their claim is that science has discovered evidence of the work of a "designer" and that they have mathematical formulae and scientific-sounding "concepts" to back this up.[5]

Not only is ID not about Biblical literalism, but almost all talk of God has been carefully removed from the discussion. In an apparent nod to the failure of "scientific creationism," ID makes no reference to scripture and proudly proclaims that some of its advocates are nonbelievers. No proof of God's existence is offered—just that of an "Intelligent Designer." Students are not to be taught who this Designer is, just that the evidence shows that the Designer exists. Presumably, they can take it from there.

This gives the newspaper op-ed pieces and public forums a new twist. All the would-be reformers can now claim to be calling for nothing more than "better science teaching." Biology and earth science teachers are portrayed as just not knowing enough about what's going on in their own fields. If this is true, of course, then state standards must be redrafted to bring everybody up to speed with the latest "science," which is Intelligent Design.[6]

Of course, it's not true. There is no such scientific revolution under way.[7] But if the public can be convinced that such a revolution exists, science teachers who object can be portrayed as the reactionary, closed-minded ones. It's as though they must answer the question, "Have you stopped teaching stale, incorrect science?" The ID proponents challenge with, "We only want you to teach more about evolution, including this ultra-modern idea that is sweeping biology." The public is left to wonder what all the fuss is about. Why shouldn't our science teachers get on with teaching all this cutting-edge stuff?

The fuss, of course, is that it isn't science. The supposed "scientific revolution" is a creation of public relations. A science teacher cannot go to any major science journal or scientific organization and find out about all this new research—because there is none. In the fall of 2004 an ID article by a Discovery Institute Fellow appeared in the *Proceedings of the Biological Association of Washington*, a venerable but formerly obscure journal dealing with subtle taxonomic issues. The flurry of responses to the article gives a good picture of the current state of ID as science: the governing council of the journal almost immediately disavowed the article's publication. The National Center for Science Education (NCSE) and the Discovery Institute websites provide contrasting views of the publication and its retraction.[8] Of course, there are several religious journals, such as the *Journal of Interdisciplinary Studies*, and journals created specifically to carry the work of the Intelligent Design movement's own authors. There is also a spate of books and articles outlining the philosophical positions that underlie Intelligent Design, and there are some buzz phrases that are meant to sound quantifiable and solidly scientific, such as "irreducible complexity."[9] Finally, and undeniably, there is the Wedge Strategy.

Watch Out for the Wedge

The Wedge Strategy, which derives from the writings of Berkeley law professor Phillip Johnson, proposes nothing less than "the salvation of Western Civilization" by, among other things, the removal of evolution from science education and the institution of a Christian belief system throughout American society.[10]

In their more aggressive postures, the advocates of Intelligent Design have proposed a reestablishment of "proper science," science that will always take into account the work of a Supreme Being, an Intelligent Designer, or even, if you catch them in an unguarded moment, God.[11] The restoration of the science that was being pursued in England prior to the Darwin/Huxley revolution—all to the greater glory of God and mindful of His great works—is central to the Wedge Strategy. And, of course, this very aim gives the lie to proclamations of a purely scientific revolution. Proponents need to have science itself redefined to include the supernatural if they are to conduct their revolution.

It's a strange scientific revolution that seeks to establish its position in secondary school curricula before the research itself has been accomplished. But this obvious impediment is removed if the revolution is based on a *redefinition* of science rather than on new research.

Additional evidence of the true purpose of this so-called scientific revolution may be found in the history of Seattle's Discovery Institute and the backgrounds of its major figures. The Discovery Institute used to feature the Wedge

Strategy on its website, and Phillip Johnson was a founding advisor of its Center for the Renewal of Science and Culture. This center, the anti-evolution arm of the Discovery Institute, originally had a very apt logo: Michelangelo's magnificent representation of God passing the spark of life to Adam. When the Wedge Strategy document was removed from the website, so too were the logo and name of the center. Now, it is simply the Center for Science and Culture, and the logo is a beautiful Hubble image that is also somewhat suggestive of an eye.[12]

The Fellows of the Center for Science and Culture have an impressive array of degrees, but you won't find a leading biologist among them. Many have degrees in philosophy, divinity, mathematics, or the law. Most have some active connection to evangelical Christian institutions. One who does have a Ph.D. in biological sciences from the University of California, Berkeley, has proclaimed his intention to follow the commission he received from the Rev. Sun Myung Moon to root out the evil of evolution. In fact, that's why he worked to earn a Ph.D. in biology.[13] But the publications and press releases of the Center for Science and Culture are "designed" to look as if they are reporting on nothing but a dispute among scientists that any up-to-date science teacher had better include in his or her teaching—or a great scientific revolution will leave the poor students behind.

Hammering the Wedge

Though the Wedge Strategy is no longer posted on the website of the Discovery Institute, its recommendations are clearly being followed. For example, the strategy details a simultaneous assault on state boards of education and on the print and broadcast media, which the Discovery Institute is carrying out. In some state battles, these Intelligent Design folks have been found out, and their efforts have been temporarily thwarted. But their tactics are sophisticated, and they understand that all publicity is good and that no defeat is real. They are more than willing to back off—even to cease advocating for the inclusion of ID—and just make sure that all science teachers are required to portray evolution as a "theory in crisis." The strategy is to move, relentlessly, from standards battles, to curriculum writing, to textbook adoption, and back again—doing whatever it takes to undermine the central position of evolution in biology.[14]

These people have money, political sophistication, experience, patience, and a wonderful user-friendly website.[15] Their carefully orchestrated campaign is designed to leave the science establishment looking close-minded, as if it is attempting to hide some dirty linen. How likely is it, after all, that the public will consult the current scientific literature or contact major scientific organizations, which would inform them that evolution is alive and well—indeed, central to virtually all biology and medicine—and not in any crisis?

In 2002, during the flap that ID advocates created surrounding the revision of the Ohio state science standards, redefining science to include God was proposed to the Ohio legislature, so that the legislature would then be able to get behind a new set of standards that would, naturally, include Intelligent Design. Imagine a state legislature defining science! Imagine a state legislature mandating the inclusion of religious content in science classes![16] Behind the elaborate ID façade, this effort was simply an attempt to bring a religious orientation into the public schools via, of all places, the science classroom. And that was just a step in the overall plan to put the U.S. on a course toward the theocracy envisioned in the Wedge Strategy.

Back to the Classroom

Intelligent Design was very much alive and well in Darwin's day, though it was then known as "natural theology." But science—through Darwin, Alfred Russel Wallace, and others—discovered a naturalistic theory by which to work, evolution by natural selection (and other mechanisms discovered over time), and, ever since the Enlightenment, has pursued scientific research without reference to religion. Scientists, of course, may be religious people, but science itself is not a religious endeavor. Science says nothing against adopting the ID outlook as a personal philosophy, but that doesn't make ID science.[17]

Meanwhile, good science is hard to teach. A teacher needs a solid background in science, sufficient time, a measure of creativity, a supportive administration, decent equipment, and sound texts. Those were the very things that T. H. Huxley was arguing for in the late 19th century, as he tried to free British science education from control by the Church of England. And those are *still* the things that science teachers need to succeed in their work, not a stealth religious agenda resurrected from Huxley's time.

But the ID folks—especially those from the Discovery Institute—make headway almost everywhere they go, because not only students and parents but teachers themselves are so poorly educated about science in general and about religion, philosophy, the history of ideas, and evolution that they have no ready defenses against the attack. It sounds so good. The major proponents of ID have doctorates, possess great media savvy, and exhibit supreme confidence. What's an educator or concerned citizen to do? Here are a few possibilities.

1. *As usual, there's no substitute for being informed.* Regularly visit the Discovery Institute's website and follow the news updates posted on the website of the NCSE, an organization that has been dedicated for over 20 years to helping teachers, administrators, school districts, and communities deal intelligently, humanely, and effectively with assaults on the teaching of evolution.[18] View the videos supported and inspired by the Discovery Institute, Icons of Evolution and Unlocking the Mystery of Life, preferably before they are shown in your area. Chances are that they are already in heavy demand at your local library, and several public broadcast stations have shown them around the country. They are excellent propaganda pieces, made up to look like NOVA-style science videos. Read the detailed critiques of these videos available through the NCSE journal and website.[19] Read an account of the history of Intelligent Design and of the Discovery

Institute. Barbara Forrest's summary article is the quickest way to learn important details, and if you want more background, you can find a gold mine in *Creationism's Trojan Horse*, which she co-authored with Paul Gross.[20]

2. *Consider some ideas to improve the teaching of evolution in your school(s).* Make no mistake about it, the ID movement and the Discovery Institute, in particular, will seize the initiative wherever possible. To prevent being always in a posture of reaction and defense, you'll need to do the best job possible of teaching real evolutionary science.[21]

3. *Learn more about religions, history, and the humanities in general, and make use of that knowledge.* One of the most significant opportunities to increase understanding of this issue is to be found in the humanities. Most students are woefully ignorant of the histories of the world's great religions, let alone the smaller ones. This makes meaningful discussions of the differences between scientific and religious thought next to impossible. Consider the example of the Scopes Trial. The fundamentalist movement is highly significant in American history and politics, and understanding its historical context helps to show how evolutionary biology, an activity of science, came to be such a target of fundamentalist ire. The "Trial of the Century" in little Dayton, Tennessee, makes all kinds of sense when the economics, politics, and Chamber of Commerce mentality of rural Tennessee are known. And William Jennings Bryan's role also makes sense in light of the struggles of the fundamentalist movement to gain the initiative in the pulpits of America. Public school science classrooms and evolution were seized upon as an attention-getting target for this denominational skirmish.[22] The proper separation of church and state makes sense only if one is aware of the great variety of religions that exist today in our communities and have existed throughout the history of this country.

   Oddly, if religion could be accorded a position of greater respect and importance in our humanities curricula, it could well be less threatening—even to fundamentalists—for students to learn in their science courses what scientists are up to. While scientists are undertaking all this evolution-based research, fundamentalists are clearly entitled to believe in a literal Biblical account. People should be strong in their faith. Meanwhile, they ought to learn what those modern biologists are doing, because it's exciting in its own right.

4. *Examine the teaching of evolution at the introductory level in colleges, especially as manifested in teacher preparation programs.* There needs to be better preparation at this level for all teachers, since this is likely to be the only background in the subject that they'll ever get. The genuine revolution in molecular biology that has taken place over the last four decades has squeezed aside such "whole organism" topics as evolution in many introductory college programs—to the delight of the anti-evolutionists.

5. *Check out the so-called Santorum Amendment.* This is believed to be a very big gun in the ID movement's arsenal, and it is easily portrayed as a federal mandate to "teach the controversy" and include Intelligent Design as a legitimate scientific theory. In reality, the

"Santorum Amendment" is only some language tucked away in an obscure text that was part of the discussions during debate on the No Child Left Behind Act. Besides being emphatically ambiguous, it never became law.[23]

6. *Prepare to be challenged if any standards writing or statewide curriculum development is about to go on.* The Discovery Institute is on the lookout for all such activity, and some of their "Fellows" are likely to show up. Consult the NCSE for local resources to help in the battle as soon as you know that any aspect of science teaching will be on the table.

An American Education

In the end, shouldn't it to be possible for fundamentalists, mainstream believers, agnostics, and atheists to have a rich understanding of, let us say, Islam, Buddhism, or any religion? It is possible to understand a great deal about these religions without adopting their belief systems. Likewise, both believers and nonbelievers could have a rich understanding of what evolutionary researchers are up to. They can understand the processes and findings of the sciences, and they need not abandon their religious or philosophical positions. They could learn that many religions promote the notion that God is an active Designer, but that many others don't. They could learn that science is silent on the subject of God.

Where I teach, the Intelligent Design movement, as a 21st-century echo of the natural theology of the mid-19th century, adds one more interesting facet to our discussions of the cultural context in which the science of evolution continues to develop.[24] But across the country, in the battles on the revision of state standards, in curriculum writing, and in textbook adoptions, Intelligent Design, especially as promoted by the Discovery Institute of Seattle, is causing great confusion. Those who care must not stand idly by. It is time for science educators and their colleagues in the humanities and in religious education to join with administrators and get into the discussions and on the appropriate committees.

And if readers who do not teach biology have gotten this far, sit back and think about the implications if the Wedge Strategy should succeed. What if science is redefined to make consistent reference to the supernatural? What if the "Intelligent Designer" becomes central to the biology curriculum in the lab down the hall? If this Designer could fabricate the basal complex of a bacterial flagellum, one of the ID supporters' favorite images, it would seem a trivial exercise for the Designer to influence the outcome of a war or a political campaign. If we apply ID to human history, will we not find that some societies are obviously chosen by the Designer over others because of their "correct" beliefs? And to ensure continuing favor with the Designer, will we not have to institute public displays of understanding so that the Designer will know that we're ready to work with Him? Her? It? A morning rendition of the Pledge of Allegiance will seem quaint and trivial compared to the dedication of public schools to the work of following the Designer's design.

References

1. John Hedley Brooke, *Science and Religion: Some Historical Perspectives* (Cambridge: Cambridge University Press, 1991).

2. Adrian Desmond, *Huxley: From Devil's Disciple to Evolution's High Priest* (Reading, Mass.: Perseus Books, 1997); Adrian Desmond and James Moore, *Darwin* (New York: Norton, 1991); and William Irvine, *Apes, Angels, and Victorians* (New York: Time, Inc., 1963).

3. Edward J. Larson, *Trial and Error: The American Controversy over Creation and Evolution* (Oxford: Oxford University Press, 2003); and Dorothy Nelkin, *The Creation Controversy: Science or Scripture in the Schools* (Boston: Beacon Press, 1982).

4. *BSCS Biology: A Molecular Approach*, 8th ed. (Columbus, Ohio: Glencoe/McGraw-Hill, 2001); *BSCS Biology: An Ecological Approach*, 9th ed. (Dubuque, Ia.: Biological Sciences Curriculum Study, Kendall/Hunt, 2002); Ken Miller and Joe Levine, *Biology* (Old Tappan, N.J.: Prentice-Hall, 2004); and George B. Johnson, *The Living World* (New York: McGraw-Hill, 2003).

5. Robert T. Pennock, ed., *Intelligent Design: Creationism and Its Critics* (Cambridge, Mass.: MIT Press, 2001).

6. *Icons of Evolution: Dismantling the Myths* (Colorado Springs, Colo.: Focus on the Family Films, 2002).

7. Barbara Forrest and Paul R. Gross, *Creationism's Trojan Horse: The Wedge of Intelligent Design* (London: Oxford University Press, 2003).

8. Stephen C. Meyer, "The Origin of Biological Information and the Higher Taxonomic Categories," *Proceedings of the Biological Society of Washington,* vol. 117, 2004, pp. 213–39. . . .

9. Michael J. Behe, *Darwin's Black Box: The Biochemical Challenge to Evolution* (New York: Free Press, 1996); William A. Dembski, *No Free Lunch: Why Specified Complexity Cannot Be Purchased Without Intelligence* (Lanham, Md.: Rowman & Littlefield, 2002); and John Angus Campbell and Stephen C. Meyer, eds., *Darwinism, Design, and Public Education* (East Lansing: Michigan State University Press, 2003).

10. Barbara Forrest, "The Wedge at Work: How Intelligent Design Creationism Is Wedging Its Way into the Cultural and Academic Mainstream," in Pennock, pp. 5–53.

11. Phillip E. Johnson, *The Wedge of Truth: Splitting the Foundations of Naturalism* (Downers Grove, Ill.: InterVarsity Press, 2000).

12. Glenn Branch, "Evolving Banners at the Discovery Institute," *Reports of the National Center for Science Education,* 12 September 2002. . . . Since this article was written, the layout and logo of the institute have changed again, and the Wedge Strategy is once more available on the website. The introductory article "The Wedge Document: So What?" asserts that the Wedge Strategy does not represent some behind-the-scenes conspiracy. But whether or not the effort is conspiratorial has little to do with whether Intelligent Design qualifies as science.

13. Jonathan Wells, "Darwinism: Why I Went for a Second Ph.D.,". . . .

14. Mark Terry and Scott Linneman, "Watching the Wedge: How the Discovery Institute Seeks to Change the Teaching of Science," *Washington State Science Teachers' Journal,* March 2003, pp. 12–15.

15. . . . .

16. Forrest and Gross, pp. 231–39.

17. Kenneth R. Miller, *Finding Darwin's God: A Scientist's Search for Common Ground Between God and Evolution* (New York: HarperCollins, 1999); and Michael Ruse, *Darwin and Design: Does Evolution Have a Purpose?* (Cambridge, Mass.: Harvard University Press, 2003).

18. . . . .

19. Illustra Media, *Unlocking the Mystery of Life: The Case for Intelligent Design* (Colorado Springs: Focus on the Family Films, 2002); . . . See also *Icons of Evolution*; and Mark Terry, "Icons of Deception," *Reports of the National Center for Science Education* (in press, 2004).

20. Forrest, op. cit.; and Forrest and Gross, op. cit.

21. See, for example, Paul Farber, "Teaching Evolution and the Nature of Science," *American Biology Teacher*, May 2003, pp. 347–54; Brian J. Alters and Sandra M. Alters, *Defending Evolution in the Classroom* (Sudbury, Mass.: Jones and Bartlett, 2001); Mark Terry, "Art and Evolution," *Science Teacher*, 2005, in press. . . .

22. Edward Larson, *Summer for the Gods: The Scopes Trial and America's Continuing Debate over Science and Religion* (New York: Basic Books, 1997).

23. Glenn Branch, "Farewell to the Santorum Amendment," *Reports of the National Center for Science Education,* vol. 22, nos. 1–2, 2002, pp. 12–14. . . .

24. Robert T. Pennock, *Tower of Babel: The Evidence Against the New Creationism* (Cambridge, Mass.: MIT Press, 1999); and Ruse, op. cit.

Dan Peterson **NO**

The Little Engine That Could . . . Undo Darwinism

Imagine a nanotechnology machine far beyond the state of the art: a micro-miniaturized rotary motor and propeller system that drives a tiny vessel through liquid. The engine and drive mechanism are composed of 40 parts, including a rotor, stator, driveshaft, bushings, universal joint, and flexible propeller. The engine is powered by a flow of ions, can rotate at up to 100,000 rpm (ten times faster than a NASCAR racing engine), and can reverse direction in a quarter of a rotation. The system comes with an automatic feedback control mechanism. The engine itself is about 1/100,000th of an inch wide—far smaller than can be seen by the human eye.

Most of us would be pleasantly surprised to learn that some genius had designed such an engineering triumph. What might come as a greater surprise is that there is a dominant faction in the scientific community that is prepared to defend, at all costs, the assertion that this marvelous device could not possibly have been designed, must have been produced blindly by unintelligent material forces, and only gives the appearance—we said *appearance!*—of being designed.

As you may have guessed, these astonishingly complex, tiny, and efficient engines exist. Millions of them exist inside you, in fact. They are true rotary motors that drive the "bacterial flagellum," a whip-like propulsion device for certain bacteria, including the famous *E. coli* that lives in your digestive system.

Oddly enough, this intricate high-speed motor is at the center of a controversy that has been kindling in scientific circles for a decade, and is now igniting hot debate outside those circles. That's because, even more oddly, the implications of whether this little engine was designed are incalculably profound. They involve questions such as: What constitutes science? Did living things "just happen" by natural causes or were they designed by an intelligence? And what follows from those two competing alternatives—in morality, education, culture, and science itself?

The controversy stems from the work of a growing cadre of scientists, mathematicians, and scholars in the field of "intelligent design," or ID for short. In the life sciences, the proponents of intelligent design are challenging the reigning orthodoxy that life developed entirely by the blind operation of natural forces. Their arguments are essentially of two kinds.

From *The American Spectator,* vol. 38, no. 5, June 2005, pp. 34–38, 42–43. Copyright © 2005 by American Spectator, LLC. Reprinted by permission.

First, building on recent discoveries in cell biology, molecular genetics, and other disciplines, they contend that life, and the complex processes by which cells do their work, cannot have been produced by that combination of chance and necessity known as Darwinian evolution. Second, using the analytical techniques of information theory, they contend that the kind of information embodied in things that are designed can only be produced by an intelligent agent, not by undirected material causes. Design, they say, is empirically detectable—and it is detectable, in fact, in living things. (Some of the ID proponents have demonstrated that the physical laws of the universe also show overwhelming evidence of being designed. For reasons of space rather than interest, I can only discuss here the work that ID is doing in the biological sciences.)

Of course, if the hypothesis that the universe and life are designed is true, the ready inference is that this designer has to be an incomprehensibly potent and awesome Intelligent Agent. A lot of influential people in science, the media, the schools, and other institutions don't much like the notion of the Big Intelligent Agent. Hence the controversy over ID, and the slanted treatment of it that is often seen.

Among certain sectors of the media, for example, it's an article of faith that those who believe in God, or advocate principles supporting that belief, are just a mob of Bible-thumping, knuckle-dragging, Scripture-spouting, hellfire and brimstone-preaching, rightwing, gun-toting, bigoted, homophobic, moralistic, paternalistic, polyester-wearing, mascara-smeared, false-eyelashed, SUV-driving, Wal-Mart shopping, big hair, big gut, fat butt, holy-rolling, snakehandling, Limbaugh-listening, Bambi-shooting, trailer-park-dwelling, uneducated, ignorant, backwater, hayseed, hick, inbred, pinhead rubes—mostly from the South, or places no better than the South—who voted for Bush.

So, many of the news stories refer to intelligent design theory as "creationism" and ignore the science behind it. They imply that ID is just religion in disguise: "Creationism in a cheap tuxedo," as one headline put it. Let's look at the science, then, because the truth about the intelligent design school could not be more different from those stereotypes. The proponents of ID base their arguments on biological and physical data generally accepted in science. They use the same kinds of analytical methods and mathematical tools as other scientists. The ID theorists do not reason from religious premises. Neither do they attempt to prove the truth of Scripture, or of any particular religious views. As a rule, they do not contest that life on Earth is billions of years old, or that evolution has occurred in the sense of "change over time" in biological forms.

What they do contest is that undirected material causes alone can explain life's origin and development. Instead, they argue that design is the best *scientific* explanation for the stunning complexity of the cellular processes that underlie life, and for the evidence of how life actually developed. That conclusion, if true, certainly has religious implications. But, as will become evident, the reasoning and methods used by the ID proponents are fact-based and scientific.

Before getting to the science, though, let's take a moment to see who the ID proponents are. Many of the prominent ID theorists are affiliated with the

Center for Science and Culture (CSC) at the Seattle-based Discovery Institute (most of them hold day jobs, too). Some background on the individuals whose work is mentioned in this article may be helpful in deciding if the ID movement is really just a confederacy of dunces allied against the enlightened.

The most prolific of the ID proponents is William Dembski. A bespectacled, youthful-looking man, Dembski has a Ph.D. in mathematics from the University of Chicago, a Ph.D. in philosophy from the University of Illinois, and a Master of Divinity from Princeton Theological Seminary. He has done postdoctoral work in mathematics at MIT, in physics at the University of Chicago, and in computer science at Princeton, as well as being a National Science Foundation doctoral and postdoctoral fellow. He is the leading thinker in applying information theory in the field of intelligent design, and has written or edited ten books.

Michael Behe, who popularized the flagellar motor as an example of intelligent design, is a professor of biochemistry at Lehigh University in Pennsylvania, with more than 35 articles in refereed scientific journals (and many popular works) to his credit. Stephen Meyer, director of the Discovery Institute's CSC, has undergraduate degrees in physics and geology, and a Ph.D. in the history and philosophy of science from Cambridge University in England for his dissertation on the history of origin of life biology.

Jonathan Wells holds a Ph.D. in molecular and cell biology from the University of California at Berkeley, and another Ph.D. in religious studies from Yale University. He got double 800s on his SATs. Phillip Johnson, whose advocacy will be mentioned in a moment, is professor of law at the University of California-Berkeley. He graduated first in his law school class at the University of Chicago Law School, clerked for Chief Justice Earl Warren on the United States Supreme Court, and published scores of articles and several books during his career.

Highly educated journalists may be forgiven for looking down their noses at hopeless dummies like these. To the rest of us, their credentials may suggest that they could be fairly intelligent men, whose arguments may be worth considering. In fact, they and others like them have put the Darwinist establishment on the defensive in the battle of ideas.

There is good reason for that, when you think about it. Throughout most of the history of Western civilization, the fact that life was designed by God was beyond any serious dispute. Genesis told the story of how God created the heavens, earth, and life. The complexity, beauty, and order we see in life and the cosmos was confirming evidence of his hand at work, and a reflection of his glory. There was no other plausible, competing explanation of how life could be so perfectly designed to fit the environment, and how the environment could be so perfect for life. But in the mid-19th century, Darwin changed all that.

Darwin posited that a purely materialist account, dispensing with God, could explain the origin of species. His central mechanism was natural selection acting on random variation. When variations in living things naturally occurred by chance, those variations that were harmful to the organism's survival would be ruthlessly weeded out. Variations that were conducive to survival or reproduction, however, would gradually come to prevail. The organisms that possessed them would, over time, outcompete those with less adaptive characteristics. This purely naturalistic mechanism—wholly devoid of any foresight, design, or purpose—could, in Darwin's view, explain the development of life and why different species were apparently so well designed for their environment.

Darwin thus provided a "creation story" for a naturalistic or materialistic view of the world. Richard Dawkins—Oxford zoologist, militant atheist, and leading exponent of materialistic Darwinism—has declared that "although atheism might have been *logically* tenable before Darwin, Darwin made it possible to be an intellectually fulfilled atheist." But if atheistic materialism is true, life on Earth by definition cannot have been designed by an intelligence (except perhaps by space aliens, whose own design would remain unexplained). Dawkins therefore asserts that "biology is the study of complicated things that give the *appearance* of having been designed for a purpose." He refers to living beings as "designoid" objects. "Designoid objects look designed," Dawkins contends, "so much so that some people—probably, alas, most people—think they are designed. These people are wrong."

Dawkins' view that we, and all life forms, are only apparently designed has been the emphatically enforced orthodoxy among biologists since not long after Darwin. But, as it turns out, increasing knowledge over the past few decades about the immensely complicated processes and structures within the cell, the operation of DNA, the fossil record of the development of species, and other pertinent evidence has not confirmed Darwinism, but radically undermined it.

Enter the intelligent design theorists. Severe difficulties with the Darwinian theory were becoming increasingly obvious by the 1980s, and some scientists began to state openly that design should be considered as an alternative theory. Then in 1991 Phillip Johnson (the Berkeley law professor mentioned above) published a powerful critique of Darwinism entitled *Darwin on Trial*. In that volume Johnson marshaled the extensive scientific evidence against Darwinism. More importantly, he showed that Darwinism has essentially become a faith in naturalism that is immune to refutation by any set of facts. Arguments or conclusions that are not Darwinian are automatically ruled out of bounds by the scientific establishment. Within the Darwinian fold, wild conjectures, surmises unsupported by facts, and arguments lacking in explanatory power are accepted as legitimate, so long as they permit a "naturalistic" explanation.

Johnson also had the temerity to point out that many of the "classic" examples of Darwinian evolution, including those often presented in textbooks, were either distorted or outright fakes. ID proponent Jonathan Wells later took up this theme in his book *Icons of Evolution*. (See also the article by Wells, "Survival of the Fakest," *TAS*, December 2000/January 2001.) Often the Darwinists knew of these falsifications, but managed to forgive themselves for the good of their mutual cause. Johnson and Wells didn't cut them any slack.

The Darwinists were outraged by Johnson, but there was worse to come. In 1996, Michael Behe (the Lehigh biochemistry professor) published a blockbuster called *Darwin's Black Box*. In that book, he explored the mind-boggling complexity of biochemical activities within the body and the cell.

Some complex structures or processes, known as *cumulatively complex*, may continue to function if some part is taken away. An army, for example, is highly complex, but it can lose soldiers, vehicles, or even whole units, and still be able to perform its function of fighting, although progressively less well. But Behe demonstrated that the molecular machines existing inside cells, and other biological processes, are sometimes *irreducibly complex*. An irreducibly complex machine or process is one that has multiple parts, and will not function if any one of the fundamental parts is taken way. All of the parts must be there, all at once, for any function to occur.

Behe's most famous example is the bacterial flagellum described above. If you take away the driveshaft from the flagellar motor, you do not end up with a motor that functions less well. You have a motor that does not function at all. All of the essential parts must be there, all at once, for the motor to perform its function of propelling the bacterium through liquid.

Why is that important? Because that is precisely what Darwinian evolution cannot accomplish. Darwinian evolution is by definition "blind." It cannot plan ahead and create parts that might be useful to assemble a biological machine in the future. For the machine to be assembled, all or nearly all the parts must already be there and be performing a function. Why must they already be performing a function? Because if a part does not confer a real, present advantage for the organism's survival or reproduction, Darwinian natural selection will not preserve the gene responsible for that part. In fact, according to Darwinian theory, that gene will actually be selected *against*. An organism that expends resources on building a part that is useless handicaps itself compared to other organisms that are not wasting resources, and will tend to get outcompeted.

Darwin himself said that "if it could be demonstrated that any complex organ existed which could not possibly have been formed by numerous, successive, slight modifications, my theory would absolutely break down." But an irreducibly complex system cannot evolve in that way, according to Behe. By definition, if an irreducibly complex system were missing just one of its essential parts, it would not function. How or why, then, would blind, purposeless evolution have created the other parts that had no prior function, just waiting for the final part to fall into place? Answer: it wouldn't. Irreducibly complex systems, which do not function if any core part is missing, can only be created by an intelligent designer who plans ahead. . . .

⚜

But why should scientists reject design as a matter of principle? And why should they do so when naturalistic explanations are lacking or deeply flawed, and the evidence of design is becoming more and more compelling?

That's the question being asked by the intelligent design theorists. William Dembski, whom we met above (the bespectacled guy with the bookcase full of advanced diplomas), has developed powerful arguments based on mathematics and information theory to show that design can be detected scientifically. He also demonstrates that as a matter of principle blind necessity—that is, the laws of nature—cannot produce design of the kind life exhibits. Neither can that kind of design be produced by the interaction of chance and necessity—that is, by the Darwinian principle of random variation filtered through the laws of nature. Only intelligence can produce what Dembski refers to as "complex specified information," and life exhibits complex specified information (or "specified complexity") to an extraordinary degree. . . .

⋅⊙⋅

How could this vast amount of complex specified information come about without intelligence? The problem for Darwinian theory is particularly acute with respect to the origins of life. But even after life gets underway, random variation and natural selection can't conceivably generate the magnitude of information necessary, the ID theorists argue.

To take just one example, a well-known (and unsolved) problem for Darwinism is the Cambrian Explosion. As noted by Stephen Meyer in the book *Debating Design*, this event might be better called the Cambrian Information Explosion. For the first three billion years of life on Earth, only single-celled organisms such as bacteria and bluegreen algae existed. Then, approximately 570 million years ago, the first multi-cellular organisms, such as sponges, began to appear in the fossil record. About 40 million years later, an astonishing explosion of life took place. Within a narrow window of about 5 million years, "at least nineteen and perhaps as many as 35 phyla (of 40 total phyla) made their first appearance on Earth. . . ." Meyer reminds us that "phyla constitute the highest categories in the animal kingdom, with each phylum exhibiting unique architecture, blueprint, or structural body plan." These high order, basic body plans include "mollusks (squids and shellfish), arthropods (crustaceans, insects, and trilobites), and chordates, the phylum to which all vertebrates belong."

These new, fundamental body plans appeared all at once, and without the expected Darwinian intermediate forms. The amount of new biological information necessary to create these abruptly emerging body plans is staggering. Meyer states that sponges such as those that existed right before the Cambrian explosion probably required about five basic cell types. More complex animals like the arthropods would have required 50 basic cell types. These in turn are dependent on new and different proteins. Citing recent research, he notes that the more complex kinds of single cell organisms might require about a million DNA base pairs to manufacture the necessary proteins. But a complex, multicellular organism such as an arthropod would require "orders of magnitude" more coding instructions. The modern fruit fly is an arthropod, and it has about 120 million base pairs. The odds that this quantity of information could be generated by random variation filtered through natural selection quickly surpass the "universal probability bound." It's not going to happen. Not even once, in the entire universe, in its whole history.

But it did happen. The preceding paragraph of this article also happened, even though the odds of it being produced by chance also far exceed the universal probability bound. That's because it's not difficult for an intelligence to produce complex specified information that would otherwise be vanishingly improbable. That's also why the ID theorists contend that only an intelligence could possibly produce the vast and detailed information base that is required for life in all its amazing complexity and variety.

This is not an "argument from ignorance" or for a "God of the gaps." The ID theorists are not saying "We don't know how something occurred, therefore God must have done it." Rather, it is an "inference to the best explanation." Naturalistic explanations have turned out to be wholly insufficient, in principle and in practice, to explain the specified complexity that characterizes life at the cellular and molecular level. We know that intelligent agents can generate complex specified information. As a matter of both experience and theory, it appears that complex specified information can *only* be generated by intelligence. So when we find living organisms that exhibit specified complexity, the best explanation is that the information was produced by an intelligent agent, and that the organism was, in fact, designed.

How has the scientific establishment reacted to the ID challenge? Variously. Some scientists have reconsidered their views, and become sympathetic to intelligent design. Others have engaged the ID theorists in debate, ranging in character from cordial to caustic.

Richard Dawkins refuses to debate Dembski, and a couple of years ago published an unfinished letter to the late Stephen Jay Gould, the renowned evolutionist from Harvard. In that letter, Dawkins proposed that they not debate "latter day creationists" who only want to share a platform with a "real scientist" (such as, presumably, himself). Dawkins is a true believer in the Darwinian faith, who characterizes his role as "Advocate for Disinterested Truth." He refers to religion as a "virus of the mind," and explicitly affirms that he is both "contemptuous" and "hostile" towards it. According to Dawkins, "It is absolutely safe to say that, if you meet somebody who claims not to believe in evolution, that person is ignorant, stupid or insane (or wicked, but I'd rather not consider that)."

It is plain to see that there is more than a disagreement over scientific techniques or reasoning here. Dawkins' commitment to materialism and atheism is a philosophical position, not a scientific one. Those who challenge materialism's creation story must be anathematized. Unfortunately, the American Association for the Advancement of Science has taken a similar position. In a board resolution adopted in 2002, that organization charges the "so-called" ID movement with, among other things, claiming "that contemporary evolutionary theory is incapable of explaining the origin of the diversity of living organisms." In other words, ID proponents are charged not merely with being wrong, but with committing heresy against contemporary evolutionary theory."

Richard M. von Sternberg holds two Ph.D.s in the area of evolutionary biology, and is not himself an advocate of intelligent design. When serving as the managing editor of the *Proceedings of the Biological Society of Washington*, he allowed a scholarly paper by the Discovery Institute's Stephen Meyer to be published in that journal. Although he had followed standard peer review procedures, the full brunt of the Darwinian establishment's wrath was brought down on him. . . . Dembski summarizes the strident reaction to ID by parts of the scientific community (and presents strategies for handling it) in "Dealing with the Backlash against Intelligent Design,". . .

The controversy has for several years been spilling into the public schools. The ID proponents do not contend that their theory ought to be taught in the public schools. All they claim is that students should be made aware that there is a controversy here. But the supporters of Darwinism are adamant. Only the Darwinian orthodoxy can be taught, and no theory critical of it can even be mentioned.

All of this suggests that what is at stake here are two competing philosophical visions: one that automatically rules out the possibility of God (and therefore a designer) as a matter of principle, and one that affirms God, or is at least willing to entertain the possibility of a designer. That division, to a great extent, underlies the "culture wars" and much else in our public life.

It is precisely because intelligent design relies upon scientific methods and evidence that it is regarded by the materialists as so extraordinarily dangerous. It threatens to allow religion to escape from the ghetto assigned to it by the dominant 19th- and 20th-century materialism. It actually claims to be true, on the same level that all science claims to be true.

If intelligent design makes good its claims, it might change the definition of science. It might change the assumptions on which we conduct our public discourse and education. It might change conceptions about whether there is an objective moral order. It might help open minds that would otherwise be closed.

It might *be* true, and be able to prove it.

POSTSCRIPT

Is "Intelligent Design" a Threat to the Curriculum?

According to Sam Harris in *The End of Faith: Religion, Terror, and the Future of Reason* (2004), "Our world is fast succumbing to the activities of men and women who would stake the future of our species on beliefs that should not survive an elementary school education. That so many of us are still dying on account of ancient myths is as bewildering as it is horrible and our own attachment to these myths, whether moderate or extreme, has kept us silent in the face of developments that could ultimately destroy us." These strong words are aimed at religious extremism as a threat to reason and could, by some, be applied to some aspects of the issue discussed here. For a more conciliatory position on the educational implications of this broader concern, see Columbia University professor Kent Greenawalt's 2005 book *Does God Belong in Public Schools?*, and for litigation background, see Martha M. McCarthy's "The Legal Evolution of Intelligent Design," *Educational Horizons* (Spring 2006). Another good review of the problem can be found in Vicki D. Johnson's "A Contemporary Controversy in American Education: Including Intelligent Design in the Science Curriculum," *Kappa Delta Pi Record* (Spring 2006).

A wealth of books has appeared in recent years that exemplify the depth of the controversy. Among the best are *Darwinism, Design, and Public Education* (2003), edited by John Angus Campbell and Stephen C. Meyer; Phillip E. Johnson's *The Wedge of Truth: Splitting the Foundations of Naturalism* (2000); *Darwin and Design: Does Evolution Have a Purpose?* (2003) by Michael Ruse; *Intelligent Design: Creationism and Its Critics* (2001), edited by Robert T. Pennock; *Creationism's Trojan Horse: The Wedge of Intelligent Design* (2003) by Barbara Forrest and Paul R. Gross; and *The Ancestor's Tale: A Pilgrimage to the Dawn of Evolution* (2004) by Richard Dawkins.

Three books on the subject appeared in 2006: *Why Intelligent Design Fails*, edited by Matt Young and Taner Edis; *Darwin and Intelligent Design* by Francisco Jose Ayala; and *Darwin Strikes Back: Defending the Science of Intelligent Design* by Thomas Woodward and William Dembski.

Some journal articles to add fuel to the fire are Donald K. Sharpes and Mary M. Peramas, "Accepting Evolution or Discarding Science," *Kappa Delta Pi Record* (Summer 2006); Gary K. Clabaugh, "Teaching Intelligent Design and the 'Bush Doctrine'," *Educational Horizons* (Spring 2006); Robert George Sprackland, "Teaching About Origins: A Scientist Explains Why 'Intelligent Design' Isn't Science," *American School Board Journal* (November 2005); Chris Mooney, "Inferior Design," *The American Prospect* (September 2005); and Lenn E. Goodman, "Science and God," *Society* (March–April 2008).

ISSUE 17

Are Single-Sex Schools and Classes Effective?

YES: **Peter Meyer,** from "Learning Separately: The Case for Single-Sex Schools," *Education Next* (Winter 2008)

NO: **Vincent A. Anfara, Jr. and Steven B. Mertens,** from "Do Single-Sex Classes and Schools Make a Difference?" *Middle School Journal* (November 2008)

ISSUE SUMMARY

YES: Journalist Peter Meyer examines the history of single-sex schools and recent concerns about "shortchanging" girls and the "crisis" in boys' education and lauds the current resurgence of single-sex schooling.

NO: Associate professor of education Vincent A. Anfara, Jr. and assistant professor of education Steven B. Mertens review research on student culture, academic climate, and attitudinal effects, concluding that the benefits of single-sex schooling remain unclear.

Gender has always been a factor in education policies and practices, both in the United States and around the world, both historically and today. Thomas Jefferson, our first "education president" deemed it appropriate to recommend three years of schooling for females to prepare them for marriage and motherhood. "Domestic arts" and "home economics" were for many decades cornerstones of the education of girls. Law schools and medical schools were predominantly male preserves historically. As recently as 1970 less than 1 percent of medical and law degrees were earned by women. The Title IX provisions passed by Congress in 1972, prohibiting discrimination on the basis of gender, opened the door of opportunity for women in professional preparation and athletic endeavors.

The 1992 study sponsored by the American Association of University Women, "How Schools Shortchange Girls," found pervasive gender bias in textbooks and classroom procedures that limited the development of girls' potential. Shortly afterward, two books, *Failing at Fairness: How America's Schools Cheat Girls* by Myra and David Sadker and Judy Mann's *The Difference: Growing*

Up Female in America, provided ideological and research-based support for the AAUW findings. Education historian Diane Ravitch at the time conceded that a gender bias is embedded in the popular culture but contended that since great strides have been made to redress patterns of historical discrimination in the schools federal gender equity legislation is not needed.

More recently attention has been paid to the ways in which boys are victimized during their school experiences. In 2000, Christina Hoff Sommers, in her book *The War Against Boys: How Misguided Feminism Is Harming Our Young Men*, declared that the typical boy is behind the typical girl in reading and writing, is less committed to school, and is less likely to go to college. In early 2006, *Newsweek* magazine featured a cover story on "The Boy Crisis," claiming that at every level of schooling boys are falling behind. Brain researcher Michael Gurian, author of *Boys and Girls Learn Differently* and *The Mind of Boys*, claims that boys make up 90 percent of discipline referrals, 70 percent of learning disabled children, and two-thirds of children on behavioral medication.

The most recent wrinkle in the on-going concern about gender factors in schooling is the movement toward single-sex classes and single-sex schools. New regulations issued by the U. S. Department of Education in 2006 have clarified the legal status of this approach. This makes it easier to establish single-sex schools than to form single-sex classes within co-educational facilities and it exempts charter schools from all stipulated requirements. A major force in the campaign to expand single-sex instruction is the National Association for Single-Sex Public Education headed by Dr. Leonard Sax. The most vocal opposition has come from the American Civil Liberties Union, the National Organization for Women, and the American Association of University Women. Emily Martin of the ACLU Women's Rights Project has said that the new regulations contradict Title IX which prohibits exclusion on the basis of gender alone. She states that schools may now "separate girls and boys for virtually any reason . . . including outdated and dangerous gender stereotypes."

Leonard Sax, in "Single-Sex Education: Ready for Prime Time," *The World & I* (August 2002), states that it is a new era in American education, that for the first time in our history an explicit legal provision exists affirming the value of single-sex schooling. Rosemary Salomone, author of *Same, Different, Equal* (2005), says that families of all incomes should at least have the option of one-sex schools. In *Successful Single-Sex Classrooms* (2009), Michael Gurian contends that such classrooms allow teachers to construct a brain-friendly environment for both boys and girls.

Among the basic concerns of the opposition are the conflict with the "separate educational facilities are inherently unequal" principle, the lack of supportive research, and the perpetuation of sex stereotyping.

In the following articles Meyer presents his arguments for single-sex education and Anfara and Mertens raise crucial points of caution.

YES

Peter Meyer

Learning Separately: The Case for Single-Sex Schools

Susan Vincent reached into the cage and pulled out a small yellow bird, saying, "This is Kiwi. He loved us, but he was lonely." It is a lovely spring day in Spanish Harlem on the Upper East Side of Manhattan and Vincent, a former children's clothing designer turned award-winning high-school science teacher, is explaining some facts about the facts of life. "We had to get Kiwi a mate. It was a perfect way for the girls to learn something about nature, about birds, about"—she smiles, holding little Kiwi up—"about the birds and the bees."

It was, as they say in the field, "a teachable moment." And for Vincent it was much more teachable because all of her 10th-grade students were girls. "There was no giggling and whispering, no holding back," she recalls. "The girls gathered round and we talked about the mating habits of birds and they asked good questions and learned a lot. Boys would have been a big distraction."

It seems so logical. Separate boys and girls so they can get their work done. It was clear to me and my classmates 40 years ago, as we gazed out the window during English class in our all-boys high school (a Catholic seminary) and watched the teenage kids from town "making out" on a stone wall; at least it was clear to Father Ignatius, who would threaten a "bastinado with salt rubbed in the wounds" if we didn't focus on the sentence that needed diagramming.

"We can concentrate a lot better without boys," is a comment I heard dozens of times in the course of researching this story. Boys seem less sure of the benefits. "Yeah, it's okay," says a student at the private all-boys Roxbury Latin School, out side of Boston. . . . But the headmaster, Kerry Brennan, is certain: "Young men are able to focus much more ably on academics without the girls."

Rosemary Salomone, professor of law at St. John's University and author of the 2003 book *Same, Different, Equal: Rethinking Single-Sex Schooling*, agrees: "Many students in single-sex classes report feeling more comfortable raising their hands and expressing uncertainty regarding a lesson or topic without fear of embarrassment or teasing from the opposite sex."

The fact that researchers like Salomone are talking about single-gender education represents a sea change in attitudes—and policies and practices, a change that was formalized by the historic rewriting of Title IX of the federal Education Amendments in 2006. The new rules give local districts the option of offering single-gender public schools and programs for the first time in more than 30 years. The regulations permit single-sex classrooms when districts "provide a rationale," "provide a coeducational class" as well, and "conduct a review every two years." Districts may operate a single-sex school as long as they provide equal services either in a coed school or a school for the opposite gender. Charter schools are exempt from all restrictions. Prior to these changes, educators lived in a vague legal world, at the mercy of a Supreme Court decision (the 1996 Virginia Military Institute [VMI] case, *United States v. Virginia*), which required an "exceedingly persuasive justification" of anyone wanting to set up single-sex schools or classes.

As late as 1990, James Coleman remarked that that it was considered suspect to even study the question of single-sex schooling. The famous University of Chicago sociologist noted that there were times when "a societal consensus" dictates that "one institution is *right*" and, he concluded, "coeducation is such an institution."

At the time, Coleman was writing to introduce a pioneering book on the subject, *Girls and Boys in School: Together or Separate?* by Providence College sociologist Cornelius Riordan. The questions Riordan was asking—"just what are the consequences of single-sex and coeducational schools for those who pass through them? Specifically, what are the intellectual consequences, the psychological consequences, and the social consequences?"—had not been asked, or answered, before. Coleman attributed the research failure to "the force of conventional values." Riordan's research compared outcomes for graduates of single-sex Catholic schools with those for graduates of coed Catholic schools. He found that single-sex schooling helps to improve academic achievement, with benefits greater for girls than boys, and that underprivileged children derived the most benefit. His book concluded that we had to "give students some measure of access to single-sex education."

Going, Going, All but Gone

While there are no reliable counts of single-gender schools in the first half of the 20th century, best estimates are that most were schools for white boys. Many of the girls' schools that did exist early on served as "finishing" schools rather than preparation for college. Coleman wrote, "Single-sex school was, at the outset, schooling for boys. Schooling for girls was an afterthought, either in single-sex institutions of their own, or with boys, where small numbers made single-sex institutions inefficient. Boys' schools, however, were dominant, and the elimination of single-sex schooling could be seen as elimination of that dominance."

In the 1960s and 1970s, the civil rights and feminist movements combined their equality crusade fervor to "open" previously exclusive men's schools to women, and white schools to blacks. Public single-gender schools were all but eliminated in the process. Boston Latin, one of the oldest and most prestigious public schools in America, succumbed to coeducation in 1972, the same year that Congress passed Title IX mandating equal education for the sexes. Central High School in Philadelphia, founded in 1838, may have been the last all-boys public school in America when it finally went coed in 1983.

Although insulated from laws governing public schools, private schools felt the pressure as well, and many single-gender institutions, often fighting for economic survival, opened their doors to both sexes after 1970. For example, the Nichols School for boys in Buffalo, founded in 1892, accepted girls in 1973. Tabor Academy in Marion, Massachusetts, began in 1876 with male and female students, was a school for boys by the 1950s, and became coed again in 1979.

Yale went coed (in 1969), as did dozens of colleges and universities. The wave of coeducation sentiment was intense: even institutions that had arisen to offer women opportunity they couldn't get in a man's world were closed. In barely more than two decades, from 1960 to 1980, over half of the 268 women-only colleges in America closed, and many others went coed. By 1993, according to the National Institute on Postsecondary Education, Libraries, and Lifelong Learning, there were just 83 women-only colleges.

"Single-sex schooling seemed to be dying a slow but certain death," writes Salomone. Coeducational institutions were considered "more socially appropriate, liberating, and enlightened."

There was ample evidence to justify feminists' skepticism about single-gender education, since for many decades (even centuries) such schooling was meant only to reinforce gender stereotypes and prejudices. "Only in recent decades have societies seriously begun to unlock the full potential of girls," wrote David Von Drehle in *Time* magazine last summer, "but the cultivation of boys has been an obsession for thousands of years."

Tinkering Around the Coed Edges

Once single-sex schools were knocked out of the ring, the gender fights occurred almost exclusively inside the coed arena. The American Association of University Women (AAUW) published a series of studies in the 1990s called *Shortchanging Girls, Shortchanging America,* which highlighted the fact that girls aged 9 to 15 suffered from lower self-esteem, less willingness to stand up for their views with teachers, and lower interest in science and mathematics than boys. The AAUW report sparked an intense national debate, with its findings that girls were disadvantaged in classrooms by, among many inequities, being called upon less frequently and encouraged less than male students.

Great efforts were made to make schools more girl-friendly—introducing new math and science curricula and teaching methods, for example—which seemed to succeed only in creating a "boys crisis." "[B]oys rather than girls are now on the short end of the gender gap in many secondary school outcomes," said Cornelius Riordan in 2000. "Currently, boys are less likely than girls to be in an academic (college preparatory) curriculum. They have lower educational and occupational expectations, have lower reading and writing test scores, and expect to complete their schooling at an earlier age". . . .

The problem has gotten so far out of hand—schools have become, some argue, anti-boy—that *Time* put Von Drehle's report on the cover with the provocative headline, "The Myth About Boys." The writer paints a bleak picture of the state of boys in our current school system. He recounts meeting Christina

Hoff Sommers, author of *The War Against Boys*. "She ticked through a familiar, but disturbing indictment," Von Drehle writes. "More boys than girls are in special education classes. More boys than girls are prescribed mood-managing drugs. This suggests to her (and others) that today's schools are built for girls, and boys are becoming misfits."

In *Same, Different, Equal*, Rosemary Salomone concludes, "The data demonstrate that the prevailing system of education (overwhelmingly mixed-sex) is failing boys as well as girls, if in different ways, regardless of resource allocations."

Back from the Brink

Initial efforts to revive single-gender public education were done in by "conventional values," buttressed by what was then a sturdy Title IX ethos. "During the early 1990s a number of school leaders tried to set up single-sex schools or single-sex classes," Riordan recalls. "That was happening in Detroit, in Ventura, California, in Rochester, and other places. In all of those cases—it was a sad story—they were driven out or shut down by principals and teachers and parents. The one in Detroit went to court, but for the most part they were shut down by political pressure and threats of legal action."

Both Riordan and Salomone say 1996 was a turning point in the single-gender school wars. In June of that year, the Supreme Court declared VMI's all-male admissions policy unconstitutional while noting the advantages of single-gender education. All the justices—from Ruth Bader Ginsburg to Antonin Scalia—agreed that single-sex education offers positive educational benefits. In writing the majority opinion, Justice Ginsburg, a long and tireless advocate for gender equality, noted that "single-sex education affords pedagogical benefits to at least some students" and concluded, "that reality is uncontested in this litigation."

A few weeks after the Supreme Court ruling, Community School District 4 in New York City announced the opening of The Young Women's Leadership School (TYWLS) in East Harlem. . . . While it was the VMI case that got most of the nation's attention by seeming to strike a final blow against single-gender schooling in the United States, TYWLS seems to have won the day. The girls' school now has two schools in Queens, and one each in the Bronx and Philadelphia.

"Twenty years ago, all-girl schools seemed headed for extinction, a footnote in the story of American education," writes Ilana DeBare, author of *Where Girls Come First*, an account of public and private schools for girls going back into the 1800s. "Today they are experiencing an extraordinary renaissance. Between 1991 and 2001, more than 30 new girls' schools opened throughout the United States from Harlem to Silicon Valley, Atlanta to Seattle."

According to Leonard Sax, executive director of the National Association for Single Sex Public Education, in 1995 there were just 3 single-gender public schools in the United States; by 2007 there were 86, with an additional 277 public schools offering all-girls or all-boys education programs within their coeducational buildings.

This reversal of fortune has been spurred in part by "a growing body of research that single-gender, especially at the middle school level, works," says South Carolina Superintendent of Education Jim Rex, who campaigned on a platform that included making single-gender schools an option in every school district in the state.

Kathy Piechura-Couture, a professor at the Institute for Educational Reform at Stetson University in Deland, Florida, has studied children at the Woodward elementary school in Deland, which has had separate classes for boys and girls for three years. She concluded that boys and girls are different enough that they demand, or should be offered, separate schools. "We looked at gain scores and concluded that there is a significant difference for boys when put in separate classes," says Piechura-Couture. Over the years, she explains, other researchers have discovered a significant number of differences between boys and girls that affect their learning abilities at any given time. "Girls have better hearing than boys, for instance," she says. "So, if you have a room full of girls you don't have to yell."

A research review undertaken by the American Institutes for Research in 2005 culled the most reliable studies from a decade of research on single-sex education. Most of the research had been done on Catholic schools and more on girls' schools than on schools for boys. The review found that roughly one-third of studies favored single-sex schools on measures of short-term academic accomplishment. The researchers characterized most of the remainder as finding no difference or having null findings. They found little support, however, for coeducational schooling being more effective. This, argue proponents of single-sex schools, suggests that parents should at least be given a choice.

More Is Equal

The resurgence of single-sex schooling has also been the result of hard-fought battles to recapture the benefits of difference and take advantage of educational choice. The rewriting of Title IX addressed confusion created by the restrictions in the original 1972 statute and the support for single-sex education in the No Child Left Behind Act of 2001. Among proponents of the changes were Senators Hillary Clinton, Kay Bailey Hutchison, and Dianne Feinstein—women who have arrived, both Clinton and Feinstein via single-sex schools. Senator Hutchison, a product of coed schooling, in a 2001 *American University Law Review* article wrote, "Talk to students and graduates of single-sex schools (mostly private or parochial), and almost all will say with gusto that they were enriched and strengthened by their experience. . . . Study after study has demonstrated that girls and boys in single-sex schools are academically more successful and ambitious than their coeducational counterparts. Minority students in single-sex schools often show dramatic improvements in attitudes toward school, greater interest among girls in math and science, and dramatically fewer behavior problems."

It is true, as Salomone says, that sometimes "same is equal," other times "different is equal," and still other times, "more is equal." Part of what single-sex schools do is redress historic and historical inequities; another part is minimizing the distractions that come from mixing the sexes; and a final ingredient is addressing gender differences in learning. James Coleman, who died in 1995, probably would have appreciated the cultural shifts that have made the single-sex school take on new meaning, since he was one of the first modern academics to propose that coed schools offered a false promise of equality. As those who have studied the racial educational gaps in our public elementary and secondary schools have noticed, throwing children together does not solve the problems of dominance; it can, in fact, exacerbate them. The two notions of peer effects—race and gender—have been joined as more and more attention is being paid to "black boys" and schools that cater to them. That is surely what Tom Carroll, chairman of the Brighter Choice Charter Schools in Albany, New York, has proved. . . . Increasingly, the single-sex school movement is seen, as Martin Luther King III told an Albany audience celebrating Brighter Choice, as a means of "liberation—liberation from prejudice, liberation from socially imposed limitations, and liberation of the dignity, capabilities, and potential for excellence that dwells in the heart of every human being." Choice is opportunity. The choice of single-sex education is affirmative action for the sexes.

In a front-page story, the *New York Times* called the 2006 amendments to Title IX "the most significant policy change on the issue" in more than 30 years. The decision, of course, came with what Martin Davis of the Thomas B. Fordham Institute characterized as "a flood of criticisms from women's groups and some civil rights organizations." But the dire predictions about the resegregation of public schools and turning back the clock on civil rights gains for women never materialized. And while various groups threatened legal actions, none have materialized. It is a new world, especially for women, and serious educators seem to realize that single-sex schools and classrooms are not a threat, but another arrow in the quiver of education quality.

. . .

Vincent A. Anfara, Jr.
and Steven B. Mertens

 NO

Do Single-Sex Classes and Schools Make a Difference?

Until the late 19th century, education in the United States was single-sex education. Coeducation gradually entered the American educational landscape in the late 1800s (Bureau of Education, 1883; Butler, 1910; Kolesnik, 1969), and since that time, single-sex education mainly has been confined to private and denominational (mostly Catholic) schools. According to Tyack and Hansot (1990) and Hawtrey (1896), economic factors were the major impetus for the rising "tide of coeducation." Simply put, it was cheaper to educate boys and girls together than to operate separate schools, which would have required duplicating expensive facilities, equipment, and personnel. Feminists of the day also valued coeducation as a necessary step in the women's rights movement and their influence contributed to the passage of Title IX of the Education Amendments of 1972, aimed at guaranteeing gender equity in federally financed schools, colleges, and universities. Finally, coeducation was considered "natural" in that it facilitated the development of positive relations with members of the opposite sex, allowed boys and girls the opportunity to learn to work together, and was conducive to happier marriages (Atherton, 1972; Hale, 1929).

In the second half of the 19th century, William Harris, superintendent of the St. Louis schools and later U.S. Commissioner of Education, argued that mixing the sexes improved instruction and discipline for boys and girls by merging their different abilities and allowing students of each gender to serve as a "countercheck" on the other (Harris, 1870). As we have seen with most educational reforms and innovations, the fanfare that welcomed coeducation very soon led to concerns and indictments. In his book, *Sex in Education,* Clarke (1873) purported that academic competition with boys overloaded girls' brains and interfered with the development of their reproductive organs.

Single-sex education (also less frequently called single gender and SS) garnered renewed interest in the 1990s from researchers, advocacy groups, and policymakers; and since 2003, there has been an extraordinary surge in interest in single-sex public education. The new regulations, issued by the U.S. Department of Education on October 25, 2006, fueled the fire of this renewed interest. Secretary Spellings, commenting on the "final rule," noted that

> Research shows that some students may learn better in single-sex education environments. The Department of Education is committed to giving communities more choice as to how they go about offering

varied learning environments to their students. These final regulations permit communities to establish single-sex schools and classes as another means of meeting the needs of students. (U.S. Department of Education, 2006)

Assessing the relative advantages and disadvantages of single-sex classes and schools is difficult. As single-sex education gains interest and appeal, educators, policymakers, and advocates continue to search for research evidence to legitimize this approach to improving student outcomes (e.g., academic, behavioral, social, attendance, self-esteem). While this review of the research will not be limited solely to middle grades schools, many of the studies that are reviewed were conducted in middle grades schools. Considerable exploration of single-sex education has occurred in the realm of legal and political issues, but there has been comparatively little examination of student outcomes and other educational implications. Salomone (2006), recognizing the problematic and inconclusive nature of this research literature, noted that most of the research originates from private and denominational schools and from abroad and tends to be anecdotal reports and scattered studies that lack scientific rigor. This installment of *What Research Says* will focus on what we currently know about single-sex education. Specifically, it will critically review in relation to single-sex education (a) what proponents and critics claim, (b) what researchers say about school culture and academic climate, (c) the attitudinal effects, (d) academic issues, and (e) problems with the research.

The Proponents and Critics of Single-Sex Programs Speak

Proponents of single-sex education cite a variety of reasons such classes or schools would be more appropriate than coeducational schools. These reasons are supported to some extent by experiential knowledge, ideological beliefs, and data and include (a) the "boy crisis," (b) biological differences, (c) achievement gaps, and (d) distractions. While concerns were expressed in the late 1990s about short-changing girls, especially in regard to mathematics, science, and technology classes, evidence began to surface that documented a "boy crisis." This crisis was characterized by lower scores by males on the National Assessment of Educational Progress (National Center for Educational Statistics, 2005), higher dropout and suspension rates for boys (Mead, 2006), a higher incidence of classification of learning disabilities, and lower test-taking rates on assessments like the SAT and ACT. In the realm of biological research, advances in brain-based research highlighted that fact that boys and girls are "wired" differently which supported the contention that they should receive differentiated educational experiences to meet their special needs. In support of biological differences, Salomone (2006) stated,

> We know that girls, as a group, enter school with more advanced verbal and fine-motor skills, have longer attention spans, and greater impulse control. This . . . puts many young boys at a disadvantage in the lower

grades. At the same time, boys tend to have more advanced visual-spatial skills through much of schooling, which puts them at an advantage in math and science. (p. 787)

Another reason to consider single-sex education relates to the achievement gap that exists between the performance of boys and girls. Frequently, the focus of this achievement gap is on the educational needs of a targeted group of students like African American and Hispanic males. Finally, removing distractions by dividing the sexes has been offered as an argument in favor of single-sex education. Gurian and Henley (2001) asked teachers to discuss their experiences in single-sex classes and schools and were told that fewer discipline problems were evident. Ferrara and Ferrara (2004), studying a New York middle school, found that participation was more widespread and students were less self-conscious in single-sex classes. Bracey (2006) added some additional reasons for implementing single-sex educational programs, including: (a) improving girls self-esteem, confidence, and leadership skills; (b) increasing attention to pedagogically significant gender differences, particularly those found through brain research; and (c) controlling the behavior of boys.

Some critics of single-sex education note that separate is always "inherently unequal." They take this phrase from the famous *Brown v. Board of Education* decision. Greenberger, from the National Women's Law Center, characterized single-sex education as "an invitation to discriminate" (cited in Green, 2006, online). The National Coalition for Women and Girls in Education also expressed opposition to single-sex education and wrote,

> Single-sex education does not guarantee improved schools. Rather, the elements that enable children to succeed in single-sex education can be replicated in coeducational settings. These elements include a focus on core academics, small class size, qualified teachers, sufficient funding, and parental involvement. (2002, online)

Additional concerns deal with the limited opportunities for male and female students to work together and socialize, the potential for limited course offerings with honors and AP courses usually not being offered in single-sex schools, and the possibility for teasing to occur. Datnow, Hubbard, and Woody (2001) noted that students in their study reported "a significant amount of teasing . . . and being labeled as bad kids, or preppy, or . . . gay" (p. 7).

The Research

For most of the 20th century there has been little interest for researchers in the United States to study the effects of single-sex schooling in contrast to coeducational setting. Single-sex schooling was a perfectly legitimate option, but one that mainly existed within the context of private and denominational schools. Jill (1993) commented that the findings on single-sex education are a mix of "passionate conviction and rather ambiguous research results" (p. 90). While this certainly seems to be an accurate characterization, what is indisputable is that research about the merits of single-sex classrooms and schools has an international flavor. Researchers in England and Wales (Bell, 1989; Byrne, 1993; Dean, 1998; Gorard, 1998), South Africa (Lee & Lockheed, 1990; Mallam, 1993), the United States (Kumagai, 1995; Lee & Marks, 1992; LePore & Warren, 1997), New Zealand (Harker & Nash, 1997; Scott, 1991), and Australia (Smith, 1994; Willis & Kenway, 1986; Young & Fraser, 1992) have all added to the debate on the relative merit of single-sex education. Other countries, including Nigeria, Thailand, and Jamaica, have single-sex schools that have been researched.

Although most of the research has focused on the benefits for females, more recent attention has been given to the academic failure of males, particularly African American males. Research on single-sex education has sought to measure the effects of single-sex schooling on student outcomes like academic performance, self-esteem, attitudes toward academic subject matter, as well as students' preferences for single or coeducation schooling. Let us turn our attention to what we know about the relationship between single-sex schooling and these student outcomes.

Student Culture, Academic Climate, and Single-Sex Education

More than 40 years ago, sociologist James Coleman was one of the first researchers to question coeducational schools in the United States. In his book, *Adolescent Society,* he noted that "coeducation may be inimical to both academic achievement and social adjustment" for adolescents (1961, p. 51). After examining the value systems of adolescents in 10 secondary schools, he found that many more students would rather be good athletes or leaders in extracurricular activities than excellent students. He concluded that this "youth culture" (which he called a "cruel jungle of rating and dating," p. 51) exerted a negative influence on intellectual endeavors. From this conclusion it was determined that this coeducational environment was particularly harmful to girls, who were overly concerned about making themselves "desirable objects for boys" (p. 52). Twenty years later, John Goodlad, in *A Place Called School* (1984), agreed with Coleman's earlier assessment. While it must be acknowledged that much has changed in light of Title IX, researchers like Salomone (2003) claimed that most of what Coleman and Goodlad found is still true in high schools and middle schools today. What is important about this discussion is that these findings have resurfaced in recent years to support single-sex education, particularly for girls and minority boys. The argument is that, at least for some middle and high school students, coeducation fosters nonacademic values and heightens social pressures that distract students from the work of school. Studies conducted in New Zealand, Canada, and the United States (Jones, Shallcrass, & Dennis, 1972; Schneider & Counts, 1982) underscore the more academic orientation of single-sex schools and document more time spent on homework and a desire on the part of the students to be remembered for their academic abilities rather than their social popularity or involvement in extracurricular activities.

Attitudinal Effects and Single-Sex Schooling

A few published studies have investigated the hypothesis that girls in single-sex schools have higher self-esteem. Cairns (1990) investigated self-esteem for 2,295 students in 76 grammar and secondary schools in Northern Ireland. He concluded that single-sex schools provide benefits in terms of self-esteem. Supporting the opposite conclusion, Foon (1988) surveyed 1,675 secondary students in private coeducational and single-sex schools in Australia and found no significant differences in self-esteem between girls from coeducational and single-sex schools, although she reported higher self-esteem for boys attending single-sex schools. In Belgium, Brutsaert and Bracke (1994) found that girls do not seem to be influenced by the gender organization of the school and that boys were negatively affected because of the preponderance of female teachers, who unwittingly contribute to lowering the boys' overall sense of well-being.

There is something of a consensus among researchers that girls in single-sex schools tend to perceive math and science classes as less "masculine," and, therefore, have stronger preferences for them. Vockell and Lobonc (1981) administered a questionnaire to 476 single-sex and 280 coeducational students in U.S. high schools. They found that girls in single-sex schools rated physical sciences as less masculine than did females in coeducational settings. In contrast, Stables (1990) studied 2,300 students (ages 13–14) and found no differences in the perception of subject importance by sex or school type. He concluded that single-sex schools reduce the polarization of attitudes between the sexes.

In regard to sex stereotyping, no consistent relationship has been found between school type and degree of sex stereotyping. Lee and Marks (1994) found that sex stereotyping occurs with as much frequency in single-sex schools as in coeducational environments. Gill (1996), studying single-sex schools in New Zealand, also noted that "teacher awareness is of much more significance than school gender context in producing or overcoming stereotypical gender limitations on students" (p. 17).

Supporters of single-sex schools and classes maintain that they offer girls a "safe place" for learning. Similar arguments hold that single-sex schools allow teachers to challenge students' gendered perceptions and enhance their self-confidence in nontraditional subjects. The evidence generated in the United States in support of these claims is largely anecdotal, with much being reported in the popular press and conference presentations. Research from abroad (e.g., Parker & Rennie, 1997), though, reports girls having more positive attitudes toward math, science, and technology, along with a higher level of comfort, in classes that do not contain boys. According to Leslie (1999), girls describe their experiences in single-sex classes as "freedom to excel without social pressure" (online). More generally, the research suggests that girls show personal growth through improved confidence (Arbor, 1998), a positive self-image (Lee, 1986), and higher self-esteem (Mael, 1998). In the classroom, girls take more risks (Streitmatter, 1997) and ask more questions (Stutler, 1997). They also show a great interest in academics (Lee, 1986) and an increased educational ambition (Lee, 1986). Boys also benefit from improved self-esteem (Mael, 1998) and tend to ask more questions in class (Arbor, 1998).

Academic Issues and Single-Sex Schooling

While girls tend to perceive single-sex classes and schools to be superior, there are a number of studies that point to the fact that these perceptions have not translated into improved academic performance for girls in single-sex schools. Among the studies that have been conducted, Rowe (1988) examined 398 middle school students in Australia and found no significant differences in mathematics achievement. These findings have been supported by the research of Leder and Forgasz (1994), Workman (1990), Young and Fraser (1992), and Harker and Nash (1997).

Some studies, though, do show gains in academic achievement. These include the work of Lee and Bryk (1986), Marsh (1989), Lee and Marks (1990), Riordan (1985), and Lee and Lockheed (1990). Riordan tested for differences between Catholic single-sex schools and public coeducational schools in relation to reading and math. He found that while Catholic single-sex schools scored consistently higher than coeducational public schools, Catholic coeducational schools differed little from public coeducational schools.

Problems with the Research

This corpus of research is not without problems. Findings conflict, as exemplified by studies done by Kenway (1995) and Sukhnandan, Lee, and Kelleher (2000). While Kenway reported that boys in mathematics classes were noisier in the classroom, spent less time on task, and complained about missing girls who could help them with their work, Sukhnandan, Lee, and Kelleher found that boys viewed single-sex classes positively and reported being more interested and motivated in their work and that the absence of girls helped improve confidence and involvement levels.

There are numerous studies, but few high-quality ones that use comparison groups, control for confounding variables, or use national databases. As an example, in 1999 a California middle school (referred to as Single Sex Academy or SSA, see Herr & Arms, 2004) opened with single-sex classes and is considered the largest experiment in single-sex schooling in the United States. It serves a low-income, urban population of students of color. It was described as "an elaborate experiment to determine whether adolescent boys and girls learn better if separated from one another" (Haynes, 1999). SSA was a reconstituted school that was under extreme pressure to improve the low ranking on the Academic Performance Index, primarily determined by student scores on standardized tests. With no staff development related to single-sex education, teachers were left to do the best they could. Herr and Arms concluded that although SSA was deemed to be a success supporting single-sex schooling, there is no way of actually attributing the improvement to the gender composition of the school. More likely, this improvement was due to substantial changes in curriculum and instruction and other variables related to being reconstituted.

In 2005, the United States Department of Education, along with the American Institute for Research, tried to weigh in on the topic, publishing a meta-analysis comparing single-sex and coeducational schools (U.S. Department of Education, 2005). The authors started with 2,221 citations, which yielded 40 usable studies. Of these 40 studies, 41% favored single-sex schools, 45% found negative effects, and 6% had mixed findings.

Many of the studies from outside the United States (e.g., England) raise concerns about internal validity due to selection bias. Single-sex schools in these studies and contexts traditionally involve private schools with brighter students from more privileged backgrounds. The schools are populated with students who self-select, and the schools engage in a process referred to as "academic weeding-out" (Salomone, 2003, p. 190). Lee and Lockheed (1990) called this validity threat a "social phenomenon and a statistical nuisance" (p. 228).

Conclusion

The benefits of single-sex schooling remain unclear (Harker, 2000; Warrington, 2002). The research comparing the merits of single-sex education and coeducation has not yielded definitive answers. In spite of this conclusion, in 2002 and again in 2004, the Bush administration signaled its intent to promote single-sex schools through the easing of a "rigid" interpretation of Title IX (Davis, 2002). Simply put, when a single-sex school works, we are not exactly sure why it works. The research seems to point in the direction of benefits for poor and minority students and girls. But the presumption in favor of coeducation is found in both the law and in the minds of most Americans.

Salomone (2003) noted that single-sex education has been ideologically tied to racial segregation, which, in effect, causes us to be more critical of it and demand far more of it than we do of other "uncertain" educational innovations. As single-sex education gains more interest and appeal, policymakers, educators, and advocates must continue to search for empirical findings to legitimize this departure from what is considered the "norm." What seems to get lost in the search for definitive evidence is that the exact nature and benefits of single-sex education are highly contextual. School characteristics (e.g., class size, percentage of male and female teachers), teaching styles and instructional practices, and the curriculum, among other factors, all have significant effects on students' achievement. It depends on the students, their backgrounds, abilities, and needs, and it also depends on what we are looking for as the desired outcome of this initiative. Findings about single-sex education must be viewed and interpreted with a healthy dose of caution. As a number of researchers (Jackson & Smith, 2000; Marsh & Rowe, 1996) cautioned, the better performance of students in single-sex classes and schools is mainly attributable to a plethora of factors like student ability, socioeconomic status, type of school (private vs. public), school characteristics (e.g., size, organizational structures), selection bias, and effective teaching. When these factors are controlled for, the academic differences between students in single-sex education and coeducational schools are neither significant nor conclusive (Lingard et al., 2001).

References

Arbor, A. (1998). Single-gender public schools. *The Education Digest, 63*(7), 54–57.

Atherton, B. F. (1972). Co-educational and single sex schooling and happiness of marriage. *Educational Research, 15,* 221–226.

Bell, J. F. (1989). A comparison of science performance and uptake by fifteen-year-old boys and girls in co-educational and single-sex schools. *Educational Studies,* 15(2), 193–203.

Bracey, G. W. (2006). *Separate but superior? A review of issues and data bearing on single-sex education* (EPSL-0611-221-EPRU). Tempe, AZ; Arizona State University, Education Policy Research Unit.

Brutsaert, H., & Bracke, P. (1994). Gender context in elementary school. *Educational Studies,* 20(1), 3, 10.

Bureau of Education. (1883). *Co-education of the sexes in the public schools of the U.S.A.* Washington, DC: United States Government Printing Office.

Butler, N. M. (Ed.). (1910). *Education in the United States.* New York: American Book Company.

Byrne, E. (1993). *Women and science: The shark syndrome.* London: Falmer Press.

Cairns, E. (1990). The relationship between adolescent perceived self-competence and attendance at single-sex secondary school. *British Journal of Educational Psychology, 60,* 207–211.

Clarke, E. H. (1873). *Sex in education.* Boston: Rand, Avery, and Company.

Coleman, J. S. (1961). *The adolescent society.* New York: The Free Press.

Datnow, A., Hubbard, L., & Woody, E. (2001). *Is single gender schooling viable in the public sector? Lessons from California's pilot program.* Retrieved June 28, 2008, from . . .

Davis, M. (2002). Department aims to promote single-sex schools. *Education Weekly, 21*(36), 24–25.

Dean, C. (1998, 27 November). Failing boys, public burden number one. *Times Educational Supplement,* p. 1.

Ferrara, P.J., & Ferrara, M. M. (2004, Summer). Single-gender classrooms: Lessons from a New York middle school. *ERS Spectrum,* 26–32.

Foon, A. (1988). The relationship between school type and adolescent self-esteem, attribution styles, and affiliation needs: implications for educational outcome. *British Journal of Educational Psychology, 58,* 44–54.

Gill, J. (1996, April). *Different contexts, similar outcomes.* Paper presented at the annual meeting of the American Educational Research Association, New York.

Goodlad, J. I. (1984). *A place called school.* New York: McGraw-Hill.

Gorard, S. (1998). Four errors . . . and a conspiracy? The effectiveness of schools in Wales. *Oxford Review of Education,* 24(4), 459–472.

Green, E. (2006, October 27). Are single-sex classrooms legal? *U.S. News and World Report.* Retrieved June 27, 2008, from . . .

Gurian, M., & Henley, P. (with Trueman, T.). (2001). *Boys and girls learn differently! A guide for teachers and parents.* San Francisco: Jossey-Bass.

Hale, B. F. (1929). A debate on coeducation. *Minnesota Chats, 11,* 7–9.

Harker, R. (2000). Achievement, gender and the single-sex/coed debate. *British Journal of the Sociology of Education,* 21(2), 203–218.

Harker, R., & Nash, R. (1997, March). *School type and the education of girls: Co-ed or girls only?* Paper presented at the annual meeting of the American Educational Research Association, Chicago.

Harris, W. T. (1870). *Sixteenth annual report* (1869–1870). St. Louis, MO: St. Louis Board of Education.

Haynes, V. D. (1999). Boys and girls in a class apart. *Chicago Tribune Internet Edition.* Retrieved June 30, 2008, from . . .

Hawtrey, M. (1896). *The coeducation of the sexes.* London: Kegan Paul, Trench, Trubner & Co.

Herr, K., & Arms, E. (2004). Accountability and single-sex schooling; A collision of reform agendas. *American Educational Research Journal, 41*, 527–555.

Jackson, C., & Smith, D. (2000). Poles apart? An exploration of single-sex and mixed-sex educational environments in Australia and England. *Educational Studies, 26*(4), 409–422.

Jill, J. (1993). Re-phrasing the question about single sex schooling. In A. Reid & B. Johnson (Eds.), *Critical issues in Australian education in the 1990s* (pp. 90–99). Adelaide, Australia: Centre for Studies in Educational Leadership, University of South Australia.

Jones, J. C., Shallcrass, J., & Dennis, C. C. (1972). Coeducation and adolescent values. *Journal of Educational Psychology, 63*(4), 334–341.

Kenway, J. (1995). Masculinities in schools; Under siege, on the defensive and under reconstruction? *Discourse: Studies in the Cultural Politics of Education, 16*, 59–79.

Kolesnik, W. B. (1969). *Co-education: Sex differences and the schools.* New York: Vantage Press.

Kumagai, J. (1995). Do single-sex classes help girls achieve in physics? *Physics Today, 48*, 73–74.

Leder, G., & Forgasz, H. (1994, April). *Single-sex mathematics classes in a co-educational setting: A case study.* Paper presented at the annual meeting of the American Educational Research Association, New Orleans, LA.

Lee, V. E. (1986). Effects of single-sex secondary schools on student achievement and attitudes. *Journal of Educational Psychology, 78*(5), 381–395.

Lee, V. E., & Bryk, A. (1986). Effects of single-sex secondary schools on student achievement and attitudes. *Journal of Educational Psychology, 78*(5), 381–395.

Lee, V. E., & Lockheed, M. M. (1990). The effects of single-sex schooling on achievement and attitudes in Nigeria. *Comparative Educational Review, 4*(2), 209–231.

Lee, V. E., & Marks, H. M. (1990). Sustained effects if the single-sex secondary school experience on attitudes, behaviors and values in college. *Journal of Educational Psychology, 82*(3), 578–592.

Lee, V. E., & Marks, H. M. (1992). Who goes where? Choice of single-sex and co-educational independent secondary schools. *Sociology of Education, 65*, 226–231.

Lee, V. E., & Marks, H. M. (1994). Sexism in single-sex and coeducational independent secondary school classrooms. *Sociology of Education, 67*(2), 92–120.

LePore, P. C., & Warren, I. R. (1997). A comparison of single-sex and co-educational Catholic secondary schooling: Evidence from the National Educational Longitudinal Study of 1988. *American Educational Research Journal, 34*(3), 485–511.

Leslie, C. (1999). Separate and unequal? *Newsweek*. Retrieved June 28, 2008, from . . .

Lingard, B., Ladwig, J., Mills, M., Bahr, M., Chant, D., Warry, M., Ailwood, J., Capeness, R., Christie, P., Gore, J., Hayes, D., & Luke, A. (2001). The Queensland school reform longitudinal study. Vols. 1 & 2. Brisbane: Educational Queensland.

Mael, F. A. (1998). Single-sex and coeducational schooling: Relationships to socioemotional and academic development. *Review of Educational Research, 68*(2), 101–129.

Mallam, W. A. (1993). Impact of school type and sex of the teacher in female students' attitudes toward mathematics in Nigerian secondary schools. *Educational Studies in Mathematics, 24*(2), 223–229.

Marsh, H. (1989). Effects of attending single-sex and coeducational high schools on achievement, attitudes, behaviors, and sex differences. *Journal of Educational Psychology, 81*(1), 70–85.

Marsh, H., & Rowe, K. (1996). The effects of single-sex and mixed-sex mathematics classes within a coeducational school: A reanalysis and comment. *Australian Journal of Education, 40*(2), 147–162.

Mead, S. (2006). *The truth about boys and girls*. Washington, DC: Education Sector.

National Center for Educational Statistics. (2005). *The nation's report card: NAEP 2004 trends in academic progress*. Washington, DC: U.S. Department of Education. Retrieved June 27, 2008, from . . .

National Coalition for Women and Girls in Education. (2002). *Single-sex notice of intent comments*. Retrieved June 19, 2008, from . . .

Parker, L. H., & Rennie, L. J. (1997). Teachers' perceptions of the implementation of single-sex classes in coeducation schools. *Australian Journal of Education, 41*(2), 119–133.

Riordan, C. (1985). Public and Catholic schooling: The effects of gender context policy. *American Journal of Education, 93*(4), 518–540.

Rowe, K. J. (1988). Single sex and mixed sex classes: The effects of class type on student achievement, confidence and participation in mathematics. *Australian Journal of Education, 32*(2), 180–202.

Salomone, R. C. (2003). *Same, different, and equal: Rethinking single-sex schooling*. New Haven, CT: Yale University Press.

Salomone, R. C. (2006). Single-sex programs: Resolving the research conundrum. *Teachers College Record, 108*, 778–802.

Schneider, F. W., & Counts, L. M. (1982). The high school environment: A comparison of coeducational and single-sex schools, *Journal of Educational Psychology, 4(6)*, 898–906.

Scott, A. C. (1991). *A girls-only science class in a co-educational secondary school*. Unpublished master's thesis, Victoria University of Wellington, New Zealand.

POSTSCRIPT

Are Single-Sex Schools and Classes Effective?

A myriad of questions remain regarding the value of single-sex education. The ACLU has raised a number of crucial questions on the topic. One of the main concerns is that sex segregation encourages teachers to oversimplify the issue of learning style differences and to ignore the more nuanced needs of both boys and girls. This and other important aspects are explored in the ACLU publication "Boys' Brains v. Girls' Brains: What Sex Segregation Teaches Students" (May 19, 2008).

In "Teaching Boys and Girls Separately," in *The New York Times* (March 2, 2008), Elizabeth Weil presents a critical exploration of the claims put forth by Leonard Sax and Michael Gurian. She states that "despite a lack of empirical evidence, a cottage industry has emerged working the 'boys and girls are essentially different, so we should educate them differently' angle." The Gurian Institute, for example, has been quite successful commercially by producing best-selling books on learning differences and providing training sessions for teachers across the country. Meanwhile, noted expert David Sadker contends that very little research actually exists on single-sex schools and their effectiveness is a big educational question mark.

Further exploration of the gender issue and the arguments over single-sex instruction may be found in "Same-Sex Schools," *American School Board Journal* (November 2002), by Kathleen Vail; "No Girls Allowed," *NEA Today* (April 2006), by Mary Ellen Flannery; "Closing the Gender Gap—Again!" *Principal* (March/April 2005), by David Sadker and Karen Zittleman; "Separating the Sexes: A New Direction for Public Education?" *The Christian Science Monitor* (May 24, 2004), by Teresa Mendez; and "Single-Sex Schooling: Is It Simply a 'Class Act'?" *Gender & Education* (March 2006), by Georgina Tsolidis and Ian R. Dobson.

A number of provocative books have been written on the topic, including Michael Ruhlman's *Boys Themselves: A Return to Single-Sex Education* (1996), Karen Stabiner's *All Girls: Single-Sex Education and Why It Matters* (2002), Leonard Sax's *Boys Adrift: The Five Factors Driving the Growing Epidemic of Unmotivated Boys and Underachieving Young Men* (2007), and Pedro A. Noguera's *The Trouble with Black Boys—and Other Reflections on Race, Equity, and the Future of Public Education* (2008). Finally, an interesting treatment of the issue is presented by E. Thomas Ewing in "The Repudiation of Single-Sex Education," *American Educational Research Journal* (Winter 2006).

ISSUE 18

Can Zero Tolerance Violate Students Rights?

YES: **Hon. David Souter,** from Majority Opinion in *Safford Unified School District #1 v. Redding* (June 25, 2009)

NO: **Hon. Clarence Thomas,** from Dissenting Opinion in *Safford Unified School District #1 v. Redding* (June 25, 2009)

ISSUE SUMMARY

YES: Supreme Court justice David Souter, delivering the opinion of the Court, hold that school officials, in carrying out a zero-tolerance policy on drug possession, violated a student's Fourth Amendment right against unreasonable search and seizure when they included a strip search of the girl.

NO: Justice Clarence Thomas, in dissent, states that the majority opinion imposes too vague a standard on school officials and that it grants judges sweeping authority to second-guess measures those officials take to maintain discipline and ensure safety.

Approximately a decade ago, after the tragedy at Columbine, school systems across the nation introduced zero-tolerance policies aimed at the curtailment of harmful student behaviors. The initial focus of these policies was on the elimination of weapons but soon spread to restrictions on any type of drugs or medication, legal or illegal, doctor-prescribed or readily available in stores. By 2006 about 95% of schools in the United States had zero-tolerance policies and nearly half of them reported taking serious action against students, including expulsion, suspension, and transfer to an alternative school.

While many of the practices involved in the enforcement of these policies have been welcomed by all members of the school community insofar as they promoted a safer environment for learning, questions have been raised in recent years about the appropriateness of some actions of school officials. Authors exploring this issue include Randall R. Beger, "Expansion of Police Power in Public Schools and the Vanishing Rights of Students," *Social Justice* (Spring/Summer 2002); Mary Ann Manos, *Knowing Where to Draw the Line: Ethical and Legal Standards for Best Classroom Practice* (2006); Kris Axtman, "Why

Tolerance Is Fading for Zero Tolerance in Schools," *The Christian Science Monitor* (March 31, 2005); Bob Herbert, "6-Year-Olds Under Arrest," *The New York Times* (April 9, 2007); and Elizabeth Frost, "Zero Privacy: Schools Are Violating Students' Fourteenth Amendment Right of Privacy Under the Guise of Enforcing Zero-Tolerance Policies," *Washington Law Review* (May 2006).

Media attention to this issue has stirred public concern and parents of students subjected to allegedly unfair treatment by school officials have initiated lawsuits. Lawyers pursuing such cases have often used a precedent established in the 1969 Supreme Court ruling in *Tinker v. Des Moines Independent School District* that students in school are still "persons" under the Constitution and are therefore possessed of fundamental rights that the state must respect. Subsequent Supreme Court cases involving First and Fourth Amendment rights are reviewed by Nelda Cambron-McCabe in "Balancing Students' Constitutional Rights," *Phi Delta Kappan* (June 2009). She concludes that while the courts have granted school officials considerable latitude in maintaining a school environment conducive to learning they must also honor students' rights in the process. An excellent source on this historical problem of appropriate balance is *From Schoolhouse to Courthouse: The Judiciary's Role in American Education* (2009), edited by Joshua M. Dunn and Martin R. West. The current period of security guards, metal detectors, surveillance cameras, locker raids, and book bag searches has captured the attention of the ACLU and other concerned groups.

The question of how far school authorities can go in fulfilling zero-tolerance policies came to a head in the Supreme Court's recent ruling in *Safford Unified School District #1 v. Redding*, argued April 21, 2009 and decided June 25, 2009. The case involved what is characterized as a strip search of a 13-year-old middle school student, Savana Redding, accused of hiding ibuprofen tablets in violation of the school's no-tolerance policy on drugs that banned the possession even of nonprescription pain relievers without explicit permission. School officials claimed that they were on high alert because a student had nearly died the year before after taking medication brought to the school by a friend and that they had good reasons to be suspicious of Savana despite her honor roll grades and spotless disciplinary record. After the event, Savana never returned to Safford Middle School. The Supreme Court ruled in her favor.

In the excerpts from the 8-1 ruling presented below, Justice Souter details the bases for the judgment, which included protection of the school officials from further suits, although Justices Stevens and Ginsburg dissented on that point. Justice Thomas, agreeing with the school official immunity point, was the lone dissenter on the central ruling regarding the violation of the student's rights.

YES

David H. Souter

Strip Search Violates 14th Amendment

J USTICE SOUTER delivered the opinion of the Court.

The issue here is whether a 13-year-old student's Fourth Amendment right was violated when she was subjected to a search of her bra and underpants by school officials acting on reasonable suspicion that she had brought forbidden prescription and over-the-counter drugs to school. Because there were no reasons to suspect the drugs presented a danger or were concealed in her underwear, we hold that the search did violate the Constitution, but because there is reason to question the clarity with which the right was established, the official who ordered the unconstitutional search is entitled to qualified immunity from liability.

. . .

The events immediately prior to the search in question began in 13-year-old Savana Redding's math class at Safford Middle School one October day in 2003. The assistant principal of the school, Kerry Wilson, came into the room and asked Savana to go to his office. There, he showed her a day planner, unzipped and open flat on his desk, in which there were several knives, lighters, a permanent marker, and a cigarette. Wilson asked Savana whether the planner was hers; she said it was, but that a few days before she had lent it to her friend, Marissa Glines. Savana stated that none of the items in the planner belonged to her.

Wilson then showed Savana four white prescription-strength ibuprofen 400-mg pills, and one over-the-counter blue naproxen 200-mg pill, all used for pain and inflammation but banned under school rules without advance permission. He asked Savana if she knew anything about the pills. Savana answered that she did not. Wilson then told Savana that he had received a report that she was giving these pills to fellow students; Savana denied it and agreed to let Wilson search her belongings. Helen Romero, an administrative assistant, came into the office, and together with Wilson they searched Savana's backpack, finding nothing.

At that point, Wilson instructed Romero to take Savana to the school nurse's office to search her clothes for pills. Romero and the nurse, Peggy Schwallier, asked Savana to remove her jacket, socks, and shoes, leaving her in stretch pants and a T-shirt (both without pockets), which she was then asked to remove. Finally, Savana was told to pull her bra out and to the side

From Supreme Court of the United States, June 25, 2009.

and shake it, and to pull out the elastic on her underpants, thus exposing her breasts and pelvic area to some degree. No pills were found.

Savana's mother filed suit against Safford Unified School District #1, Wilson, Romero, and Schwallier for conducting a strip search in violation of Savana's Fourth Amendment rights. The individuals (hereinafter petitioners) moved for summary judgment, raising a defense of qualified immunity. The District Court for the District of Arizona granted the motion on the ground that there was no Fourth Amendment violation, and a panel of the Ninth Circuit affirmed. . . .

A closely divided Circuit sitting en banc, however, reversed. Following the two-step protocol for evaluating claims of qualified immunity, . . . the Ninth Circuit held that the strip search was unjustified under the Fourth Amendment test for searches of children by school officials set out in *New Jersey* v. *T. L. O.,* . . . (1985). . . . The Circuit then applied the test for qualified immunity, and found that Savana's right was clearly established at the time of the search: "'[t]hese notions of personal privacy are "clearly established" in that they inhere in all of us, particularly middle school teenagers, and are inherent in the privacy component of the Fourth Amendment's proscription against unreasonable searches'" . . . . The upshot was reversal of summary judgment as to Wilson, while affirming the judgments in favor of Schwallier, the school nurse, and Romero, the administrative assistant, since they had not acted as independent decisionmakers. . . .

. . .

The Fourth Amendment "right of the people to be secure in their persons . . . against unreasonable searches and seizures" generally requires a law enforcement officer to have probable cause for conducting a search. "Probable cause exists where 'the facts and circumstances within [an officer's] knowledge and of which [he] had reasonably trustworthy information [are] sufficient in themselves to warrant a man of reasonable caution in the belief that' an offense has been or is being committed," . . . and that evidence bearing on that offense will be found in the place to be searched.

In *T. L. O.,* we recognized that the school setting "requires some modification of the level of suspicion of illicit activity needed to justify a search," . . . and held that for searches by school officials "a careful balancing of governmental and private interests suggests that the public interest is best served by a Fourth Amendment standard of reasonableness that stops short of probable cause" . . . . We have thus applied a standard of reasonable suspicion to determine the legality of a school administrator's search of a student, . . . and have held that a school search "will be permissible in its scope when the measures adopted are reasonably related to the objectives of the search and not excessively intrusive in light of the age and sex of the student and the nature of the infraction" . . . .

A number of our cases on probable cause have an implicit bearing on the reliable knowledge element of reasonable suspicion, as we have attempted to flesh out the knowledge component by looking to the degree to which known facts imply prohibited conduct, . . . the specificity of the information received, . . . and the reliability of its source. . . . At the end of the day, however, we have realized that these factors cannot rigidly control, . . . and we have come back to saying that the standards are "fluid concepts that take their substantive content from the particular contexts" in which they are being assessed. . . .

Perhaps the best that can be said generally about the required knowledge component of probable cause for a law enforcement officer's evidence search is that it raise a "fair probability" . . . or a "substantial chance" . . . of discovering evidence of criminal activity. The lesser standard for school searches could as readily be described as a moderate chance of finding evidence of wrongdoing.

. . .

In this case, the school's policies strictly prohibit the nonmedical use, possession, or sale of any drug on school grounds, including "'[a]ny prescription or over-the-counter drug, except those for which permission to use in school has been granted pursuant to Board policy.'" . . . A week before Savana was searched, another student, Jordan Romero (no relation of the school's administrative assistant), told the principal and Assistant Principal Wilson that "certain students were bringing drugs and weapons on campus," and that he had been sick after taking some pills that "he got from a classmate." . . . On the morning of October 8, the same boy handed Wilson a white pill that he said Marissa Glines had given him. He told Wilson that students were planning to take the pills at lunch.

Wilson learned from Peggy Schwallier, the school nurse, that the pill was Ibuprofen 400 mg, available only by prescription. Wilson then called Marissa out of class. Outside the classroom, Marissa's teacher handed Wilson the day planner, found within Marissa's reach, containing various contraband items. Wilson escorted Marissa back to his office.

In the presence of Helen Romero, Wilson requested Marissa to turn out her pockets and open her wallet. Marissa produced a blue pill, several white ones, and a razor blade. Wilson asked where the blue pill came from, and Marissa answered, "'I guess it slipped in when *she* gave me the IBU 400s.'" . . . When Wilson asked whom she meant, Marissa replied, "'Savana Redding.'" . . . Wilson then enquired about the day planner and its contents; Marissa denied knowing anything about them. Wilson did not ask Marissa any followup questions to determine whether there was any likelihood that Savana presently had pills: neither asking when Marissa received the pills from Savana nor where Savana might be hiding them.

Schwallier did not immediately recognize the blue pill, but information provided through a poison control hotline indicated that the pill was a 200-mg dose of an anti-inflammatory drug, generically called naproxen, available over the counter. At Wilson's direction, Marissa was then subjected to a search of her bra and underpants by Romero and Schwallier, as Savana was later on. The search revealed no additional pills.

It was at this juncture that Wilson called Savana into his office and showed her the day planner. Their conversation established that Savana and Marissa were on friendly terms: while she denied knowledge of the contraband, Savana admitted that the day planner was hers and that she had lent it to

Marissa. Wilson had other reports of their friendship from staff members, who had identified Savana and Marissa as part of an unusually rowdy group at the school's opening dance in August, during which alcohol and cigarettes were found in the girls' bathroom. Wilson had reason to connect the girls with this contraband, for Wilson knew that Jordan Romero had told the principal that before the dance, he had been at a party at Savana's house where alcohol was served. Marissa's statement that the pills came from Savana was thus sufficiently plausible to warrant suspicion that Savana was involved in pill distribution.

This suspicion of Wilson's was enough to justify a search of Savana's backpack and outer clothing. If a student is reasonably suspected of giving out contraband pills, she is reasonably suspected of carrying them on her person and in the carryall that has become an item of student uniform in most places today. If Wilson's reasonable suspicion of pill distribution were not understood to support searches of outer clothes and backpack, it would not justify any search worth making. And the look into Savana's bag, in her presence and in the relative privacy of Wilson's office, was not excessively intrusive, any more than Romero's subsequent search of her outer clothing.

. . .

Here it is that the parties part company, with Savana's claim that extending the search at Wilson's behest to the point of making her pull out her underwear was constitutionally unreasonable. The exact label for this final step in the intrusion is not important, though strip search is a fair way to speak of it. Romero and Schwallier directed Savana to remove her clothes down to her underwear, and then "pull out" her bra and the elastic band on her underpants. . . . Although Romero and Schwallier stated that they did not see anything when Savana followed their instructions, . . . we would not define strip search and its Fourth Amendment consequences in a way that would guarantee litigation about who was looking and how much was seen. The very fact of Savana's pulling her underwear away from her body in the presence of the two officials who were able to see her necessarily exposed her breasts and pelvic area to some degree, and both subjective and reasonable societal expectations of personal privacy support the treatment of such a search as categorically distinct, requiring distinct elements of justification on the part of school authorities for going beyond a search of outer clothing and belongings.

Savana's subjective expectation of privacy against such a search is inherent in her account of it as embarrassing, frightening, and humiliating. The reasonableness of her expectation (required by the Fourth Amendment standard) is indicated by the consistent experiences of other young people similarly searched, whose adolescent vulnerability intensifies the patent intrusiveness of the exposure. . . . The common reaction of these adolescents simply registers the obviously different meaning of a search exposing the body from the experience of nakedness or near undress in other school circumstances. Changing for gym is getting ready for play; exposing for a search is responding to an accusation reserved for suspected wrongdoers and fairly understood as so degrading that a number of communities have decided that strip searches in schools are never reasonable and have banned them no matter what the facts may be. . . .

The indignity of the search does not, of course, outlaw it, but it does implicate the rule of reasonableness as stated in *T. L. O.,* that "the search as actually conducted [be] reasonably related in scope to the circumstances which justified the interference in the first place." . . . The scope will be permissible, that is, when it is "not excessively intrusive in light of the age and sex of the student and the nature of the infraction." . . .

Here, the content of the suspicion failed to match the degree of intrusion. Wilson knew beforehand that the pills were prescription-strength ibuprofen and over-the-counter naproxen, common pain relievers equivalent to two Advil, or one Aleve. He must have been aware of the nature and limited threat of the specific drugs he was searching for, and while just about anything can be taken in quantities that will do real harm, Wilson had no reason to suspect that large amounts of the drugs were being passed around, or that individual students were receiving great numbers of pills.

Nor could Wilson have suspected that Savana was hiding common pain-killers in her underwear. Petitioners suggest, as a truth universally acknowledged, that "students . . . hid[e] contraband in or under their clothing," . . . and cite a smattering of cases of students with contraband in their underwear. . . . But when the categorically extreme intrusiveness of a search down to the body of an adolescent requires some justification in suspected facts, general background possibilities fall short; a reasonable search that extensive calls for suspicion that it will pay off. But nondangerous school contraband does not raise the specter of stashes in intimate places, and there is no evidence in the record of any general practice among Safford Middle School students of hiding that sort of thing in underwear; neither Jordan nor Marissa suggested to Wilson that Savana was doing that, and the preceding search of Marissa that Wilson ordered yielded nothing. Wilson never even determined when Marissa had received the pills from Savana; if it had been a few days before, that would weigh heavily against any reasonable conclusion that Savana presently had the pills on her person, much less in her underwear.

In sum, what was missing from the suspected facts that pointed to Savana was any indication of danger to the students from the power of the drugs or their quantity, and any reason to suppose that Savana was carrying pills in her underwear. We think that the combination of these deficiencies was fatal to finding the search reasonable.

In so holding, we mean to cast no ill reflection on the assistant principal, for the record raises no doubt that his motive throughout was to eliminate drugs from his school and protect students from what Jordan Romero had gone through. Parents are known to overreact to protect their children from danger, and a school official with responsibility for safety may tend to do the same. The difference is that the Fourth Amendment places limits on the official, even with the high degree of deference that courts must pay to the educator's professional judgment.

We do mean, though, to make it clear that the *T. L. O.* concern to limit a school search to reasonable scope requires the support of reasonable suspicion of danger or of resort to underwear for hiding evidence of wrongdoing before a search can reasonably make the quantum leap from outer clothes and backpacks to exposure of intimate parts. The meaning of such a search, and the degradation its subject may reasonably feel, place a search that intrusive in a category of its own demanding its own specific suspicions.

. . .

❧

The strip search of Savana Redding was unreasonable and a violation of the Fourth Amendment, but petitioners Wilson, Romero, and Schwallier are nevertheless protected from liability through qualified immunity. . . .

NO

School Officials Deserve Leeway

J USTICE THOMAS, concurring in the judgment in part and dissenting in part.

    I agree with the Court that the judgment against the school officials with respect to qualified immunity should be reversed. . . . Unlike the majority, however, I would hold that the search of Savana Redding did not violate the Fourth Amendment. The majority imposes a vague and amorphous standard on school administrators. It also grants judges sweeping authority to second-guess the measures that these officials take to maintain discipline in their schools and ensure the health and safety of the students in their charge. This deep intrusion into the administration of public schools exemplifies why the Court should return to the common-law doctrine of *in loco parentis* under which "the judiciary was reluctant to interfere in the routine business of school adminis-tration, allowing schools and teachers to set and enforce rules and to maintain order." . . . But even under the prevailing Fourth Amendment test established by *New Jersey* v. *T. L. O.,* . . . all petitioners, including the school district, are entitled to judgment as a matter of law in their favor.

. . .

    "Although the underlying command of the Fourth Amendment is always that searches and seizures be reasonable, what is reasonable depends on the context within which a search takes place." . . . Thus, although pub-lic school students retain Fourth Amendment rights under this Court's prec-edent, . . . those rights "are different . . . than elsewhere; the 'reasonableness' inquiry cannot disregard the schools' custodial and tutelary responsibility for children." . . . For nearly 25 years this Court has understood that "[m]aintaining order in the classroom has never been easy, but in more recent years, school disorder has often taken particularly ugly forms: drug use and violent crime in the schools have become major social problems." . . . In schools, "[e]vents calling for discipline are frequent occurrences and sometimes require immedi-ate, effective action." . . .

    For this reason, school officials retain broad authority to protect students and preserve "order and a proper educational environment" under the Fourth Amendment. . . . This authority requires that school officials be able to engage in the "close supervision of schoolchildren, as well as . . . enforc[e] rules against conduct that would be perfectly permissible if undertaken by an adult." . . . Seeking to reconcile the Fourth Amendment with this unique public school setting, the Court in *T. L. O.* held that a school search is "reason-able" if it is "'justified at its inception'" and "'reasonably related in scope to

From Supreme Court of the United States, June 25, 2009.

the circumstances which justified the interference in the first place.'" . . . The search under review easily meets this standard.

. . .

A "search of a student by a teacher or other school official will be 'justified at its inception' when there are reasonable grounds for suspecting that the search will turn up evidence that the student has violated or is violating either the law or the rules of the school." . . . As the majority rightly concedes, this search was justified at its inception because there were reasonable grounds to suspect that Redding possessed medication that violated school rules. . . . A finding of reasonable suspicion "does not deal with hard certainties, but with probabilities." . . . To satisfy this standard, more than a mere "hunch" of wrongdoing is required, but "considerably" less suspicion is needed than would be required to "satisf[y] a preponderance of the evidence standard." . . .

Furthermore, in evaluating whether there is a reasonable "particularized and objective" basis for conducting a search based on suspected wrongdoing, government officials must consider the "totality of the circumstances." . . . School officials have a specialized understanding of the school environment, the habits of the students, and the concerns of the community, which enables them to "'formulat[e] certain common-sense conclusions about human behavior.'" . . . And like police officers, school officials are "entitled to make an assessment of the situation in light of [this] specialized training and familiarity with the customs of the [school]." . . .

Here, petitioners had reasonable grounds to suspect that Redding was in possession of prescription and nonprescription drugs in violation of the school's prohibition of the "non-medical use, possession, or sale of a drug" on school property or at school events. . . . As an initial matter, school officials were aware that a few years earlier, a student had become "seriously ill" and "spent several days in intensive care" after ingesting prescription medication obtained from a classmate. . . . Fourth Amendment searches do not occur in a vacuum; rather, context must inform the judicial inquiry. . . . In this instance, the suspicion of drug possession arose at a middle school that had "a history of problems with students using and distributing prohibited and illegal substances on campus." . . .

The school's substance-abuse problems had not abated by the 2003–2004 school year, which is when the challenged search of Redding took place. School officials had found alcohol and cigarettes in the girls' bathroom during the first school dance of the year and noticed that a group of students including Redding and Marissa Glines smelled of alcohol. . . . Several weeks later, another student, Jordan Romero, reported that Redding had hosted a party before the dance where she served whiskey, vodka, and tequila. . . . Romero had provided this report to school officials as a result of a meeting his mother scheduled with the officials after Romero "bec[a]me violent" and "sick to his stomach" one night and admitted that "he had taken some pills that he had got[ten] from a classmate." . . . At that meeting, Romero admitted that "certain students were bringing drugs and weapons on campus." . . . One week later, Romero handed the assistant principal a white pill that he said he had received from Glines. . . . He reported "that a group of students [were] planning on taking the pills at lunch." . . .

School officials justifiably took quick action in light of the lunchtime deadline. The assistant principal took the pill to the school nurse who identified it as prescription-strength 400-mg Ibuprofen. . . . A subsequent search of Glines and her belongings produced a razor blade, a Naproxen 200-mg pill, and several Ibuprofen 400-mg pills. . . . When asked, Glines claimed that she had received the pills from Redding. . . . A search of Redding's planner, which Glines had borrowed, then uncovered "several knives, several lighters, a cigarette, and a permanent marker." . . . Thus, as the majority acknowledges, . . . the totality of relevant circumstances justified a search of Redding for pills.

. . .

The remaining question is whether the search was reasonable in scope. Under *T. L. O.,* "a search will be permissible in its scope when the measures adopted are reasonably related to the objectives of the search and not excessively intrusive in light of the age and sex of the student and the nature of the infraction." . . . The majority concludes that the school officials' search of Redding's underwear was not "'reasonably related in scope to the circumstances which justified the interference in the first place,'" . . . notwithstanding the officials' reasonable suspicion that Redding "was involved in pill distribution," . . . . According to the majority, to be reasonable, this school search required a showing of "danger to the students from the power of the drugs or their quantity" or a "reason to suppose that [Redding] was carrying pills in her underwear." . . . Each of these additional requirements is an unjustifiable departure from bedrock Fourth Amendment law in the school setting, where this Court has heretofore read the Fourth Amendment to grant considerable leeway to school officials. Because the school officials searched in a location where the pills could have been hidden, the search was reasonable in scope under *T. L. O.*

. . .

The majority finds that "subjective and reasonable societal expectations of personal privacy support . . . treat[ing]" this type of search, which it labels a "strip search," as "categorically distinct, requiring distinct elements of justification on the part of school authorities for going beyond a search of clothing and belongings." . . . Thus, in the majority's view, although the school officials had reasonable suspicion to believe that Redding had the pills on her person, . . . they needed some greater level of particularized suspicion to conduct this "strip search." There is no support for this contortion of the Fourth Amendment.

. . .

❧

The analysis of whether the scope of the search here was permissible under that standard is straightforward. Indeed, the majority does not dispute that "general background possibilities" establish that students conceal "contraband in their underwear." . . . It acknowledges that school officials had reasonable suspicion to look in Redding's backpack and outer clothing because if "Wilson's reasonable suspicion of pill distribution were not understood to support searches of outer clothes and backpack, it would not justify any search worth making." . . . The majority nevertheless concludes that proceeding any further with the search was unreasonable. . . . But there is no support for this conclusion. The reasonable suspicion that Redding possessed the pills for distribution purposes did not dissipate simply because the search of her backpack turned up nothing. It was eminently reasonable to conclude that the backpack was empty because Redding was secreting the pills in a place she thought no one would look. . . .

Redding would not have been the first person to conceal pills in her undergarments. . . . Nor will she be the last after today's decision, which announces the safest place to secrete contraband in school.

. . .

The majority compounds its error by reading the "nature of the infraction" aspect of the *T. L. O.* test as a license to limit searches based on a judge's assessment of a particular school policy. According to the majority, the scope of the search was impermissible because the school official "must have been aware of the nature and limited threat of the specific drugs he was searching for" and because he "had no reason to suspect that large amounts of the drugs were being passed around, or that individual students were receiving great numbers of pills." . . . Thus, in order to locate a rationale for finding a Fourth Amendment violation in this case, the majority retreats from its observation that the school's firm no-drug policy "makes sense, and there is no basis to claim that the search was unreasonable owing to some defect or shortcoming of the rule it was aimed at enforcing." . . .

Even accepting the majority's assurances that it is not attacking the rule's reasonableness, it certainly is attacking the rule's importance. This approach directly conflicts with *T. L. O.* in which the Court was "unwilling to adopt a standard under which the legality of a search is dependent upon a judge's evaluation of the relative importance of school rules." . . . Indeed, the Court in *T. L. O.* expressly rejected the proposition that the majority seemingly endorses—that "some rules regarding student conduct are by nature too 'trivial' to justify a search based upon reasonable suspicion." . . .

The majority's decision in this regard also departs from another basic principle of the Fourth Amendment: that law enforcement officials can enforce with the same vigor all rules and regulations irrespective of the perceived importance of any of those rules. "In a long line of cases, we have said that when an officer has probable cause to believe a person committed even a minor crime in his presence, the balancing of private and public interests is not in doubt. The arrest is constitutionally reasonable." . . . The Fourth Amendment rule for searches is the same: Police officers are entitled to search regardless of the perceived triviality of the underlying law. As we have explained, requiring police to make "sensitive, case-by-case determinations of government need," . . . for a particular prohibition before conducting a search would "place police in an almost impossible spot" . . . .

The majority has placed school officials in this "impossible spot" by questioning whether possession of Ibuprofen and Naproxen causes a severe enough threat to warrant investigation. Had the suspected infraction involved a street drug, the majority implies that it would have approved the scope of the search. . . . In effect, then, the majority has replaced a school rule that draws no distinction among drugs with a new one that does. As a result, a full search of a student's person for prohibited drugs will be permitted only if the Court agrees that the drug in question was sufficiently dangerous. Such a test is unworkable and unsound. School officials cannot be expected to halt searches based on the possibility that a court might later find that the particular infraction at issue is not severe enough to warrant an intrusive investigation. . . .

⋅◉⋅

In determining whether the search's scope was reasonable under the Fourth Amendment, it is therefore irrelevant whether officials suspected Redding of possessing prescription-strength Ibuprofen, nonprescription-strength Naproxen, or some harder street drug. Safford prohibited its possession on school property. Reasonable suspicion that Redding was in possession of drugs in violation of these policies, therefore, justified a search extending to any area where small pills could be concealed. The search did not violate the Fourth Amendment.

. . .

POSTSCRIPT

Can Zero Tolerance Violate Student Rights?

While public sentiment and media commentary tended to side with the final ruling in *Safford Unified School District #1 v. Redding*, the conduct of school officials charged with the responsibility of carrying out zero-tolerance policies will most likely come under further legal scrutiny. Does the Fourth Amendment require a stricter standard than "reasonableness" for justifying actions such as student strip searches? Is the zero-tolerance basis for school discipline itself faulty and in need of modification? Does the principle enunciated by Justice Stephen Breyer in an earlier case continue to guide legal opinions, namely that "school officials need a degree of flexible authority to respond to disciplinary challenges and the law has always considered the relationship between teachers and students special"?

These and related questions are explored in depth in "Law and Order in the Classroom" by Richard Arum and Doreet Preiss in *Education Next* (Fall 2009); *Zero-Tolerance Policies in Schools* (2009), edited by Peggy Daniels; and Bryan R. Warnick's "Surveillance Cameras in Schools: An Ethical Analysis," *Harvard Educational Review* (Fall 2007).

Additional perspectives on the privacy issue at hand and important subtopics can be found in these sources: Ross W. Greene, *Lost at School* (2008), which explores the need for changing the culture and practice of discipline in the schools; Joseph A. Lieberman, *School Shootings: What Every Parent and Educator Needs to Know to Protect Our Children* (2008), which identifies characteristics of the antisocial personality; Justin M. Bathon and Martha M. McCarthy, "Student Expression: The Uncertain Future," *Educational Horizons* (Winter 2008); Alfie Kohn, "Safety from the Inside Out: Rethinking Traditional Approaches," *Educational Horizons* (Fall 2004); Pedro A. Noguera, "Rethinking Disciplinary Practices," *Theory Into Practice* (Autumn 2003); Alfie Kohn, *Beyond Discipline: From Compliance to Community* (2006); and Anne Gregory and Dewey Cornell, "'Tolerating' Adolescent Needs: Moving Beyond Zero-Tolerance Policies in High School," *Theory Into Practice* (Spring 2009).

Discipline and classroom management are among the primary concerns of beginning teachers. No foolproof theories of discipline exist, but a wide-ranging exploration of ideas such as those in the sources cited above and those in first-hand anecdotal accounts by first-year teachers can help in the construction of a reasonable approach when coupled with the sage advice of veteran educators.

ISSUE 19

Do Computers Negatively Affect Student Growth?

YES: Lowell Monke, from "The Human Touch," *Education Next* (Fall 2004)

NO: Frederick M. Hess, from "Technical Difficulties," *Education Next* (Fall 2004)

ISSUE SUMMARY

YES: Lowell Monke, an assistant professor of education, expresses deep concerns that the uncritical faith in computer technology in schools has led to sacrifices in intellectual growth and creativity.

NO: Frederick M. Hess, while sharing some of Monke's observations, believes that the tools of technology, used appropriately, can support innovation and reinvention in education.

T he schools have not always used or responded to new media constructively, so it is crucial that media experts help teachers, administrators, and curriculum designers carve out appropriate strategies for dealing with new technologies. Some experts—while seeing many exciting possibilities in computer-based instruction, particularly in the realm of individualization and self-pacing—caution that we need far more sophisticated understanding of the processes of learning, human motivation, and factors involved in concentration. Others fear the controlling force of computer programs because it could lead to the diminution of the spontaneity and instinctive responses of the learner. The ultimate effect of the new technology could be a complete transformation of learning and the conception of organized education—but similar predictions were made with the advent of television and even radio.

In 1984 MIT professor Seymour Papert predicted, "There won't be schools in the future; I think that the computer will blow up the school." But Larry Cuban, in "Revolutions That Fizzled," *The Washington Post* (October 27, 1996), warns that the persistent urge to reengineer the schools has continually failed to transform teaching practices. Papert, writing in the same issue, counters that the computer makes possible John Dewey's depiction of learning through experimentation and exposure to the real world of social experience. Computer enthusiasts Jim Cummins of New York University and Dennis Sayers of the Ontario Institute for Studies in Education, in their 1996 book *Brave New Schools*, urge heavy investment in an Internet-wired nationwide school system.

On the negative side, Richard P. Lookatch, in "The Ill-Considered Dash to Technology," *The School Administrator* (April 1996), warns that "hardware hucksters have found K–12 schools to be open landfills for outdated central processing units, while software pushers find technology-zealous media specialists ideal targets for software, much of which ultimately ends up in a storage cabinet because it is either too frustrating, too complicated, or too poorly correlated to the curriculum." His position is that educational media offer no unique benefits and may well lead to inequity, lower standards, and wasted financial resources.

In "The Emperor's New Computer: A Critical Look at Our Appetite for Computer Technology," *Journal of Teacher Education* (May–June 1996), David Pepi and Geoffrey Schuerman pose several crucial questions, including the following:

- Is technology an effective catalyst for educational reform?
- Are past, current, and anticipated uses of technology consistent with contemporary theories of learning?
- Is using computers synonymous with good teaching?
- Does technology promote critical thinking?
- Does technology build cooperation?
- How much information can we tolerate?

In considering responses to such questions, the authors draw on Neil Postman's 1993 book *Technopoly*, in which "technopoly" is defined as a culture in which all aspects of human life must find meaning in terms of the current technology and in which there is no tolerance of alternative worldviews. It is Postman's opinion that we are moving toward that culture.

Books addressing the issue include Jane M. Healy's *Failure to Connect* (1998); Frederick Bennett's *Computers as Tutors: Solving the Crisis in Education* (1999); Clifford Stoll's *High Tech Heretic* (1999); Andrea A. DiSessa's *Changing Minds: Computers, Learning, and Literacy* (2000); Larry Cuban's *Oversold and Underused* (2001); and Seymour Papert's *The Connected Family* (1996). In his book, Papert states, "Despite frequent predictions that a technological revolution in education is imminent, school remains in essential respects very much what it has always been, and what changes have occurred (for better or for worse) cannot be attributed to technology."

The opinions that follow pit Lowell Monke, who feels that the computer's emphasis on information acquisition reconstitutes learning and shifts our values, against Frederick Hess, who holds out hope that the efficiencies of computer technology can free students and teachers for more creative exploration.

YES

Lowell Monke

The Human Touch

In 1922 Thomas Edison proclaimed, "I believe the motion picture is destined to revolutionize our educational system and that in a few years it will supplant largely, if not entirely, the use of textbooks." Thus began a long string of spectacularly wrong predictions regarding the capacity of various technologies to revolutionize education.

What betrayed Edison and his successors was an uncritical faith in technology itself. This faith has become a sort of ideology increasingly dominating K–12 education. In the past two decades, school systems, with generous financial and moral support from foundations and all levels of government, have made massive investments in computer technology and in creating "wired" schools. The goal is twofold: to provide children with the computer skills necessary to flourish in a high-tech world and to give them access to tools and information that will enhance their learning in subjects like mathematics and history.

However, in recent years a number of scholars have questioned the vast sums being devoted to educational technology. They rarely quibble with the need for children to learn how to use computers, but find little evidence that making technology more available leads to higher student achievement in core subjects. As Stanford University professor Larry Cuban writes in *Oversold and Underused,* "There have been no advances (measured by higher academic achievement of urban, suburban, or rural students) over the past decade that can be confidently attributed to broader access to computers. . . . The link between test-score improvements and computer availability and use is even more contested."

While it is important to examine the relationship between technology and learning, that debate often devolves into a tit-for-tat of dueling studies and anecdotes. The problem with framing the issue merely as a question of whether technology boosts test scores is that it fails to address the interaction between technology and the values learned in school. In short, we need to ask what kind of learning tends to take place with the computer and what kind gets left out.

The Need for Firsthand Experience

A computer can inundate a child with mountains of information. However, all of this learning takes place the same way: through abstract symbols,

From *Education Next*, Fall 2004, pp. 10–14. Copyright © 2004 by Education Next. Reprinted by permission of Hoover Institution, Stanford University.

decontextualized and cast on a two-dimensional screen. Contrast that with the way children come to know a tree—by peeling its bark, climbing its branches, sitting under its shade, jumping into its piled-up leaves. Just as important, these firsthand experiences are enveloped by feelings and associations—muscles being used, sun warming the skin, blossoms scenting the air. The computer cannot even approximate any of this.

There is a huge qualitative difference between learning about something, which requires only information, and learning from something, which requires that the learner enter into a rich and complex relationship with the subject at hand. For smaller children especially, that relationship is as physical as it is mental. Rousseau pointed out long ago that the child's first and most important teacher is his hands. Every time I walk through a store with my sons and grow tired of saying, "Don't touch that!" I am reminded of Rousseau's wisdom.

What "Information Age" values tempt us to forget is that all of the information gushing through our electronic networks is abstract; that is, it is all representations, one or more symbolic steps removed from any concrete object or personal experience. Abstract information must somehow connect to a child's concrete experiences if it is to be meaningful. If there is little personal, concrete experience with which to connect, those abstractions become inert bits of data, unlikely to mobilize genuine interest or to generate comprehension of the objects and ideas they represent. Furthermore, making meaning of new experiences—and the ideas that grow out of them—requires quiet contemplation. By pumping information at children at phenomenal speed, the computer short-circuits that process. As social critic Theodore Roszak states in *The Cult of Information*, "An excess of information may actually crowd out ideas, leaving the mind (young minds especially) distracted by sterile, disconnected facts, lost among the shapeless heaps of data."

This deluge of shapeless heaps of data caused the late social critic Marshall McLuhan to conclude that schools would have to become "recognized as civil defense against media fallout." McLuhan understood that the consumption and manipulation of symbolic, abstract information is not an adequate substitute for concrete, firsthand involvement with objects, people, nature, and community, for it ignores the child's primary educational need—to make meaning out of experience.

Simulation's Limits

Of course, computers can simulate experience. However, one of the by-products of these simulations is the replacement of values inherent in real experience with a different set of abstract values that are compatible with the technological ideology. For example, "Oregon Trail," a computer game that helps children simulate the exploration of the American frontier, teaches students that the pioneers' success in crossing the Great Plains depended most decisively on managing their resources. This is the message implicit in the game's structure, which asks students, in order to survive, to make a series of rational, calculated decisions based on precise measurements of their resources. In other words, good pioneers were good accountants.

But this completely misses the deeper significance of this great American migration, which lies not in the computational capabilities of the pioneers but in their determination, courage, ingenuity, and faith as they overcame extreme conditions and their almost constant miscalculations. Because the computer cannot traffic in these deeply human qualities, the resilient souls of the pioneers are absent from the simulation.

Here we encounter the ambiguity of technology: its propensity to promote certain qualities while sidelining others. McLuhan called this process amplification and amputation. He used the microphone as an example. The microphone can literally amplify one's voice, but in doing so it reduces the speaker's need to exercise his own lung power. Thus one's inner capacities may atrophy.

This phenomenon is of particular concern with children, who are in the process of developing all kinds of inner capacities. Examples abound of technology's circumventing the developmental process: the student who uses a spell checker instead of learning to spell, the student who uses a calculator instead of learning to add—young people sacrificing internal growth for external power.

Often, however, this process is not so easily identified. An example is the widespread use of computers in preschools and elementary schools to improve sagging literacy skills. What could be wrong with that? Quite a bit, if we consider the prerequisites to reading and writing. We know that face-to-face conversation is a crucial element in the development of both oral and written communication skills. On the one hand, conversation forces children to generate their own images, which provide connections to the language they hear and eventually will read. This is one reason why reading to children and telling them stories is so important. Television and computers, on the other hand, generally require nothing more than the passive acceptance of prefabricated images.

Now consider that a study reported in *U.S. News & World Report* estimated that the current generation of children, with its legions of struggling readers, would experience one-third fewer face-to-face conversations during their school years than the generation of 30 years ago. It may well be that educators are trying to solve the problem of illiteracy by turning to the very technology that has diminished the experiences children need to become literate.

Obsolete Lessons

But students need to start using computers early in order to prepare for the high-tech future, don't they? Consider that the vast majority of students graduating from college this past spring started kindergarten in 1986, two years after the Macintosh was invented. If they used computers at all in elementary school, they were probably command-line machines with no mouse, no hard drive, and only rudimentary graphics. By the time these students graduated from college, whatever computer skills they picked up in primary school had long been rendered obsolete by the frenetic pace of technological innovation.

The general computer skills a youth needs to enter the workplace or college can easily be learned in one year of instruction during high school. During the nine years that I taught Advanced Computer Technology for the Des Moines public schools, I discovered that the level of computer skills students brought to the class had little bearing on their success. Teaching them the computer skills was the easy part. What I was not able to provide were the rich and varied firsthand experiences students needed in order to connect the abstract symbols they had to manipulate on the screen to the world around them. Students with scant computer experience but rich ideas and life experiences were, by the end of the year, generating sophisticated relational databases, designing marketable websites, and creating music videos. Ironically, it was the students who had curtailed their time climbing the trees, rolling the dough, and conversing with friends and adults in order to become computer "wizards" who typically had the most trouble finding creative things to do with the computer.

Certainly, many of these highly skilled young people (almost exclusively young men) find opportunities to work on computer and software design at prestigious universities and corporations. But such jobs represent a minuscule percentage of the occupations in this nation. And in any case, the task of early education is not merely to prepare students for making a living; it is to help them learn how to make a life. For that purpose, the computer wizards in my class seemed particularly ill prepared.

So why is it that schools persist in believing they must expose children to computers early? I think it is for the same reason that we take our children to church, to Fourth of July parades, and indeed to rituals of all types: to initiate them into a culture—in this case, the culture of high technology. The purpose is to infuse them with a set of values that supports the high-tech culture that has spread so rapidly across our society. And this, as we shall see, is perhaps the most disturbing trend of all.

The Ecological Impact of Technology

As the promise of a computer revolution in education fades, I often hear promoters fall back on what I'll term the neutrality argument: "Computers are just tools; it's what you do with them that matters." In some sense this is no more than a tautology: Of course it matters *how* we use computers in schools. What matters more, however, is that we use them *at all*. Every tool demands that we somehow change our environment or values in order to accommodate its use. For instance, the building of highways to accommodate the automobile hastened the flight to the suburbs and the decline of inner cities. And over the past 50 years we have radically altered our social landscape to accommodate the television set. In his seminal book *Autonomous Technology*, Langdon Winner dubbed this characteristic "reverse adaptation."

Consider the school personnel who already understand, intuitively, how this principle works: the music teacher whose program has been cut in order to fund computer labs; the principal who has had to beef up security in order to protect high-priced technology; the superintendent who has had to craft an "acceptable use" agreement that governs children's use of the Internet (and for the first time in our history renounces the school's responsibility for the material children are exposed to while in school). What the computers-are-just-tools argument ignores is the ecological nature of powerful technologies—that is, their introduction into an environment reconstitutes all of the relationships in that environment, some for better and some for worse. Clinging to the belief that computers have no effect on us allows us to turn a blind eye to the sacrifices that schools have made to accommodate them.

Not only do computers send structural ripples throughout a school system, but they also subtly alter the way we think about education. The old saw, "To a man with a hammer everything looks like a nail," has many corollaries (the walls of my home once testified to one of my favorites: to a four-year-old with a crayon, everything looks like drawing paper). One that fits here is, "To an educator with a computer, everything looks like information." And the more prominent we make computers in schools (and in our own lives), the more we see the rapid accumulation, manipulation, and sharing of information as central to the learning process—edging out the contemplation and expression of ideas and the gradual development of meaningful connections to the world.

In reconstituting learning as the acquisition of information, the computer also shifts our values. The computer embodies a particular value system, a technological thought world first articulated by Francis Bacon and Rene Descartes four hundred years ago, that turns our attention outward toward asserting control over our environment (that is essentially what technologies do—extend our power to control from a distance). As it has gradually come to dominate Western thinking, this ideology has entered our educational institutions. Its growing dominance is witnessed in the language that abounds in education: talk of empowerment, student control of learning, standards, assessment tools, and productivity. Almost gone from the conversation are those inner concerns—wisdom, truth, character, imagination, creativity, and meaning—that once formed the core values of education. Outcomes have replaced insights as the yardstick of learning, while standardized tests are replacing human judgment as the means of assessment. No tool supports this technological shift more than computers.

In the Wrong Hands

There are some grave consequences in pushing technological values too far and too soon. Soon after my high-school computer lab was hooked up to the Internet, I realized that my students suddenly had more power to do more damage to more people than any teenagers in history. Had they been carefully prepared to assume responsibility for that power through the arduous process of developing self-discipline, ethical and moral strength, compassion, and connection with the community around them? Hardly. They and their teachers had been too busy putting that power to use.

We must help our young people develop the considerable moral and ethical strength needed to resist abusing the enormous power these machines give them. Those qualities take a great deal of time and effort to develop in a child, but they ought to be as much a prerequisite to using powerful computer tools as is learning how to type. Trying to teach a student to use the power of computer technology appropriately without those moral and ethical traits is like trying to grow a tree without roots.

Rather than nurture those roots, we hand our smallest children machines and then gush about the power and control they display over that rarefied environment. From the earliest years we teach our children that if they have a problem, we have an external tool that will fix it (computers are not the only tools; Ritalin, for example, is a powerful technology that has been scandalously overprescribed to "fix" behavior problems). After years of this training, when our teenagers find themselves confused, angry, depressed, or overwhelmed, we wonder why so many of them don't reach out to the community for help or dig deep within themselves to find the internal strength to persevere, but rather reach for the most powerful (and often deadly) tool they can find to "fix" their problems. Our attempts to use powerful machines to accelerate or remediate learning are part of a pattern that sacrifices the growth of our children's inner resources and deep connectedness to community for the ability to extend their power outward into the world. The world pays a high price for the trade-off.

The response that I often hear to this criticism—that we just need to balance computer use in school with more "hands-on" activities (and maybe a little character education)—sounds reasonable. Certainly schools should help young people develop balanced lives. But the call for balance within schools ignores the massive commitment of resources required to make computers work at all and the resultant need to keep them constantly in use to justify that expense. Furthermore, that view of balance completely discounts the enormous imbalance of children's lives outside of school. Children typically spend nearly half their waking life outside of school sitting in front of screens. Their world is saturated with the artificial, the abstract, the mechanical. Whereas the intellectual focus of schools in the rural society of the 19th century compensated for a childhood steeped in nature and concrete activity, balance today requires a reversal of roles, with schools compensating for the overly abstract, symbolic, and artificial environment that children experience outside of school.

Technology with a Human Purpose

None of this is to say that we should banish computers from all levels of K–12 education. As young people move into subject areas like advanced mathematics and chemistry that rely on highly abstract concepts, computers have much to offer. Young people will also need computer skills when they graduate. But computer-based learning needs to grow out of years of concrete experience and a fundamental appreciation for the world apart from the machine, a world in which nature and human beings are able to speak for and through themselves to the child. Experiences with the computer need to grow out of early reliance on simple tools that depend on and develop the skills of the child rather than complex tools, which have so many skills already built in. By concentrating high technology in the upper grades, we honor the natural developmental stages of childhood. And there is a bonus: the release of massive amounts of resources currently tied up in expensive machinery that can be redirected toward helping young children develop the inner resources needed to put that machinery to good use when they become adults.

There remains a problem, however. When Bacon began pushing the technological ideology, Western civilization was full of meaning and wretchedly short on the material means of survival. Today we face the reverse situation: a society saturated in material comforts but almost devoid of meaning. Schools that see their job as preparing young people to meet the demands of a technology-driven world merely embrace and advance the idea that human needs are no longer our highest priority, that we must adapt to meet the demands of our machines. We may deliver our children into the world with tremendous technical power, but it is rarely with a well-developed sense of human purpose to guide its use.

If we are to alter that relationship, we will have to think of technological literacy in a new way. Perhaps we could call it technology awareness. Whatever its name, that kind of study, rather than technology training, is what needs to be integrated into the school curriculum. I am currently working with the Alliance for Childhood on a set of developmental guidelines to help educators create technology-awareness programs that help young people think about, not just with, technology. This is not the place to go into the details of those guidelines. What I want to emphasize here is that they share one fundamental feature: They situate technology within a set of human values rather than out in front of those values. They do not start by asking what children need to do to adapt to a machine world, but rather, which technologies can best serve human purposes at every educational level and how we can prepare children to make wise decisions about their use in the future.

The most daunting problems facing our society—drugs, violence, racism, poverty, the dissolution of family and community, and certainly war—are all matters of human purpose and meaning. Filling schools with computers will not help find the answers to why the freest nation in the world has the highest percentage of citizens behind bars or why the wealthiest nation in history condemns a sixth of its children to poverty.

So it seems that we are faced with a remarkable irony: that in an age of increasing artificiality, children first need to sink their hands deeply into what is real; that in an age of light-speed communication, it is crucial that children take the time to develop their own inner voice; that in an age of incredibly powerful machines we must first teach our children how to use the incredible powers that lie deep within themselves.

Frederick M. Hess **NO**

Technical Difficulties

In 2000, at the height of the technology boom, Maine governor Angus King made a splash by proposing to give laptops to all of the state's 7th graders. His stated purpose was to "do something different from what everybody else is doing." Missing from the $50 million proposal, however, was any rationale related to school performance. No evident thought had been put into how this major investment in new technology would make schools more efficient, produce future savings, or enhance the learning process.

King's proposal was typical of the way in which technologies like the personal computer and the Internet have been used in public education. The tendency has been to sprinkle computers and Internet connections across classrooms in the pleasant hope that teachers will integrate them into their lessons. The purpose is seldom to make teachers more productive or to rethink the way in which lessons are delivered. Indeed, PCs often serve as little more than high-priced typewriters, sitting in the back of classrooms unused for most of the school day.

This state of affairs stands in sharp contrast to how technology is used by business and government enterprises that engage in competition with other manufacturers and service providers. To them, technology is not an end in itself, something to be adopted merely because it exists, but a tool for self-improvement. A competitive enterprise adopts new technologies when these enable workers to tackle new problems or to do the *same thing* as before, but in a *cheaper and more efficient* fashion. For example, technology investments enabled the U.S. Postal Service, under heavy competitive pressure from United Parcel Service and Federal Express, to trim its workforce by 16,000 in 2003. These cuts followed layoffs of 23,000 employees over the preceding two years. The cuts were made possible not by reducing service, but by substituting technology in areas where people were performing either routine tasks or roles that automated machines could handle more efficiently.

At a broader level, in recent years the nation's 100 largest companies improved productivity so rapidly that in 2003 it took only nine workers to do what ten workers had done in 2001. Economists have long recognized that the potential for growth in productivity is more limited in service sectors like education than in manufacturing or retail. Nonetheless, even the service sector has witnessed productivity gains of about 1 percent a year during the past three decades.

Public schools, by contrast, have steadily *added* to the ranks of teachers and reduced class sizes even as they make ever-larger investments in new technologies. Spending on technology in public schools increased from essentially zero in 1970 to $118 per student in 2002 and $89 per student in 2003, according to *Education Week*. In 1998 there were 12.1 students for every computer connected to the Internet; by 2002, the ratio had dropped to 4.8 students per computer, according to the Department of Education. In the past five years alone, the nation has spent more than $20 billion linking schools and classrooms to the Internet through the federal E-rate program with little to show for it in the way of instructional changes or improved outcomes. Meanwhile, despite these huge new investments in technology, massive increases in the workforce of teachers drove the student-teacher ratio from 22 students per teacher to 16 students per teacher between 1970 and 2001.

Cultural Bias

Why have public schools failed so far to put all this fancy new technology to good use? One clear reason is that they face no pressure to do so. Organizations like the Postal Service make effective use of technology because they must keep up with FedEx, UPS, and other delivery services. Competitive enterprises are on a constant search for ways of boosting their productivity, holding down their costs, and developing innovative products—because they know that their competitors are always on the lookout for similar advantages. No executive wants to adopt a painful course like downsizing the workforce or imposing wrenching change. They take these steps only when compelled.

Public schools, however, are insulated from the pressures of competition. They thus have no reason to regard technology as a tool to trim their workforce or to rethink the ways in which they deliver education. This problem is compounded by the fact that collective-bargaining agreements between school districts and employee unions have made using technology to displace workers or reinvent processes extraordinarily difficult.

There is also a bias within the culture of education against ideas that seem too "businesslike." Indeed, the very words "efficiency" and "cost-effectiveness" can set the teeth of parents and educators on edge. Proposals to use technology to downsize the workforce, alter instructional delivery, or improve managerial efficiency are inevitably attacked by education authorities as part of an effort to, in the words of Henry Giroux, "Transform public education . . . [in order] to expand the profits of investors, educate students as consumers, and train young people for the low-paying jobs of the new global marketplace." The notion that the responsible use of public money is the work of some shadowy global conspiracy evinces a fundamental lack of seriousness about educating children.

Traditionalists insist that it is impossible to educate children more efficiently, that there is no way technology can be substituted for anything that educators do. They frequently compare the act of teaching to the arts: where the act of creation itself is the end product, it can be difficult or impossible to use technology to improve performance. As the late Daniel Patrick Moynihan, the legendary U.S. senator, was fond of saying, producing a Mozart quartet two centuries ago required four musicians, four stringed instruments, and, say, 35 minutes. Producing the same Mozart quartet today requires the same resources. Despite breathtaking technological advances, productivity has not changed.

In the case of schooling, however, this analogy is incomplete and ultimately misleading. In the arts, what has changed over two centuries is that, through radio, CDs, television, and digital media, the number of people able to *hear and appreciate* a given performance has increased dramatically, at an ever-decreasing cost. Improved technology has now made available to the general public what was once the preserve of the elite.

The spread of the Internet and other technological advances has created similar opportunities in education. For instance, during the 2002–03 school year, the Florida Virtual School enrolled more than 6,800 students in its 75 course offerings. Florida Virtual is a public entity that provides instruction to students in schools and districts throughout the state. The school provides web-based classes, instruction, and assessments to students in a variety of academic subjects and electives. Like virtual schools operating in 15 other states, Florida Virtual allows faculty to provide courses to a scattered student population. Programs like Florida Virtual may make it possible to provide some academic instruction more cheaply and more effectively, freeing up resources for other needs.

At the university level, nearly 2 million students took at least one course online in the fall of 2003. In a national survey of nearly 1,000 college administrators conducted by the Sloan Consortium, 57 percent of the administrators reported that Internet-based courses were already at least equivalent to traditional courses in quality. And a third of the administrators thought that the web-based courses would be superior to in-class instruction within three years. Such improvements are to be expected among the many colleges and universities now competing for students' distance-learning dollars. However, efforts to use the Internet in an effective manner are few and far between among K–12 public schools.

Technology and Data Management

Used wisely, information technology does have the capacity to help schools become dramatically more effective. Data systems that track information on individual students permit teachers to quickly check the performance of individual students on specific tasks. Information technology can also give school-site personnel unprecedented control over budgets and hiring and can increase their flexibility regarding resource allocation. The Learning First Alliance, a consortium that includes the National Education Association and the American Federation of Teachers, has highlighted how this has worked in districts like Long Beach and Chula Vista, California, and Aldine, Texas.

Outside of schooling, a compelling illustration of how accountability and technology can together improve public services comes from the remarkable success that New York City and other cities enjoyed using new tools to combat crime in the 1990s. The New York City Police Department introduced a system called CompStat, short for "comparative statistics." CompStat compiled data from police reports, crime complaints, arrests, and crime patterns. Over time, the system was broadened to include 734 categories of concern, measuring even the incidence of loud parties and of police overtime.

In the first five years after the 1993 introduction of CompStat, the number of homicides in New York City fell from 1,946 to 629—a rate of decrease three times that of the nation as a whole. Similar results were experienced in other cities that implemented the system, from Philadelphia to Los Angeles. Why did the system work? It helped to hold officers accountable, to pinpoint areas of concern, and to provide the information that can help all police focus on using their skills. In New York City, precincts were required to update their crime statistics on a weekly or daily basis, rather than on the monthly or quarterly basis that had traditionally been the norm. New software allowed department officials to precisely map clusters of crimes, correlating them with drug sale sites, areas of gang activity, schools, public housing, and other relevant locations, and to share the information department-wide within seconds.

In K–12 education, by contrast, we generally manage most information the same way stores managed inventory in the 1960s. Almost unbelievably in this day and age, the typical district spends 40 or more minutes a year per student collecting, processing, and reporting the data required by the U.S. Department of Education under the No Child Left Behind Act. That equates to more than 6,000 hours of employee time in a district with 10,000 students. The tremendous delays in processing data and the staff time consumed are the consequence of districts' having personnel fill out written forms and retyping data from one software package to another. Simply equipping districts to report data electronically and acquire data from existing databases is a daunting challenge.

When principals or teachers are asked for this information, those that have it available almost inevitably turn to large binders rather than more nimble electronic interfaces. When asked if he could pull some data on teacher absenteeism or staff training costs, one veteran principal in a well-regarded district spluttered, "Do you know what I do if I want substitute teacher data? I have [my secretary] go through the files and tally it up. She keeps a running total on a piece of graph paper for me. . . . If I want to check on a supply order, I call the deputy [superintendent] for services because we're old friends, and I know he'll actually have someone pull it for me."

Modern information technology offers a wealth of straight-forward, time-tested ways to make the necessary data widely and instantly available. There is an array of systems, produced by firms like Scantron and IntelliTools, that allow teachers to call up simple graphs detailing the performance of individual students at the push of a button. However, using these systems requires the consistent collection of information on student learning. Assigning paper-based quizzes ensures that almost all of the information on student mastery will be lost, while the software produced by a dozen or more firms is able to quickly read the results from electronically administered tests into an evolving portfolio of data that tracks student learning.

Ultimately, to be useful, this information has to be at people's fingertips. This is an eminently solvable technical challenge. Huge, complicated organizations, from Wal-Mart to the Internal Revenue Service, routinely track productivity figures, costs, and evaluative measures.

A New Role for Teachers

How else can technology support innovation and reinvention in education? Consider that, historically, teachers have been expected to perform a wide range of responsibilities. Each teacher is expected to design lesson plans, lecture, run class discussions, grade essays and exams, mentor colleagues, supervise homeroom, and patrol the cafeteria. Every year our high schools have tens of thousands of teachers giving variations of the same lectures on the Civil War, the digestive system, and the properties of quadratic equations. In fact, the job description of a teacher today is pretty similar to that of a teacher in 1950.

In medicine, by contrast, progress has been marked by specialization. Doctors with different types of training have taken on more precisely defined roles while less expensive professionals like registered nurses and physical therapists are now performing tasks that don't require a doctor's training. Similarly, 16-year-old volunteers using handheld scanners are able to track medical supplies and hospital inventory with a precision that would have been unimaginable even in the best-managed enterprise just two decades ago.

Imagine a hospital with no nurses or physicians' assistants or physical therapists, where doctors performed every task. We would need a slew of additional doctors, each would have less time to devote to any particular specialty, and costs would skyrocket.

How can technology enable teachers to specialize in the same manner as, say, doctors? Let's consider one classroom example in order to understand how technology can help teachers use their time more productively. Teachers know it is useful to have students write on a regular basis. When I taught high-school social studies, like so many of my colleagues, I required students to write at least three pages a week commenting on what we had read and discussed in class.

The problem is that, at a minimum, this meant my 150 students would turn in 450 pages a week of writing. A teacher who reads, marks, and comments on each student's weekly work in just five minutes will spend more than 12 hours a week simply providing feedback on such writing assignments. Most of this time isn't spent providing particularly cerebral feedback, but instead flagging obvious grammatical and structural problems and reminding students to write in complete sentences. Meanwhile, teachers also need to prepare for teaching, assess other assignments, assist and advise students, and lead a personal life. The result is often that teachers provide limited feedback, read student work sporadically, or (most commonly) assign less writing than might be ideal.

Once, such compromises were unavoidable. That is no longer the case. Today, for instance, there is essay-grading software, commercially available from companies like Vantage Learning or the Educational Testing Service, that can quickly and efficiently analyze pieces of writing on dimensions such as sentence construction, language, and mechanics. Several of these programs match the scores given by expert human raters more than 90 percent of the time, which is actually *higher* in some cases than the rate of agreement among multiple human readers. How can this be? In most cases, we're not talking about evaluating Proustian prose; we're talking about helping the typical 4th grader learn to write clearly and effectively. Most of the mistakes that students make and most of the feedback they need are pretty predictable.

Clearly technological tools cannot imitate the full range of skills that a teacher brings when reading a student's essay. Technology cannot gauge a student's growth, analytic prowess, possible interests, or unexpected developments. However, assessment software can replicate the routine elements of evaluation, providing more complete feedback on the essentials while freeing up teachers to make fuller use of their expertise. The result is that teachers spend less time on trivia while adding more value. Rather than requiring hundreds of thousands of teachers to spend hundreds of hours a year circling dangling participles or errant commas, the sensible substitution of technology can help ensure quality feedback while allowing teachers more time for preparation, instruction, and tutoring.

Human ingenuity is the most expensive commodity in the developed world. People are costly to employ; no well-run organization hires reams of bodies when it is possible to hire more selectively and use employees more thoughtfully. This is why efforts to reduce class size are a static, unimaginative, and inefficient way to improve schooling. These efforts presume that teachers need to perform all the duties and tasks now in place; helping them accomplish these tasks more effectively thus requires shrinking the number of students they must teach. However, if we were to retool the teacher's role in a way that used scarce resources like teachers' time and expertise more carefully, teachers could spend more time on the areas where they add value even while working with larger classes of students. If grading essays or examining student performance on weekly quizzes took only half as much time as it currently does, a teacher could work with more students and still have *more* instructional time for each student in that class.

A Tool, Not a Miracle Cure

The nation continues to blithely operate schools in a fashion that was dated in the 1970s and that today would be deemed irresponsible in a toothpaste factory. Rather than demand that education dollars be invested with particular care, we pour money into technology with little thought to how these tools might be used most sensibly.

The ability to instantly share full information on student performance, school performance, and costs across vast distances permits a focus on results that was simply not feasible until the most recent decade. The information technology that makes the easy sharing of information possible is the engine that makes tough-minded accountability, school choice, and visionary leadership a possibility.

Using new technological tools to relieve educators of routine functions will help them focus on those roles that add substantial value—enhancing their contribution, making the organization more productive, and thereby increasing both the benefit to the customer and the resources available to reward employees. Reducing rote demands allows people to focus on what they do best and reduces the number of talented workers who need to be hired—which, in turn, allows us to pay employees more.

Ultimately, if leaders lack the tools to increase efficiency, streamline their workforce, or sensibly reallocate resources, they won't. Technology is not a miracle cure. It is a tool. Used wisely, it can help professionals to take full advantage of their skills, slash the time spent on rote tasks, and concentrate resources and effort where they are needed most.

POSTSCRIPT

Do Computers Negatively Affect Student Growth?

A few years ago educational reformer John I. Goodlad declared that "school" should be considered a concept rather than a place and that this formulation would seem to be an appropriate keynote for education in the twenty-first century. Certainly, advocates of computerization and global networking would be comfortable with the idea. But today, as more school systems are being "wired," questions of initial cost, hardware obsolescence, variable availability, software quality and appropriateness, teacher reluctance, and productive utilization remain to be discussed and resolved.

Help in exploring these and related questions may be found in Gary Kidd's "Using the Internet as a School," *The Educational Forum* (Spring 1996); "Unfilled Promises," by Jane McDonald, William Lynch, and Greg Kearsley, *The American School Board Journal* (July 1996); Frederick Bennett's *Computers as Tutors* (1999); Leon Botstein's "A Brave New World?" *The School Administrator* (March 2001); Craig A. Cunningham's "Improving Our Nation's Schools Through Computers and Connectivity," *Brookings Review* (Winter 2001); R. W. Burniske's "When Computer Literacy Goes Too Far," *Phi Delta Kappan* (March 2001); and Frederick Bennett's "The Future of Computer Technology in K–12 Education," *Phi Delta Kappan* (April 2002). The April 1996 issue of *The School Administrator* contains a number of articles on such topics as Internet access and technology's usefulness in the inclusion of disabled students. Other journal issues devoted to the controversy include *Educational Leadership* (November 1997), *Contemporary Education* (Winter 1997), *NASSP Bulletin* (November 1997), *Theory Into Practice* (Winter 1998), *The School Administrator* (April 1999), *NASSP Bulletin* (May 1999 and September 1999), *Principal* (January 2000), *The Futurist* (March–April 2000), *Educational Leadership* (October 2000), *Kappa Delta Pi Record* (Fall 2000), *American Educator* (Fall 2001), *The School Administrator* (October 2001), *NASSP Bulletin* (November 2001) and *The School Administrator* (August 2005). Recent sources of special interest include Todd Oppenheimer's *The Flickering Mind: The False Promise of Technology in the Classroom and How Learning Can Be Saved* (2003), Gene I. Maeroff's *A Classroom of One: How Online Learning Is Changing Our Schools and Colleges* (2002), Jane M. Healy's "Young Children Don't Need Computers," *Principal* (May–June 2003) and Mark Bauerlein's book, *The Dumbest Generation: How the Digital Age Stupifies Young Americans and Jeopardizes Our Future* (2008).

Finally, educational psychologist Richard P. Lookatch has argued that multimedia use in school offers students the opportunity to interact with the images behind a glass screen, but the looming danger is that it replaces students' interaction with each other and their environment.

ISSUE 20

Should Alternative Teacher Training Be Encouraged?

YES: Robert Holland, from "How to Build a Better Teacher," *Policy Review* (April & May 2001)

NO: Linda Darling-Hammond, from "How Teacher Education Matters," *Journal of Teacher Education* (May/June 2000)

ISSUE SUMMARY

YES: Public policy researcher Robert Holland argues that current certification programs are inadequate, especially given the growing shortage of teachers.

NO: Educational professor Linda Darling-Hammond offers evidence of failure among alternative programs and responds to criticism of standard professional preparation.

The quality and appropriateness of teacher preparation programs have long been topics of discussion in academic and professional circles, as well as in the media. From the appraisals by educators James Bryant Conant, Sterling McMurrin, and James Koerner in the 1960s to recent critiques by James Coleman, Ernest Boyer, John I. Goodlad, and William J. Bennett, the education of future teachers has consistently been under careful scrutiny. Rita Kramer called for the closing of all schools of education in her 1991 book *Ed School Follies: The Miseducation of America's Teachers.* Education dean Donald J. Stedman, in "Re-inventing the Schools of Education," *Vital Speeches of the Day* (April 15, 1991), recommended a serious restructuring of teacher preparation to replace the current bureaucratic rigidity with a flexible interdisciplinary approach.

In 1985 the Carnegie Forum released its agenda for wide-ranging improvements, and the American Association of Colleges of Teacher Education published *A Call for Change in Teacher Education.* Of greater impact was the formation of the Holmes Group by deans of education schools at almost all of the leading universities in the country. In 1986 a report released by this organization entitled *Tomorrow's Teachers* called for a stronger preparation in the liberal arts and academic majors and for moving teacher certification courses to the master's degree level. A National Board of Professional Standards was established in 1987, offering the prospect of a higher level of certification and status enhancement for teachers. In 1995 the Holmes Group, in *Tomorrow's Schools of Education*, supported the concept of professional development schools run jointly by universities and public school systems and fueled by applied research. A firm message was sent: "Reform—or get out of business!"

While many internal reforms have been carried out in the past two decades, pressures from the outside for alternatives to the usual paths of entry into the profession have been steadily building. Frederick M. Hess, in "Break the Link," *Education Next* (Spring 2002), contends that anyone who has not completed the specified training is unsuited to enter a classroom and must be prohibited from applying for a job, regardless of any other qualifications. About 10 years ago, Wendy Kopp launched Teach for America in an attempt to bring bright and dedicated teacher candidates into disadvantaged schools by providing an abbreviated training program. In her 2001 book *One Day All Children . . . The Unlikely Triumph of Teach for America and What I Learned Along the Way*, she explains the program and offers a self-appraisal.

The growing undersupply of teachers has created more urgent calls for change. The 1998 report of the National Center for Education Information, *Alternative Teacher Certification—An Overview*, documents the evolution of alternative routes and the rapid growth in the number of individuals pursuing them. Articles that examine this issue include Linda Darling-Hammond, "The Challenge of Staffing Our Schools," *Educational Leadership* (May 2001); Mary E. Diez, "The Certification Connection," *Education Next* (Spring 2002); Arthur E. Wise, "Creating a High-Quality Teaching Force," *Educational Leadership* (December 2000–January 2001); and Richard M. Ingersoll, "Holes in the Teacher Supply Bucket," *The School Administrator* (March 2002). The Summer 2006 issue of *American Educator* has articles on the theme "Why Teachers Leave," and *Phi Delta Kappan* (January 2007) features a controversial article by Sharilyn C. Steadman and John S. Simmons, "Teachers Not Certified by Universities Burden Our Best Teachers."

In the following selection, Robert Holland reviews the criticism of traditional teacher certification programs, critiques the profession's attempts at internal reform, and suggests a "value-added" approach. In the second selection, Darling-Hammond presents evidence that internal reforms have strengthened the programs and that alternatives such as Teach for America are woefully inadequate.

YES

Robert Holland

How to Build a Better Teacher

American schools need more teachers. American schools need better teachers. Practically everyone with a stake in the education debate agrees with those two premises. However, there is sharp disagreement as to whether more regulation or less is the way to go.

The differences of perspective begin over just how vital to transmitting knowledge a teacher is. No one is more certain about the overriding importance of a teacher in a child's academic progress than Tennessee statistician William Sanders, who has developed a value-added instrument that might revolutionize how good teachers are found and rewarded for productive careers. Speaking before the metropolitan school board in Nashville in January [2001], Sanders risked friendly fire when he disputed the connection much of the education world makes between poverty and low student performance: "Of all the factors we study—class size, ethnicity, location, poverty—they all pale to triviality in the face of teacher effectiveness."

That flies in the face of a widespread conviction in the education world that poverty is such a powerful depressant on learning that even the greatest teachers may only partially overcome its effects. As Diane Ravitch documents in her recent book *Left Back* (Simon & Schuster), education "progressives" long have believed that many children shouldn't be pushed to absorb knowledge beyond their limited innate capacities; that they are better off with teachers who help them get in touch with their feelings and find a socially useful niche.

But Sanders has volumes of data to back up his contention. While at the University of Tennessee, he developed a sophisticated longitudinal measurement called "value-added assessment" that pinpoints how effective each district, school, and teacher has been in raising individual students' achievement over time. His complex formula factors out demographic variables that often make comparisons problematic. Among other things, he found that students unlucky enough to have a succession of poor teachers are virtually doomed to the education cellar. Three consecutive years of first quintile (least effective) teachers in Grades 3 to 5 yield math scores from the thirty-fifth to forty-fifth percentile. Conversely, three straight years of fifth quintile teachers result in scores at the eighty-fifth to ninety-fifth percentile.

The state of Tennessee began using value-added assessment in its public schools in 1992, and Sanders is in demand in many other states where legislators are considering importing the system. The "No Excuses" schools identified

From *Policy Review*, April & May 2001, pp. 37–47. Copyright © 2001 by Robert Holland. Reprinted by permission of The Hoover Institution, Stanford University and Robert Holland. www.policyreview.org

by an ongoing Heritage Foundation project—high-poverty schools where outstanding pupil achievement defies stereotypes about race and poverty—buttress Sanders' contention that the quality of teaching is what matters most. Consider, for instance, Frederick Douglass Academy, a public school in central Harlem that has a student population 80 percent black and 19 percent Hispanic. The *New York Times* recently reported that all of Frederick Douglass's students passed a new, rigorous English Regents exam last year, and 96 percent passed the math Regents. The Grades 6–12 school ranks among the top 10 schools in New York City in reading and math, despite having class sizes of 30 to 34.

And what makes the difference? "Committed teachers," said principal Gregory M. Hodge—teachers, he said, who come to work early, stay late, and call parents if children don't show up for extra tutoring. The disciplined yet caring climate for learning set by Hodge and principals of other No Excuses schools also is due much credit.

Those who believe in deregulation of teacher licensing see in value-added assessment a potential breakthrough. Principals (like Hodge) could hire and evaluate their teachers not necessarily on the basis of credit-hours amassed in professional schools of education but in terms of objective differences instructors make when actually placed before classrooms of children. The Thomas B. Fordham Foundation published in April 1999 a manifesto on teacher quality that argues strongly for a "results-based accountability system," disaggregated by teacher, along the lines of what Sanders has devised.

However, much of the education establishment—those in and around education school faculties nationwide, the professional development specialists at teacher unions and associations, state and local boards of education, and education specialists in much of the foundation world—takes a very different view. They argue that what is needed is much more centralized control of teacher preparation and licensing to ensure that teachers are better and more uniformly qualified when they enter the classroom. They propose to ensure this by placing professional licensing under the aegis of a single accreditation body, one that would be controlled to a great extent by the teachers themselves—or, more precisely, their national unions.

Which side prevails in this dispute over how to get the best teachers into schools—the Sanders model of ongoing evaluation of effectiveness or the establishment preference for centralized credentialing—may tell us more than anything else about the quality of instruction American pupils and their parents can expect from their schools for a generation. This is the key battleground in public education today.

Teacher Certification: A Primer

The one point on which both camps agree is that the existing system of teacher certification badly needs reform. Hence, a brief survey of that system may be helpful. Currently, state departments of education and collegiate schools of education are the gatekeepers to teaching careers in America's public schools. This is a collaboration dedicated to the use of government power to standardize and centralize education, or, in the economists' term, "regulatory capture." Government licensing agencies that are charged with protecting the public interest are effectively controlled by the interests—in this case, the teacher-trainers—they are supposed to be regulating.

As a result, an aspiring teacher typically must complete a state-approved program of teacher education that is heavy on how-to-teach or pedagogical courses. All 50 states require new teachers to obtain a bachelor's degree, and all 50 require course work in pedagogy. In some states, the teacher's degree must be in education, while other states require an academic major but specify that within that degree there must be a considerable number of education courses (about a semester's worth) and also a period of student teaching (another semester). In addition, many teacher colleges tack on additional training requirements, so that fulfilling requirements for the study of pedagogy can consume well over a year of college. Most states require prospective teachers to pass one or more subject-area tests, but these often ask for regurgitation of nostrums taught by education professors.

Critics of the schools of pedagogy are legion. Seventy years ago, H.L. Mencken (never one to mince words) asserted that most pedagogues "have trained themselves to swallow any imaginable fad or folly, and always with enthusiasm. The schools reek with this puerile nonsense."

In the early 1990s, Rita Kramer took a nationwide tour of leading schools of education, from Teachers College at Columbia to the University of Washington, and reported in *Ed School Follies* on the intellectual emptiness of teacher preparation—hours spent on how to teach Tootles the Locomotive with the proper attitude, but precious little depth in history, mathematics, science, or literature. Recently Heather Mac Donald took a close look at ed schools for *City Journal* and summed up teacher educators' dogma in the phrase "Anything But Knowledge." She found teachers of teachers still holding fast to the doctrine laid out in 1925 by Teachers College icon William Heard Kilpatrick: Schools should instill "critical thinking" in children instead of teaching them facts and figures, which (he surmised) they could always look up for themselves as they became "lifelong learners." Today, Teachers College mandates courses in multicultural diversity and has students act out ways to "usurp the existing power structure."

Jerry Jesness, a special education teacher in a south Texas elementary school, observes that "every profession has its gatekeepers, the college professors who not only teach, but also sift out the slow, the lazy, and the mediocre, those unfit to practice the profession for which they are preparing. One must have intelligence, drive, and stamina, especially to get through schools of engineering, law, or medicine.

"In colleges of education, the reverse seems to be the case. After a few weeks of Ed 101, the students most possessed of those qualities begin to slip away. By the time education students begin their semester of student teaching, the best and brightest have already defected to other disciplines. Colleges and departments of education separate the wheat from the chaff, but unlike those of the other disciplines, they then throw away the wheat."

The current system does allow for a semblance of public accountability. At least in theory, citizens—by their votes for governors and state legislators, and in some states, the state education boards and superintendents of public instruction—can pressure education bureaucrats to adopt more sensible rules for preparing and employing teachers. One state in which the political process has recently yielded reform is Georgia, where Democratic Gov. Roy Barnes last year won legislative approval for eliminating seniority-based teacher tenure.

At the center of the school of thought that believes tighter national regulation is key to reform is a foundation-funded entity called the National Commission on Teaching and America's Future (NCTAF). NCTAF is the latest incarnation of a Carnegie Corporation commission—the first was the 1986 Carnegie Task Force on Teaching as a Profession—advocating a centralized, national system of teacher licensing controlled by private organizations with stakes in the process. With North Carolina Gov. James Hunt as its chairman and Stanford education professor Linda Darling-Hammond as its director, NCTAF issued its report, "What Matters Most: Teaching for America's Future," in 1996. (The Rockefeller Foundation joined Carnegie in bankrolling the commission.) NCTAF, which stayed active to lobby for its proposals, drew raves in the press for its "action agenda" to reform the training and certifying of teachers. Little ink went toward exploring the deeper implications of nationalizing control of teaching.

NCTAF called for, among other things:

- Mandatory accreditation by an organization called the National Council for Accreditation of Teacher Education (NCATE) of all teacher training programs in the country.
- National Board for Professional Teaching Standards (NBPTS) certification of more than 100,000 "master" teachers.
- Formation of "independent" professional boards in each state to set policies on teacher preparation, testing, and licensing, in tune with the nationalized policy.

In December 1999, Linda Darling-Hammond forcefully stated the case for the pro-regulatory proposition that education credentials do make a difference. "It stands to reason," she wrote, "that student learning should be enhanced by the efforts of teachers who are more knowledgeable in their field and are skillful at teaching it to others. Substantial evidence from prior reform efforts indicates that changes in course taking, curriculum content, testing, or textbooks make little difference if teachers do not know how to use these tools well and how to diagnose their students' learning needs."

The Union Interest

The National Education Association [NEA], the nation's largest teacher union, has emerged as a leading advocate of the NCTAF model of "reforming" the system by stripping control of teacher certification from the state departments of education. The NEA touts this as "professionalization," meaning self-regulation by teachers or benign-sounding "peer review." But critics dispute how much rank-and-file teachers would be empowered. Education Consumers Clearinghouse founder John Stone, a professor of education at East Tennessee State University, believes "the parties serving up these bold proposals represent the interests that have governed teacher training and licensure all along. Since publication of *A Nation at Risk* in 1983, teacher training and licensure have undergone repeated rewrites, none of which has produced any noticeable improvements in schooling."

The NEA likes the idea of all teachers having to graduate from a teacher training program certified by NCATE. This is perhaps unsurprising, given that NCATE has been tightly linked to the NEA since the former's founding in 1954. NCATE's director, Arthur E. Wise, also heads the NEA's 31-year-old non-profit subsidiary, the National Foundation for the Improvement of Education. Meanwhile, NEA president Robert F. Chase chairs the Executive Committee of NCATE. Furthermore, Wise sat on the national commission, NCTAF, that would grant NCATE control of all teacher accreditation that it has not been able to gain on a voluntary basis over the past 40 years.

An important link in the pro-regulatory reformers' plan is the National Board for Professional Teaching Standards (NBPTS), an outgrowth of the 1986 Carnegie report. NBPTS subsequently received Carnegie Corporation outlays of several million dollars. In the 1990s, the federal government also began subsidizing the NBPTS heavily, at the urging of President Clinton. The board is a key element in today's strategy to centralize control of the gates to teaching. The privately operated NBPTS confers national certification on teachers who submit portfolios (videotapes of the teaching, lesson plans, samples of student work) for evaluation. The teachers also must pay a $2,300 application fee, but sometimes their school boards pay it for them.

The NBPTS purports to identify excellence through this process, but economists Dale Ballou of the University of Massachusetts and Michael Podgursky of the University of Missouri—who called "professionalization" into question after careful analysis—point out that there has been no evidence to show that students of NBPTS-certified teachers learn any more than students of other teachers. Researchers at the Consortium for Policy Studies at the University of Wisconsin at Madison recently found that NBPTS-certified teachers tend to become more reflective about their teaching, but their principals found it difficult to link any improvements in student achievement to the teachers' national certification.

From the perspective of economists Ballou and Podgursky, "The activities over which the profession seeks control—accreditation of teacher education programs and teacher licensing—are well-recognized means of restricting supply," which puts upward pressure on salaries. They add there can be no doubt that teacher unions see the professionalization movement "as a means to increase salaries." For further evidence of how tightly linked some of the regulatory reform is, consider that NEA president Chase serves as a member of NCTAF, which seeks to greatly augment the powers of NCATE, on which Chase is a major power—and all this would confer more economic muscle on the NEA.

NCTAF was remarkably successful using the rhetoric of reform to persuade business leaders and the media that its program actually was a "scathing indictment" of the system for training and certifying teachers. The *New Republic* begged to differ: "Forcing teachers," the journal's editors commented, "to attend NCATE certification programs that douse them with pedagogical blather (NCATE's 'vision of quality' seeks to promote 'equity' and 'diversity' but says nothing about academic achievement) will likely scare off math and science specialists in droves."

The NEA stepped up its campaign in spring 2000. Chase and his associates unveiled revised NCATE standards for accreditation at a Washington news conference. NCATE stated that schools of education it accredits will have to meet "rigorous new performance-based standards" in order to win NCATE accreditation.

By focusing on "candidate performance," said NCATE president Wise, the "standards represent a revolution in teacher preparation." But skeptics wonder how "revolutionary" it is to assess candidates largely according to videotaped activities, portfolios of projects, personal journals, or their compatibility with a team. That's the emphasis of the NBPTS, but portfolio assessment relies heavily on subjective judgment, as opposed to testing a teacher's knowledge of the subject being taught.

"In spite of claims to the contrary," notes Podgursky, "at present there exists no reliable evidence indicating whether or not graduates of NCATE accredited teacher training programs are better teachers." Although several states have responded by mandating NCATE accreditation, Podgursky added, "mandatory accreditation would almost certainly restrict the supply of teachers and exacerbate teacher shortages, yet its effect on the teacher quality pool is uncertain. It may also stifle promising state-level experiments with alternative teacher certification and the entry of new teacher-training institutions into the market."

For his part, Wise claims: "As more institutions meet NCATE's national professional standards, more qualified teacher candidates will be available, since candidates from accredited institutions pass licensing examinations at a higher rate than do those from unaccredited institutions or those with no teacher preparation." Wise based that assertion on a recent Educational Testing Service (ETS) study of the rates at which teacher candidates pass the Praxis II licensing exams. However, the same study shows that the SAT and ACT scores of NCATE graduates who passed licensing exams are lower than those of non-NCATE peers. In addition, Podgursky observed that the released ETS data are so flawed as to make any comparisons problematic. For instance, 14 percent of the sample of Praxis II test-takers never enrolled in a teacher-training program—yet the researchers sorted them into NCATE categories based on the colleges they attended. The study also failed to take into account wide variations in how states test prospective teachers.

The new standards condense NCATE's 1995 version of standards from 20 categories into six. Examiners will look at teacher-candidates' knowledge, skills, and "dispositions"; the school's assessment system; the inclusion of field experience and clinical practice; the institution's devotion to "diversity"; how faculty model "best practices"; and unit governance, including the wise use of information technology.

Actually, notes Professor Stone, the "new" standards implement mostly old ideas about teaching from existing standards. As for the portfolios, classroom observations, and emphasis on Praxis II, "performance on these various assessments reflects nothing more than a grasp of the same old faulty teaching practices that education professors have been espousing right along."

Most parents—the primary consumers of education—want schools to stress academic achievement, as studies by the nonpartisan Public Agenda have shown. However, as Public Agenda's surveys also reveal, many education professors believe "best practice" is a teacher not teaching, but facilitating in the progressive tradition, while children construct their own meaning, an approach called constructivism. "Social justice" is valued more highly than achievement. Arguably, that's the approach NCATE accreditation would enshrine.

As Podgursky and Ballou note in a recent Brookings Institution paper, public education already is a regulated monopoly. In most school districts, parents have little or no choice of their children's schools or teachers. In addition, unlike in medicine or other service markets, education consumers lack the protection of antitrust or malpractice lawsuits. Within this structure, the teacher unions already exercise enormous economic power as their well-organized affiliates bargain with fragmented local school boards.

If, next, teacher unions win control of the gates to teaching through their domination of such organizations as NCATE, they arguably would possess "market power not enjoyed by producers or unions in any major industry in our economy." That would not bode well for efforts to expand consumer choice and to get fresh blood into the teaching profession. Moreover, when a monopoly can restrict supply, prices will rise—in this case, teacher salaries. That would fulfill a primary objective of the teacher unions, but without any guarantee of increased quality.

Another Approach

What kind of persons might be attracted to teaching were the doors to teaching careers open to people with a wide variety of backgrounds that didn't necessarily include sitting through hundreds of hours of education courses, whether NCATE-accredited or not? Suppose principals could hire their own teaching staffs without having to follow the credits-hours prescribed by education bureacracies?

Well, there would be more teachers like Scott (Taki) Sidley, who taught English at T.C. Williams High School in Alexandria, Va., the past three years, but ran athwart the state bureaucracy's insistence that he take additional prescribed courses in order to be "certified." In a piece of Sunday commentary in the *Washington Post* (June 25, 2000), long-time teacher Patrick Welsh lamented the "bureaucratic narrow-mindedness" that pushes people like Sidley out of teaching.

Welsh noted that Sidley, a University of Virginia graduate who has served in the Peace Corps, won acclaim from students and parents and was considered "one of our [T.C. Williams'] finest teachers." But he must leave the young people he was teaching so well because he lacks on his resume 30 credit-hours that regulators insist he must have—one being a low-level composition course, even though he took 48 graduate hours in creative writing at U.Va. and the university exempted him from introductory composition because of his Advanced Placement English score in high school.

Many young teachers like Sidley, Welsh notes, "see the petty adherence to the certification rules as symptomatic of a pervasive problem." For an alternative vision, he quoted Dave Keener, head of the school's science department and the 1998 Virginia winner of the Presidential Award for Excellence in Science and Mathematics Teaching: "The process of getting the best has to be streamlined. Individual high schools should be given the power to advertise positions and do their own recruiting. . . . Principals, with advice of teachers, should be able to do all the hiring on the spot without having to get approval from the central office, which often takes weeks. De-emphasize the education courses. Once we get the kind of people we want, we could train them in the schools."

That's the sensible approach that one kind of education reform, the charter school, facilitates. Organizers of charter schools—often teachers with a common vision—receive waivers from certification and other bureaucratic rules. In exchange for independence, they agree to be accountable for academic results. Many charter schools freely hire teachers who know their subjects but haven't been through the education-school mill. Only a small fraction of charter school teachers choose to belong to the national teacher unions.

In its 1996 report, NCTAF gave the impression with its sharp attack on the current state-controlled certification system that it wanted a thorough-going reform that would bring bright young teachers into the classroom. But as Professors Ballou and Podgursky observe, NCTAF focuses not on recruiting more talented individuals but on beefing up the system of teacher training—and shifting its control from political bodies to organizations, like NCATE, that may also reflect private agendas, such as the NEA'S.

There are a few small-scale programs designed to deepen the pool of teaching talent by going outside the certification routine. One is Teach for America, which places liberal arts graduates in high-need urban and rural districts. Another is Troops to Teachers, which assists retiring military personnel in becoming teachers. In both instances, the newly minted teachers obtain provisional certification and then work toward obtaining enough professional education credits to gain full certification.

New Jersey is one state that has taken seriously the desirability of offering alternative routes to teaching. In 1984, the state reduced the number of education courses required for traditional certification, while putting new teachers under the tutelage of a mentor teacher. At the same time, it allowed teachers to recruit liberal arts graduates who hadn't been through education schools at all. These teachers were also put under the supervision of a mentor. They would get on-the-job training in applied teaching. The new approach has resulted in higher scores on licensing tests, a lower attrition rate, and a more diverse teaching force, notes former New Jersey Education Commissioner Leo Klagholz in a Fordham Foundation paper.

Such programs are fine as far as they go—but they don't go nearly far enough nationwide. Strict regulation of K–12 teaching has yielded pervasive mediocrity. It is time to deregulate and to emphasize results. Instead of screening teachers according to courses taken and degrees earned, school administrations should free principals to hire the most intellectually promising material—English majors to teach English, history majors to teach history—and then let the schools assimilate them in the nitty-gritty of preparing lesson plans and monitoring lunchrooms.

Value-Added Assessment

The quest for reform based on proof of good teaching brings us back to William Sanders and the Tennessee Value-Added Assessment System (TVAAS), which generates annual reports of gains in student achievement produced by each teacher, school, and school district. Progress is broken down by core subject, and gains are compared to national, state, and local benchmarks.

Professor John Stone explains the significance of using such a system:

> By comparing each student's current achievement to his or her past performance and aggregating the results, value-added assessment statistically isolates the impact of individual teachers, schools, and school systems on the average progress of the students for which they are responsible. Not incidentally, value-added assessment can also be used by education's decisionmakers to isolate and assess the effectiveness of everything from the latest curricular innovations, to the preparedness of novice teachers, to the quality of the programs in which teachers were trained.

Here, in short, is a real-world way to assess the performance of teachers—as opposed to the paperwork realm of NCATE, which deems credentials and licensure hoops to be the equivalent of quality assurance.

The most thoroughgoing reform of teacher licensing and hiring could come through a combination of the New Jersey and Tennessee approaches. Schools could hire teachers with liberal-arts educations and/or valuable working-world experiences, then give them on-the-job mentoring, and finally evaluate their teaching prowess according to a value-added assessment.

It's known from Sanders's research, the No Excuses schools, and plain common sense that teachers make a profound difference in students' lives. Deregulated teacher hiring combined with value-added assessment could bring an infusion of fresh talent into teaching and provide a basis for rewarding those teachers who do the most to help children learn. Such a system also could quickly identify teachers who needed extra training, or those who ought to be pursuing a different line of work. Such a change would deserve to be called reform; mandatory accreditation locking in the status quo in teaching preparation does not.

Three days into his administration, President George W. Bush unveiled an accountability plan for federal education spending that sparked hope for a fresh approach to bringing good teachers to K–12 schools. He proposed that

Congress revise Title II of the Elementary and Secondary Education Act so that school districts can come up with alternative ways to certify teachers. And he would reserve a chunk of funding for grants to states that develop systems to measure teacher effectiveness according to student academic achievement.

That's value-added, and it may turn out to be the most significant education tool since chalk.

Linda Darling-Hammond

 NO

How Teacher Education Matters

Over the past decade, public dissatisfaction with schools has included dissatisfaction with teacher education. Education schools have been variously criticized as ineffective in preparing teachers for their work, unresponsive to new demands, remote from practice, and barriers to the recruitment of bright college students into teaching. In more than 40 states, policy makers have enacted alternative routes to teacher certification to create pathways into teaching other than those provided by traditional 4-year undergraduate teacher education programs. Whereas some of these are carefully structured postbaccalaureate programs, others are little more than emergency hiring options. Upon his election in 1988, President Bush's only education proposal was the encouragement of alternative teacher certification. In 1995, Newt Gingrich proposed the elimination of teacher certification rules as his major education initiative. In 1999, Chester Finn and the Thomas B. Fordham Foundation issued a manifesto arguing against teacher education requirements as a "barrier" to entering teaching.

Voices of dissatisfaction have been raised from within the profession as well (Goodlad, 1990; Holmes Group, 1986). These voices, however, have urged the redesign of teacher education to strengthen its knowledge base, its connections to both practice and theory, and its capacity to support the development of powerful teaching. Proposals at the far ends of this continuum stand in stark contrast to one another. One approach would replace university-based preparation with on-the-job training that focuses on the pragmatics of teaching, whereas the other would expand professional training to prepare teachers for more adaptive, knowledge-based practice, while simultaneously tackling the redesign of schools and teaching. Which of these routes holds the most promise? What are the implications for teachers' capacities, and, most important, for the education of children?

Although the debates on these questions have been largely ideological, there is a growing body of empirical evidence about the outcomes of different approaches to teacher education and recruitment. This research suggests that the extent and quality of teacher education matter for teachers' effectiveness, perhaps now even more than before. The expectations that schools teach a much more diverse group of students to much higher standards create much greater demands on teachers. Teaching for problem solving, invention, and application of knowledge requires teachers with deep and flexible knowledge of subject matter who understand how to represent ideas in powerful ways

[and] can organize a productive learning process for students who start with different levels and kinds of prior knowledge, assess how and what students are learning, and adapt instruction to different learning approaches.

Do Education Schools Help Teachers Learn?

Even if one agrees that there are desirable knowledge and skills for teaching, many people believe that anyone can teach, or, at least, that knowing a subject is enough to allow one to teach it well. Others believe that teaching is best learned, to the extent that it can be learned at all, by trial and error on the job. The evidence strongly suggests otherwise. Reviews of research over the past 30 years have concluded that even with the shortcomings of current teacher education and licensing, fully prepared and certified teachers are generally better rated and more successful with students than teachers without this preparation (Ashton & Crocker, 1986; Evertson, Hawley, & Zlotnik, 1985; Greenberg, 1983; Haberman, 1984; Olsen, 1985).

In fields ranging from mathematics and science to vocational education, reading, elementary education, and early childhood education, researchers have found that teachers who have greater knowledge of teaching and learning are more highly rated and are more effective with students, especially at tasks requiring higher order thinking and problem solving. (For a review of this literature, see Darling-Hammond, 1996b.) Interestingly, whereas subject-matter knowledge is often found to be an important factor in teaching effectiveness, it appears that its relationship to teaching performance is curvilinear; that is, it exerts a positive effect up to a threshold level and then tapers off in influence. Furthermore, measures of pedagogical knowledge, including knowledge of learning, teaching methods, and curriculum, are more frequently found to influence teaching performance and often exert even stronger effects than subject-matter knowledge (Ashton & Crocker, 1986; Begle & Geeslin, 1972; Byrne, 1983; Evertson et al., 1985; Ferguson & Womack, 1993; Guyton & Farokhi, 1987; Monk, 1994; Perkes, 1967–1968). It seems logical that pedagogical skill would interact with subject matter knowledge to bolster or undermine teacher performance. As Byrne (1983) suggests,

> insofar as a teacher's knowledge provides the basis for his or her effectiveness, the most relevant knowledge will be that which concerns the particular topic being taught and the relevant pedagogical strategies for teaching it to the particular types of pupils to whom it will be taught. (p. 14)

Meanwhile, studies of teachers admitted with less than full preparation find that recruits tend to be less satisfied with their training and have greater difficulties planning curriculum, teaching, managing the classroom, and diagnosing students' learning needs. They are less able to adapt their instruction to promote student learning and less likely to see it as their job to do so, blaming students if their teaching is not effective. Principals and colleagues rate these teachers less highly on their instructional skills, and they leave teaching at higher-than-average rates. Most important is that their students learn less, especially in areas such as reading, writing, and mathematics, which are critical to later school success (Darling-Hammond, 1999b).

Illustrating these findings, Gomez and Grobe's (1990) study of the performance of alternate certification (AC) candidates in Dallas, who receive a few weeks of summer training before they assume full teaching responsibilities, found that their performance was much more uneven than that of traditionally trained entrants who had equivalent scores on the state's subject matter exams. From 2 to 16 times as many AC recruits were rated "poor" on each teaching factor evaluated, and their students showed significantly lower achievement gains in language arts and writing.

Perhaps it is not surprising that alternate route teachers from short-term programs report less satisfaction with their preparation and less commitment to remaining in teaching than other recruits (Darling-Hammond, Hudson, & Kirby, 1989; Lutz & Hutton, 1989). Problems resulting from inadequate preparation headed the list of complaints of the 20% of Los Angeles AC candidates who quit before they completed their summer training programs in 1984 and 1985, as well as many of those who remained but voiced dissatisfaction (Wright, McKibbon, & Walton, 1987). Stoddart's (1992) analysis reveals that 53% of these recruits had left teaching within the first 6 years of program operation. Among AC candidates in Dallas, only half successfully "graduated" to become full-fledged teachers after their first year as interns. Only 40% said that they planned to stay in teaching, as compared to 72% of traditionally trained recruits (Lutz & Hutton, 1989).

Even very intelligent people who are enthusiastic about teaching find that they cannot easily succeed without preparation, especially if they are assigned to work with children who most need skillful teaching. The best-publicized program founded on this idea is Teach for America (TFA), created to recruit bright college graduates to disadvantaged schools en route to careers in other professions. If anyone could prove the claim that teachers are born and not made, these bright eager students might have been the ones to do it. Yet, four separate evaluations found that TFA's 3-to-8-week summer training program did not prepare candidates adequately (Grady, Collins, & Grady, 1991; Popkewitz, 1995; Roth, 1993; Texas Education Agency, 1993), despite the intelligence and enthusiasm of many of the recruits. Many recruits knew that their success—and that of their students—had been compromised by their lack of access to the knowledge needed to teach. Yale University graduate Schorr (1993) was one of many to raise this concern:

> I—perhaps like most TFAers—harbored dreams of liberating my students from public school mediocrity and offering them as good an education as I had received. But I was not ready. . . . As bad as it was for me, it was worse for the students. Many of mine . . . took long steps on the path toward dropping out . . . . I was not a successful teacher and the loss to the students was real and large. (pp. 317–318)

These feelings contribute to the program's high attrition rate. Even though many recruits report that they initially entered the program with the intention of exploring teaching as a career, many also indicate that they left in discouragement because they felt unsuccessful. TFA statistics show that of those who started in 1990, 58% had left before the third year, a 2-year attrition rate nearly three times the national average for new teachers. The Maryland State Department of Education found that 62% of corps members who started in Baltimore in 1992 left within 2 years.

Aside from high attrition, studies of short-term alternative programs have also noted that what little pedagogical training they provide tends to focus on generic teaching skills rather than subject-specific pedagogy, on singular techniques rather than a range of methods, and on specific, immediate advice rather than research or theory (Bliss, 1992; Stoddart, 1992; Zumwalt, 1990).

The lack of traditional coursework and student teaching in these programs are generally supposed to be compensated for by intensive mentoring and supervision in the initial months of full-time teaching. Ironically, however, most studies have found that promised mentors did not often materialize (Darling-Hammond, 1992).

Unfortunately, the least well-prepared recruits are disproportionately assigned to teach the least advantaged students in high-minority and low-income schools (National Commission on Teaching and America's Future [NCTAF], 1996). In the aggregate, this can make a substantial difference in what children learn. Recent multivariate studies of student achievement at the school and district level have found a substantial influence of teachers' qualifications on what students learn. Ferguson's (1991) analysis of Texas school districts found that teachers' expertise, including their scores on a licensing examination measuring basic skills and teaching knowledge; master's degrees' and experience accounted for more of the interdistrict variation in students' reading and mathematics achievement in grades 1 through 11 than student socioeconomic status. The effects were so strong, and the variations in teacher expertise so great, that after controlling for socioeconomic status, the large disparities in achievement between Black and White students were almost entirely accounted for by differences in the qualifications of their teachers. This finding contravenes the common presumption that students' school achievement is largely a function of their socioeconomic status and that school variables make little difference in educational outcomes.

A more recent Texas study (Fuller, 1999) found that students in districts with greater proportions of fully licensed teachers were significantly more likely to pass the Texas state achievement tests after controlling for student socioeconomic status, school wealth, and teacher experience. Similar to this, a North Carolina study (Strauss & Sawyer, 1986) found that teachers' average scores on the National Teacher Examinations measuring subject matter and teaching knowledge had a large effect on students' pass rates on the state competency examinations. A 1% increase in teacher quality (as measured by NTE scores) was associated with a 3% to 5% decline in the percentage of students failing the exam.

A recent school-level analysis of mathematics test performance in California high schools (Fetler, 1999) found a strong negative relationship between average student scores and the percentage of teachers on emergency certificates, after controlling for student poverty rates. Another California study found that across all income levels, elementary students' reading achievement is strongly related to the proportions of fully trained and certified teachers (Los Angeles County Office of Education, 1999), much more so than to the proportion of beginners in the school. The study concluded that "this supports the finding that differing test scores are a teacher training issue and not merely due to new teachers' lack of classroom experience."

Responses to Critiques of Traditional Teacher Education

Lest schools of education become sanguine, however, there are grounds for concern about traditional preparation programs as well. The often-repeated critiques of traditional teacher education programs include the pressure of inadequate time within a 4-year undergraduate degree, which makes it hard to learn enough about both subject matter and pedagogy; the fragmentation of content and pedagogical coursework and the divide between university- and school-based training; the weak content of many courses that pass on folklore instead of systematically developed knowledge; the lack of adequate clinical training; and the lack of resources in many education programs that serve as "cash cows" for their universities, which perpetuates much of the above.

Over the past decade, many schools of education and school districts have begun to change these conditions. Stimulated by the efforts of the Holmes Group and the National Network for Educational Renewal, more than 300 schools of education have created programs that extend beyond the confines of the traditional 4-year bachelor's degree program, thus allowing more extensive study of the disciplines to be taught along with education coursework that is integrated with more extensive clinical training in schools. Some are 1- or 2-year graduate programs that serve recent graduates or midcareer recruits. Others are 5-year models that allow an extended program of preparation for prospective teachers who enter teacher education during their undergraduate years. In either case, because the 5th year allows students to devote their energies exclusively to the task of preparing to teach, such programs allow for year-long school-based clinical experiences that are woven together with coursework on learning and teaching.

Many of these programs have joined with local school districts to create professional development schools where novices' clinical preparation can be more purposefully structured. Like teaching hospitals in medicine, these schools aim to provide sites for state-of-the-art practice that are also organized to support the training of new professionals, extend the professional development of veteran teachers, and sponsor collaborative research and inquiry. These approaches resemble reforms in teacher education abroad. Countries such as Germany, Belgium, France, and Luxembourg have long required from 2 to 3 years of graduate-level study in addition to an undergraduate degree for prospective teachers, including an intensively supervised internship in a school affiliated with the university.

A number of recent studies have found that graduates of extended programs (typically 5-year programs) are not only more satisfied with their preparation, they are viewed by their colleagues, principals, and cooperating teachers as better prepared, are as effective with students as much more experienced teachers, and are much more likely to enter and stay in teaching than their peers prepared in traditional 4-year programs (Andrew, 1990; Andrew & Schwab, 1995; Arch, 1989; Denton & Peters, 1988; Dyal, 1993; Shin, 1994). In fact, the entry and retention rates of these programs are so much higher than those of 4-year programs—which are, in turn, much higher than short-term alternative programs—that it is actually less expensive to prepare career teachers in this way once the costs of preparation, recruitment, induction, and replacement due to attrition are taken into account (Darling-Hammond, 1999a).

These new programs typically engage prospective teachers in studying research and conducting their own inquiries through cases, action research, and the development of structured portfolios about practice. They envision the professional teacher as one who learns from teaching rather than one who has finished learning how to teach, and the job of teacher education as developing the capacity to inquire sensitively and systematically into the nature of learning and the effects of teaching. This is an approach to knowledge production like the one that Dewey (1929) sought, one that aims to empower teachers with greater understanding of complex situations rather than to control them with simplistic formulas or cookie-cutter routines for teaching:

> Command of scientific methods and systematized subject matter liberates individuals; it enables them to see new problems, devise new procedures, and in general, makes for diversification rather than for set uniformity. (p. 12)
>
> This knowledge and understanding render (the teacher's) practice more intelligent, more flexible, and better adapted to deal effectively with concrete phenomena or practice. . . . Seeing more relations he sees more possibilities, more opportunities. His ability to judge being enriched, he has a wider range of alternatives to select from in dealing with individual situations. (pp. 20–21)

Dewey's notion of knowledge for teaching is one that features inquiry into problems of practice as the basis for professional judgment grounded in both theoretical and practical knowledge. If teachers investigate the effects of their teaching on students' learning, and if they study what others have learned, they come to understand teaching to be an inherently nonroutine endeavor. They become sensitive to variation and more aware of what works for what purposes in what situations. Access to contingent knowledge allows them to become more thoughtful decision makers.

Training in inquiry also helps teachers learn how to look at the world from multiple perspectives, including those of students whose experiences are quite different from their own, and to use this knowledge in developing pedagogies that can reach diverse learners. Learning to reach out to students, those who are difficult to know as well as those who are easy to know, requires boundary crossing, the ability to elicit knowledge of others, and to understand it when it is offered. As Delpit (1995) notes, "We all interpret behaviors, information, and situations through our own cultural lenses; these lenses operate involuntarily, below the level of conscious awareness, making it seem that our own view is simply 'the way it is' " (p. 1512). Good teachers must develop an awareness of their perspectives and how these can be enlarged to avoid a "communicentric bias" (Gordon, 1990), which limits their understanding of those whom they teach.

Developing the ability to see beyond one's own perspective, to put oneself in the shoes of the learner and to understand the meaning of that experience in terms of learning, is perhaps the most important role of universities in the preparation of teachers. One of the great flaws of the "bright person myth" of teaching is that it presumes that anyone can teach what he or she knows to anyone else. However, people who have never studied teaching or learning often have a very difficult time understanding how to convey material that they themselves learned effortlessly and almost subconsciously. When others do not learn merely by being told, the intuitive teacher often becomes frustrated and powerless to proceed. This frequently leads to resentment of students for not validating the untrained teacher's efforts. Furthermore, individuals who have had no powerful teacher education intervention often maintain a single cognitive and cultural perspective that makes it difficult for them to understand the experiences, perceptions, and knowledge bases that deeply influence the approaches to learning of students who are different from themselves. The capacity to understand another is not innate; it is developed through study, reflection, guided experience, and inquiry.

Among the tools teacher educators increasingly use for this purpose are inquiries that engage prospective teachers in investigating learning and the lives of learners and evaluating the many different outcomes of teaching. These include prospective teachers conducting case studies of children while studying development and learning, thus coming to better understand the children's thinking and experiences; conducting community studies that investigate local neighborhoods in ways that illuminate culture, customs, and life experiences of different groups of people; conducting investigations of student learning, like the National Board for Professional Teaching Standards' student learning commentaries that evaluate artifacts of the learning of 3 diverse students over time; assembling portfolios that use artifacts of teaching and learning to analyze the effects of practice; and pursuing problem-based inquiries that seek to identify problems of practice and understand them through action research coupled with reviews of others' research. These tools allow the application of theoretical principles to problems in specific contexts while appropriately complicating efforts to draw generalizations about practice. A small but growing body of research suggests that such strategies can help teachers understand more deeply the many variables that influence their work. For example, in the case of cases and portfolios that require teachers to examine student learning in relation to their teaching, teachers claim that the process of engaging in such analysis ultimately enriches their ability to understand the effects of their actions and helps them better meet the needs of diverse students. (For a review of this literature, see Darling-Hammond and Snyder, in press.) One of the ways in which this occurs is through the process of trying to view teaching and classroom events from the perspectives of the students who experience them. As teachers look beyond their own actions to appreciate the understandings and experiences of their students, and evaluate these in light of their self-developed knowledge of individual learners and their professional knowledge of factors influencing development and learning, they grow wiser about the many ways in which learning and teaching interact.

A commitment to open inquiry, the enlargement of perspectives, and the crossing of boundaries are critical features of the ideal of university education. In fact, the basis of the very earliest universities was that they tried to bring together scholars from all over the known world. They sought to create ways to share diverse perspectives from various geographic areas, cultures, and disciplines as the basis for developing knowledge and finding truth. If universities are to continue to make the important contribution to the education of teachers that they can make, they need to pursue these ideals of knowledge building and truth finding by creating a genuine praxis between ideas and experiences, by honoring practice in conjunction with reflection and research, and by helping teachers reach beyond their personal boundaries to appreciate the perspectives of those whom they would teach.

References

Andrew, M. (1990). The differences between graduates of four-year and five-year teacher preparation programs. *Journal of Teacher Education, 41,* 45–51.

Andrew, M., & Schwab, R. L. (1995). Has reform in teacher education influenced teacher performance? An outcome assessment of graduates of eleven teacher education programs. *Action in Teacher Education, 17,* 43–53.

Arch, E. C. (1989, April). *Comparison of student attainment of teaching competence in traditional preservice and fifth-year master of arts in teaching programs.* Paper presented at the annual meeting of the American Educational Research Association, San Francisco.

Ashton, P., & Crocker, L. (1986). Does teacher certification make a difference? *Florida Journal of Teacher Education, 3,* 73–83.

Begle, E. G., & Geeslin, W. (1972). *Teacher effectiveness in mathematics instruction.* (National Longitudinal Study of Mathematical Abilities Reports No. 28). Washington, DC: Mathematical Association of America and National Council of Teachers of Mathematics.

Bliss, T. (1992). Alternate certification in Connecticut: Reshaping the profession. *Peabody Journal of Education, 67*(3), 35–54.

Byrne. (1983). *Teacher knowledge and teacher effectiveness: A literature review, theoretical analysis, and discussion of research strategy.* Paper presented at the meeting of the Northeastern Educational Research Association, Ellenville, NY.

Darling-Hammond, L. (1992). Teaching and knowledge: Policy issues posed by alternative certification for teachers. *Peabody Journal of Education, 67*(3), 123–154.

Darling-Hammond, L. (1999a). *Solving the dilemmas of teacher supply, demand, and standards: How we can ensure a competent, caring, and qualified teacher for every child.* New York: National Commission on Teaching and America's Future.

Darling-Hammond, L. (1999b). *Teaching quality and student achievement: A review of state policy evidence.* Seattle, WA: Center for the Study of Teaching and Policy, University of Washington.

Darling-Hammond, L., Hudson, L., & Kirby, S. (1989). *Redesigning teacher education: Opening the door for new recruits to science and mathematics teaching.* Santa Monica, CA: RAND.

Darling-Hammond, L., & Snyder, J. (in press). Authentic assessment of teaching in context. *Journal of Teaching and Teacher Education.*

Denton, J. J., & Peters, W. H. (1988). *Program assessment report: Curriculum evaluation of a non-traditional program for certifying teachers.* College Station, TX: Texas A & M University.

Dewey, J. (1929). *The sources of a science of education.* New York: Horace Liveright.

Dyal, A. B. (1993). *An exploratory study to determine principals' perceptions concerning the effectiveness of a fifth-year preparation program.* Paper presented at the annual meeting of the Mid-South Educational Research Association, New Orleans, LA.

Evertson, C., Hawley, W., & Zlotnick, M. (1985). Making a difference in educational quality through teacher education. *Journal of Teacher Education, 36*(3), 2–12.

Ferguson, R. F. (1991). Paying for public education: New evidence on how and why money matters. *Harvard Journal on Legislation, 28*(2), 465–498.

Ferguson, P., & Womack, S. T. (1993). The impact of subject matter and education coursework on teaching performance. *Journal of Teacher Education, 44*(1), 55–63.

Fetler, M. (1999, March 24). High school staff characteristics and mathematics test results. *Education Policy Analysis Archives,* 7 [Online]. . . .

Fuller, E. J. (1999). *Does teacher certification matter? A comparison of TAAS performance in 1997 between schools with low and high percentages of certified teachers.* Austin: Charles A. Dana Center, University of Texas at Austin.

Gomez, D. L., & Grobe, R. P. (1990, April). *Three years of alternative certification in Dallas: Where are we?* Paper presented at the Annual Meeting of the American Educational Research Association, Boston.

Goodlad, J. (1990). *Teachers for our nation's schools.* San Francisco: Jossey-Bass.

Gordon, E. W. (1990). Coping with communicentric bias in knowledge production in the social sciences. *Educational Researcher, 19.*

Grady, M. P., Collins, P., & Grady, E. L. (1991). *Teach for America 1991 Summer Institute evaluation report.* Unpublished manuscript.

Greenberg, J. D. (1983). The case for teacher education: Open and shut. *Journal of Teacher Education, 34*(4), 2–5.

Guyton, E., & Farokhi, E. (1987, September–October). Relationships among academic performance, basic skills, subject matter knowledge and teaching skills of teacher education graduates. *Journal of Teacher Education, 37*–42.

Haberman, M. (1984, September). *An evaluation of the rationale for required teacher education: Beginning teachers with or without teacher preparation.* Paper prepared for the National Commission on Excellence in Teacher Education, University of Wisconsin-Milwaukee.

Holmes Group. (1996). *Tomorrow's teachers: A report of the Holmes Group.* East Lansing, MI: Author.

Los Angeles County Office Of Education. (1999).

Lutz, F. W., & Hutton, J. B. (1989). Alternative teacher certification: Its policy implications for classroom and personnel practice. *Educational Evaluation and Policy Analysis, 11*(3), 237–254.

Monk, D. H. (1994). Subject matter preparation of secondary mathematics and science teachers and student achievement. *Economics of Education Review, 13*(2), 125–145.

National Commission on Teaching and America's Future. (1996). *What matters most: Teaching for America's future.* NY: Author.

Olsen, D. G. (1985). The quality of prospective teachers: Education vs. noneducation graduates. *Journal of Teacher Education, 36*(5), 56–59.

Perkes, V. A. (1967–1968). Junior high school science teacher preparation, teaching behavior, and student achievement. *Journal of Research in Science Teaching, 6*(4), 121–126.

Popkewitz, T. S. (1995). Policy, knowledge, and power: Some issues for the study of educational reform. In P. Cookson & B. Schneider (Eds.), *Transforming schools: Trends, dilemmas and prospects.* Garland Press.

Roth, R. A. (1993). *Teach for America 1993 summer institute: Program review.* Unpublished report.

Schorr, J. (1993, December). Class action: What Clinton's National Service Program could learn from "Teach for America." *Phi Delta Kappan,* 315–318.

Shin, H.-S. (1994). *Estimating future teacher supply: An application of survival analysis.* Paper presented at the annual meeting of the American Educational Research Association, New Orleans, LA.

Strauss, R. P., & Sawyer, E. A. (1986). Some new evidence on teacher and student competencies. *Economics of Education Review, 5*(1), 41–48.

Stoddart, T. (1992). An alternative route to teacher certification: Preliminary findings from the Los Angeles Unified School District Intern Program. *Peabody Journal of Education, 67*(3).

Texas Education Agency. (1993). Teach for America visiting team report. Meeting minutes of Texas State Board of Education Meeting (Appendix B), Austin.

Wright, D. P., McKibbon, M., & Walton, P. (1987). *The effectiveness of the teacher trainee program: An alternate route into teaching in California.* Sacramento: California Commission on Teacher Credentialing.

Zumwalt, K. (1990). *Alternate routes to teaching: Three alternative approaches.* New York: Teachers College, Columbia University.

POSTSCRIPT

Should Alternative Teacher Training Be Encouraged?

The present shortage of teachers, which has brought about the admission of college graduates without indoctrination in "methods," is an opportunity not to be missed. Liberal arts majors, if their courses were truly liberal, will be free of crippling ideas about how to teach.

—Jacques Barzun

This sentiment, of course, is in direct contrast to Darling-Hammond's position expressed in *The Right to Learn* (1997): "Many people sincerely believe that anyone can teach, or, at least, that knowing a subject is enough to allow one to teach it well. Others believe that teaching is best learned, to the extent that it can be learned at all, by trial and error on the job. The evidence, however, strongly suggests otherwise."

Further argumentation on this basic issue can be found in the following sources: Chester E. Finn, Jr., and Kathleen Madigan, "Removing Barriers for Teacher Candidates," *Educational Leadership* (May 2001); Carol Tell, "Making Room for Alternative Routes," *Educational Leadership* (May 2001); David C. Berliner, "A Personal Response to Those Who Bash Teacher Education," *Journal of Teacher Education* (November/December 2000); and Susan Moore Johnson, "Can Professional Certification for Teachers Reshape Teaching as a Career?" *Phi Delta Kappan* (January 2001).

Articles related to the Wendy Kopp alternative include Molly Ness, "Lessons of a First-Year Teacher," *Phi Delta Kappan* (May 2001); . . .; and Margaret Raymond and Stephen Fletcher, "The Teach for America Evolution," *Education Next* (Spring 2002). Molly Ness has . . . expanded her ideas into book form with *Lesson To Learn: Voices from the Front Lines of Teach for America* (2004) and two recent books are noteworthy: *Relentless Pursuit* (2008) by Donna Foote and *Work Hard, Be Nice* (2009) by Jay Mathews.

Special theme issues may be found in *Educational Horizons* (Fall 1999 and Spring 2000), *Kappa Delta Pi Record* (Spring 2000), *The School Administrator* (January 2001), *Educational Leadership* (March 2002), and *Education Next* (Spring 2002).

In the midst of all of this wrangling about the components and length of teacher preparation, perhaps what is needed is a reconceptualization of teaching as a career. We need to address what is needed before entry into the profession, what is needed in the formative stages of the developing professional, and, most important, what is needed in the various fulfillment stages along the path to retirement and beyond.

ISSUE 21

Can Merit Pay Accelerate School Improvement?

YES: Steven Malanga, from "Why Merit Pay Will Improve Teaching," *City Journal* (Summer 2001)

NO: Al Ramirez, from "How Merit Pay Undermines Education," *Educational Leadership* (February 2001)

ISSUE SUMMARY

YES: Steven Malanga, a senior fellow of the Manhattan Institute, draws on examples from the corporate world and from public school systems in Cincinnati, Iowa, and Denver to make his case for performance-based merit pay for teachers.

NO: Associate professor of education Al Ramirez contends that merit pay programs misconstrue human motivation and devalue the work of teachers.

T he issue of merit pay, or pay-for-performance, for teachers is certainly not new, but as Steven Malanga, one of the combatants presented in the pairing offered here, says, it is "one of the bitterest controversies in today's school reform debate." The current push to improve public education, particularly in impoverished areas, and to hold individual schools more accountable for achieving desired results has rekindled the argument over merit pay as a replacement for a reward system based primarily on seniority and earned course credits.

Although some forms of merit plans were widely used in the early part of the twentieth century, the economic depression of the 1930s prompted conversions to uniform pay scales. Teachers' unions, which gained strength throughout the remainder of the century, were not supportive of incentive pay schemes. They expressed doubts about the fairness of various evaluation methods and concerns about possible threats to collegiality and the standardization of teaching practices. Since the 1980s, and particularly since the passage of the "No Child Left Behind" legislation, pressure for an accountability system containing specific rewards for teachers and schools that meet desired outcomes has vastly increased.

The matter of how to appropriately and fairly evaluate teacher performance remains a major stumbling block in the adoption of merit pay plans. Local socioeconomic factors and the unevenness of support structures among school systems and states add complexity to the process. According to Sandra McCollum, in "How Merit Pay Improves Education," *Educational Leadership* (February 2001), merit pay programs are often discontinued because of one or more of the following reasons: they are unfairly implemented, teachers' unions refuse to endorse them, they create poor teacher morale, legislators who support them leave office, and they are simply too costly and difficult to administer.

An economist's view is offered by Darius Lakdawalla in "Quantity Over Quality," *Education Next* (Fall 2002). He contends that schools have been hiring more teachers in an effort to reduce class sizes but have not been rewarding them for quality performance. In the past few decades, serious opportunities outside teaching have opened up, and school systems have not risen to challenge the competition. The problem of retaining and attracting top-quality teachers is addressed in Marge Scherer, "Improving the Quality of the Teaching Force: A Conversation With David C. Berliner," *Educational Leadership* (May 2001). Berliner states that 7 of 23 nations surveyed exceed the United States in starting salaries for teachers and that 9 of 21 nations exceed the United States in top teacher salaries. In the realm of pay, status, and working conditions, says Berliner, "The U.S. is saying to its educators that they are not really important; if we thought they were important, we'd pay them a larger share of our gross domestic product, as other nations do." Yet Berliner is also worried that a merit pay plan based primarily on student achievement could lead to teachers' doing the wrong thing in their classrooms—cheating and narrowing the curriculum.

Some guidelines for the fair evaluation of teacher performance are put forth by Thomas R. Hoerr in "A Case for Merit Pay," *Phi Delta Kappan* (December 1998). In Hoerr's view, there must be trust between the administration and the faculty, judgments must be treated with confidentiality, there must be recognition that both what is valued and how it is measured will vary by context, and teachers who do not perform satisfactorily and do not respond to supportive intervention should not be rehired. Getting rid of ineffective teachers, however, is so arduous and expensive that many school systems do not attempt it. So says Peter Schweizer in "Firing Offenses," *National Review* (August 17, 1998). He analyzes the companion issue of teacher tenure, a system that was originally designed to protect the best teachers from wrongful termination but that Schweizer says now protects the worst teachers from rightful termination.

In the following selections, Steven Malanga argues that merit pay is essential to meaningful teacher evaluation and school improvement, while Al Ramirez contends that merit pay is a misguided policy with numerous unintended consequences.

YES

Steven Malanga

Why Merit Pay Will Improve Teaching

One of the bitterest controversies in today's school-reform debate is merit pay—rewarding teachers not for seniority and the number of ed-school credits they've piled up, as public schools have done since the early 1920s, but for what they actually achieve in the classroom. Education reformers argue that merit pay will give encouragement to good teachers and drive away bad ones, and thus improve under-performing public schools. But most teachers' unions adamantly oppose the idea. We don't have reliable means to measure a teacher's classroom performance, the unions charge, so merit plans will inevitably result in supervisor bias and favoritism: "Just too many cliques in the system," one teacher typically complains in a recent survey.

Nowhere is the incentives debate raging more fiercely than in New York City, where teachers' contract negotiations have been at an impasse for months. Mayor Rudolph Giuliani has demanded that merit pay for individual teachers be part of any deal; the teachers' union response (at least so far): fuhgeddaboudit.

Missing from the argument, though, are lessons from the private sector, where sophisticated, effective performance-based compensation has been *de rigueur* since the 1980s—part and parcel, experts believe, of corporate America's hugely successful restructuring. Also ignored are experiments with comprehensive merit-pay plans that are under way in a few innovative school districts across the country—districts burdened with much less political resistance than Gotham.

⌀

To get a sense of what merit pay could do for the public schools, consider the benefits it has showered on American industry over the last two decades. Before the eighties, merit pay in U.S. firms—if it existed at all—was pretty simple: the boss gave you a fat bonus if you (or your unit) met sales or production goals. But as international economic competition pummeled them in the early 1980s, U.S. corporations, desperate to regain their competitiveness, began to experiment with measuring individual worker performance. They established pay incentives to improve it in formerly hard-to-measure categories of output and in previously intangible areas like customer service or product quality. Of course, the bottom line was still the bottom line, but these intangibles, companies now reasoned, mattered to the long-term economic health of the firm, even if they didn't show up right away in the quarter-by-quarter numbers.

Familiar today, the new performance criteria—and the multi-faceted compensation plans built on their foundation—were strikingly original at the time. Retailers hired "mystery" shoppers to check out how employees treated customers, and based salaries, in part, on what they found. Businesses built into sales contracts "integrity" clauses that gauged not just how many widgets an employee sold but how long clients stuck with him. Banks remunerated loan officers not just for the lending they brought in but for the long-term quality of their loan portfolios. Some auto dealers tied part of salesmen's pay to how customers rated them in follow-up surveys. Companies combined these kinds of individualized incentives with rewards for everybody if the whole firm did well. Airlines, for example, gave the entire crew bonuses if the fleet's on-time performance improved.

Predictably, when U.S. businesses first introduced these innovations, workers grumbled, especially in heavily unionized industries like auto manufacturing, where any change threatened cushy labor arrangements. "They said that you couldn't measure some things, that the pay systems were too subjective, that supervisors were too subjective—in short, everything that teachers today are saying," observes Alan Johnson, a New York-based compensation consultant. Many efforts stumbled at first, too, and companies had to discard or overhaul them. Creating effective programs, it became clear, would not be an overnight fix. "Even today, with all we know, it takes three years to start up an effective incentive-pay program," cautions Martha Glantz, a compensation expert with Buck Consultants in Manhattan. "You can spend the first year just deciding what the company's goals and missions are, and collecting the data."

But American firms, needing to change or perish, forged ahead, winning over employees who liked the challenge of incentive pay and, through trial and error, developing pay plans that worked. By the mid-1990s, half of all major American corporations used such incentives. "It's no longer credible to say you can't measure something or that the only thing you can measure is a simple output," says Johnson. Merit pay played a crucial role, most observers believe, in generating the zooming productivity gains and superior product quality that American firms began recording in the late 1980s and that have been central to the nation's economic prosperity ever since.

❧

The public education monopoly has long resisted merit pay with the same ferocity with which private-sector workers at first greeted it. Opponents have constantly invoked previous attempts that failed—though their only examples have been two experiments that are over 100 years old, and another from the 1960s, before modern notions of performance pay emerged. The conventional wisdom among educators had long been that any attempt to pin down exactly what makes for good teaching, let alone measure and reward it fairly, was doomed to fail. "There was a general feeling that you were either gifted as a teacher or you weren't, and that good teaching wasn't something you could define," says Charlotte Danielson, an expert on teaching at the Educational Testing Service in New Jersey. As a last-ditch defense, some educators even argued that factors outside school, especially a student's socioeconomic and family situation, had a much greater impact on student performance than teachers did, so that using merit pay based on student performance to promote good teaching, even if it could be defined, wasn't fair. The unasked question was why teachers should ever receive salary hikes if what they do doesn't matter.

Over the last decade, these views have utterly collapsed, undermining the intellectual case—weak as it was—against merit pay. A key figure has been University of Tennessee statistician William Sanders, who discovered how to measure a teacher's effect on student performance. Rather than try to filter out the myriad sociological influences on pupils, a nearly impossible task, Sanders used complex statistical methods to chart the progress of students against themselves over the course of a school year and measure how much "value" different teachers added. Now called the Tennessee Value-Added Assessment System, Sanders's approach proved what every parent already knew: not only did teachers matter, but some were lots better than others. Other education experts, including Danielson, author of several popular books on pedagogy, developed widely accepted criteria to judge good teaching, which put paid to the absurd notion that it was too elusive to define.

⋅✦⋅

If the 1990s helped re-establish the centrality of teaching in the education debate, however, that victory hasn't melted away the teachers' unions' political opposition to merit pay. Even so, a small number of school systems across the country, under intense pressure from parents, politicians, and administrators to improve student performance, have turned to merit pay to promote better teaching. And, after some give-and-take, they've managed to get the teachers' unions on board.

Cincinnati's public school system, the first to experiment with performance incentives, persuaded its teachers' union in 1997 to do a test run of merit pay. Two years later, a ten-school pilot program, designed by administrators and teachers, got under way. Essential to union support was the pilot's proposed use of peers to evaluate teachers. "The peer evaluators, who have no stake in how teachers are judged, are important to the perception of the fairness of the system," observes Kathleen Ware, associate superintendent of Cincinnati schools. Using Danielson's criteria of good teaching—they include class preparation and clarity of presentation—the principals and peer evaluators devoted 20 to 30 hours to assessing every teacher in the ten chosen schools. Based on how they scored, teachers then wound up in one of five salary categories, with "novices" making the least money and "accomplished" teachers the most.

The pilot proved successful. A majority of teachers involved found it fair and judged the standards used as appropriate for the whole school district. The city's board of education adopted it in the spring of 2000, and, in a subsequent election, union members signed on. Teachers will go through evaluations every five years, though those looking to move up quickly can request an appraisal after just two years. New teachers and one-fifth of all experienced teachers [had] evaluations done [in 2001], but no one [started] getting paid under the new system until 2002.

Unfortunately, Cincinnati's new program doesn't directly use student test scores in its evaluations. Bringing in scores would have generated too much union hostility for the plan to gain acceptance, reports school superintendent Steven Adamowski. And in all likelihood, tying pay solely to test scores is a bad idea; nobody would call meritorious a teacher who boosted scores but left his students psychological wrecks because of his bullying. Yet leaving tests out altogether also makes no sense. After all, what better way to determine how well students are doing—the only reason for the concern over teaching quality in the first place—than test scores? Cincinnati's program recognizes this implicitly. The district will monitor test results of students whose teachers score the highest ratings. If those students don't show substantial improvement, school officials will toughen the program's standards. In addition, the district will rely on student tests to award bonuses to all teachers in a school whose kids take big strides.

꾸�‒

One major benefit of merit systems is that they enable schools to pay teachers—especially young and ambitious teachers—fatter salaries. That's the overriding rationale behind Iowa's new incentives program, enacted by the state legislature to keep better-paying nearby states from spiriting away top teachers. The state has anted up $40 million for salary increases, but, in a program similar to Cincinnati's, Iowa will now evaluate teachers thoroughly to make sure the extra dough goes only to the good classroom performers, not the duds. "We believe this system will help us retain the best people by re-professionalizing teaching," enthuses John Forsyth, chief executive of the Des Moines-based Wellmark Blue Cross and Blue Shield. Forsyth helped the state dream up the new system, looking to the market for inspiration. "We know good teachers make a difference," he continues, "and we're going to pay those who do make a difference." How much more reasonable this is than the New York union's claim that, because a few city teachers jump to higher-paying suburban schools each year, all teachers—the good and the bad alike—need equal raises to make them stay.

In Iowa's new system, good teachers will now be able to reach higher salary levels much earlier in their careers than before. "The private pay consultants who looked at our old seniority system thought it must have been designed specifically to keep teacher pay low and save school districts money," says Ted Stilwill, director of Iowa's Department of Education. "The only way for teachers to get paid more under that system was for them to stick it out for years." As in Cincinnati, union opposition means that Iowa won't rely on test scores to evaluate teachers—at least not directly. But in addition to paying teachers based on their performance evaluations, the state will also offer modest yearly bonuses to all teachers in a school whose students do well on standardized tests, with the biggest bonuses going to the school's best instructors, rather than all teachers getting equal rewards.

Helping to develop Iowa's plan has been an eye-opener for the state's education chief. "Private-sector compensation experts taught me that businesses use pay as a way of getting everyone to follow common goals," Stilwill says. "Being in the public sector most of my life, I never understood that."

Though Cincinnati and Iowa have skirted the controversy of using student test scores, Denver is confronting it head-on. The city has launched two pilot plans that link pay directly to scores. One pilot program uses student scores in standardized tests of basic skills; another relies on scores in specific subjects. Principals and teachers agree at the beginning of the school year on what kinds of improvements in test scores they'll shoot for and then face evaluation at the end of the year to see if they've met their goals. Denver is also instituting a third merit-pay pilot program that instructs teachers in the principles of good teaching and then evaluates their teaching skills and rewards them accordingly. Denver will later measure how their students perform on tests to see if its criteria for good teaching really produce results. Through these experiments, Denver hopes to figure out what motivates teachers best and what works best for students.

Denver's teachers' union, surprisingly, has contributed mightily to developing the pilots; the head of the project's design team, Brad Jupp, is a union negotiator. He says the union is participating because the demand to make schools more accountable is so intense that teachers would rather help create performance systems than have them imposed from above. "If you believe that your union members are doing a good job—and we do—then you want a system that accurately measures that," says Jupp.

Experiences from the private sector suggest that it will take several years before these imaginative programs work out all their kinks. In the meantime, controversy will dog the new programs. Critics will pounce on their every mistake as evidence that paying teachers for performance is a bad idea. And unions are likely to push for watered-down plans in order to deflect criticism without giving up too much.

This last is exactly what's happening in New York. The teachers' union has offered the mayor a compromise: pay every teacher in a school or district a bonus if the school's or district's test scores rise. A trial run of such a system, supported by Gotham's business community, is under way in two urban districts; other states, including California and Georgia, already have school-based bonuses.

But group bonuses will never substitute adequately for true performance pay, compensation experts believe, since they don't single out good and bad teachers. All they're likely to do is to frustrate first-rate teachers working in schools with mediocre staffs. "If you have four workers doing well in a unit that is not otherwise performing, over time those four will leave the company and go somewhere that they can be rewarded for their superior work," says consultant Glantz. And since schoolwide bonuses don't put any pay at risk—poor performance doesn't mean less money—they won't help rid schools of lousy teachers either. By contrast, teachers who score poorly in, say, Cincinnati, now find themselves shunted into the lowest salary level, discouraging them from sticking around. Mayor Giuliani, rightly, has rejected the union's offer.

Of course, smaller cities like Cincinnati are far removed from the we don't-do-windows union obstructionism of a New York or a Los Angeles. For 15 years, Cincinnati's teachers' union has accepted some kind of peer evaluation of teachers; it's easily one of the nation's most flexible teachers' unions. Unions in New York and Los Angeles, conversely, have fought almost every education reform tooth and nail. Last year in Los Angeles, thousands of teachers ferociously protested against a proposed merit-pay plan, eventually killing it. Moreover, in the current public school monopoly, there's nothing really comparable to the outside economic pressure that forced American industry to develop its merit programs—one more argument for school choice.

Without individualized merit pay, teacher evaluations will remain perfunctory at best. Today, New York principals fail less than 1 percent of all teachers in annual evaluations. New York hopes to get principals to crack down on bad teaching by rewarding them financially when their schools do well. That will eliminate one of the main objections to teacher merit pay—that it leads to supervisor favoritism: even if a principal hates an effective teacher's guts, he's not going to want to lose someone who's helping him sweeten his own salary. But until teachers are part of any performance-pay system, the impact of such innovations will be severely limited—and students will continue to get shortchanged, regardless of how much their teachers take to the bank.

Al Ramirez **NO**

How Merit Pay Undermines Education

Proposals for merit pay, including pay-for-performance, continue to surface as policymakers search for ways to motivate administrators and teachers to be more effective—and to make educators do what policymakers want them to do. These types of remuneration plans are different from paying a teacher extra for taking on additional duties, such as running an after-school computer laboratory or serving as a mentor or master teacher. Instead, these merit pay policies give individual employees extra compensation, above and beyond the base salary, for work and contributions that exceed some pre-established criteria. These criteria often include achieving higher student test scores on standardized tests.

Carrots and Sticks

Why can't teachers and administrators be "incentivized" like aluminum-siding salespeople? Not all lawyers in a legal firm take home the same annual salary and bonuses, so why can't policymakers for public education find a way to pay similar classifications of employees different rates of pay on the basis of their job performance? Professional sports teams pay their players on the basis of their performance and perceived potential value to the team, so why can't school districts do the same?

But do compensation decisions really reflect employees' contributions? As Rosabeth Moss Kanter (1987) points out, "Status, not contribution, has traditionally been the basis for the numbers on employees' paychecks. Pay has reflected where jobs rank in the corporation hierarchy—not what comes out of them" (p. 60). Despite centuries of experience with employee compensation plans, status still wins out over contribution. Contrast the pay of corporate CEOs in the United States, some of whom earn more than 600 times as much as their typical non-management employees, to the much smaller differential between the pay of employees and CEOs in Europe and Japan. Do American corporate boards know something about compensation plans that their foreign competitors don't?

In fact, the seemingly logical link between employee production and compensation is often debatable and highly subjective. We can understand why new approaches to determining pay are so difficult to establish in public school districts today if we look at the historical development of educators' most common compensation approach—uniform salary schedules with steps and lanes. This compensation system rewards professionals for their years of experience on the job and level of educational attainment. Incentives are structured to encourage teachers and some administrators to remain loyal to the school district and to improve their skills and knowledge by pursuing additional training, usually by attending approved workshops and courses or earning graduate degrees.

In the ideal situation, this system rewards a teacher or principal who, for example, participates in a workshop, typically on his or her own time, about the educational uses of computers. This employee is building on a knowledge base and thus is able to make a greater contribution to the school district's mission to prepare students for success in our democratic society. In theory, this compensation system motivates employees to get better at their jobs. Critics argue that the theory behind this system doesn't hold up. They point to the lack of linkage between the incentive system and outcomes in schools and classrooms. They also challenge the abuses in such systems, where employees are rewarded for taking courses in wok cooking or given graduate credit by diploma mills for signing up for the walking tour of downtown Los Angeles.

But the tenacious attachment to this system has deep roots. In the past, policy leaders set up teacher compensation systems according to criteria that they felt were justified and appropriate, and boards of education, city councils, and other similar deliberative bodies used democratic means to arrive at pay policies. Nonetheless, some of these decisions look strange to us today. Consider the Chicago school system in the early 1900s. As the school system matured, policymakers moved to standardize the employee compensation system. One of the components of their system was a substantial pay differential between male and female employees (Peterson, 1985), and the gender pay differential continued even when women started to assume administrative roles. At the beginning of the 20th century, pay differentials in Atlanta, Georgia, were based on race. Although the African American community had managed to secure minimal services from the Atlanta school board, the dual system of education determined that African American and white teachers would not have the same rate of pay (Peterson, 1985). History has demonstrated that governing bodies are capable of establishing unfair practices. The legacy of such compensation systems in public education has been to elevate one criterion—fairness—as the paramount consideration in all pay decisions.

Logic would dictate that a teacher's years of experience in the classroom and level of educational attainment are somewhat related to the academic performance of students. In theory, a first-year chemistry teacher fresh out of college is not as effective with high school students as is a 10-year veteran with a master's degree in science teaching or organic chemistry. But critics counter that empirical evidence doesn't support such logic. They assert that a teacher's training is irrelevant and that experience counts for nothing. What matters, they say, are the results a teacher gets with students; outcomes, not inputs, should determine rewards. Using an outcome-based criterion, they claim, is the only fair approach to rewarding teachers.

Educators point out that such proposals for output-based compensation are not fair, reverting once again to the fairness issue. How can teachers be held accountable for school conditions that they cannot control? Unless all inputs are equalized for all teachers and administrators, how can policymakers judge the value of the outcome? Educators further argue that their jobs involve more than teaching academic subjects and often extend beyond the measurable—for example, consoling a child whose parents are going through a divorce or advising a student about options for college.

Understanding Human Motivation

The problem with both the input-reward system and the outcome-reward system is that they ignore the basic dynamics of what motivates human beings. The approach of focusing on fairness above all else has inhibited the contribution of some members of the group—for example, those with exceptional abilities who may not fit the mold. In contrast, the outcome-centered motivation system devalues the significance of an individual's contribution and oversimplifies the role of the educator. Neither system considers the body of research related to the psychology of human motivation.

Consider the work of Frederick Herzberg (1987) and his studies of employee motivation. He and his colleagues identified a series of more than 3,000 items that either motivated workers or diminished employees' enthusiasm for their jobs. The "satisfiers" and "dissatisfiers" will surprise policymakers who view money as the sole motivator on the job. Organizational policy and administrative procedures, supervisory practices, employee-employer relations, working conditions, and salary proved to have greater potential to be dissatisfiers than satisfiers. These dissatisfiers are important and need the attention of employers. But the satisfiers—the motivators that are essential to spurring performance to higher levels—included achievement on the job, recognition for one's contribution or for a job well done, the work itself, job responsibility, opportunities for career advancement, and professional growth.

Abraham Maslow's (1970) study of human motivation should also inform policymakers who are intent on lighting a fire under professional educators. Maslow bases his theory on a hierarchy of needs to which all humans respond. This hierarchy ascends from basic needs (water, shelter, and food) to complex needs (advancement, growth, and achievement). Money, benefits, and job security appear at the lower end of the hierarchy. Merit pay systems that attempt to use money alone as a lever for improvement are more likely to cause educators who have other employment options to leave the school district than to strive for the desired results of their supervisors.

William Glasser (1997) presents an articulate explanation of human motivation through his Choice Theory. Glasser points out that all people are motivated to meet their needs for belonging to groups, maintaining a sense of self-efficacy or power, and having fun. These are natural and intrinsic needs that humans are driven to meet. When institutions use extrinsic motivation devices to manipulate their members, they often divert their members from meeting these intrinsic human needs. The frustration and anger that often result are destructive to the organization. Ill-conceived reward systems that diminish employee loyalty and increase resentment toward management can cause incalculable productivity losses in organizations. Here again, money alone does not work as a motivator.

Perhaps no one has been more eloquent than the late W. Edwards Deming (1993) in addressing the destructive nature of extrinsic reward systems

> that squeeze out from an individual, over his lifetime, his innate intrinsic motivation, self-esteem, dignity. They build into him fear, self-defense, extrinsic motivation. We have been destroying our people, from toddlers on through the university, and on the job. (p. 124)

According to Deming, the forces of destruction include grade rankings; merit systems, particularly ones that categorize people; contrived competition among people within organizations; schemes for incentive pay and pay-for-performance; and numerical goals, targets, and quotas—without any guidelines on how to achieve them. These forces suboptimize the system and cause humiliation, resentment, and fear. Using such approaches also shifts the burden to produce results from management to the employees. Deming asserts that such practices belie the fact that more than 90 percent of the organization's outcomes are the result of the leadership and governance structure of the organization and not the effort of individual workers who work in the system.

Extrinsic reward systems create the illusion of employer control but at the expense of the full involvement and commitment of dedicated, enthusiastic employees. Extrinsic reward systems divert resources and energy from what is much more likely to move the organization to higher levels of performance. They discard the most valuable resources in the organization: the brainpower, problem-solving ability, and innovative thinking that every employee brings to the job.

Dud Silver Bullets

A growing number of legislators, governors, mayors, superintendents, school board members, and business people advocate programs for merit pay or pay-for-performance. Their good intentions to make schools better often lead them to quick-fix solutions and seemingly obvious, but wrong, answers. Perhaps one of the biggest ironies encountered by school leaders is the ill-informed advice they receive, often unsolicited, from business leaders who proffer "real-world" solutions—like merit pay—to fix school problems. These business leaders are ignorant of the research literature that does not support such practices; ironically, these findings often come out of business leaders' own university-based business colleges. In some cases, unfortunately, the political leaders know better but cannot resist the temptation to scapegoat the less powerful members of the organization—teachers—and pander to an ignorant public and news media. And in the worst cases, leaders are so cynical about the public education system that they blame and punish employees as a way of diverting attention from the real, and typically more costly, issues confronting the schools.

Donald Campbell, Kathleen Campbell, and Ho-Beng Chia (1998) conducted a thorough investigation of merit pay systems. They concluded that pay-for-performance programs raise problematic issues related to measurement, performance appraisal and feedback, and the desirability of the rewards. For example, questions arise about the validity either of the instrument used to measure performance or the nature of the work. Attempts to address these issues through training or better measures fall short. Additionally, the researchers found that employees tend to reject most or all of the evaluation systems, regardless of what adjustments are made. Money, the key factor in such systems, is usually in short supply, so the potential impact of rewards is minimal and does not outweigh the negative effects of the merit pay system. Finally, the authors conclude that the implementation of merit pay systems becomes unwieldy, contributes to mission drift, and often leads to unintended consequences, such as enormous pay differentials between subordinates and supervisors, or the ignoring of work assignments that do not earn consideration for merit.

Questions to Ask

Policymakers and school leaders are supposed to make changes that improve the education systems for which they are responsible. The penchant to move to action and make sweeping changes without proper policy analysis and policy development techniques contributes to the dysfunction of many school systems. The one-step-forward-two-steps-back method of creating education policy, so common today, is certainly irresponsible, if not unethical. Flashy or feel-good policies make the system worse. Policymakers, leaders, and deliberative bodies that are interested in investigating the value of merit pay systems should ask themselves these questions:

- Do I understand the nature of human motivation? Why have our teachers and administrators chosen to work in our school district? It is often difficult to tap into the employee's motivation for employment, and some appraisal and reward systems may even reduce enthusiasm for the job and productivity.
- Can a school district be run like a business? Do business practices readily transfer to a publicly held organization run by highly trained professionals with an educational mission? Do the culture and structure of a school district support or deter the use of business-like evaluation and merit systems?
- Is this evaluation and reward system fair? How would I feel if my employer instituted such a program at my job? Fairness in the design and implementation of appraisal and reward systems is both crucial and complex. The fairness issue will permeate any proposed system and must apply to the employee, the appraiser, the organization, and the organizational stakeholders, including students, parents, and taxpayers.
- Can my organization find an evaluation and compensation system that is not excessively burdensome and that operates effectively? Do I understand that some important job functions may not be measurable?

Do I understand that some elaborate evaluation systems may distract staff from their duties?
- Have I explored the unintended consequences of a new system? Organization leaders must be careful about what is rewarded in a merit pay system—because they will get it! Have I considered what won't get done because it doesn't count for merit pay? The goal is to move forward, not to suboptimize the organization.
- Am I clear about whom to reward? This central question must be part of policymakers' considerations. Will the system reward individuals or teams? Enterprises that are highly collaborative should be cautious about setting compensation systems in motion that promote destructive competition.

A candid discussion of these questions among policymakers, school leaders, and stakeholders will go a long way toward forming sound education policy. Employee evaluation and reward systems are complicated matters that require thoughtful deliberation. They have the potential to be as destructive as they are constructive. Our schools are too important to operate with misguided policies.

References

Campbell, D. J., Campbell, K. M., & Chia, H. B. (1998). Merit pay, performance appraisal, and individual motivation: An analysis and alternative. *Human Resources Management, 37*(2), 131–146.

Deming, W. E. (1993). *The new economics for industry, government, education.* Cambridge, MA: Massachusetts Institute of Technology Center for Advanced Engineering Study.

Glasser, W. (1997). A new look at school failure and school success. *Phi Delta Kappan, 78*(8), 596–602.

Herzberg, F. (1987). One more time: How do you motivate employees? *Harvard Business Review, 65,* 109–120.

Kanter, R. M. (1987, March/April). Attack on pay. *Harvard Business Review, 65,* 60–67.

Maslow, A. H. (1970). *Motivation and personality.* New York: Harper & Row.

Peterson, P. E. (1985). *The politics of school reform, 1870–1940.* Chicago: University of Chicago Press.

POSTSCRIPT

Can Merit Pay Accelerate School Improvement?

After the Soviet Union's challenge to America's technological superiority manifested itself in the late 1950s, financial incentives were given to present and recruited teachers of math and science under a federal initiative. Currently, the "crisis" focus is on underperforming public schools located primarily in districts with high percentages of minority students. Some critics have made the argument that a maximum federal effort should be directed at schools with the greatest need in order to close the existing achievement gaps. This idea is elaborated upon by Cynthia D. Prince in "Attracting Well-Qualified Teachers to Struggling Schools," *American Educator* (Winter 2002). "Today," she explains, "both the ATF [American Federation of Teachers] and the NEA [National Education Association] favor offering locally-developed financial incentives to qualified teachers who choose to work in hard-to-staff schools."

In "The Teacher Shortage: A Case of Wrong Diagnosis and Wrong Prescription," *NASSP Bulletin* (June 2002), Richard M. Ingersoll offers an analysis of reasons why large numbers of qualified teachers are departing their jobs for reasons other than retirement. In "Why Are Experienced Teachers Leaving the Profession?" *Phi Delta Kappan* (September 2002), Barbara Benham Tye and Lisa O'Brien report on their survey of teachers who have already left the profession and those who are considering leaving. They found that those who had left ranked the pressure of increased accountability (high-stakes testing and standards) as the number one reason. Salary considerations ranked seventh. Of those who were considering leaving, however, salary considerations ranked first.

A stinging indictment of merit pay can be found in Maurice Holt's "Performance Pay for Teachers: The Standards Movement's Last Stand?" *Phi Delta Kappan* (December 2001). In it, Holt states, "Having done their best to demoralize schools and give the phrase 'testing to destruction' a new meaning, there's one last aspect of civilized education that the Standardistos have in their sights: the sense of trust and cooperation among teachers." Their ammunition: "competitive salary structures."

Further resources on the topic of merit pay for teachers include Lawrence Hardy, "What's a Teacher Worth?" *American School Board Journal* (August 2002); . . . Cynthia D. Prince, "Higher Pay in Hard-to-Staff Schools: The Case for Financial Incentives," *The School Administrator* (June 2002); . . . Sam Coleman, "Fault Lines in Merit Pay," *Rethinking Schools* (Summer 2008); and Jacob Vigdot, "Scrap the Sacrosanct Salary Schedule," *Education Next* (Fall 2008).

Contributors to This Volume

EDITOR

JAMES WM. NOLL has retired from his professorial position in the College of Education at the University of Maryland in College Park, Maryland, where he taught philosophy of education and chaired the Social Foundations of Education unit. He has been affiliated with the American Educational Studies Association, the National Society for the Study of Education, the Association for Supervision and Curriculum Development, and the World Future Society. He received a B.A. in English and history from the University of Wisconsin-Milwaukee, an M.S. in educational administration from the University of Wisconsin, and a Ph.D. in philosophy of education from the University of Chicago. His articles have appeared in several education journals, and he is co-author, with Sam P. Kelly, of *Foundations of Education in America: An Anthology of Major Thought and Significant Actions* (Harper & Row, 1970). He also has served as editor and editorial board member for McGraw-Hill/Dushkin's *Annual Editions: Education Series*.

AUTHORS

MORTIMER J. ADLER (1902–2001) taught philosophy at the University of Chicago, served on the board of the Encyclopedia Britannica, founded the Aspen Institute, and co-edited *The Great Books of the Western World*.

VINCENT A. ANFARA, JR. is associate professor in the Department of Theory and Practice in Teacher Education, University of Tennessee, Knoxville, and is co-editor (with Steve Mertens and Kathleen Roney) of *An International Look at Educating Young Adolescents* (2009).

RAY BACCHETTI is a former vice president for planning and management at Stanford University and is a scholar at the Carnegie Foundation for the Advancement of Teaching.

DAVID C. BERLINER is Regents' professor in the Mary Lou Fulton College of Education at Arizona State University. He is the co-author, with Sharon L. Nichols, of *Collateral Damage: How High-Stakes Testing Corrupts America's Schools* (2007).

DOUGLAS J. BESHAROV is a professor at the University of Maryland's School of Public Policy and a scholar at the American Enterprise Institute for Public Policy Research.

WILLIAM J. BRENNAN, JR. (1906–1997) was an associate justice of the Supreme Court for 34 years during the administrations of eight presidents.

WARREN BURGER (1907–1995) was the chief justice of the United States from 1969 to 1986.

DOUGLAS M. CALL is a research associate at the University of Maryland's School of Public Policy.

WADE A. CARPENTER is associate professor of education at Berry College, Mount Berry, Georgia.

JAMIN CARSON is an assistant professor at East Carolina University. His research interest is in the philosophical foundations of education.

HERB CHILDRESS is director of liberal studies at the Boston Architectural College and author of *Landscapes of Betrayal, Landscapes of Joy* (2000).

GARY K. CLAYBAUGH is professor of education at La Salle University in Philadelphia and co-founder (with Edward G. Rozycki) of *newfoundations .com* which explores reflective educational practice.

EVANS CLINCHY is a senior consultant at the Institute for Responsive Education at Northeastern University in Boston and editor of *Transforming Public Education*.

LINDA DARLING-HAMMOND is the Charles E. Ducommun professor of education at Stanford University and executive director of the National Commission on Teaching and America's Future.

JOHN DEWEY (1859–1952) was a leading American philosopher who taught at the University of Michigan, the University of Chicago (where he founded a laboratory school to test his ideas), and Columbia University (where he spawned the progressive education movement). His most famous book is *Democracy and Education* (1916).

ERIN DILLON is a policy analyst at Education Sector in Washington, DC and a former researcher at the Beginning with Children Foundation in New York.

DAVID ELKIND is a professor of child development at Tufts University where he conducts research in the cognitive, perceptual, and social growth of children based on the theories of Jean Piaget.

ROBERT EPSTEIN is former editor-in-chief of *Psychology Today* and founder of the Cambridge Center for Behavioral Studies. He is author of *The Case Against Adolescence* (2007).

CHARLES L. GLENN is professor of administration, training, and policy studies and fellow of the University Professors Program at Boston University.

FREDERICK M. HESS is a resident scholar at the American Enterprise Institute in Washington, DC and author of *Common Sense School Reform.*

ROBERT HOLLAND is a senior fellow of the Lexington Institute in Arlington, Virginia. A journalist, he served as op-ed editor for the Richmond Times-Dispatch.

JOHN HOLT (1923–1985) was an educator and a critic of public schooling who authored several influential books on education and promoted home schooling.

ROBERT M. HUTCHINS (1879–1977) was chancellor of the University of Chicago, co-compiler of *The Great Books of the Western World*, and director of the Center for the Study of Democratic Institutions.

CRAIG D. JERALD is president of Break the Curve Consulting, specializing in education policy and has been affiliated with The Education Trust and Education Sector.

DAVID L. KIRP is a professor at the Goldman School of Public Policy at the University of California at Berkeley. Author of *The Sandbox Investment: The Preschool Movement and Kids-First Politics* (2007).

TIMOTHY J. LENSMIRE is an associate professor of curriculum and instruction at the University of Minnesota, Twin Cities.

HENRY LEVIN is the William Heard Kilpatrick professor of economics and education at Teachers College, Columbia University, and director of the National Center for the Study of Privatization in Education.

STEVEN MALANGA is a contributing editor at *City Journal* and a senior fellow at the Manhattan Institute for Policy Research.

PETER MEYER, a former news editor of *Life* magazine, is a freelance writer and a contributing editor of *Education Next*.

LOWELL MONKE teaches at Wittenberg University in Ohio and is co-author of *Breaking Down the Digital Walls: Learning to Teach in the Post-Modern World* (2001).

KRISTAN A. MORRISON is associate professor in the School of Teacher Education and Leadership at Radford University. Author of *Free School Teaching: A Journey Into Radical Progressive Education* (2007).

JOE NATHAN is director of the Center for School Change in the Hubert H. Humphrey Institute of Public Affairs at the University of Minnesota, Minneapolis.

LINDA NATHAN is headmaster of the Boston Arts Academy, a public high school for the visual and performing arts.

SHARON L. NICHOLS is an assistant professor in the College of Education and Human Development at the University of Texas at San Antonio.

RUBY PAYNE is president of aha! Process, Inc., a nationwide provider of workshops and materials for educators in poverty-area schools. Author of *Under-resourced Learners: Eight Strategies to Boost Student Achievement* (2008).

DAN PETERSON is an attorney and writer who claims to have been destined to live in Northern Virginia.

PAUL E. PETERSON is the Henry Lee Shattuck professor of government and director of the Program on Education, Policy, and Governance at Harvard University. He is a senior fellow at the Hoover Institution and editor-in-chief of Education Next.

DIANNE PICHÉ is a civil rights lawyer, teacher, and advocate who serves as executive director of the Citizens' Commission on Civil Rights in Washington, DC.

AL RAMIREZ is a retired education professor from the University of Colorado at Colorado Springs, specializing in the leadership program. He formerly was the chief state school officer in Iowa.

CARL R. ROGERS (1902–1987), a noted psychologist and educator, taught at the University of Chicago and the University of Wisconsin-Madison. He introduced the client-centered approach to psychotherapy in 1942, and he was the first psychologist to record and transcribe therapy sessions verbatim. He authored *On Becoming a Person* (1972), among many other influential works.

MARA SAPON-SHEVIN is professor of inclusive education in the Teaching and Leadership Department in the School of Education at Syracuse University. Author of *Widening the Circle: The Power of Inclusive Classrooms* (2007).

MISTILINA SATO is an assistant professor of teacher development at the University of Minnesota, Twin Cities.

B. F. SKINNER (1904–1990), a noted psychologist and exponent of behaviorism, held the William James Chair in the Department of Psychology at Harvard University. His major works include *About Behaviorism* (1976) and *Reflections on Behaviorism and Society* (1978). His most widely read book is *Walden Two* (1948).

DAVID SOUTER served on the U. S. Supreme Court as associate justice from 1990, when he was nominated by President George H. W. Bush, until his retirement in 2009.

MARK TERRY is chair of the science department at the Northwest School in Seattle, Washington. He has been a teacher in public and independent schools for over three decades.

CLARENCE THOMAS is an associate justice on the U. S. Supreme Court, having been nominated in 1991 by President George H. W. Bush.

THOMAS TOCH is co-founder and co-director of Education Sector, a think tank based in Washington, DC, and author of *High Schools on a Human Scale* (2003).

MARC TUCKER is president of the National Center on Education and the Economy and was vice-chair of the New Commission on the Skills of the American Workforce.

CHRIS WHITTLE is chairman of Whittle Communications, founder of Channel One, and CEO of Edison Schools, Inc. He is author of *Crash Course: Imagining a Better Future for Public Education* (2006).